STONE BARNS
OF AMERICA

Historic Icons East of the Mississippi

ROBERT KROEGER

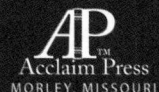

Acclaim Press
MORLEY, MISSOURI

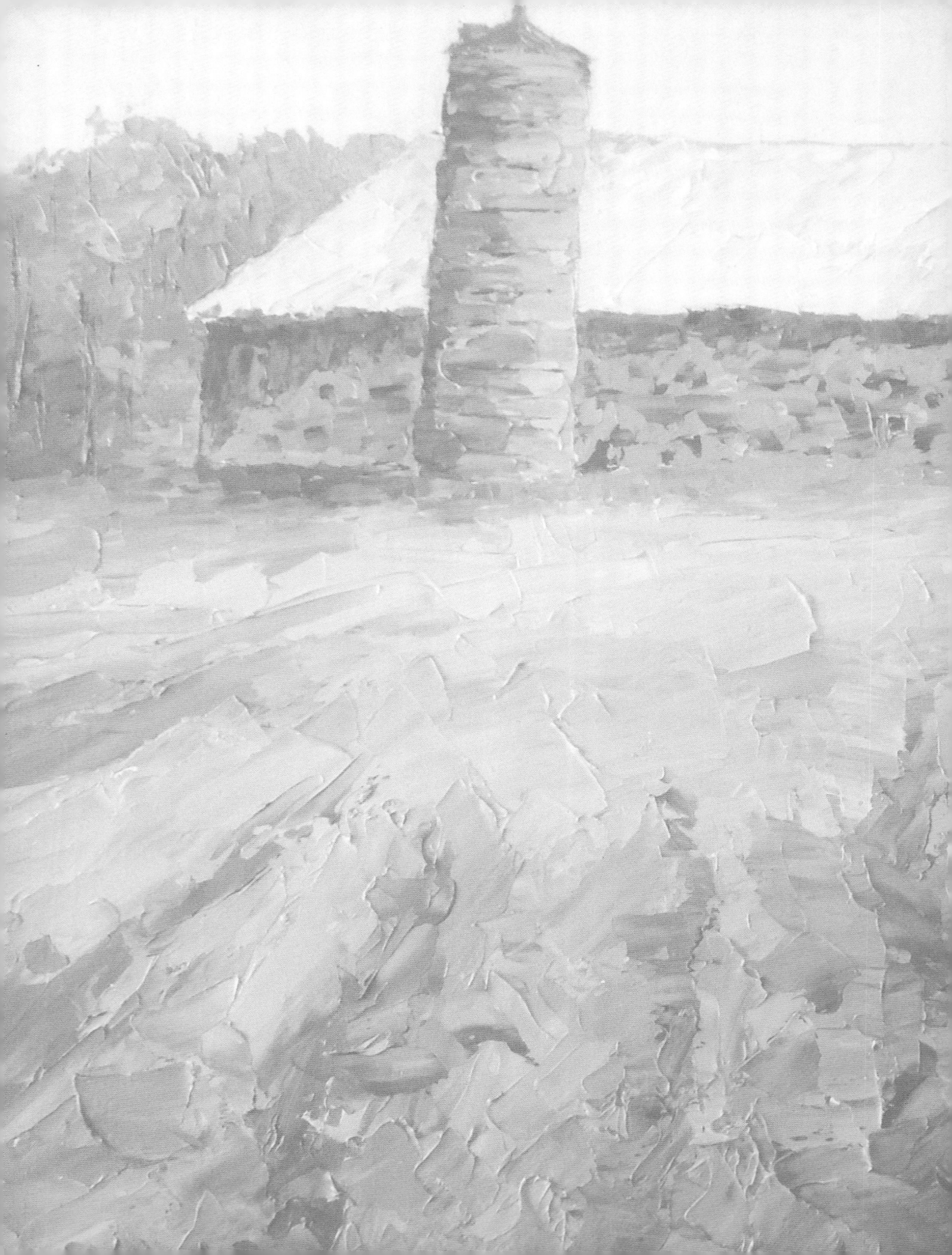

WHAT OTHERS HAVE SAID

Stone barns were built to occupy a farmstead with optimistic permanence, establishing a legacy. Bob Kroeger brings these barns to life by carefully researching and telling the stories of the families who built, restored and preserved them as well as sensitively capturing their essence with his paintings.

— Joe Mischka, Publisher, *Rural Heritage*, RFD-TV

It was a frigid February Saturday morning in 2021 when I found out the family barn built in the 1870s had caught fire and was a total loss. Though grieving, I kept returning to one thought: thank the good Lord for Robert Kroeger for so carefully documenting and immortalizing our barn through his beautiful painting and storytelling. I'm glad to see him continue to preserve the legacy of these incredible structures with this new book on stone barns.

— Matt Reese, Editor, *Ohio's Country Journal*

So many of our old structures, built using materials and techniques rarely used today, have been lost due to neglect, lack of funds for their upkeep and maintenance, apathy or "progress." Thanks to historians like Bob Kroeger who showcase these treasures, perhaps many more will be saved.

— Joan DiMaria – President, Heckler Plains Folklife Society, Pennsylvania

The stone barns at Glen Farm in Portsmouth, Rhode Island, were "state of the art" when they were built around 1910. Robert Kroeger does an excellent job of telling the story of this "Gentleman's Farm" and its barns.

— Gloria Schmidt, historian, Portsmouth, Rhode Island

Robert's work has helped bring some needed attention to a disappearing species of building in America – the barn. The more we learn about barns the more we will understand about the evolution of American history.

— Tom O'Grady, Editor, *Friends of Ohio Barns Newsletter*

The time and expense of constructing a stone barn invariably means there is a tale surrounding it. Robert Kroeger digs deep into the history behind these magnificent structures, most built well over a hundred years ago, uncovering stories every bit as fascinating as the barns.

— Dr. Bruce Baker, Witness of the Times podcaster, and member, History Cherokee, Georgia

"Robert Kroeger's love of barns is matched by his determination to document the historical barns still standing. I highly recommend his books for wonderful photography and well researched stories about the barns."

— Linda Mueller, owner of Michigan's Loeb stone barn in Charlevoix and author of *For the Love of a Castle*

"Dr. Robert Kroeger humanizes the built barn landscape in a way that both captivates and fascinates by documenting the structures in his paintings and telling poignant stories of our ancestors that intersect with the present to guide future generations. On the cusp of America250, this book illustrates the strong, nay we say stone, foundation of which our great nation with its agricultural roots was laid by native peoples and immigrants who shared their skills and culture, survived with sheer determination, and succeeded due to an inspiring work ethic."

—Leianne Neff Heppner, president and CEO, Summit County Historical Society, Akron, Ohio

"As an historic architect and fortunate owner of a rare Chester County barn – one with conical stone supports under the forebay – I was pleased to host Dr. Kroeger for not only a look at my barn, but also to take him to several others in Chester and Lancaster counties. His attention to detail and understanding the stories behind these treasures reflects his passion to preserve important pieces of American history for future generations to appreciate."

—Warren I. Claytor, A.I.A. & NCARB, Warren Claytor Architects, Inc., Wayne, Pennsylvania

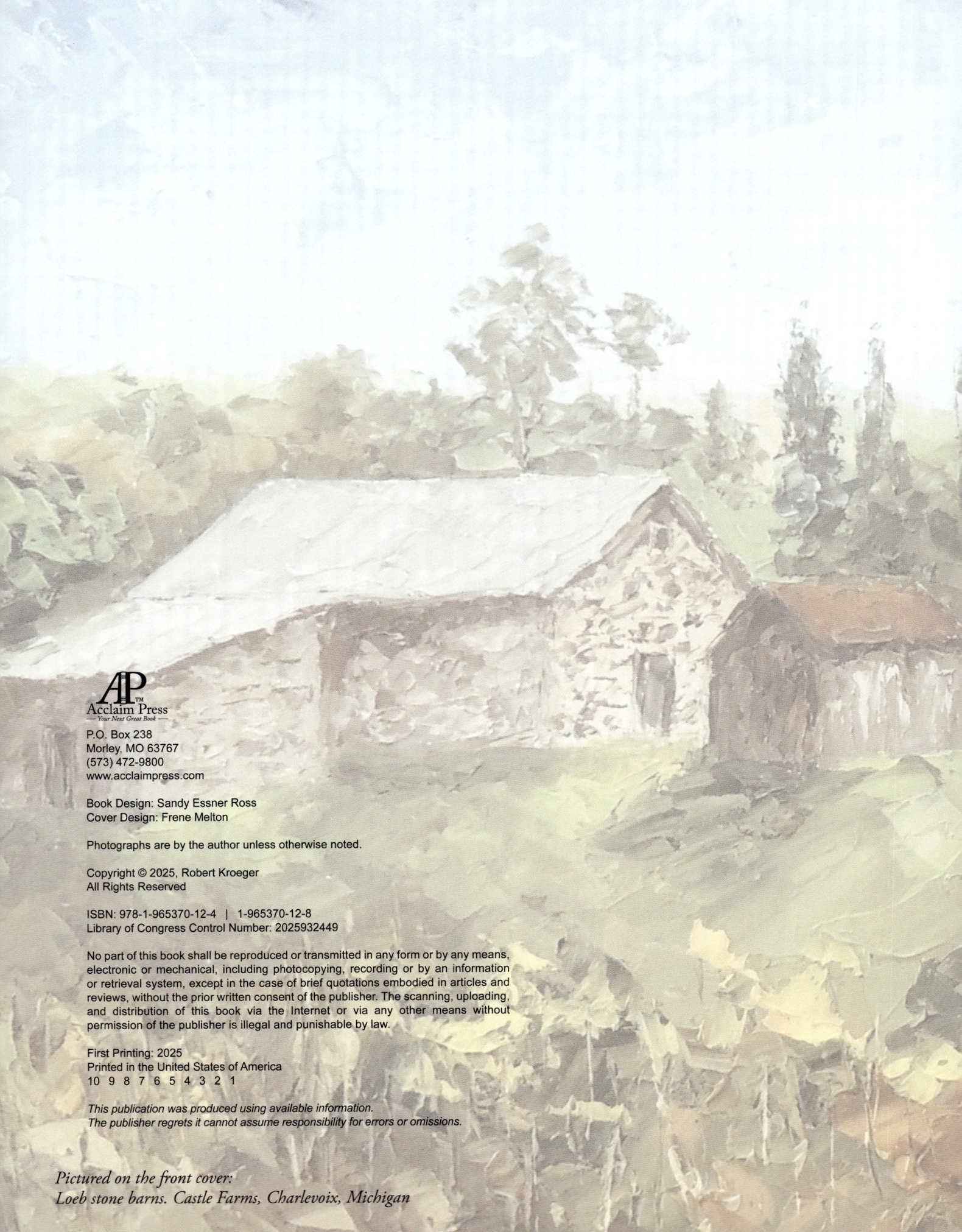

Acclaim Press
— Your Next Great Book —

P.O. Box 238
Morley, MO 63767
(573) 472-9800
www.acclaimpress.com

Book Design: Sandy Essner Ross
Cover Design: Frene Melton

Photographs are by the author unless otherwise noted.

ISBN: 978-1-965370-12-4 | 1-965370-12-8
Library of Congress Control Number: 2025932449

First Printing: 2025
Printed in the United States of America
10 9 8 7 6 5 4 3 2 1

This publication was produced using available information.
The publisher regrets it cannot assume responsibility for errors or omissions.

Pictured on the front cover:
Loeb stone barns. Castle Farms, Charlevoix, Michigan

CONTENTS

Dedication 6

Foreword. 7

Acknowledgements 8

Introduction 9

Part I – Beginnings

1. Stonemasonry 14
2. Evolution of Stone Barns 21
3. Stone Barns of Early America 26

Part II – The Barns

4. Northeast 30
5. Mid-Atlantic 57
6. Mid-South 105
7. Midwest 121

Part III – Modern Era

8. Contemporary Stone Barns 152

Afterword 154

Bibliography 156

About the Author 160

Index. 162

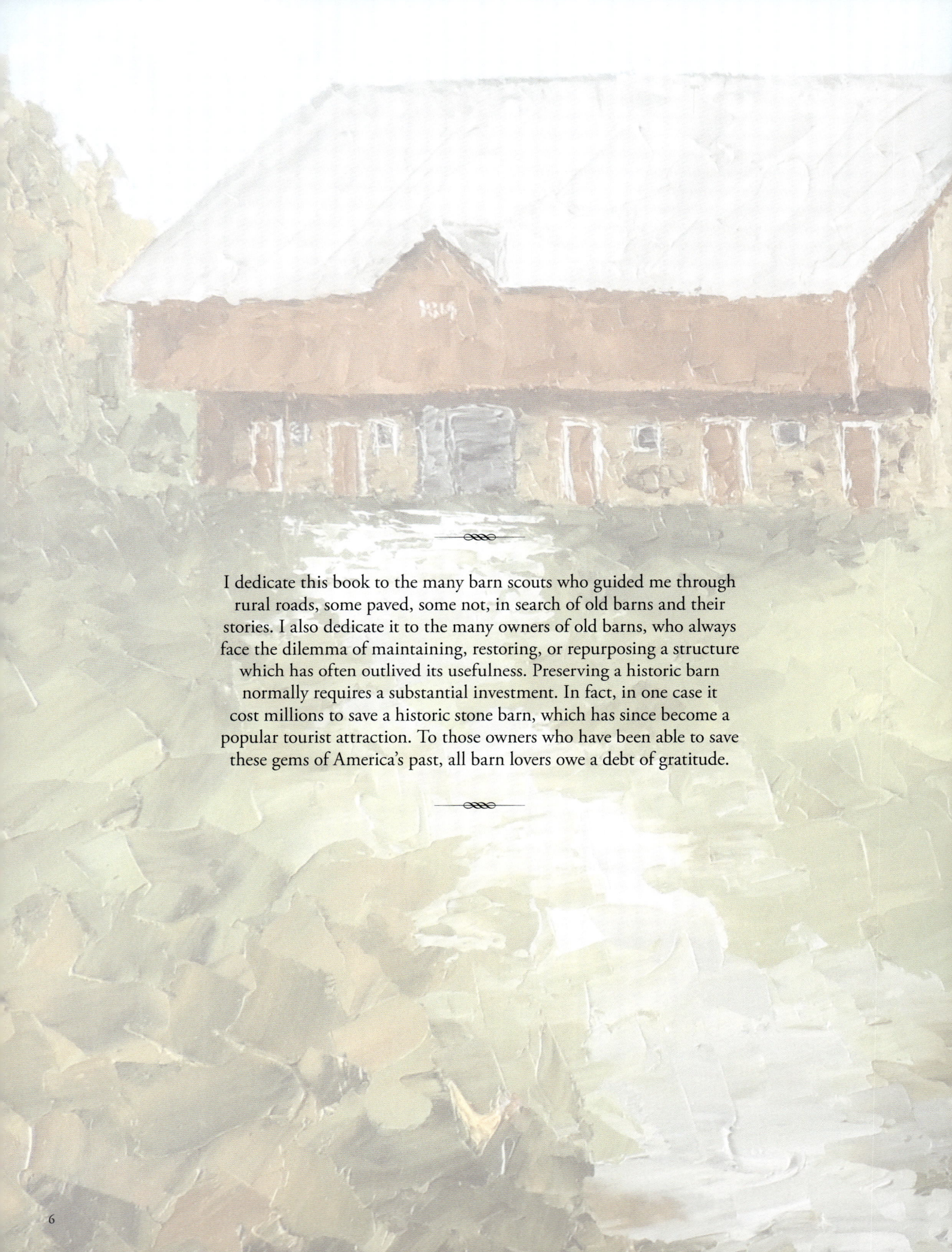

I dedicate this book to the many barn scouts who guided me through rural roads, some paved, some not, in search of old barns and their stories. I also dedicate it to the many owners of old barns, who always face the dilemma of maintaining, restoring, or repurposing a structure which has often outlived its usefulness. Preserving a historic barn normally requires a substantial investment. In fact, in one case it cost millions to save a historic stone barn, which has since become a popular tourist attraction. To those owners who have been able to save these gems of America's past, all barn lovers owe a debt of gratitude.

FOREWORD

Although often right before our eyes, especially in rural areas, certain things lie dormant for years as far as a scrutiny of their nature is concerned. It seems that we take these things for granted and they are simply overlooked. We ask ourselves – *What do they have to offer us that might be of particular interest?* They are the old buildings, particularly often abandoned ones, that basically collect dust and are frequently just repositories for people's stuff and, not uncommonly, objects of no real utility.

But along comes the mid-1970s and what starts to appear are books on barns, a few of the scholarly type and others essentially picture publications about barns of many ages. These buildings had critical practicality at countless homesteads in the 18th and 19th centuries across America. Contemporary reactions to barns are often "They can be pleasant to look at, but they belong to another age." Or "Sometimes they are eyesores." Normal reactions from the uninformed.

Prior to about 1975, few books on barns in North America had materialized. However, Eric Sloane, the dean of paintings of Americana, had written two books on these rapidly disappearing structures: the first in 1954, *American Barns and Covered Bridges*, and the second, *An Age of Barns*, in 1966. In the latter, he covered a broad diversity of barn types with various construction materials. At that time, only two or three books described barns in Pennsylvania – the greatest area of these quintessential agri-buildings, whether of log, stone, frame or combinations of these materials.

From 1975 to the mid-2020s, dozens of books appeared that focused on a wide array of barns, a good majority of them about barns in a particular geographic area or in a certain state. But few of them focused sole attention on one construction material of any kind – such as stone … until Robert Kroeger, a writer and artist from Ohio, made a commitment to include descriptions of stone barns in 41 states from coast to coast. He visited many of them himself – in recording their stories, taking photographs, and doing oil paintings of these old vernacular barns. That he did – by extensively documenting the history of each homestead, the people who occupied those lands, and their mostly neglected and unknown stories.

In facing daunting tasks, some of us do our homework and others of us do not. But Kroeger, in assembling everything together in this book on stone barns, did his and

pre-eminently so. And perhaps the best and quickest way we can tell this is by simply looking at his original compilation of 95 stone barns and their stories. All of this will appeal to a nationally broad-based audience and very little in almost any way is gone unnoticed in this seminal book. In treating many diverse geographical regions in America, he has exposed the manifold appearances of these stone buildings of eras that have spanned nearly 175 years – from what may be the oldest existing stone barn in the country, built in 1745 on the Silver Linden Farm in Loudon County, Virginia, to one in Meigs County, Tennessee, built at the onset of the Great Depression in 1930.

When an author writes about historic homesteads anywhere in North America and especially about the barns that were built at such locales, many specific topics about these individual places need to be addressed. In treating 95 barn sites, Kroeger's research embraces so many aspects that it seems like little is omitted. After finishing a rough draft of this substantial material, he conferred with the publisher; they both decided that splitting the book into two volumes would make each more affordable. So, the manuscript was divided – east and west of the Mississippi River. Each speaks eloquently about a piece of early American history.

Since we first connected in 2022, Kroeger has gained an especially keen awareness of the high concentration of stone-built barns in southeastern Pennsylvania. He calls this area "the mother lode" of stone barns in North America. In May 2024, I guided him on a tour of several of these barns within 25 miles of my home near Allentown. In addition to visiting these barns, he witnessed several dozen more stone barns as we drove towards the barns scheduled on the tour.

Kroeger's experiences in the past decade with barn construction have fostered what can be called a profound appreciation of the prodigious efforts of many early craftsmen who fashioned these lasting structures, using centuries-old European traditions. He set his eyes upon the various and prominent features of each of the barns in its individual architectural expression.

He told the stories of the early and later occupants of the homesteads. Like the proverbial kid in a candy store, Kroeger, with little exaggeration, could almost not contain himself. And who are we to blame him? The area in southeastern Pennsylvania has been and persistently maintains itself as a singular area as far as a myriad of stone barn construction is concerned. Stone barns here number in the thousands. For comparison, the author's home state of Ohio has less than a dozen stone barns and only three are included in this book.

I am fortunate and almost feel like being born under a lucky star when Robert Kroeger asked me to be a part of his barn sleuthing efforts. He's used his barn experiences to explain how America's pioneering people built these stone barns and he has covered a broad array of barns built to endure for generations. May his book on this much needed subject last as long. Barn people for the first time can make broad comparisons among many states in how these structures relate to each other and how they differ in construction. Kroeger's legacy stands as a profound tribute to these rural icons.

—**Greg Huber**
Author, *The Historic Barns of Southeastern Pennsylvania*
Allentown, Pennsylvania

ACKNOWLEDGEMENTS

I owe much gratitude to many who helped me in my research for this book. First, I thank those barn owners who took time to show me their barns and who occasionally supplied me with old barn siding to frame the painting, one more touch of nostalgia. And I must recognize my dental school roommate and friend, Dr. Pat Lang, for showing me how to make a barnwood frame.

Thanks also to the many local and state historical societies, state preservation offices, and barn foundations for giving me images, sending me newspaper and magazine articles, and connecting me with owners.

My barn scouts helped enormously, too, in directing me to stone barns. They include Jenny and Jack Clark of Michigan, Jim Dierberg of Missouri, Jack Smith of Iowa, Greg Huber and Warren Claytor of Pennsylvania, and Dr. Pat Lang of Massachusetts. These wonderful scouts not only provided leads but drove me around, allowing me to take notes, make compositions, and see several barns in a relatively short time. England's Ken Bonham has been helpful, thanks to his 14 Internet flip books on various aspects of stone barns in England and Wales.

The National Register of Historic Places, which, for brevity's sake, I'll refer to as simply the National Register, holds an enormous amount of information on barns, which helped me write their stories as did the many newspaper articles cited in the Register's nominations. Also, I relied on barn books, written by barn scholars, including Greg Huber, who kindly wrote this book's foreword. If I have omitted anyone who helped, I apologize deeply.

Traveling many miles to see these barns and meet their owners, spending countless hours in researching their history, and capturing them in paintings and essays became a labor of love. It's my hope that if, many years from now, someone sees one of these paintings and reads its essay, he or she will understand a little bit about the early pioneers, who sculpted our raw land into America, the land of the free and the home of the brave.

INTRODUCTION

Many might wonder why a retired dentist would be interested in old barns, begin painting them and documenting their stories, and feature them in three books, *Historic Barns of Ohio*, *Round Barns of America*, and now *Stone Barns of America*. The transition happened mysteriously in 2012.

After I lost my first wife to cancer, I remarried. Laura decided that we should start a tradition of an annual surprise trip on our wedding anniversary. And so, in 2012, she chose a rural B&B in Licking County, about an hour east of Columbus. As we turned down the country road, I noticed a small gray barn, perched on a hillside, its roof sagging, boards missing, and tilted about 10 degrees. As I looked up, it sent a message to me, almost like a thunderbolt: *You're going to do a painting of me, write an essay about my story, and preserve Ohio history.* Wow. It was startlingly real. Now, years later, the memory of that message is still vivid.

That night at dinner Laura and I talked about this supernatural epiphany and we decided to try to meet the barn owner. The next morning, Saturday, I knocked on the door of the circa 1830 farmhouse and met Mr. Herbert Hall, who at first was skeptical of my unannounced visit. After I explained his barn's message, he lightened up and told me how Welsh farmers moved here from the east coast, about the land grants for Civil War soldiers, and about the old gun shop across the street. His barn, one I call "Granville Gray," was full of hand-hewn timbers, some with bark still attached, joined in mortise and tenon fashion and connected with wooden nails. My Ohio Barn Project had begun.

Although my father had a fine art degree from Notre Dame and worked as a commercial artist for Truscon Steel in Youngstown, he didn't mentor me in art. So, I had to head back to the basics, studying, reading, practicing, taking workshops and learning much from an accomplished Cincinnati artist, all of which took time. Along the way, I fell in love with impasto (thick) oil painting with a palette knife, which gives a three-dimensional, rustic look, fitting for an old barn. Thanks to my dental school roommate, an accomplished carpenter, I learned how to make frames out of old barn siding, which seemed appropriate – a rustic barn, thick paint, a frame of weathered wood.

After starting my quest for barns on my own, which, luckily for me, didn't involve getting attacked by a vicious guard dog, I eventually reached out to historical societies, where I met locals who would guide me through their counties, showing me the barns and introducing me to the owners. Without these barn scouts, my project would have died.

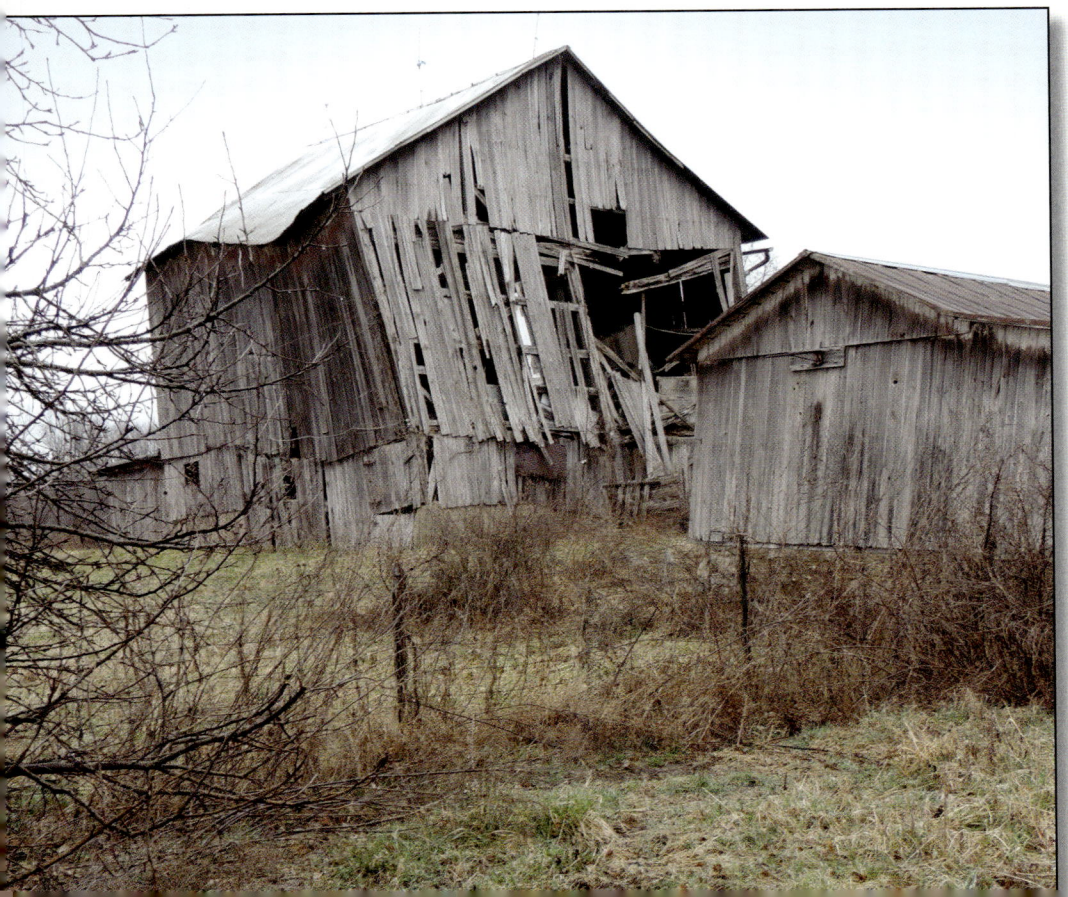

Now, armed with paintings, I decided to put them into fundraisers, at first for 4-H groups, but eventually – and now – in events for historical societies and museums throughout Ohio and Indiana. After doing fundraisers for many years, it finally dawned on me why I was doing this project: historical preservation. Accordingly, my focus became oriented towards local history or human-interest vignettes associated with the barn and its farm. Since old barns are vanishing – and their stories with

Granville Gray, 2020

9

them – my purpose was to preserve them while they still stood. The old barn of the 19th century was the "money maker," a structure that housed livestock and crops and, early on, sometimes the farm family, too. In a nutshell, this was subsistence farming and the barn was an essential part of it. So, being task oriented, I set a goal of 5,000 barn paintings. I'm about halfway there.

When I began this stone barn project, I decided to include only those barns with all four walls of stone. In the case of the Pennsylvania German bank barn with its forebay, the extended forebay is often wooden. But, as long as the walls supporting the forebay were stone, it qualified.

Unlike in the round barn project, I didn't have a comprehensive website cataloging stone barns to rely on – like the round barn site of Dale Travis – which made finding such barns easy. So, I relied on search engines, state historical societies, and state preservation offices for help. Many responded. Occasionally, when a stone barn owner would contact me, I'd look into each case thoroughly before deciding. And, at first, I was skeptical that I would find stories as compelling as those in the round barn project. But, as the years passed, the stories emerged and, with them, marvelous insights not only into the barns but into the development of our country – from the era of the colonies, through the Revolutionary War, the settlement of western territories, and into the Gilded Age of America.

Each barn had a story to tell, beginning with my first one, the Kindelberger stone barn in Monroe County, Ohio, listed on the National Register in 1980. The Kindelbergers, emigrants from Germany in 1846, were stonemasons and, although their first barn was wooden, it has a still-extant stone foundation, inscribed 1855 in stone. Later, Frederick, Jr. decided to build one that would last and, while searching for a well, he found a spot of 65 feet of bedrock, quarried huge blocks of sandstone, and placed them on top of each other, 20 rows high. The family worked on the barn for three years before finishing it in 1886.

After finding stone barns in 41 states, I had to decide how many to feature – 85, 90, 100? I based my selection of 95 barns on three criteria: esthetics, history, and the human-interest factor. Five have been named National Landmarks and 45 have been listed on the National Register, giving glimpses into regional history as well as into the lives of farmers who built them. And many that aren't listed on the Register clearly deserve to be. But, as some owners explained, they didn't want to deal with the regulations imposed on such a listing. After finishing my research in the fall of 2024 – one trip to the Shaker barns in New York and western Massachusetts and the stone barn in Cooperstown and the other to England's stone-barn-rich counties of Somerset, Devon, and Cornwall – I again conferred with the publisher.

He explained that the voluminous work would require a price close to $60, a cost that eliminates many barn book lovers. So, I split the work into two volumes – one east of the Mississippi and the other to the west of the river. Both books would be fairly equal in size and would be priced reasonably so that the message of the old stone barns could be shared with as many readers as possible.

The stories painted a colorful picture of early America. Hundreds of stone barns still exist in southeastern Pennsylvania and adjacent regions and many of those reflect tales of Revolutionary War battles. A barn in Rhode Island features a family heavily involved in the slave trade well after the state outlawed it. A Maine stone and gravel company built a stone barn to advertise their trade. New York's Shaker community built what was – and still is – the largest stone barn in America. Further south in Otsego County, a stone barn was built on a farm once owned by James Fenimore Cooper, author of beloved novels, *The Deerslayer and Last of the Mohicans.*

The Gilded Age, a term coined by humorist Mark Twain, ranged from about 1880 to 1920, a time of great wealth and monumental mansions … and stone barns. Fortunes were made by self-made men like Andrew Carnegie, immigrant son of a poor weaver, who left Scotland for America in 1848. In 1901 he sold his steel company to J.P. Morgan for $480 million and, though he had plans to build a stone barn, he never did – unlike many of his fellow millionaires.

Though these men and women of great wealth were concentrated mostly on the east coast, midwestern and western entrepreneurs built stone barns to show off their affluence, too. But not all builders of stone barns were wealthy. The German-Russians and Czechs of the Dakotas were subsistence farmers and they also were stonemasons. Living on treeless prairies, they resorted to stone. Outcroppings of stone on the grasslands of Iowa, Nebraska and Kansas led to more stone barns.

Cattle barons, another source of new wealth, often built stunning stone barns. One of them, Charles Goodnight, built one in 1870 in Pueblo, Colorado, on a route he devised to drive longhorn cattle from Texas to markets in the north. His life was featured in the television mini-series, Lonesome Dove. In another western story, perhaps fodder for another documentary, an Oregon rancher, fearing Indian attacks, hired Scottish stonemasons to build a barn to protect his prized champion stallion. Yes, a stone barn exclusively for one horse.

Many builders of stone barns had German heritage, especially those in southeastern Pennsylvania and in pockets of Germanic settlements, such as in Hermann, Missouri, and in the communities along the Ohio river in northern Kentucky. Frequently, during the massive immigration of seven million Germans during the 19th century, surnames would become Americanized. In 1882, my own great-grandfather, Gerhardt Kröger, emigrated from Germany to South Bend, Indiana, bringing my grandfather Joseph, aged seven. Around 1900, the family changed its name, deleting the umlaut in Kröger and changing it to Kroeger – to make pronunciation and spelling easier for fellow Americans. But, trust me, it still gets mispronounced and misspelled.

It's also important to realize that Germany didn't become Germany until 1871. Though many immigrated from these lands before 1871, it's easier to call them Germans from Germany instead of from one of the feudal states such as Prussia, Saxony, Bavaria, Würtemberg, and many others.

If old historic wooden barns can be likened to the insides of a cake and if round barns can be regarded as icing, then surely barns of stone would be the cake's glowing candles. The fairy tale, *The Three Little Pigs*, showed that the big, bad wolf couldn't huff and puff the brick house down. He'd have trouble with a stone house, too.

Stone barns were built to last. And often they stood the test of time, even if the roof burned. The stone shell of the massive Shaker barn in New Lebanon, New York, still stands, waiting for locals to restore it someday.

Initially, most farmers in early America built log barns since gigantic trees were abundant. According to Eric Sloane in *An Age of Barns*, by the end of the 1700s, there were about 9,000 log barns on the tax records of Pennsylvania. Less than 2,000 were stone and presumably about half of all American barns during the Revolutionary years were made of logs.

As farmers in southeastern Pennsylvania and in nearby states began to prosper in the late 18th and early 19th century, they began using stone. Huge trees were vanishing and stone was abundant and, let's face it, a stone barn was much more appealing and durable than one made of wood. The barn's beautiful stonework often flaunted the wealth of the farmer.

Yet not all owners were wealthy. In fact, most in the 19th century were subsistence farmers and had to be frugal. In northern climates, the freeze and thaw cycles would raise stones to the surface, which had to be cleared before planting crops. Often farmers would use these stones and rocks for building. But for others the stones were a nuisance. In Michigan Albert Loeb, whose restored stone barn graces the cover of this book, came up with an ingenious idea when he decided to build a stone mansion and barn complex. He offered to accept the rock piles from area farms, which meant that the farmer would be rid of the stones and have his fields cleared for planting. Loeb used the stones to build probably the most impressive barn complex in the Midwest. Thankfully, it's been restored and is open to the public.

Did I visit each barn? No. Although I visited many, it would have taken me several more years to see all the stone barns in this book. And, unlike those who are younger than I am, my clock doesn't have a lot of time left in it. And it's ticking.

The barns are arranged geographically, beginning in the northeast and ending in Wisconsin; the second volume of stone barns will feature barns west of the Mississippi. Some states have only one barn represented, but others have multiple barns, which are listed alphabetically by county. I found only a few in southern states; with mild winters, farmers didn't need barns in the South, much less stone barns.

I'm also fortunate that Greg Huber and Warren Claytor gave me tours of the stone barns in southeastern Pennsylvania, where thousands of old stone barns still stand. Like Ohio's Hubert Wilhelm and Allen Noble and Pennsylvania's Robert Ensminger, Huber is a barn scholar, having traveled to Europe to explore the stone barns of the U.K. and the wooden barns of Germany, precedents for traditional timber-framed American barns.

— **Robert Kroeger**
Cincinnati

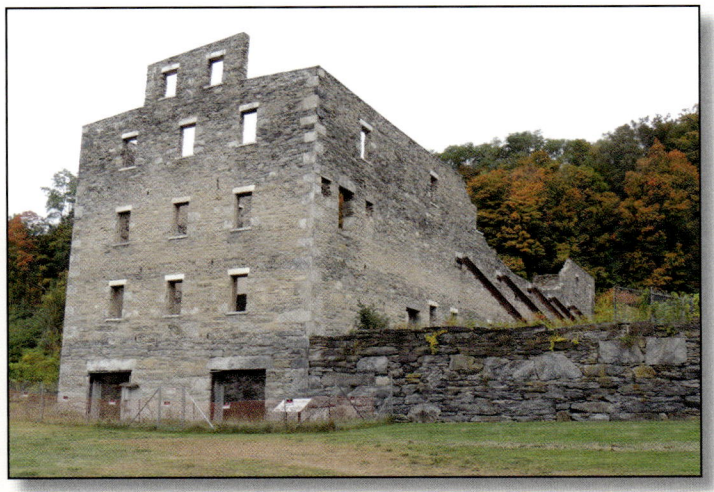

Stone wall shell, Shaker stone barn, Mt. Lebanon, New York, 2024.

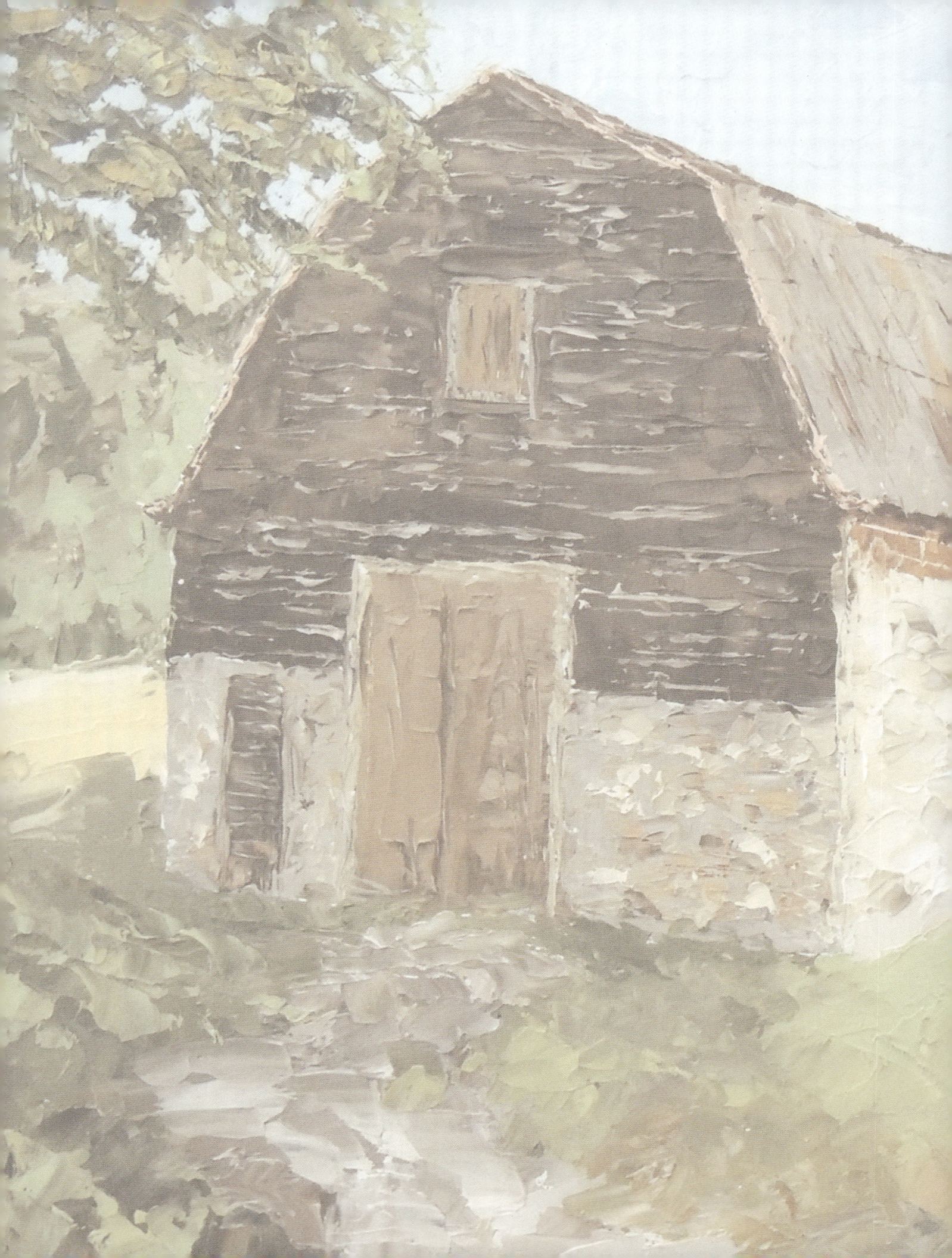

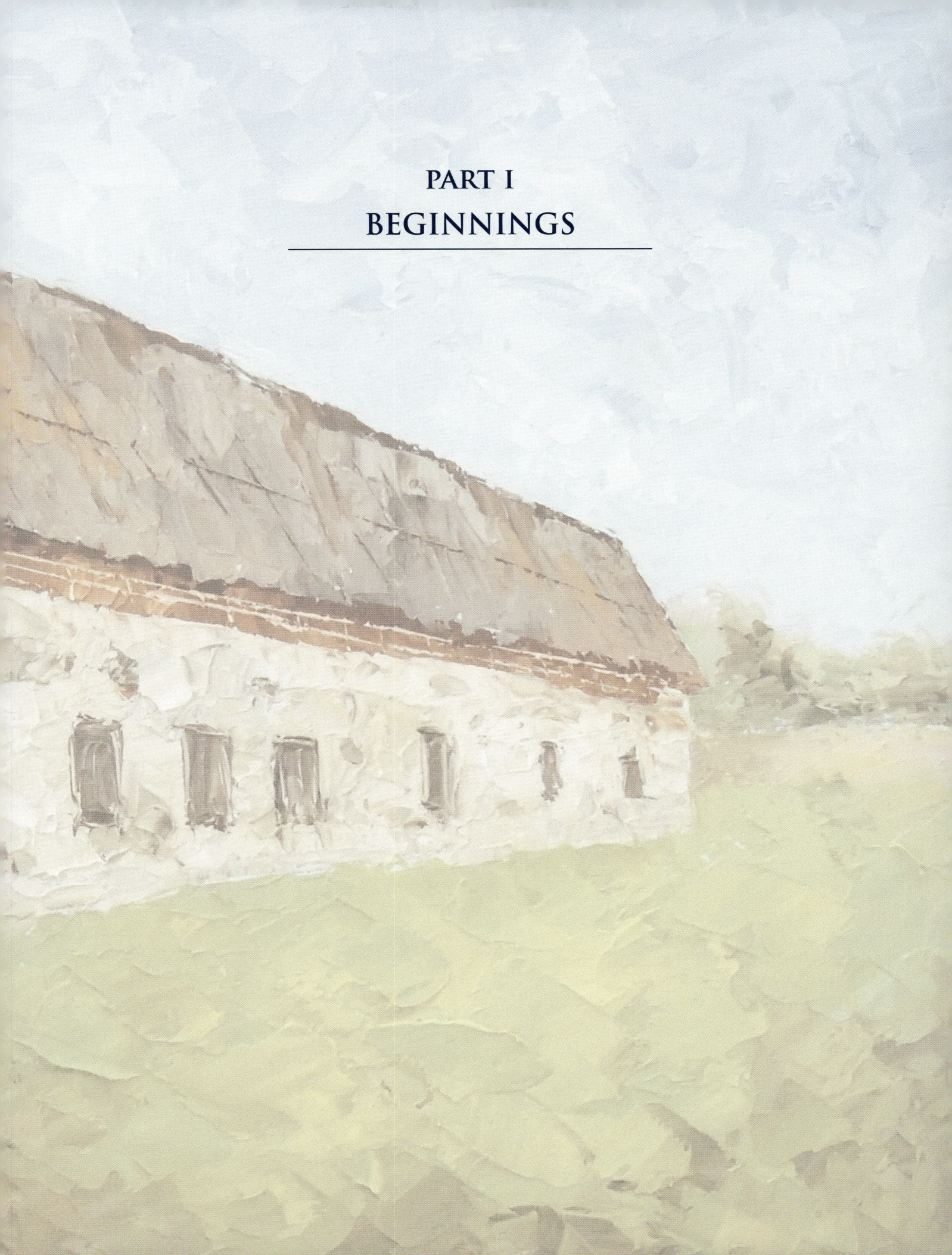

PART I
BEGINNINGS

1. STONEMASONRY

Like old barns, the art and craft of stonemasonry is fading into the sunset. Anyone who looks at a well-constructed fieldstone barn will enjoy its beauty, the randomness of the arrangement of the stones, and the variations of color. Master stonemasons, like famous artists, have left their legacies, though they're often forgotten, unlike Claude Monet, the Wyeths, and John Singer Sargent, whose painting, *Group with Parasols*, sold for $23.5 million in 2004. The advent of stone-cutting machines and artificial man-made stone has begun to eclipse the artistry and craftmanship of the stonemasons.

In fact, these days master stonemasons are few and far between. Ian Cramb, the Scottish author of *The Art of the Stonemason*, explained that he attained the mastership level after his work in restoring stonework at the historic Abbey of Iona, an island off the western coast of Scotland, visited by pilgrims from around the world.

By the 12th century in western Europe, as religious fervor heightened, thousands of stone churches and cathedrals had been built – a lucrative industry for those who built them. Guilds were formed and included three classes of stonemasons: the apprentice, the journeyman, and the master stonemason. Apprentices were often indentured to experienced masons as the price for their training. Journeymen, at the next level, were skilled enough to travel on projects with a master. If a journeyman aspired to move up, he had to present his "masterpiece" to the guild for approval before being certified. And master stonemasons could travel freely to work on buildings for their patrons. They often carved their signature marks onto stone walls, especially to make sure they received payment for their work.

Prior to 1220 masons used an axe to cut stone but after this date they used chisels, which allowed the mason to become an artist as well as a craftsman. Over the centuries stonemasonry in Europe evolved into a beautiful art form; but masons didn't leave behind any written records of their methods. Skills in cutting and laying stone were passed down from one generation to the next – without instruction manuals.

TYPES OF STONE

Though there are many types of stone and rock, the three main classifications are sedimentary, igneous, and metamorphic. Since the last category includes marble and quartzite, which are seldom seen in stone barn construction, there's no need to describe them. The most common stones used in barns are sedimentary: limestone and its softer cousin sandstone. These stones come in a variety of colors – the Smithsonian Castle is built with red Seneca sandstone from Maryland. Shale and slate are parts of this group, but seldom seen in barn walls, though slate roofs on barns became popular in America in the late 19th century. Sedimentary stones are often found in farmers' fields and appropriately called fieldstones, which often surface after a thaw in springtime. Farmers must deal with these stones before they plow their fields. Some are small – like the cobblestones of northern New York state.

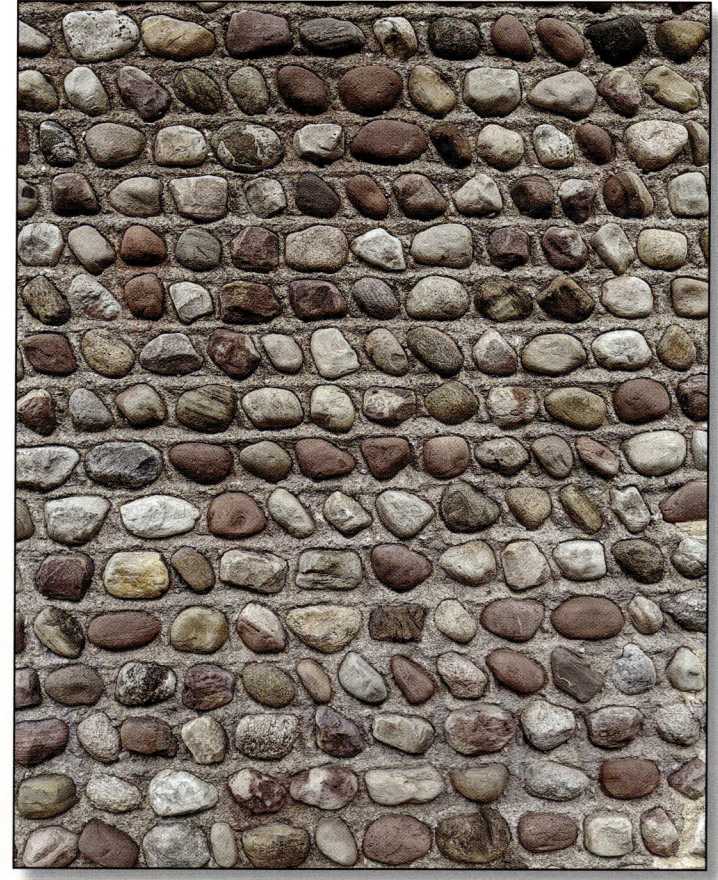

Cobblestone wall, Roe Cobblestone Schoolhouse, circa 1820. Wayne County, New York. Wikimedia Commons.

The densest rock is igneous; it's difficult to cut and shape, a challenge for anyone with skills less than those of a master stonemason. In Cornwall, southwestern England, granite was abundant and homes and barns built here hundreds of years ago still display masterful granite stonemasonry. Northern New England is full of granite, which was used in a barn in Maine that's described in this book's fourth chapter. Volcanic rock, seen mostly in the far western states, adorns stone barns of the late 1800s and the early 1900s. Called lava rock or basalt, it's extremely demanding to work with, though readily available in outcroppings, especially in Idaho.

Though there are other variations of stone used in old barns, one striking example is Pennsylvania Bluestone, which was used in historic barns of southeastern Pennsylvania. Found mostly in Susquehanna County, about 150 miles north of Philadelphia, it's a strong stone but can be worked easily and its colors include green, beige, and lilac, a veritable artist's palette.

SOURCES OF STONE

Masons found their stone in three locations. The easiest source – and possibly the earliest – was stone found in the farmer's own field. In northern climates, the combination of freezing and thawing would thrust stones up, creating a cumbersome task for the farmer before planting each spring. Frost heave, as this phenomenon is called, requires three factors: porous glacial soil, water, and freezing temperatures. The cycle of freezing and thawing is powerful enough to displace giant boulders.

Another source of stone occurs naturally in outcroppings or ledges. These are the products of the glaciers of 11,000 years ago and soil erosion, which exposes the rock over time. Small to large outcroppings provided stone to masons throughout America and were often found in cliffs, streams and riverbanks, or on hillsides. Formations of black lava rock, or basalt, still dot the highways of south-central Idaho, not far from the Craters of the Moon National Monument.

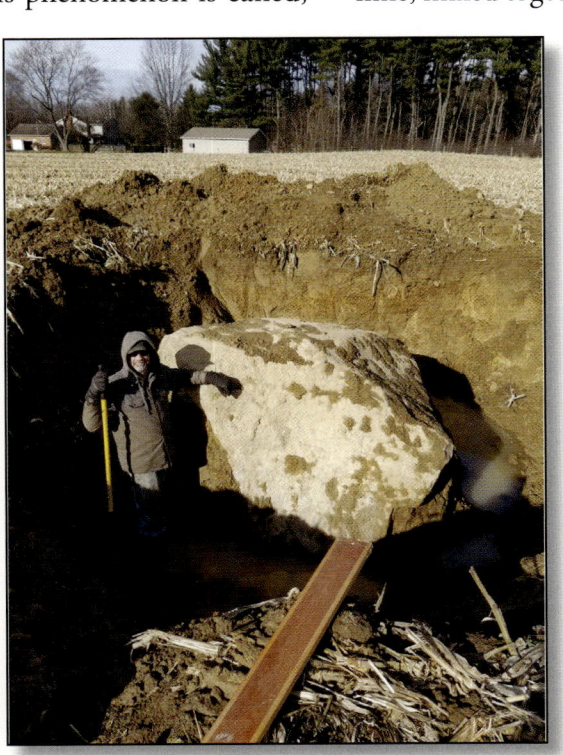

A springtime surprise of fieldstone in a farmer's field. Mahoning County, Ohio. Courtesy of Wayne Anderson.

Sometimes the barn builder would have to travel only a short distance from the farm and haul the stone in wagons or stoneboats, an example of vernacular construction.

The third source was the stone quarry. In America sandstone quarrying first took place in 1639 in Hartford, Connecticut. Two more quarries followed in 17th century Connecticut and, as settlers moved westwards, more quarries were established. The productive 19th century quarries of Iowa and Kansas supplied stone for many bridges, roads, and buildings as far west as California, thanks to railroad shipping. However, those structures, made with stone from locations far away, would not qualify as vernacular buildings. And some farms – like Ohio's Kindelberger – had their own quarries, meaning that their stone barns were built in the vernacular sense.

MORTAR

Going back to 2,500 BC, Egyptians used lime in mixing mortar for their Great Pyramid of Giza, the oldest of the Seven Wonders of the Ancient World. The Romans used it extensively throughout their vast empires, although they sometimes constructed their buildings with precisely cut blocks and stones – without mortar. Dry stone construction required exact measurement, expert stone cutting, and meticulous design. In 30 BC Roman engineer Marcus Vitruvius formulated a recipe for mortar: volcanic ash and lime, mixed together with volcanic rocks and seawater. He wrote, "… When it [the lime] is slaked, let it be mingled with the sand in such a way that, if it is pit sand, three of sand and one of lime is poured in." Over 2,000 years later, Roman mortar has stood the test of time.

In the 18th and 19th centuries farmers in the South began using lime as a fertilizer, a practice that spread into Delaware and southeastern Pennsylvania. Chester County's Samuel W. Pennypacker wrote that in 1798 a farmer named Christian Maris had successfully experimented with lime in his soil-deficient farm. And, thanks to the region's abundant limestone and old growth forests – the marble and limestone deposits in the Pike Creek Valley were the largest in Delaware – the lime business flourished. Farmers quickly realized that the limestone-rich soil was productive and stone kilns, used to extract lime from limestone, were common by 1750.

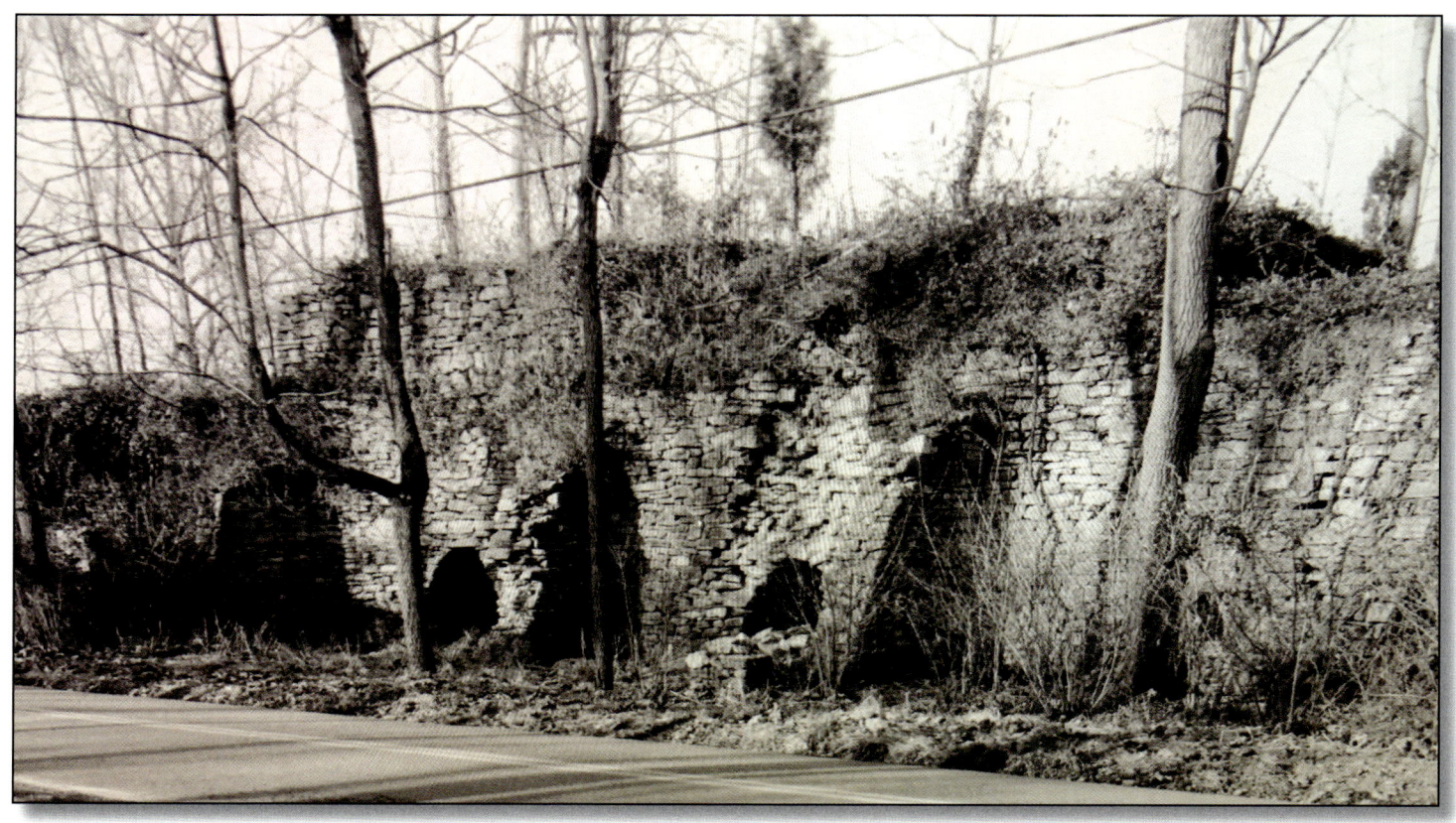

Ruins of lime kilns, Delaware, circa 1800. Wikimedia Commons.

Masons often had their own formula for mixing mortar. Many learned from their fathers or from master stonemasons. Some would taste the mix, not a pleasant thought, but probably effective. If the mortar was mixed correctly and contained sufficient lime, it could breathe, which would help it avoid cracking when temperatures would fluctuate. Author Ian Cramb comments on the necessity of a stone wall to breathe, "With a mix [of mortar] that is too strong, the moisture will stay in, and the wall will be damaged when colder temperatures come."

PORTLAND CEMENT

England's Joseph Aspdin, a stonemason and builder, patented a material called Portland cement in 1824. It consisted of a blend of limestone, clay and other minerals to produce fine particles, which became a strong building material when mixed with water. He named it after Portland stone, which was quarried on the Isle of Portland, just off the southern shore of England. Aspdin's son improved the product in the 1840s.

By the spring of 1886 the Coplay Cement Company of Lehigh County, Pennsylvania, began to produce Portland cement and built nine 90-foot-tall kilns between 1892 and 1893, making this the center of this industry in the country. By the early 1890s, the use of Portland cement

had spread westwards and eventually curtailed the use of stone, shutting down quarries in limestone-rich Iowa and Kansas. Building walls and foundations out of this cement was faster and cheaper than using quarried stone.

Unlike lime mortar, Portland cement is rigid and can lead to cracking in stonework, especially if used in tuckpointing over lime mortar. This error is sometimes seen when historic buildings are repaired incorrectly. Good stonemasons know that the right mixture of lime putty mortar has a lower compressive strength than cement and will allow the old mortar to expand and contract without causing damage.

TOOLS

A stonemason's tools evolved over time, and, compared to those used today, may seem primitive. However, judging by the attractiveness of stone barns of the 18th and 19th centuries, they must have worked well in the hands of a master stonemason. Iron wedges of various sizes were used to split stone. Early Egyptian workers used chisels of copper, bronze, and stone. Eventually, chisels were made from iron and steel. Some had flat edges; others had serrated edges. Each had a purpose and each had a name: pitching chisel, drove, splitting chisel, and splitter.

One of the more interesting tools in the 19th century

stonemason's bag was the cran-dall, a hammer-like tool used for finishing. Usually, it measured 20 to 30 inches long, weighed about 10 pounds, and had teeth on both sides. One was recently for sale on Ebay for $295.00. When Marge and Gary Baumberger, the fifth genera-tion of Ohio's historic Kindelberger farm, took ownership in the 1970s, they explored the barn's attic and discovered the stonemason's tools that were used to build this barn in the 1880s. In the photo, Gary holds a crandall and Marge holds a pick, used by her great-grandfather to build the barn in 1886.

As basic as these tools were, they still worked well in the hands of a skilled mason. However, in those days there weren't any safety regula-tions nor any protective gear. Often, when cutting or smoothing stone, dust would fill the air, entering the mason's lungs – sometimes resulting in fatalities.

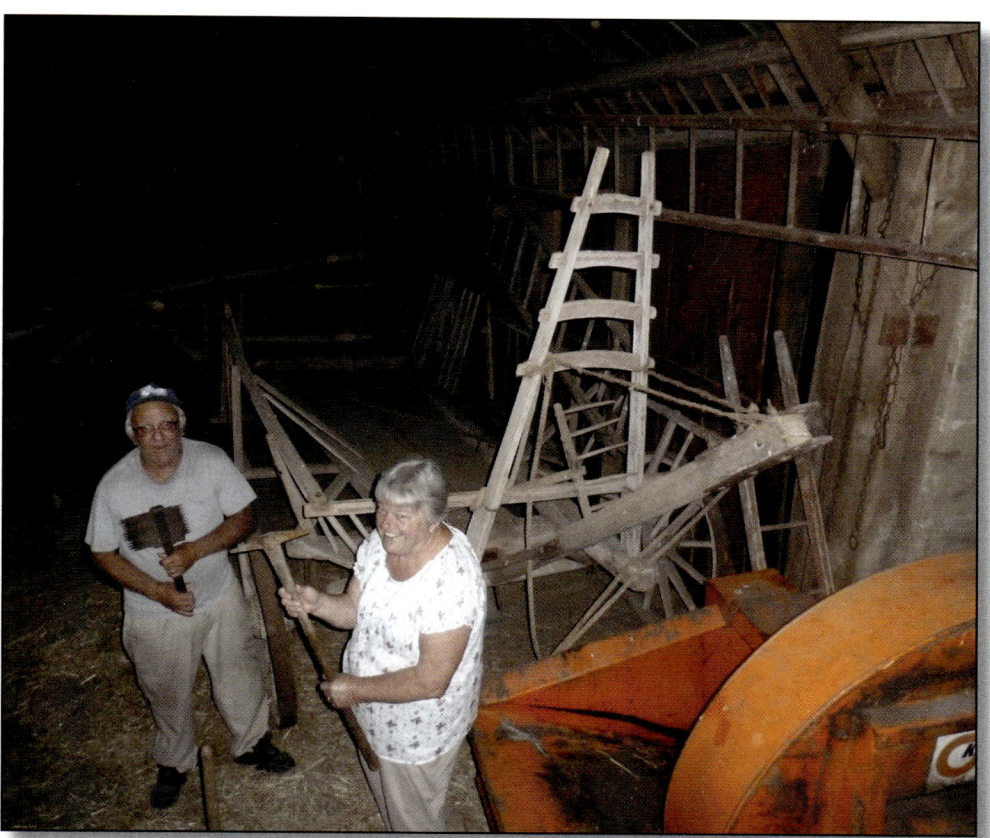

Gary holds a crandall and Marge holds a pick. Kindelberger stone barn, Ohio

ARCHITECTURE OF STONEMASONRY

Stone was abundant in medieval Great Britain and was used to in building thousands of stone barns. In fact, stone often covered the roof, which required sturdy internal support. Early in stone barn construction, an unknown builder ingeniously invented the cruck, a curved wooden support for a stone barn's roof. However, wood became scarce as early as the 17th century, when, in

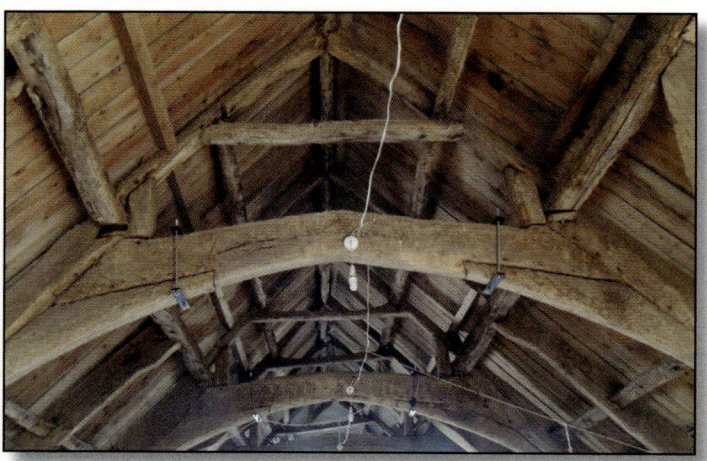

French oak crucks in the Cargoll barn.

order to supply trees for ship building for the Royal Navy, England passed acts that forbade the pruning of oak trees. As its fleet grew in numbers, so did the need for trees. To build a single 100-gun ship in the late 1700s, it took about 4,000 mature oak trees. That slowed down the use of crucks in barns, which peaked in the 17th century.

Crucks are curved blades, often ranging in width from one to two feet, that help support the roof, which usually was covered initially with thatch but later with slate, stone, or clay tiles, a heavy load. The builder would fell a tall tree that had a bend in it, hew it with an axe, and then split or saw it down the middle, which produced two matching crucks. These wooden blades would reach from the apex of the roof, braced by a ridge pole or a cross beam, and extend to the floor where the cruck would rest on a stone foundation, called a plinth. Using crucks meant that the walls were usually not load bearing since the cruck delivered the weight of the roof to the ground, which prevented the heavy roof from spreading the walls outward.

British researcher Dr. Nat Alcock, a pioneer in the sub-ject of medieval cruck-built structures, has suggested that crucks whose blades are embedded in the bottom third of that moved to America, though there are rare examples of a curved support known as a ship's knee. In almost all stone barns in the United States, the roof rests directly on the stone walls. Many phrases can be used to describe the way a stonemason would lay a stone wall and this assortment of language can be confusing. Stones can be arranged randomly, which adds appealing artistry as do variations in the color of the stones. However, even though the stones appear to be placed without rhyme or reason, there is order. Scottish master stone-mason Ian Cramb argues that masonry is a science as well as an artform. His book, *The Art of the Stonemason*, at times reads more like an engineering text.

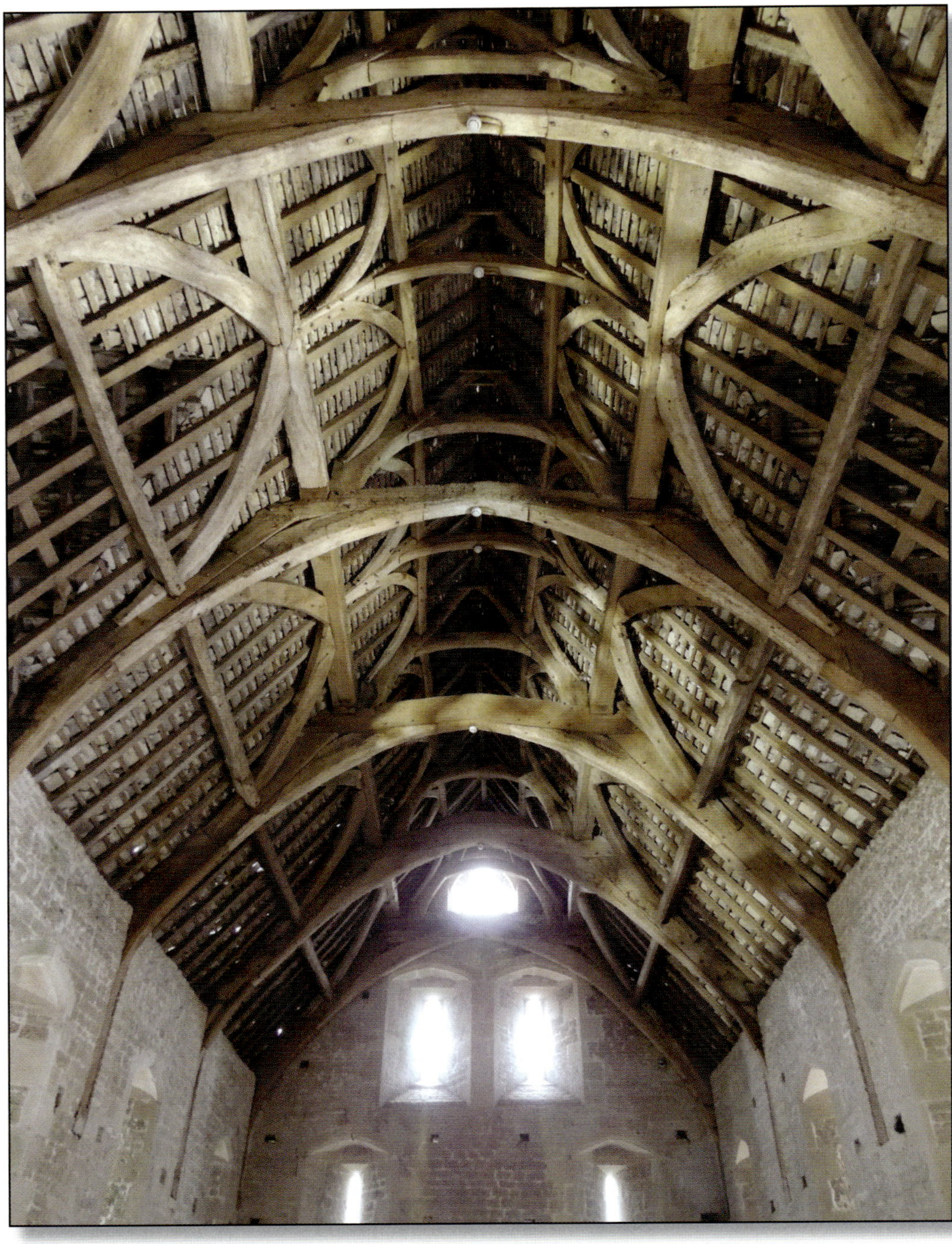

Though masonry construction varies – random rubble construction, dressed sandstone, coursed ashlar, random ashlar – it usually shares one common ingredient – the quoins. These are large stones, placed on the corners, often extending on both sides. While some quoins are primarily decorative, most deliver support to the corners. Occasionally, masons would extend stones outwards from the corners, making any stone barn expert wonder what their purpose was.

Crucks resting on stone walls, Glastonbury Abbey barn, circa 1340 AD. Somerset. 2024

the stone wall can be called "full crucks" while those with feet embedded in the middle third can be labeled "raised crucks." Crucks with feet set in post holes or in the ground may have been common once, but are rarely seen today since wood touching ground normally rots. According to Alcock in *A Catalogue of Cruck Buildings*, there were 3,845 barns with crucks in England in 2002.

For some reason, when immigrants from England arrived in America, though familiar with cruck construction, they chose to build wooden, timber-framed barns. Even when they started building stone barns, they did not make crucks. Perhaps that skill set did not travel down to the generations

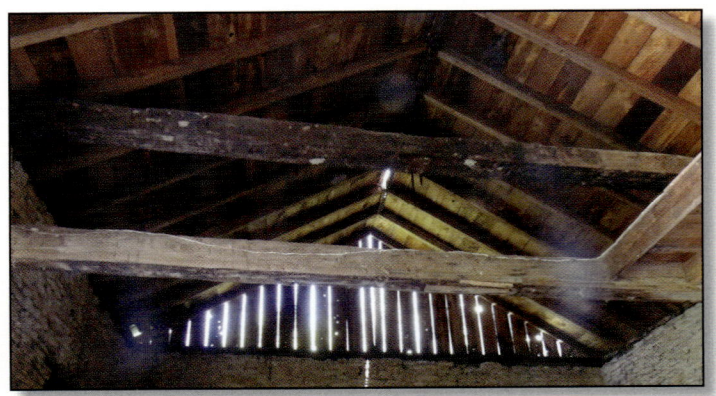

Roof rafters resting on stone walls, barn circa 1800. Hamilton County, Ohio.

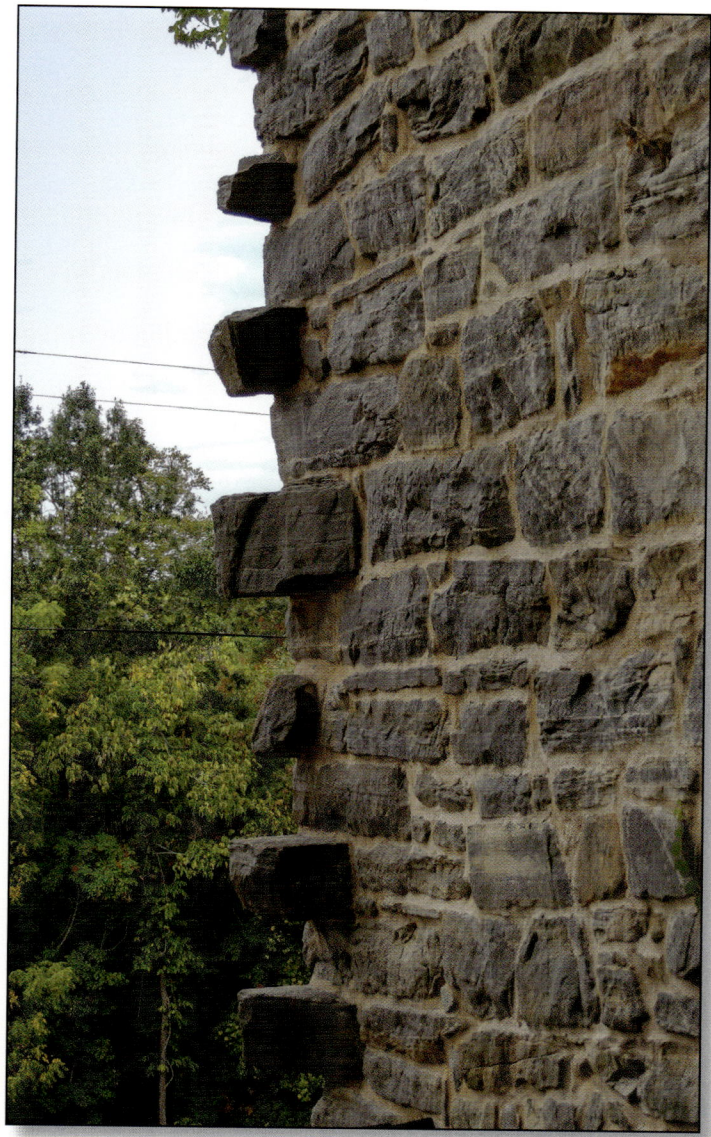

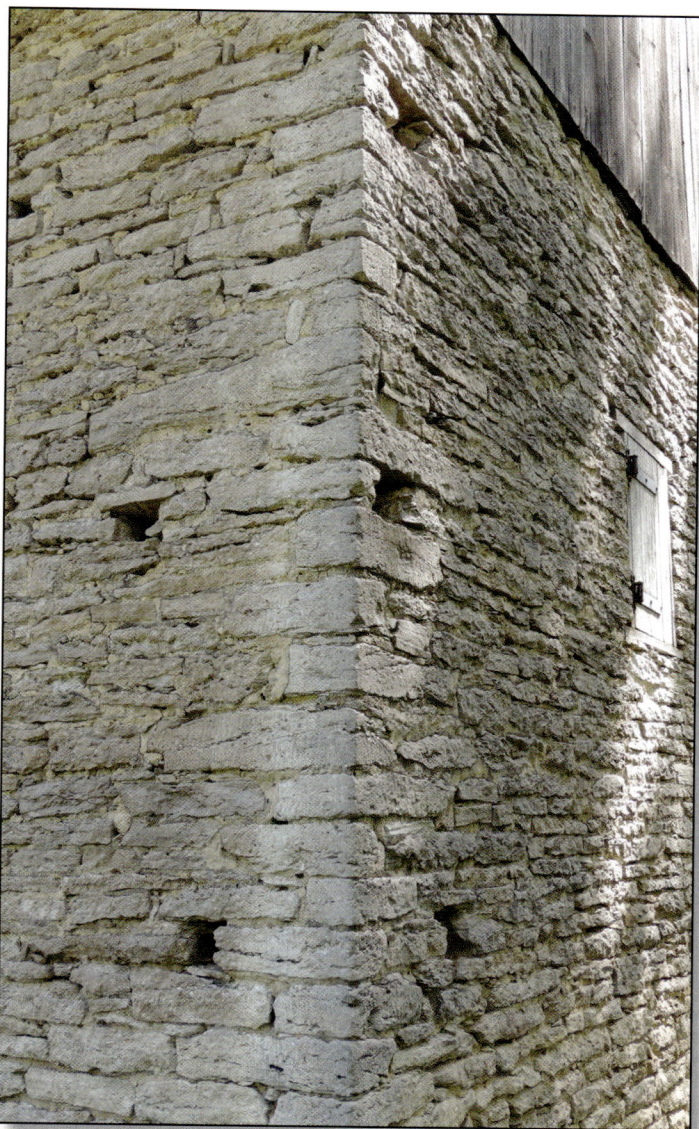

Corner extensions on a stone barn, circa 1850, Gasconade County, Missouri.

Open holes for scaffolding, barn circa 1800. Hamilton County, Ohio.

Though many masons erected scaffolding as they laid stone upwards on a barn wall, they usually would fill in the holes where their ladders and planks would rest. Occasionally the masons would leave the holes exposed, open only on the outside.

Another important consideration in building a stone barn was the foundation. Without ground support, heavy stone walls would crack or shift. In Ohio, when the Kindelbergers were exploring for a well for water, they chanced upon a plateau of 65 feet of flint bedrock. Taking advantage of this foundation, they laid one of America's most impressive stone barns, listed on the National Register in 1980. Excavating a quarry on the farm, the masons cut and dressed sandstone blocks, four to seven feet long, each weighing hundreds of pounds and laid them in rows to a height of 35 feet. Completed in 1886 – after three years of labor – the barn hasn't shifted and it remains a classic achievement in dry stonemasonry, reminiscent of mortarless Roman aqueducts.

DEFINITIONS

Since stonemasonry, especially the kind done in the 18th through early 20th century in America, is a complex subject, definitions are in order.

Ashlar—This term is used in a number of ways and perhaps is used too often. It refers to quarried stone that has been cut to specific dimensions and has been laid precisely, often with little mortar.

Buttress—A stone structure leaning against the outside wall of a building to provide support against lateral forces. Many of Great Britain's medieval barns have supporting buttresses, though not as elaborate as the "flying" buttresses of Notre-Dame Cathedral in Paris, built in the 12th century.

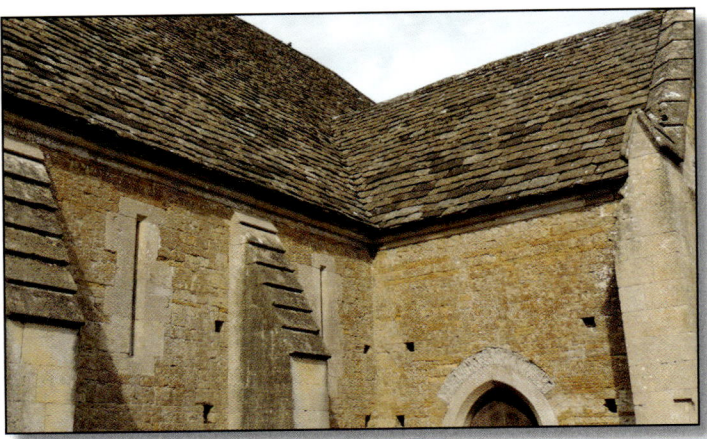

Buttresses supporting crucks and a 100-ton stone-tile roof. Glastonbury Abbey, Somerset County. 1340

Courses—These are the rows of stone, sometimes regular and sometimes apparently irregular, though Ian Cramb claims that there's always some regularity in any row.

Cruck—In medieval Britain, barn builders would select a tall tree with a curve at the top, cut it down, saw or axe it in half, and use the mating pieces to support the roof.

Dressed Stone—Masons can shape and smooth a stone's face before laying it. Or they can leave it rough and rustic-looking. Each has its advantages.

Gentleman Farmer—Compared to the small subsistence farmer, the gentleman farmer had substantial assets, making his farm essentially a hobby or a philanthropic way to experiment with agriculture for the benefit of all farmers.

Quoins—These are rocks, stones, or cut blocks that are used on the corners of the walls, often for support, but sometimes mainly for decoration. They are usually larger than other stones in the wall and are always visible on both sides of the corner.

Rubble—Such stones are rough, though sometimes they have been cut on the side that's hidden. Most attractive stone walls are built in coursed random rubble. According to Cramb, "There is no such thing as uncoursed random rubble." All random rubble walls are built in courses.

Vernacular—This refers to using locally available materials in construction. For example, the quarries of 19th century Kansas and Iowa would often ship their limestone to California for construction there, where the masonry would not be vernacular. However, if the same stone were used locally in Iowa or Kansas, that would be vernacular construction.

Some writers choose to describe stonework with many phrases, which can confuse the reader, unless he or she happens to be a stonemason. Charles Ravenswaay in his book, *The Arts and Architecture of German Settlements in Missouri: A Survey of a Vanishing Culture*, lists 10 different terms for stonework: square dressed stones, random rubble with exposed surface, random rubble with mortar finish, random rubble without quoins, coursed rubble with slushed joints, coursed random rubble, coursed rubble with square joints, rectangular stones of uniform thickness, and dry walls of random rubble. Regardless of how randomly a stone pattern appears, Cramb argues that there is no such thing as uncoursed random rubble. Stone walls in Scotland, mortarless and appearing in a haphazard pattern, have held up for centuries. And that reflects the art and the skill of a stonemason.

DRY STONE MASONRY

The farm fields of Ireland, Scotland, and parts of northeastern America are lined with rustic stone fences, laid without mortar. Such structures have many advantages over mortared walls. However, construction of mortarless walls requires skilled stonemasons since their work depends mostly on gravity and the arrangement of the stones. The non-profit Dry Stone Conservancy was established in 1996 to preserve historic dry stone structures and to revive and promote the ancient craft of dry-laid masonry. They offer workshops in this field.

Yes, dry-laid stone walls can often last for centuries without repair. However, since most walls of America's stone barns bear the weight of the roof, few of them show dry stone masonry.

2. EVOLUTION OF STONE BARNS

Stone is the most durable material used in vernacular construction of barns. Consider Mt. Rushmore in the Black Hills of South Dakota. When state historian Doane Robinson got an idea to build a monument to attract tourists, he hired sculptor Gutzon Borglum to design and supervise the project. From 1927 to 1941, Borglum and 400 stonemasons chiseled the faces of four presidents out of sheer granite. Today, over two million visit the national park each year.

Stone is also one of the oldest types of building materials. El Paraíso, located on the central coast of Peru, has 10 stone buildings that date to 3,500 BC and stretch over 123 acres. In what is now Mosul, Iraq, archaeologists discovered the stone-walled city of Nineveh, with its coursed walls of gypsum and mud, built around 3,000 BC. The Egyptians used lime in mixing mortar circa 2,500 BC to build their pyramids. And one of the most impressive stone structures, the Great Wall of China, started in the 7th century BC, stretched for 13,171 miles. Roman architects and engineers built many structures with stones that remain today – 2,000 years later – some without mortar.

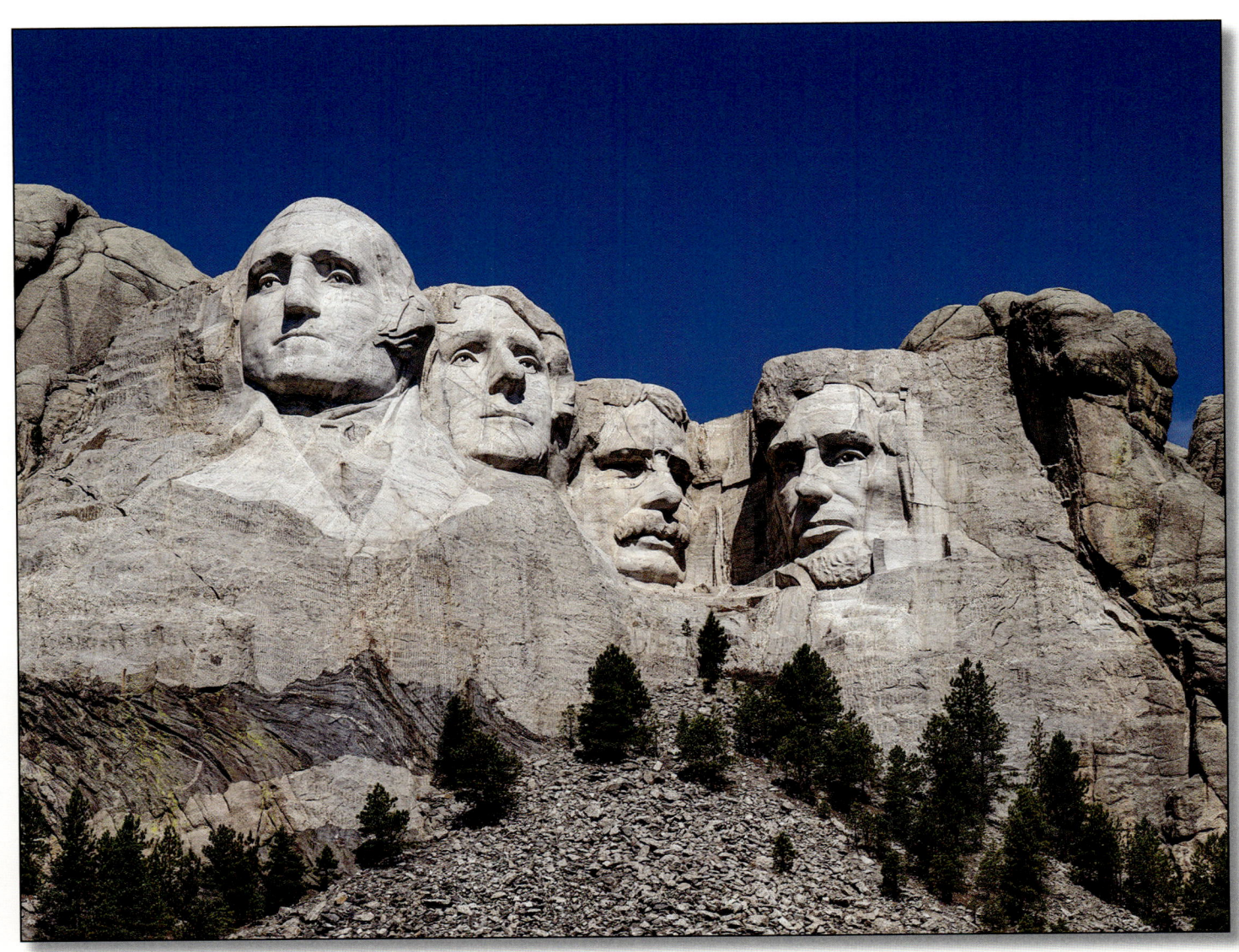

Mt. Rushmore and presidents Washington, Jefferson, Theodore Roosevelt, and Lincoln. Wikimedia Commons

After Julius Caesar invaded Britain in 54 BC, Romans continued their conquest in this new land and by AD 87 they were established. Along with legions of soldiers came Roman stonemasons, who began to build rectangular homes and barns out of stone, a drastic change from the typical Briton dwelling of a timbered and thatched roundhouse. For nearly 400 years Roman stonemasons and engineers built roads, buildings, and barns. The Roman bath complex in Somerset County, built between AD 60 and 70 and used by Romans until they left Britain, shows a high degree of stonemasonry.

The Emperor Trajan, who ruled Rome from AD 98 to 117 and expanded the empire to its furthest boundaries, ordered wooden barns be rebuilt with stone, even the roofs. Yes, the Romans and, later, the monastic orders feared fire, which often reduced their wooden barns to ashes. Stone doesn't burn. But even though the Romans built stone buildings, the majority of the population lived in wooden housing, most of which has been lost in time.

The countries of England and Wales, with thousands of stone barns still standing, probably had the biggest influence on stone barn construction in America. After the Romans, who introduced Christianity, left the British Isles in 410, Christian missionaries such as St. Augustine from mainland Europe and Sts. Columba and Columban sailed from Ireland to found abbeys in the sixth century. And, though Viking invasions wreaked havoc, they couldn't stop Christianity as it spread throughout this region.

However, when the Romans withdrew from Britain, they took with them their skilled engineers and stonemasons and stone building declined. The invaders (Germanic tribes such as the Angles, Saxons, and Jutes) built homes and barns out of timber.

The next major influence in stone barn construction was St. Benedict of Nursia, born in 480, less than 200 years after Emperor Constantine adopted the Christian religion, which became the official religion of Rome. Circa 530 St. Benedict formulated a manual of instruction for monks, which became known as The Rule of St. Benedict and was followed by the Benedictines and Cistercian monks. From his monastery at Monte Cassino in Italy, monasticism spread throughout Europe and into the British Isles. For his work Benedict is considered the founder of Western Christian monasticism. And thanks to Roman roads, monasteries spread. Pope Gregory the Great was so impressed with Benedict's Rule that in 594 he sent monks to England, where they founded England's first Benedictine monastery at Canterbury. In 597 St. Augustine arrived in Kent and converted King Aethelbert. Later, the monks brought the Romano-Christian stone culture with them. Eventually, stonework transitioned from homes and churches to include agricultural buildings, such as barns.

Charlemagne, who united and ruled most of western and central Europe circa 800, ordered all monasteries in his realm to adopt the Benedictine Rule, which all followed until the end of the 11th century, when the Cistercians were founded. Together with the Benedictines, they built between ten thousand and twenty thousand stone barns throughout Europe and Great Britain.

If he won the Battle of Hastings, William the Conqueror vowed that he would build a monastery, which he did in 1071, five years after his victory. The first monks came from the Benedictine Abbey of Marmoutier, France; the abbey was designed for 140 monks. French abbeys had stone barns.

As the monastic culture grew in England and Wales, the head monks, called abbots, often became the political kings of their estates and built huge stone buildings, including churches, residences, and barns. Most were built by the Benedictines and Cistercians. Other orders followed. Thousands of medieval stone buildings, including barns, have survived in Great Britain.

Tithe barns were built to store grain, a tribute paid by farmers, a tradition that traces back to the Romans and their taxation system. British farmers paid their tax by giving 10 percent of their harvest, which the monastery stored in tithe barns. On a trip to England in 2024 I visited two monastic stone barns, each well over 600 years old.

Located in Somerset County – and only 50 miles west of Stonehenge – Glastonbury Abbey is often considered the oldest extant abbey in England, as well as perhaps the wealthiest; its four barns represent one of the best-preserved stone farm complexes in Great Britain. Though St. Dunstan re-founded the monastery as a Benedictine abbey in 940 A.D., the main barn wasn't finished until 1340. Two hundred years later, Henry VIII dissolved the monasteries throughout Great Britain and Ireland, expelled or executed the monks, and sold or gave the abbeys to private landowners. Glastonbury continued to be used as a farm building until 1972. Today it's part of the Somerset Rural Life Museum, managed by the National Trust and open to visitors.

During restoration in 1976, dendrochronology was done, which dated the wood to the years 1343-1361. The limestone was likely taken from local quarries and the master stonemasons distinguished themselves by

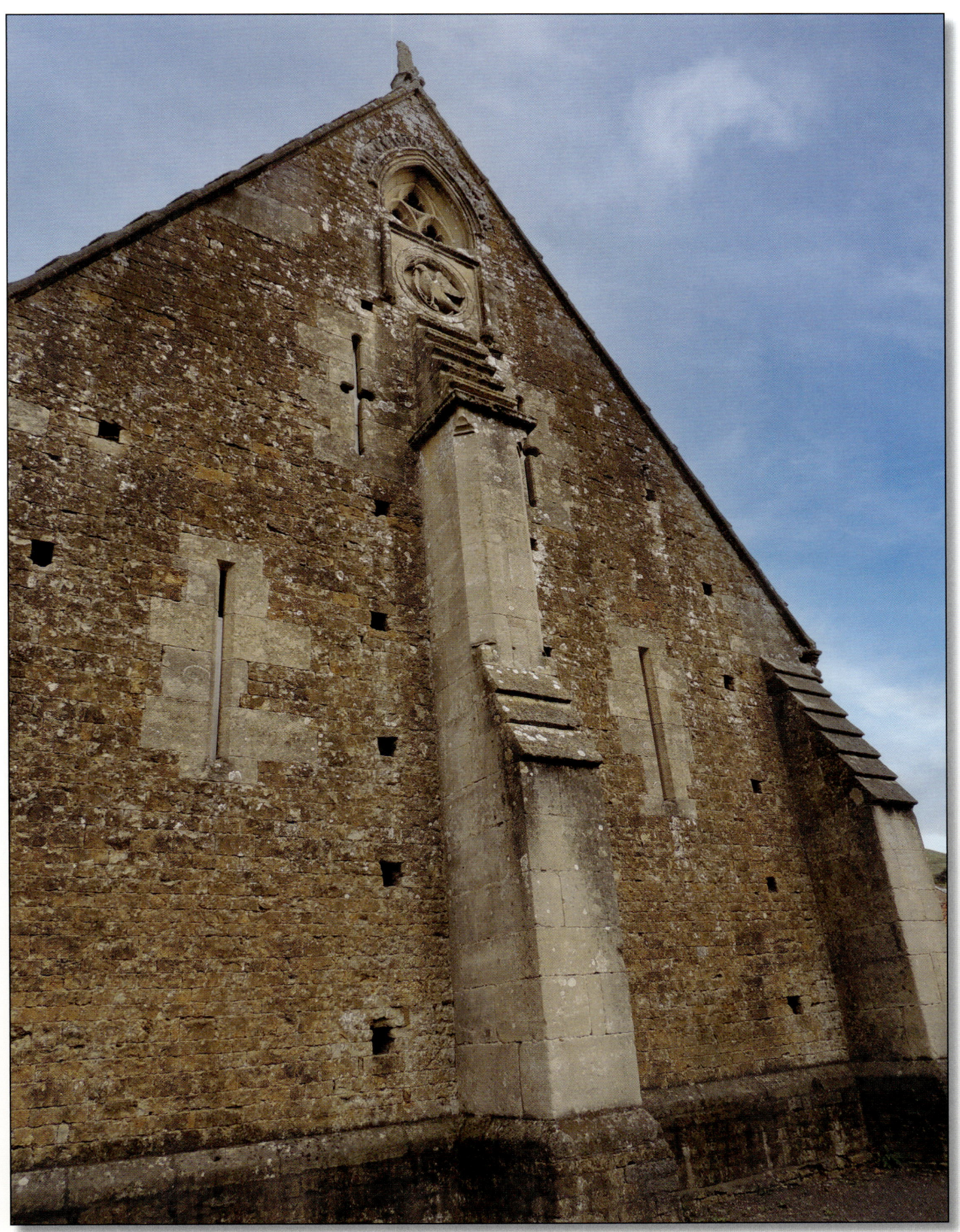

Glastonbury Abbey barn, 2024

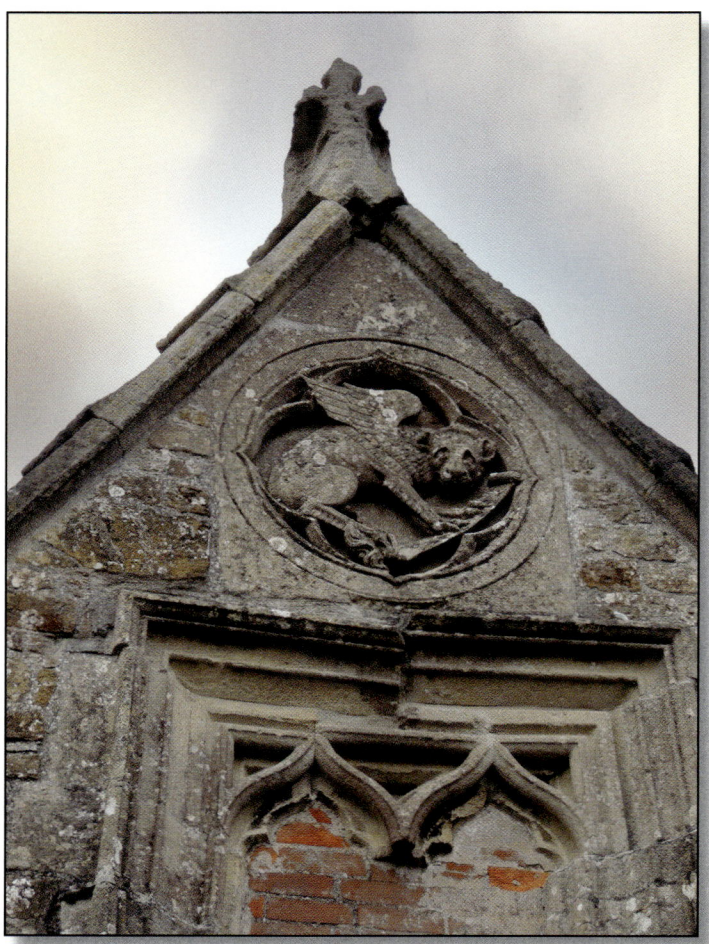

Glastonbury Abbey barn, stone carving of a winged lion, the symbol of St. Mark.

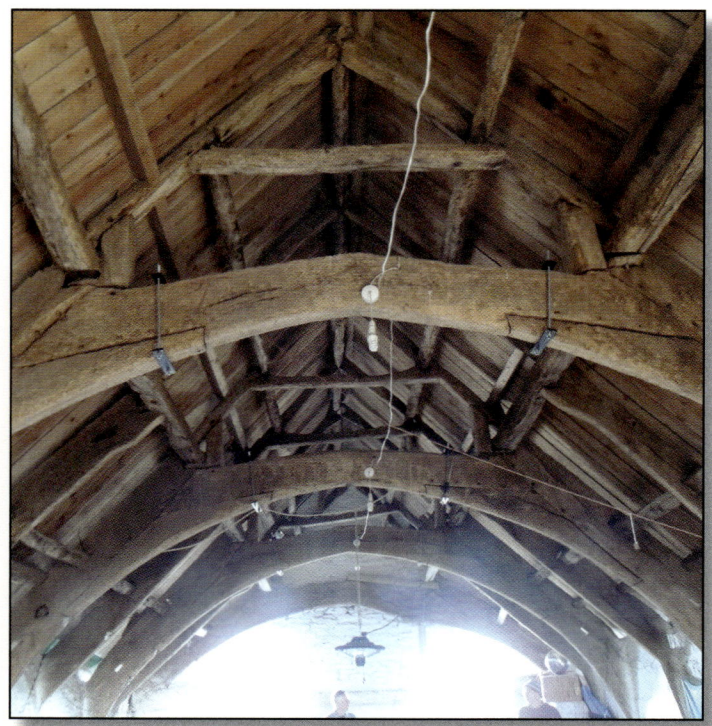

French oak crucks in the Cargoll barn. 14th century, Cornwall, England.

carving stone symbols of the four evangelists, Matthew, Mark, Luke, and John high on the exterior walls.

The barn features stone buttresses as well as wooden crucks, made of oak, elm, and chestnut, sturdy supports for the heavy stone tiled roof. The barn's interior is one of the best examples of medieval carpentry. Eight raised-base-cruck trusses, each double-tiered, brace the roof and are reinforced by exterior buttresses. At 95x33 feet, the barn is larger than most medieval stone barns and suggests that it stored crops from the monastery's estate.

The second barn I visited, this one near Newquay in Cornwall and privately owned, is a tithe barn – with an interesting story. It's the only survivor of an estate of the Bishops of Exeter, a town 80 miles eastwards. Bishop Walter Bronescombe "The Goode" purchased the land in 1269. A grant of a Thursday market was given in 1312.

Julian Odgers, a tenant, has been farming here on 425 acres since 1984. He explained that the Trewithen Estate, which purchased the farm in the early 1960s and continued buying adjacent farms, now owns 12,500 acres. Though the National Trust and English Heritage have classified the Cargoll barn as a Grade 1 listing, which recognizes it as an important building, neither organization is willing to restore it – for liability reasons. The wooden crucks are deteriorating.

In fact, the crucks are French oak, which begs the question of why would lumber be imported from France when Cornwall had plenty of its own timber in the 14th century. Julian explained that in 2019 French and British scientists examined the barn and took core samples for dendrochronology, which dated the wood to 1365. However, chances are that the bishop did not import this wood but rather repurposed it – salvaging it from a French ship that had shipwrecked on the Cornwall coast. It's been estimated that over the centuries as many as 6,000 ships have wrecked on this rocky coastline of approximately 250 miles. Although the origin of crucks may be debatable, one researcher suggested that it might have begun in boat building.

In the Cargoll barn crucks have been scribed with marriage marks, but the numeral one is missing, hinting that the barn had been shortened at some point. Mortise and tenon joints, fixed with wooden pegs, connect some of the trusses, though the original thatched roof has been replaced with corrugated metal and asbestos. Julian has added metal braces to secure the crucks, which fasten into the stone walls. On the exterior, buttresses support the crucks and the stonework, which is Killas rubble (a mining term for sedimentary rocks of the

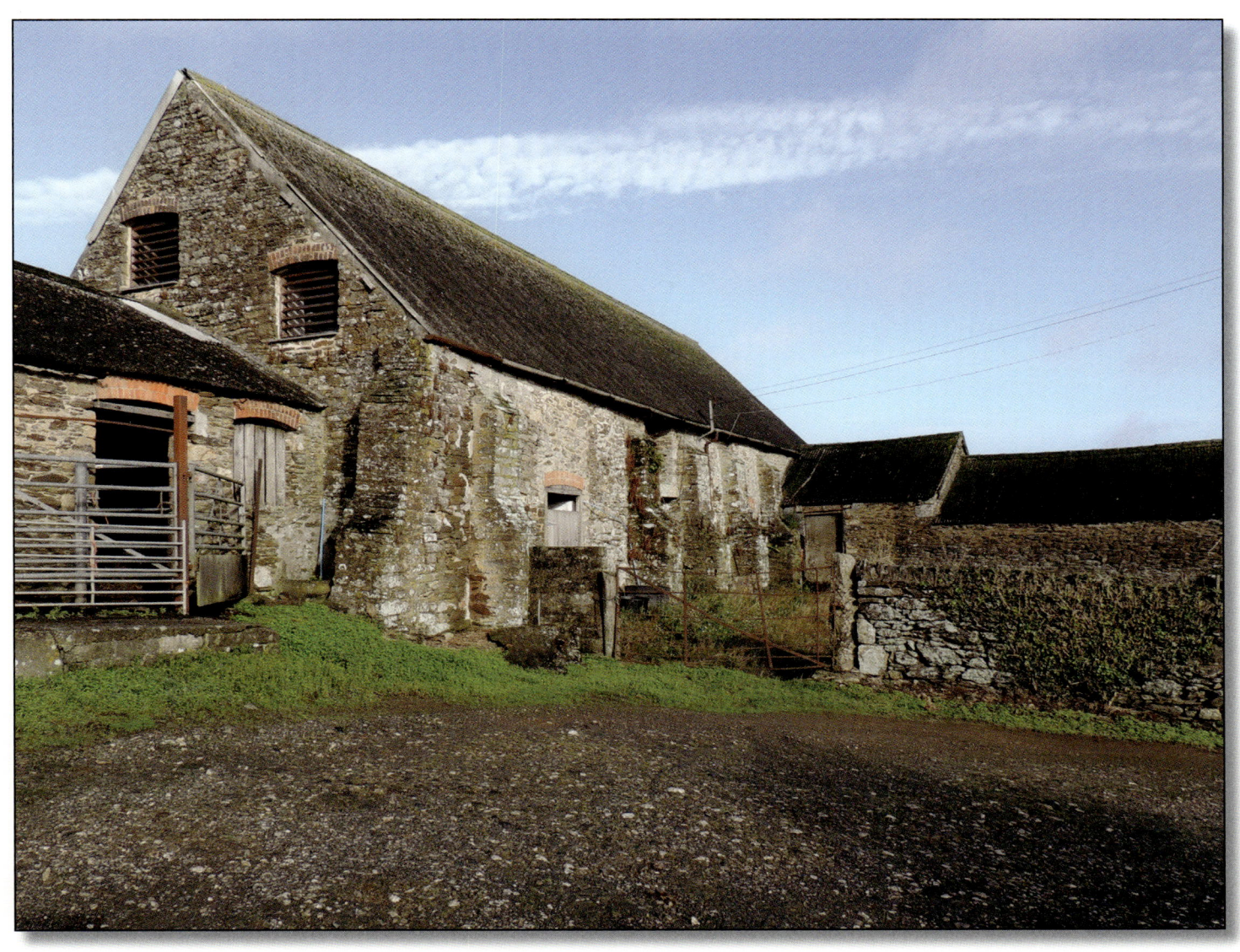

Cornwall's Cargoll barn, circa 1365

Cornwall region, much of which is granite), has been tuckpointed. Clearly, master stonemasons built this barn. Today, though the French oak is languishing, the lightweight roof will help extend the barn's longevity. Julian cherishes this piece of antiquity and, inside, he has built a long table for entertaining friends.

Meanwhile, in mainland Europe during the 16th century, Italian Andrea Palladio, at the insistence of his father, became an apprentice stonecutter when he was 13. Though he rebelled and ran away, he eventually returned, finished his apprenticeship, and joined the guild of stonemasons. For a number of years he worked as a mason, making sculptures and monuments before evolving into one of the most influential architects of history, influencing many, including President Thomas Jefferson, who incorporated his designs into American buildings in the early 19th century.

Though, initially, most barns in colonial America were built with logs or with wooden timber-framed designs, farmers eventually used stone and, if they did make crucks, no examples of this ancient craft exist today in America. Regardless, many stone barns, still standing today, are architectural and artistic masterpieces.

3. STONE BARNS OF EARLY AMERICA

When the Dutch settled in New York and in the Hudson Bay valley in the 1600s, they built barns of wood, as did early English and German immigrants, probably because wood was readily available, especially compared to their homeland. America, even on its eastern coast, was a classic virgin forest. But eventually in the 18th and 19th centuries, when tall trees were less abundant, farmers used stone. Of course, using stone meant durability and it could also show off the farmer's wealth.

Though one would expect the first stone barns to be built in New York or in the New England colonies, this wasn't the case. Instead, English and German farmers built the first stone barns in southeastern Pennsylvania and the adjacent colonies of New Jersey and Maryland. Thanks to vast forests and, borrowing traditional barn building from European prototypes, they initially built log barns and then later moved into stone. Pennsylvania's direct tax record of 1798 listed 6,813 log bans, 685 log and stone barns, and 1,829 stone barns.

The Taylor barn in Chester County, southeastern Pennsylvania, most likely built a year after its dendro-date of 1753, is one of the oldest stone barns in America and it's the oldest in the state. According to Greg Huber, most stone barns in this region weren't built until after 1770. However, when stone barns took off, accomplished stone masons had a chance to display their skills. And thousands of their attractive barns still stand here today, relatively close to the metropolis of Philadelphia (within 50 to 75 miles), making this the motherlode of stone barns. Elsewhere, there weren't many stone barns built. Rarities like the Shaker barns (the round one in Massachusetts built in 1826 and the massive one in nearby Mt. Lebanon built in 1859) were notable anomalies. Stone barns mirrored the case of the quirky round barns of the late 19th and early 20th centuries in that farmers didn't copy them; instead, they built conventional rectangular wooden barns, which were much less expensive to construct.

The cobblestone barns came next. After the Erie Canal

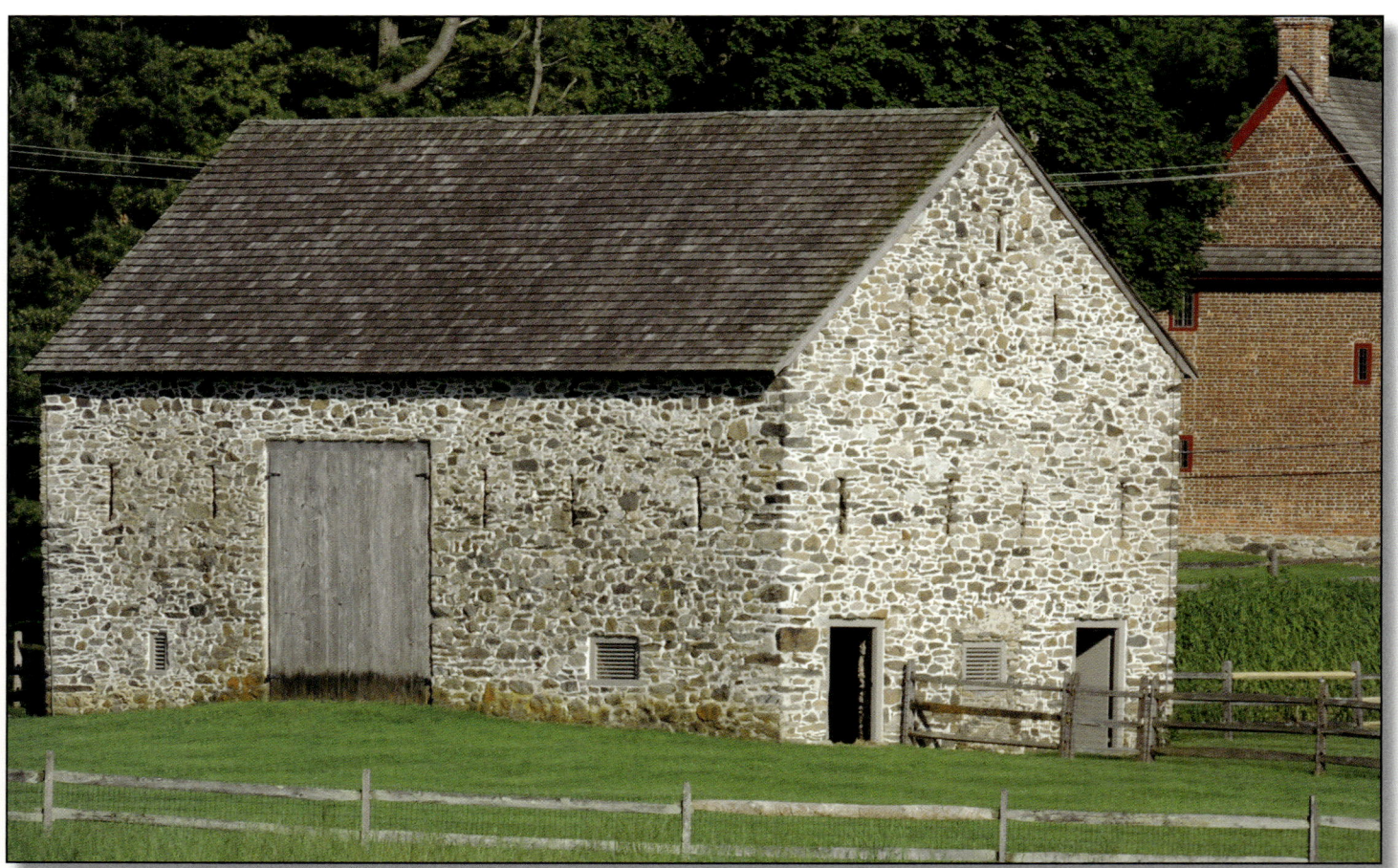

Taylor barn, 1754, Chester County, Pennsylvania

was completed in Wayne County, New York, stone masons were no longer needed and were willing to work for low wages. As a result, according to Sue and Rich Freeman, authors of *Cobblestone Quest: Road Tours of New York's Historic Buildings*, these skilled masons built over 700 cobblestone buildings, including barns, in western New York from the 1820s to the 1860s. In northeastern Ohio two cobblestone homes still exist – the only two in the state.

When the Northwest Territory opened for settlement in 1787, settlers gradually headed for this land west of Pennsylvania, northwest of the Ohio River, east of the Mississippi River, and below the Great Lakes. But they weren't inclined to build stone barns. The Ohio Country and beyond was a veritable forest – with towering trees almost asking to be part of a barn. And building a timber-framed barn was usually easier, faster, and cheaper than building one of stone.

As more land opened up, especially after the Battle of Fallen Timbers in 1794, settlers moved westwards, yearning for fertile farmland and escaping the "crowded" conditions of the east coast. Veterans of the Revolutionary War received land grants for their service. European immigrants followed, notably the Germans, seven million of them during the 19th century.

When deciding where to live in the new country, Germans often followed fellow countrymen. One isolated pocket of stone barns lies in Missouri – in Gasconade County – which became heavily settled by German immigrants in the mid-19th century, thanks to the Philadelphia-based German Settlement Society, whose goal was to establish a German colony that would preserve its heritage. Many of these immigrants were stonemasons, who built hundreds of stone homes and barns. Dozens remain today, including allied stone outbuildings such as a wineries, gristmills, smokehouses, springhouses, summer kitchens, bake ovens, and fruit storage buildings. They vary in construction from cut sandstone block to coursed rubble.

Late in the 19th century, Scandinavian immigrants began settling in the upper Midwest – in Minnesota, Wisconsin, the Dakotas, and northern Michigan. Many had stonemasonry skills and they used the abundant glacier rocks – which they had to clear from their fields after each spring thaw – to construct homes, barns, and stone walls. Many of these barns feature attractive fieldstone foundations. Some are made entirely of stone.

When western and southwestern lands became available, settlers and immigrants moved there, thanks to government land grants, which offered 160 acres of free land to those who would farm it for at least five years.

Lastly, the Gilded Age of Architecture – from about 1875 to the 1920s – was a memorable era of stone barn building. Fabulously wealthy families like the Vanderbilts, the Colts and the Taylors of Rhode Island, to name a few, joined the ranks of gentlemen farmers and built stone barns that often evoked images of the grand castles of Europe. After that time, the popularity of Portland cement, the agricultural depression of the 1920s, and the Great Depression of the 1930s spelled an end to stone barns in America (with the exception of the Rockefeller stone barn complex in New York).

Timeline – Stone Barns in the United States

1745
Stone barn on Silver Linden Farm, Loudon County, Virginia

1754
Taylor stone barn, Chester County, Pennsylvania

1798
Pennsylvania's direct tax record lists 1,829 stone barns

1770-1900
Stone barns built in southeastern Pennsylvania, Maryland, New Jersey

1826
Shaker round stone barn, Pittsfield, Massachusetts

1859
Shaker stone barn, Mt. Lebanon, New York

1864-1900
Stone barns of the western states

1875-1910s
Gilded Age of stone barns

1933
Rockefeller stone barns, New York

1991-2009
Dick Schwab builds six stone round barns in Iowa

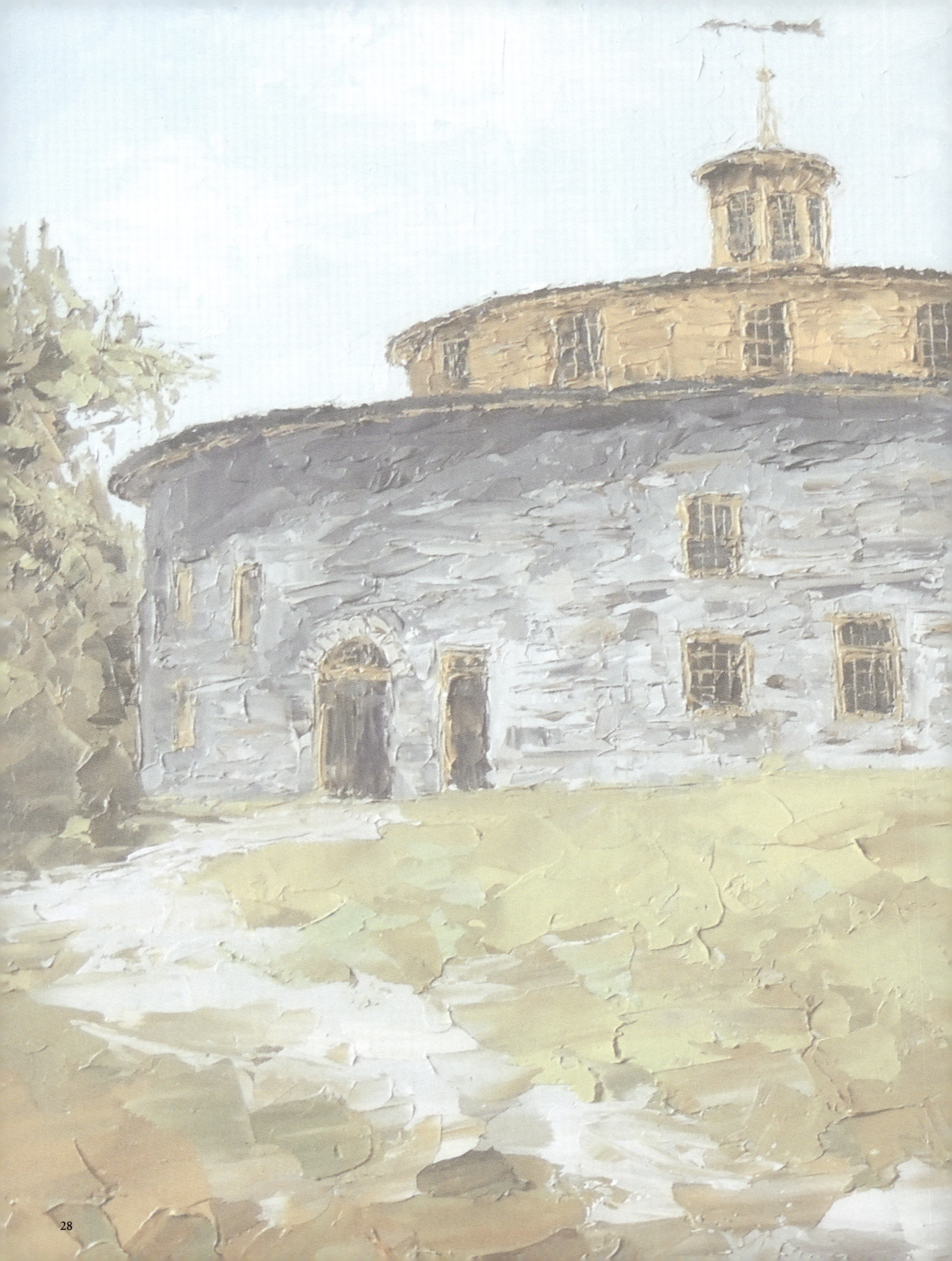

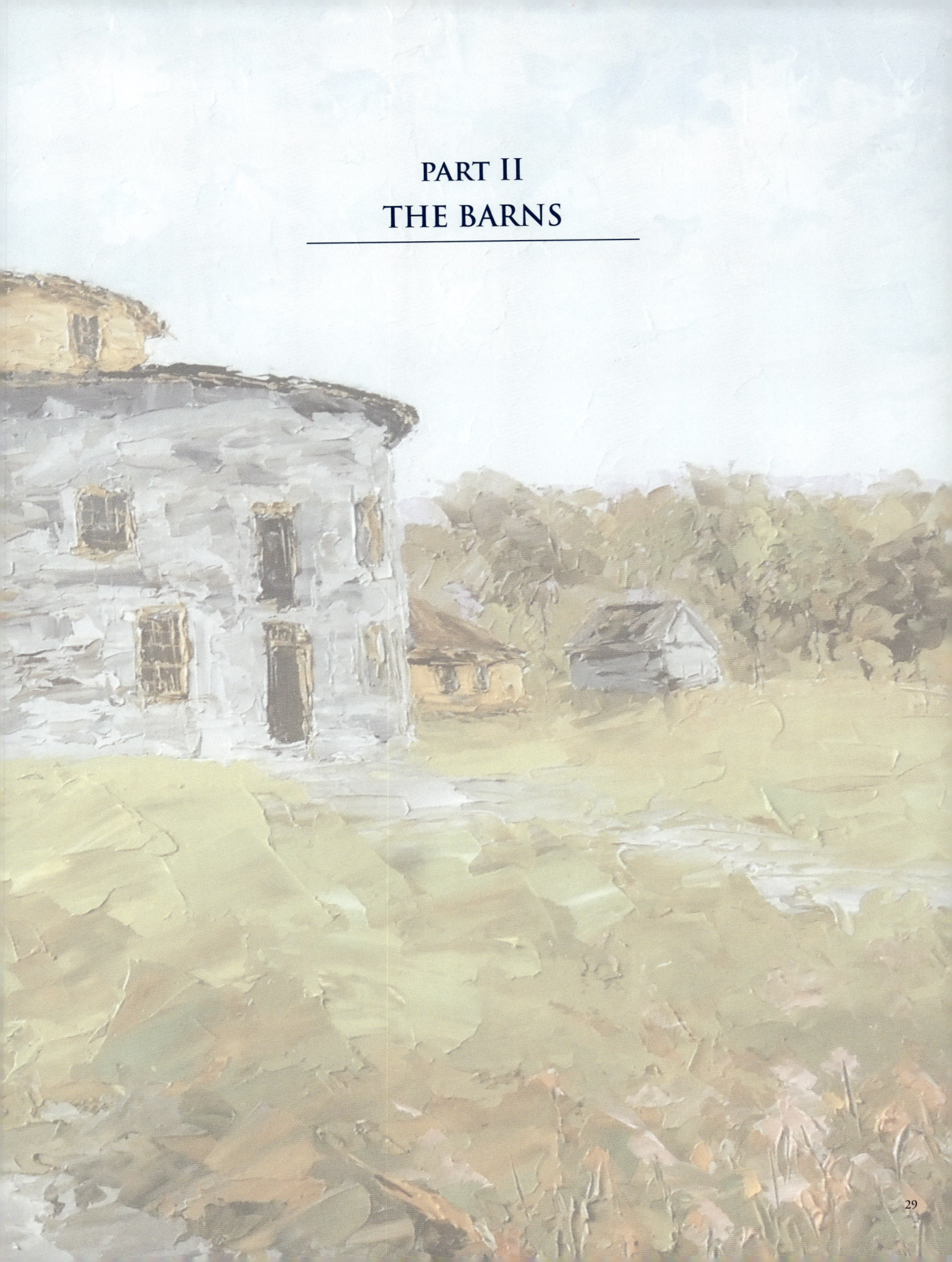

PART II
THE BARNS

4. NORTHEAST

MAINE

HANCOCK COUNTY
The Billboard Barn

Some states are known for their mountains, such as Colorado and Wyoming, some are known for their abundant lakes, such as Minnesota, some are known for their deserts, such as Nevada and Utah, and others are known for agricultural production, such as those in the corn belt throughout the Midwest. Besides blueberries and lobsters, Maine is known for its forests, which cover 91 percent of the state.

Originally part of the northern section of Massachusetts, Maine did not gain statehood until 1820, though its history goes back much further. The earliest inhabitants, approximately 3000 BC to 1000 BC, were the Red Paint People, a seafaring culture known for elaborate burials using red ochre. Over the centuries, tribes were essentially hunter-gatherers that migrated and survived on wild game, such as deer, moose, and birds as well as seals, porpoises, and fish. Today, people from the four tribes of Maine – the Maliseet, Micmac, Passamaquoddy and Penobscot (collectively known as the Wabanaki) – live both in and outside of reservations in the state.

Though explorers of several countries sailed the coastline in the 16th century, the first European settlement in the area was made on St. Croix Island in 1604 by a French party that included Samuel de Champlain and Mathieu da Costa. After naming the area Acadia, they barely survived the winter and, a year later, moved to Port-Royal in present-day Nova Scotia. By comparison, the Dutch settled Manhattan in 1614 and the pilgrims, after sailing on the Mayflower for

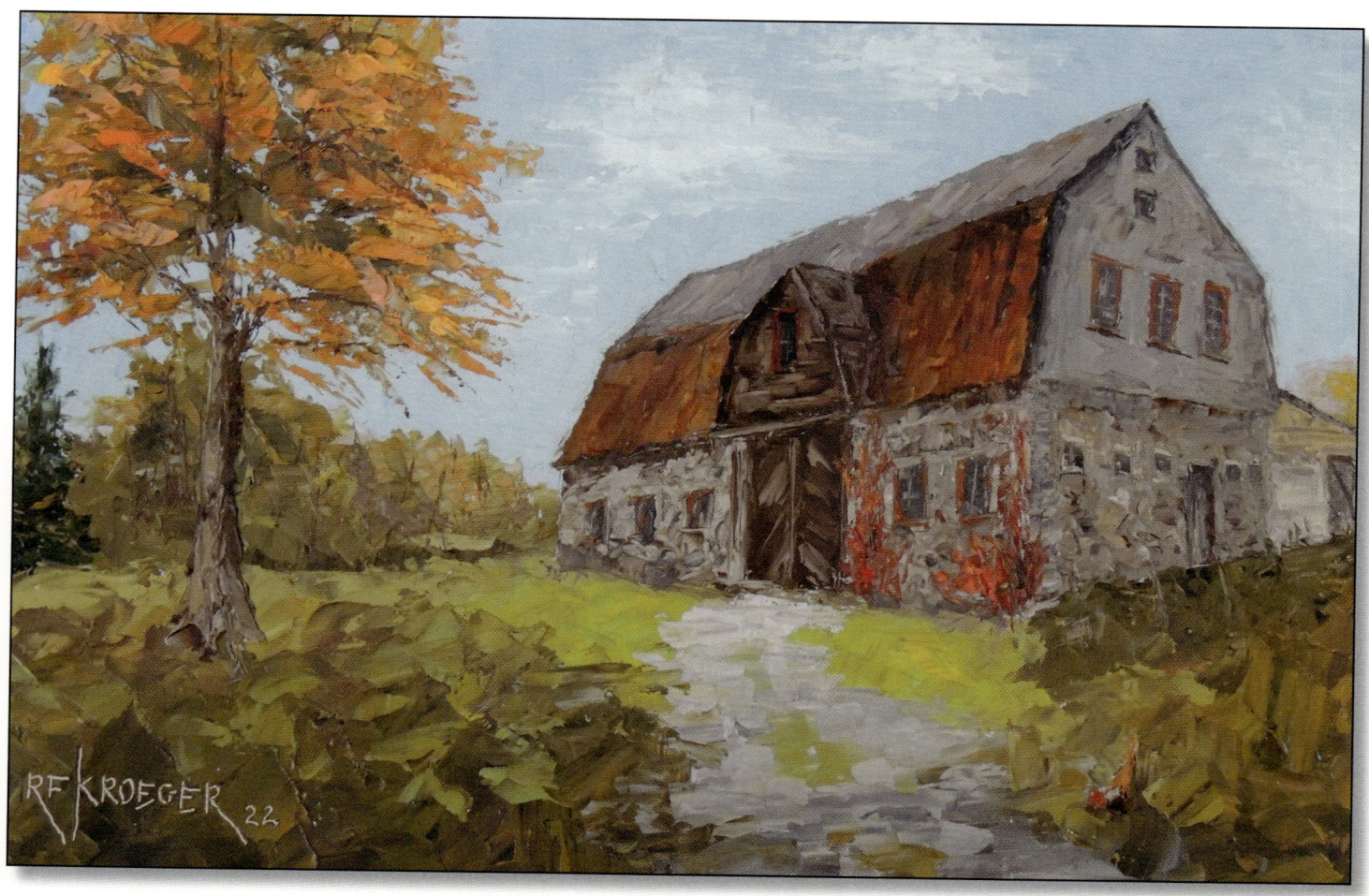

The Billboard Barn

over two months, arrived at Plymouth Rock in December 1620. Europeans had begun settling northeastern America.

Over a century later, in 1761, Abraham Somes established the first European village on Mount Desert Island and called it Somesville. Next, Israel Higgins and John Thomas founded Bar Harbor, which became incorporated in 1796. However, unlike the fertile soil of southeastern Pennsylvania, where English, Dutch, and Germans raised crops and built thousands of barns, Maine's soil was not a farmer's dream come true.

So, faced with rocky soil and poor yields, settlers relied on timbering, whale hunting, fishing, and shipbuilding, which they could do nearly all year round. Those who wanted to raise crops had to move westwards, where, in the early 19th century, land was cheap and ideal for farming. Spurred on by government homestead acts, many moved from the hilly and rocky states of Maine, New Hampshire (the Granite State), and Vermont to greener pastures in the Midwest.

Today, the Maine Farmland Trust estimates that the state has one million acres of farmland, most of which is forested. Potatoes are the state's largest crop, followed by corn, hay, oats, and vegetables. However, the Maine climate is also good for growing apples, cranberries, and, most famously, blueberries. What Maine lacks in agricultural production, it makes up for in tourism. Millions of visitors travel here each year – for a vacation or to spend the summer – by car, plane, or cruise ship.

As the major metropolitan areas of Boston, New York City, and Philadelphia grew, city dwellers looked to New England to find a break from hectic life in the cities. They chose Vermont and New Hampshire for ski trips, but the allure of Maine's rugged coastline and the individuality of its people was irresistible to those who could afford to travel here for a summer vacation.

Conservationist George B. Dorr, known as "the father of Acadia National Park," became concerned with vacationing crowds and destruction of forests and quickly established the Hancock County Trustees of Public Reservations in 1901. Later, Dorr convinced President Woodrow Wilson to establish a national park on Mt. Desert Island, which, in 1929, became Acadia National Park, portions of which sit close to this farmstead, known as the Stone Barn Farm.

With a listed address of Salisbury Cove, the farm, originally only 45 acres, is now located on 167 acres of flat land near Thomas Bay. Though the farm founding is sketchy, an 1807 plat map suggests that Eben Salisbury was the first white settler to own the land where the stone barn now stands. From minimal information in the 1810 census, Salisbury lived here with his wife and two children.

The Paine family was next to own this farm. In 1793 Thomas Jr. was the first of the family to be born on Mount Desert Island, three years before Eden (today's Bar Harbor) was established. His marriage to Olive Hadley produced 12 children, seven of whom survived past childhood. In the pre-Civil War era Thomas or one of his sons may have built the original farmhouse and barns, which were connected, common in New England – due to heavy snows and Nor'easter storms. Today the connection is gone, but the farmhouse, the carriage barn, and the stone barn survive.

Thomas and Olive's fifth child, Richard H. Paine, was born in 1828. Sometime between 1850 and 1860 Richard took over the farm, perhaps after he married. His wife, Sophia, came from the Emery family, whose name was given to the "Emery District," a tract of six farms surrounding the headwaters of Northeast Creek. According to local historians, raising livestock was the cash business of these farms, and all farmers had a few milk cows, oxen, and a horse. Though they also grew hay for feed, sold wood from forests, and raised apples in order to supplement their meager income, the young men worked as carpenters, general laborers, or fishermen. In the 1860 agricultural census, Richard's livestock consisted of two milk cows, two oxen, one hog, and eight sheep. His production that year yielded 30 pounds of wool, 35 bushels of Irish potatoes, 60 pounds of butter, and eight tons of hay.

After the Civil War began, Richard enlisted and served in the 26th Maine Regiment. Enlistment bonuses, steady wages, and patriotic fervor were hard to pass up. During the war, young Sophia worked the farm, along with raising two children under three and being pregnant with yet another. She grew potatoes, took care of the oxen, two dairy cows, eight sheep, and a hog. She was a busy lady: the farm produced 100 pounds of butter and five tons of hay.

The Maine regiment deployed to Louisiana, where miserable living conditions contributed to illness among the soldiers, including Richard, who was discharged in August, 1863. A year later Sophia died. But, determined and hardy, as most pioneering farmers were in those years, Richard continued farming, raised his children, and remarried. Unlucky in love again, he lost his second wife, who died in 1884 and then his third wife, who died in 1892. But he didn't give up: Richard, 66 in 1894, married Julia Gott. She lived until 1908.

According to a history about the men who served in Maine's 26th regiment, at 71 years old in 1899, Richard had occupations of a policeman, a carpenter, and a stonemason. But farm work being strenuous, Richard had turned the farm over to his son Willis, who sold it to James and Charles Shea. After an adventurous life, 84-year-old Richard died at a Veterans Home in Augusta in 1913.

The same year as they bought the farm in 1907, the Shea brothers built this stone barn, located on a highly visible intersection of two roads – Norway Drive and Crooked

Road, an excellent spot to showcase their masonry skills. James M. and Charles W. Shea operated a masonry business, located on Cottage Street in Bar Harbor. Their ad in the 1910-11 edition of the Maine Register stated that they were "Dealers in Lime, Cement and Sand …"

Their other work remains on the island. In 1907, when they bought the farm and built the stone barn, they got a contract to build the foundation for a greenhouse at the Turrets, a summer home that John Josiah Emery Sr. built in 1895. Emery, a real estate millionaire and banker from Cincinnati, spared no expense to construct his mansion, hiring New York architect Bruce Price, who designed it in the French Chateauesque style, a marvelous example of the Gilded Age of architecture. Today it serves as part of the College of the Atlantic.

Although it's tempting to list this barn as mere advertising strategy, the Shea brothers, besides renting the barn for income, also raised livestock – for dairy production and breeding Ayrshire cattle. They gave the bulls names such as Wilson, Kebo, and Dandy of Eden.

Several years later, the brothers rented the farm to the Paine family, who had returned from Oregon. For the Paines, who had been gone for about eight years, seeing the new stone barn must have been a thrill. In the 19th century few farmers could afford to use stone for all four barn walls, although many built wooden barns with fieldstone foundations. A stone barn was not only a good investment for durability but also a mark of distinction. In the case of the Shea Brothers' stonemasonry business, it was also a fine calling card.

They used granite from a quarry at Otter Creek as well as stones from the farm fields, which were plentiful. The stonemasons chose gray granite fieldstones, arranged in a random design – with gaps to demonstrate the power of their mortar, which has survived for over a century without tuck-pointing. Since there's no evidence of foundation cracking, the barn may be sitting on solid bedrock, possibly another hint that the builders chose the location wisely. Of course, most of Mt. Desert Island is rock. With dimensions of 36x54 feet, the barn was large enough to support a modest farm.

Large granite quoins support the corners and gray granite lintels and sills protect ground-level windows, which are bordered in red. A central dormer over the wide barn door features a six-over-six window that might have been a former haymow opening. The gambrel roof, which provides more storage than the simple gable variety, also suggests that the Sheas wanted room for hay storage. Two small man doors, one of which I painted, provide easy entry, especially on snowy days.

It's interesting that they used metal, instead of slate, for the roof and that they didn't add cupolas for ventilation, a necessary component of all barns. Inside, the 18-inch-thick walls have no interior bracing and are the major support for the roof, whose boards, irregular in size, have been through a sawmill. Our guide Renee Duncan explained that there was a mill nearby. Sometime later, the owners attached a small shed to the rear of the barn – for sheep. Outside, a circular cement pad was probably where a silo once sat. During our visit in the fall of 2022, workers were repairing the roof and installing steel beams for internal support. Renee showed us the architect's plans for restoration.

Over the years several owners took over the property until 1963 when Harry and Cindy Owen purchased it. Though they both worked outside the farm – Harry as a teacher and Cindy as a registered nurse – they raised goats and chickens, producing milk, cheese, and eggs. They also grew vegetables. Most importantly, they took care of the farm and its unique stone barn. In fact, a German tourist, obviously impressed, sent a postcard, addressed simply to the "Gentleman who grows beautiful sunflowers near the grey stone barn, Crooked Road, Bar Harbor, Maine." The card got delivered.

As the years passed, Harry and Cindy witnessed increased tourism and rapid development of the island, making them worry that the rustic character of Maine farmland would be lost. Bar Harbor zoning regulations would have allowed the farm to be divided into 42 lots for housing. But making a huge profit wasn't what the Owens wanted.

Instead, they placed the farm under a conservation easement and listed the stone barn, the 1840ish farmhouse, and the carriage barn on the National Register in 2001. The Bangor Daily News reported that Cindy Owen said, "It's our way of giving back to our friends and our community for all the happy times we've had here."

After Cindy passed in 2018, Harry sold the farm for $625,000 to the Maine Coast Heritage Trust, a state-wide land conservation organization, which intends to restore the stone barn, farmhouse, and carriage barn. After making its purchase, the trust started a fundraising campaign and launched its rehab plan in the summer of 2021. Thanks to the trust and to Cindy and Harry Owens, this historic farmstead of Civil War Veteran Richard Paine has escaped the fate of coastal farms that have been sadly consumed by development.

With 100 acres of woodland, two miles of hiking trails, a mile of frontage on Northeast Creek, blueberry bushes, and a pond, this site has a lot of potential. Hopefully, the trust will preserve most of the forested land; after all, this is the Pine Tree State. And, with good fortune, Maine's only surviving stone barn, whether a billboard barn or not, will be around for another century to memorialize its owners.

NEW HAMPSHIRE

HILLSBOROUGH COUNTY
The Granite State

New Hampshire, one of the original 13 colonies of the United States, was founded in 1623, thanks to a grant from the English Crown to Captain John Mason, who named the new settlement after his boyhood home in Hampshire County, England. Though he had been governor of Newfoundland, he never lived in New England; instead, he dispatched settlers to start a fishing village there. In 1635 he was appointed first vice-admiral of New England, but he died that year – after making plans to take his first voyage to the new colony.

In the late 1700s granite mining flourished in New Hampshire and Vermont, which led to the development of small quarries and, later, to larger ones. Local legend has it that in 1825 the French general, Marquis De Layfette, a hero during the American Revolution, made a remark that New Hampshire was a granite state. The name stuck.

Today many quarries dot the state and one, started in 1883, remained in the Swenson family until it was sold in 2016.

Benjamin Pierce Cheney, born in 1815 in Hillsborough County, began working in his father's blacksmith shop when only 10. Two years later he took jobs in a tavern and then in a general store, but his career took off in 1831. Only 16, he worked as a stagecoach driver on a 45-mile route between Nashua and Exeter. Without railroads, which would come soon enough, the stagecoach business thrived. He built friendships with passengers, one of whom, Daniel Webster, would become the United States Secretary of State in 1850.

Cheney's reputation for reliability led to banks entrusting

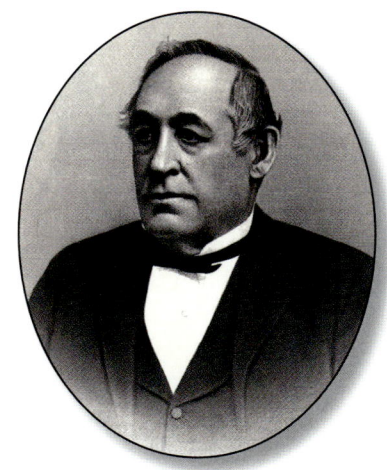

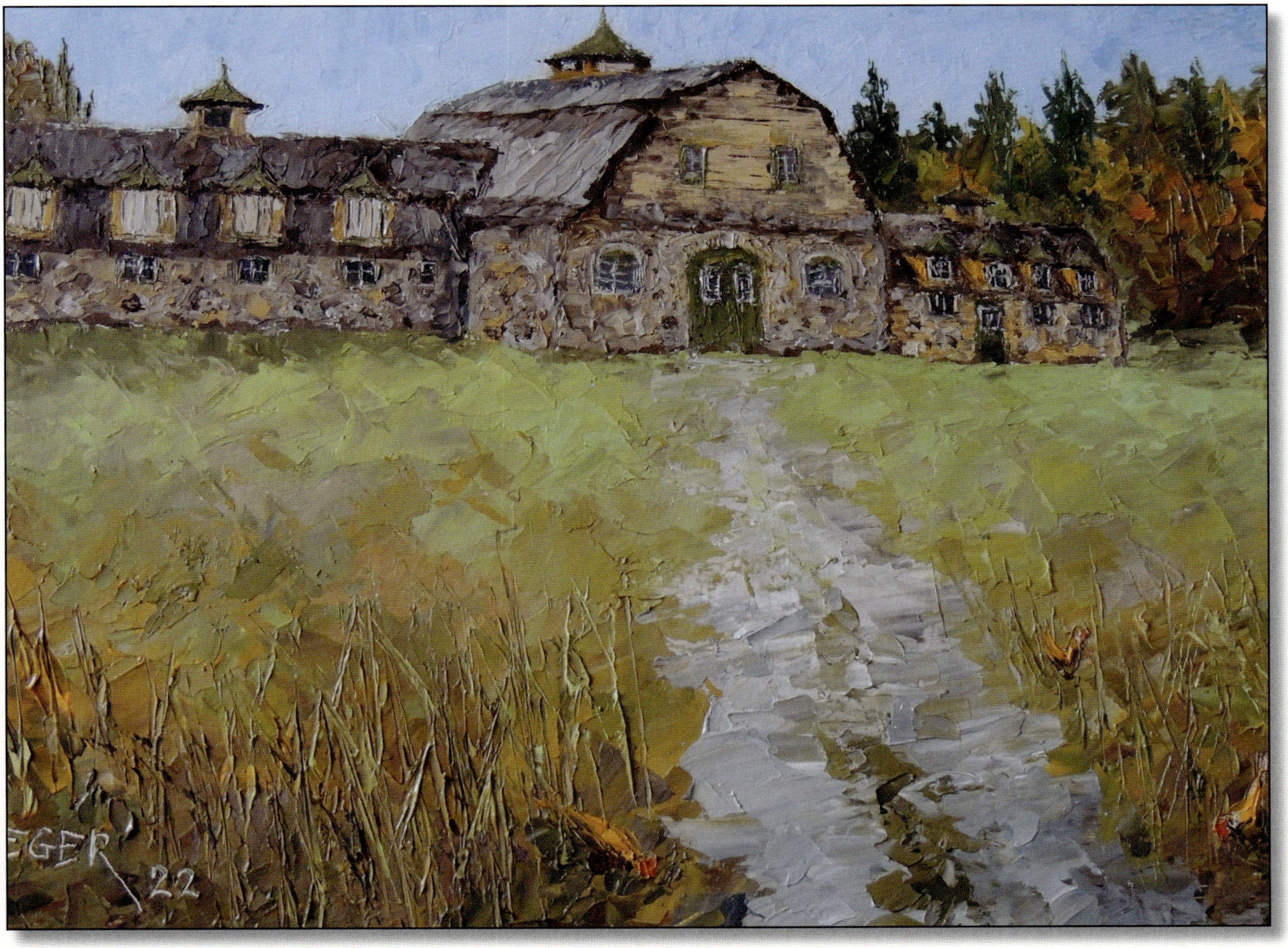

Benjamin Pierce Cheney, courtesy Wikicommons

The Granite State

him with large sums, which he delivered on his stagecoach. In 1836, now 21, the young man became a stage agent in Boston, as he rose up the ranks in this business. Six years later he and two others organized an express stagecoach line between Boston and Montreal and in 1854 he founded the United States and Canada Express Company. But by that time, railroad lines were beginning to multiply. Unfortunately, a railroad accident cost Cheney his right arm. However, on the brighter side, he was elected a director of the Wells Fargo Company in the same year. Not quite 40, he became the company's largest shareholder as well as treasurer and a director.

As railroads took over transportation, Cheney switched from stagecoaches to trains and in 1879 he sold his United States and Canada Express to American Express, a company founded in 1852 by William Fargo and Henry Wells. Under his direction, the company prospered in not only deliveries but banking – as it offered rapid transport of gold and paper money. By this time, fabulously wealthy – his fortune was estimated at $10 million – he retired from the Wells Fargo board in 1877, though he returned as a director from 1882 to1884.

Even though he lived on a 198-acre estate on the Charles River in Wellesley, Massachusetts (which has since become the Elm Bank Horticulture Center), he wanted a summer home away from the hectic life around Boston. So, in the early 1880s, he and his wife Elizabeth and their five children founded Highland Farm in Peterborough, not far from his boyhood home in the same county. It's likely that they built a traditional wooden barn and began farming, spending summers here. Benjamin Cheney died in 1895.

His wife and family continued to farm in New Hampshire, though their massive inheritance made this essentially a hobby. Elizabeth, perhaps wanting to honor the career of her late husband, built this magnificent stone barn in 1912, a time when agriculture was still the main occupation of most Americans. Local legend suggests that Forrest Mercer, a foreman on the farm, built the barn. However, from its elegant design, a well-trained and established architect must have prepared the plans.

The barn's design reflects Shingle Style architecture, the first modern American style and an offshoot of the Victorian Queen Anne style of architecture, originated by England's architects and popularized in America from 1880 to 1910. In Shingle Style, horizontal continuity was emphasized – both in exterior details and in interior rooms. Often, castle-like turrets – as in this barn's cupolas – added a European flair. Many wealthy families in New York, Boston, and other large cities in the Northeast built vacation homes in this style in resort areas such as Newport, Rhode Island, the Hamptons of Long Island, and along the coastlines of Massachusetts, New Hampshire, and Maine. The design was a mark of affluence.

The 9,000-square-foot barn was built under the supervision of farm manager Forrest Mercer and his 16-year-old helper Henry Nyland. Italian stonemasons came from Canada, quarried stone on the property, and erected stone walls, which, a century later, still reflect the builders' expertise. Multicolored fieldstones were placed randomly – with minimal mortar – showing masterful stonemasonry. Arched stone lintels sit above the main door and adjacent windows, which have large granite sills. Initially, slate covered the roofs, though they're shingle now. For those who love stone buildings, the barn is a marvel to behold. Construction took three years, finished in 1912.

It was designed to house 12 work horses, 24 dairy cows, and a piggery, although the hogs may have been kept in a separate building. Hay and grain were stored on the second level and a dairy was built on the first floor. The farm also had an orchard and a vegetable garden. Having 24 dairy cows hints that the family either supplied milk, gratis, to neighbors or sold it in local towns. The family continued to farm the land until the early 1940s, when they gifted it to a Boston dentist, Dr. Favre, a friend of the husband of Elizabeth Cheney Kaufmann. The other siblings apparently weren't interested in keeping their grandparents' farm in family hands.

Over the years, without use and with several changes in ownership, the barn deteriorated, though plans to repurpose it ranged from converting it to a hotel, a restaurant, or condominiums – all without success. In 2014, Highland Farm was for sale once again and local businessman Stan Fry – with two others – purchased it for $400,000, anxious to save it from collapse. They completed structural restorations, improving the barn significantly, while hoping to attract a developer. Two young women stepped forward, took an option on the property, planning to convert the barn to 30 condominiums and designed the complex on an "agrihood" ideal, which combines sustainable agriculture and living accommodations. The town approved their plan in 2018, but their company could not sell the units and their option expired. The development business is not an easy one.

In 2022 the property was once again for sale, this time for $2.2 million. As of the summer of 2024, the current developer has received the town's final approval for its plan to convert the stone barn into 67 luxury condominium units – as a 55-and-over active adult community. They did not have an estimate of when they'd begin sales.

The 33-acre site is appealing. The Monadnock Conservancy worked with private landowners to build a 2.6-mile trail, which goes past the barn and into wetlands and forests,

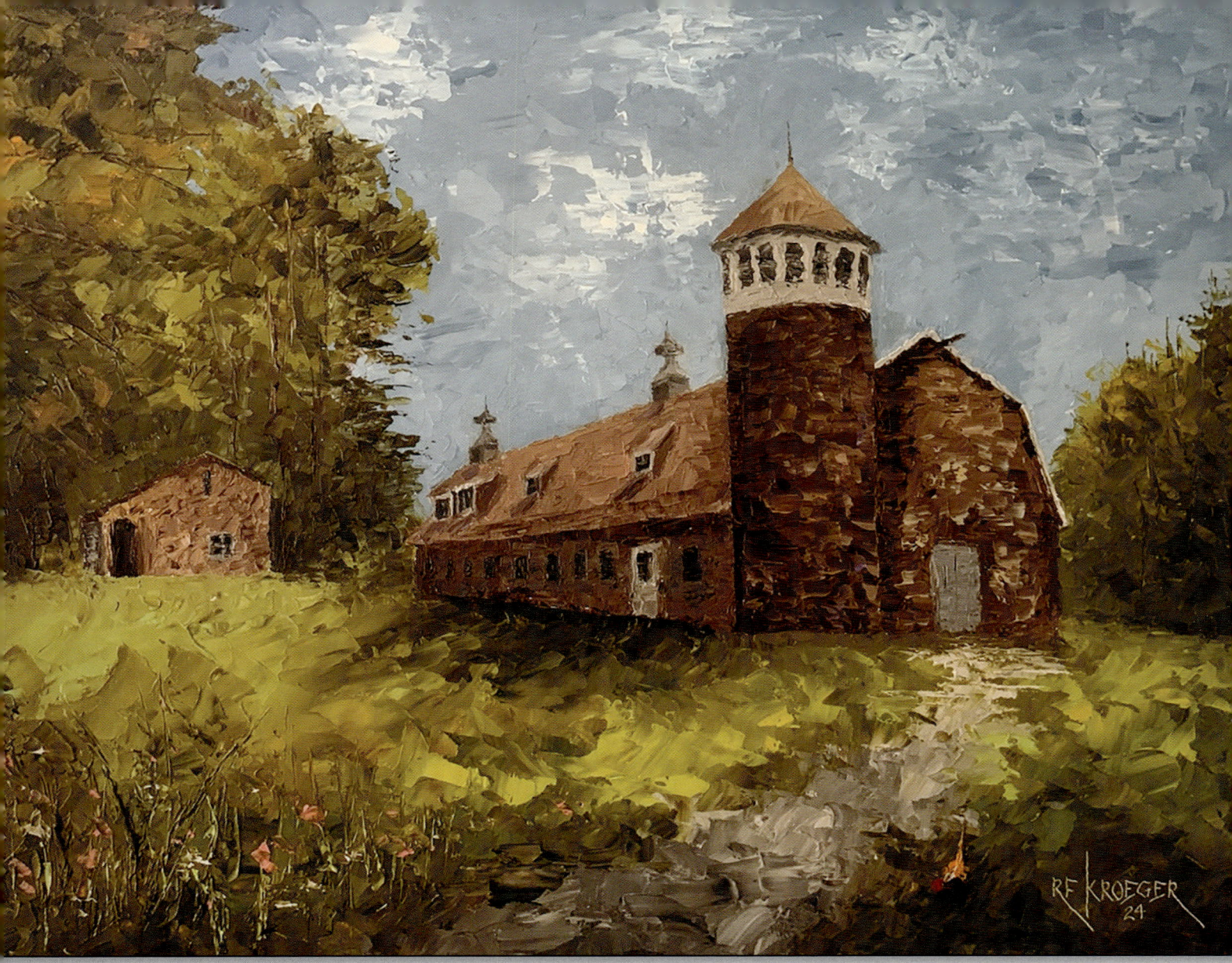

Hays Heavenly Haven

joining another longer trail from the town of Peterborough. It passes over a boardwalk through a cranberry bog and has become popular for birding, hiking, running, and general relaxation. Viewers from behind the barn can catch sunsets over 3,200-foot high Mt. Monadnock in the distance.

Although the National Register lists 107 properties in Hillsborough County, the Cheney stone barn, oddly enough, is not one of them, though it deserves to be there – not only a local gem but a national one as well – a bright feather in the history of the Granite State.

MERRIMACK COUNTY

Hays Heavenly Haven

Thousands of years ago the Abenaki Native Americans lived in this region, their name of Penacook derived from the Native word "pannukog," which means "bend in the river," referring to the Merrimack. Swerving often, it courses for 117 miles from northern New Hampshire and through Massachusetts before it empties into the Atlantic Ocean. The first Europeans settled here in 1659 and, after Merrimack County was established in 1823, its city of Concord became the state capital. This magnificent stone barn, located near Lake Sunapee, traces back to John Hay, whose son Clarence built it in 1916.

John Milton Hay was born in 1838 in Salem, Indiana, to Helen and Charles Hay. Dr. Hay, a physician, was from Lexington, Kentucky but, abhorring slavery, he moved his family to Indiana and then to Illinois. After John attended local schools, his wealthy uncle, Milton Hay, took him in and sent him to a more prestigious academy. His uncle also financed his nephew's college education at Brown University, where he finished with a master's degree in 1858. Upon returning to Illinois, he worked as a clerk, while studying law with his uncle Milton, who had a successful law practice in Springfield. There, the young Hay met John Nicolay,

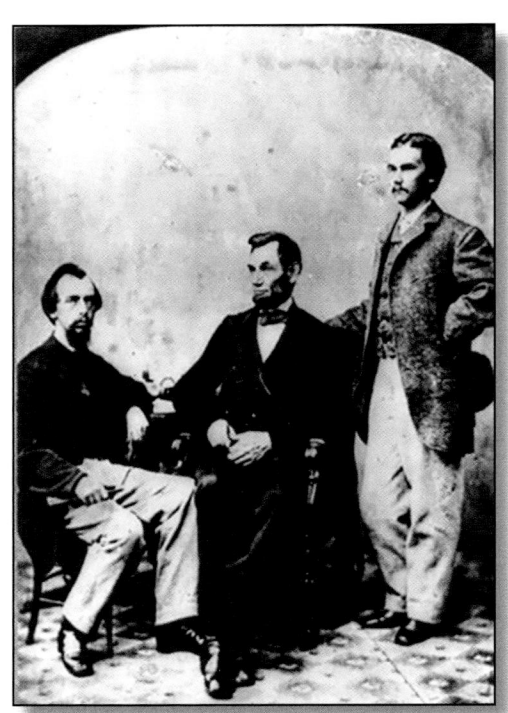

Lincoln and His Secretaries, Hays on the right. Circa 1863. Wikimedia Commons.

a newspaper reporter, who would become a life-long colleague and friend. Next door to Milton's law practice was another lawyer, Abraham Lincoln.

When Nicolay was hired to be Lincoln's private secretary for his presidential campaign, he needed help and asked John to join him, which he did. John and Nicolay wrote speeches and articles throughout the campaign. After the election, Lincoln took Nicolay with him – as his personal secretary – and invited Hay to come, too. However, Uncle Milton wanted his nephew to go to Washington as a full-fledged attorney. In February 1861 John Hay was admitted to the Illinois bar.

Nicolay and Hay moved to Washington in March and, after the inauguration, began living in the White House, where they shared a no-frills room and subsisted on a spartan salary. They worked with Lincoln non-stop seven days a week since he took no vacations. Perhaps aware of this historic time, they asked permission to write his biography, which Lincoln granted. Much later in 1874, after Robert Lincoln gave them permission to review the president's papers, the two began their research and finally published their work, which appeared initially in a series of articles in *The Century* magazine in 1890. The 10-volume biography, *Abraham Lincoln: A History*, was not sold in bookstores. As was the custom in those days, it was sold door to door and, despite a hefty price tag of $50, the print run of 5,000 copies quickly sold out. Today Amazon offers the 10 volumes in Kindle format for $2.99.

In 1862 Lincoln lost his son Willie to typhoid fever and began to view John Hay – who looked as if he were only 17 – as a surrogate son. Hay was with Lincoln when he died three years later. After the war, John remained in politics, which took him to Paris and then to Spain, where

Horace Greeley, editor of the *New York Tribune*, convinced him to join its staff, which he did, writing editorials

By 1873 bachelor Hay began courting Clara Stone, daughter of a Cleveland multimillionaire, and married her a year later. They raised four children, including Clarence, who eventually built this stone barn. In 1875 Clara and John built a mansion in Cleveland's Millionaire's Row, next door to Clara's father on Euclid Avenue. When Clara's dad died in 1883, they became fabulously wealthy.

At the time and following the years of the Civil War, eastern farmers began falling behind their Midwestern counterparts, who could sell livestock and farm produce less expensively and ship them eastwards, thanks to the development of railroads. Agriculture suffered in New Hampshire. Many young men left the state for farming in the Midwest or West or for industrial jobs in the northeastern cities. Many older farmers abandoned their farms or lost them to the cities for unpaid taxes. Well aware of this discouraging trend, the state of New Hampshire began a campaign to transform the formerly agricultural land into a mecca for summer tourists. Farmers agreed, hoping to augment their income with summer boarders. The strategy paid off: by 1890 there were 1,500 summer tourists. And the trend caught the attention of John and Clara Hays.

Now, busy writing Lincoln's biography and flush with his wife's family money, around 1866 John sent his long-time friend Clarence King to scout for old farms on the eastern shore of Lake Sunapee, in Newbury. Two years later, Hay purchased the 178-acre Rowe Farm, which became the core of a holding that would eventually include nearly 1,000 acres. Hay acquired another 30 acres in 1889, which may have been part of the Well Sweep Farm, where this barn still sits. In honor of his Scottish heritage, he named his estate, "The Fells," a word derived from the old Norse language, meaning mountainous ground, often used to describe the rocky topography of Northern England and Scotland. The term described the land perfectly – well-forested with abundant outcroppings of massive granite boulders. That autumn Hays sent 34-year-old Cleveland architect, George Francis Hammond, to Newbury to examine the site and to begin designing a summer home that was finished during the summer of 1891. Again in 1897, Clara and John commissioned Hammond to expand the house and add a semi-detached wing for their servants. Reaching this remote location was complicated and time-consuming; the family would travel first by rail and then by steamboat. No cars or helicopters in those days.

John returned to politics in 1897, when he served as ambassador to Great Britain and then as Secretary of State under President William McKinley. Two of his major contributions were promoting the Open Door policy and the retention of the Philippines after the Spanish-American War. When McKinley was assassinated, Hays continued as Secretary of State under President Theodore Roosevelt, who visited the Fells in the summer of 1902, during a campaign trip. Hays continued to serve under Roosevelt until he died in 1905. He was buried in Cleveland's Lake View Cemetery, near the grave of President James Garfield. For many summers Hays and his family spent considerable time in their palatial estate, an escape from the heat and crowds in Washington.

New Hampshire, realizing the impact a summer estate owned by the Secretary of State could have, began publicizing the Fells. In 1899 Samuel Eastman published an article, "Hon. John Hay – A Summer Sojourner" in *The Granite Monthly*, a popular New Hampshire magazine. The publicity worked: in the next 15 years many affluent families – the political elite from Chicago to Boston to Washington – bought failing farms and turned them into sumptuous summer estates, including some with stone castles and 75-mile views. One had a 28,000-acre game preserve. Today, these still dot the rural landscape of New Hampshire.

After John Hays passed, his son Clarence, then a 21-year-old student at Harvard, inherited the estate in 1906. After he graduated in 1908, he made only a few changes to the estate. However, his marriage to Alice in 1914 seemed to have sparked interest in the Fells and, wealthy from inheritance, they began building cottages and remodeling, this time with a new architect, 35-year-old Prentice Sanger, based out of New York. The architect had finished a home for his parents on Lake Sunapee in 1908, possibly endearing him to Clarence and Alice.

In 1915 the Hays commissioned Sanger to remodel the house extensively, design major landscaping, and turn the cottages into a mansion setting. Photographs, taken in 1915, showed the rocky ground around the house stripped of boulders, plowed, and planted with potatoes – as a temporary measure to prepare the soil for grass. At this time Sanger also designed a farm complex, which included this fieldstone barn and a stone milkhouse, suggesting a

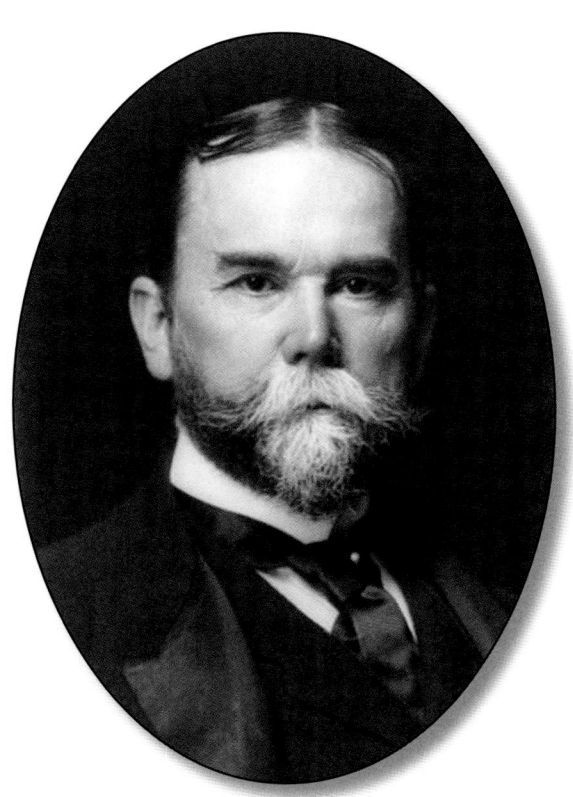

John Hay, 1897.
Wikimedia Commons

small dairy operation. The complex – the round stone silo, a stone milkhouse, and the barn – took three stonemasons three years to complete and was finished in 1916, about the same time that Sanger built his own summer home on Lake Sunapee.

During the Great Depression, an era when many wealthy family fortunes collapsed, the Hays held onto their land. But, after World War II, they felt the need to lower the expense of maintaining their estate and gardens and once again hired architect Sanger for a redesign of the main house to cut costs. In 1960 Clarence and Alice bequeathed 675 acres of woodland to a nonprofit, the Society for the Protection of New Hampshire Forests. After Clarence died in 1969, Clara eventually donated the remaining 164 acres of the estate to the United States Fish and Wildlife Service. This agency listed the Fells on the National Register in 2000. Clara reserved 143 acres, including the summer house, garage, and gate lodge, for her own use during her lifetime and another 20.5 acres, including the lakeshore cottage and boathouse, for her children during their lifetimes. Upon her death in 1987, this tract of land became the John Hay National Wildlife Refuge. A Congressional appropriation of $491,000 in 1990 funded repairs to the summer house, gate lodge, and garage, which had public toilets added in 1992.

In the late 1940s Clarence partitioned the farm buildings from the estate and sold 40 acres of the land to Max Wasserman, a civil engineer from Newton, Massachusetts. He began converting the farmhouse into a contemporary summer retreat, complete with a shallow roof and expansive glass windows. At the time, Wasserman continued to raise sheep and house them in the barn, just as Clarence did years earlier. Then, he split the property again, putting the barn and stone milkhouse on a separate seven-acre parcel. In the October 2001 issue of *Yankee Magazine*, an article titled, "Hay is For Horses," described the Hay farmhouse and the stone barn, which were for sale. Two years later the property sold for $807,500.

The new owners have restored the stone barn and have given it a new purpose – a rental for reunions, weddings, and special events. Its 22 bedrooms can accommodate a large extended family, a group of friends looking for a charming New England vacation, or folks just wanting to retrace the steps of the John Hay family a century earlier. The attractive fieldstone barn and attached round fieldstone silo, now over a century old, both the work of three master stonemasons, have been preserved, though the farmhouse is gone. Also missing are the cows, goats, oxen, and mules that were housed in the barn, the orchards that supplied fruit for the family, and the maple trees that yielded maple syrup. The owners took three years – 2005 to 2008 – to restore the barn and the stone milkhouse, being careful to retain the character of the farmstead. An old photograph, circa 1920, shows a large adjacent frame barn, big enough to hold a sizeable number of livestock and sufficient hay to feed them. It's gone, too.

Adjacent to the barn and part of the Hay estate are the gardens and the main house, which are listed on the National Register. A nonprofit called The Fells, established in 1996, is run these days by a large group of volunteers, including garden staff and administrators. The nonprofit continues to maintain the house and grounds and keep them open to the public as well as hosting educational events. Such exemplary volunteerism would make John Milton Hays, former Secretary of State and biographer of Lincoln, well pleased – now, a century removed from when John, Clara, and their children enjoyed what once was the Hays heavenly haven.

VERMONT

CHITTENDEN COUNTY
On the Shores of Shelburne

The town of Shelburne lies nestled on the eastern shore of Lake Champlain. Chartered in 1763, it was named in honor of William Petty, 2nd Earl of Shelburne and Britain's prime minister during the tail end of the American Revolution. Despite the rocky ground, hills, and cold winters, the economy in Shelburne was farming at first, then sheep raising, and, finally, orchards, followed by lake commerce. Over a century later – in 1890 – this magnificent barn was built. The estate of Shelburne Farms was founded by a young couple, Dr. William Webb and Eliza "Lila" Vanderbilt. Each has a story to tell.

William Seward Webb, born in 1851, was the son of James Watson Webb, a New York newspaper publisher, who served as the U.S. ambassador to Brazil. Seward, as he was known, studied medicine in Europe and graduated from the College of Physicians and Surgeons of Columbia University in 1875. Dr. Webb was a founder and former president of the Sons of the American Revolution.

Seward first met 17-year-old Lila Vanderbilt in 1877 at a dance class. Four years later – after having practiced medicine for six years – he married her. For a wedding present, her father gave the couple a mansion at 680 Fifth Avenue in New York City, which was later sold to John D. Rockefeller. At the request of Lila's father, Seward left his medical practice for a career in finance, eventually establishing the Wall Street firm of W. S. Webb & Company.

After the president of the Wagner Palace Car Company died, William Vanderbilt, who had controlling interest in this railroad company, appointed his new son-in-law to take its helm. Thus began Webb's career in this new business, which seemed to agree with him – his railroads opened the Adirondacks to tourism.

His wife, Lila, was a daughter of William Vanderbilt, who, in turn, was the son of Cornelius Vanderbilt, patriarch of the family line and a businessman who gained tremendous wealth in railroads and shipping, becoming one of the richest Americans in history. Vanderbilt University is named after him.

William died in 1885, leaving behind a fortune, which he shared with his children. Lila, who turned 30 in 1890, inherited 10 million dollars – an incredible sum in those days – that allowed them to build a summer estate in Shelburne. She bore four children and ran the household – hiring servants, taking care of guests (including President William Howard Taft), interior decorating, meal planning, and garden design. She also liked to play golf and bridge.

Between 1886 and 1905, the Webbs, by acquiring 32 small farms, some dating to the 18th century, amassed a tract of 3,880 acres on the shoreline of Lake Champlain. After Seward successfully petitioned the town to close off public roads to assure privacy, he hired Frederick Law Olmsted, then in his late 60s and regarded as the father of landscape architecture in America, to lay out the grounds. Olmsted also designed Central Park in New York City.

Another renowned New York architect Robert H. Robertson designed the buildings – mostly of stone, brick, and timber – beginning in 1888, using red Monkton quartzite (redstone), quarried on the farm. The barn's design reflects the trend of Shingle Style architecture, the first modern American style and an offshoot of the Victorian Queen Anne style of architecture. The work of these two architects was recognized when Shelburne Farms was listed as a National Historic Landmark, an honor conveyed in 2001.

The five-story barn complex, begun in 1886 and known now as the "Farm Barn," was constructed in randomly coursed ashlar masonry and took four years to finish. It is one of three monumental barns designed by Robertson which survive today. It's a national treasure and another example of wealth and architecture of the Gilded Age.

Opposite: *On the Shores of Shelburne*

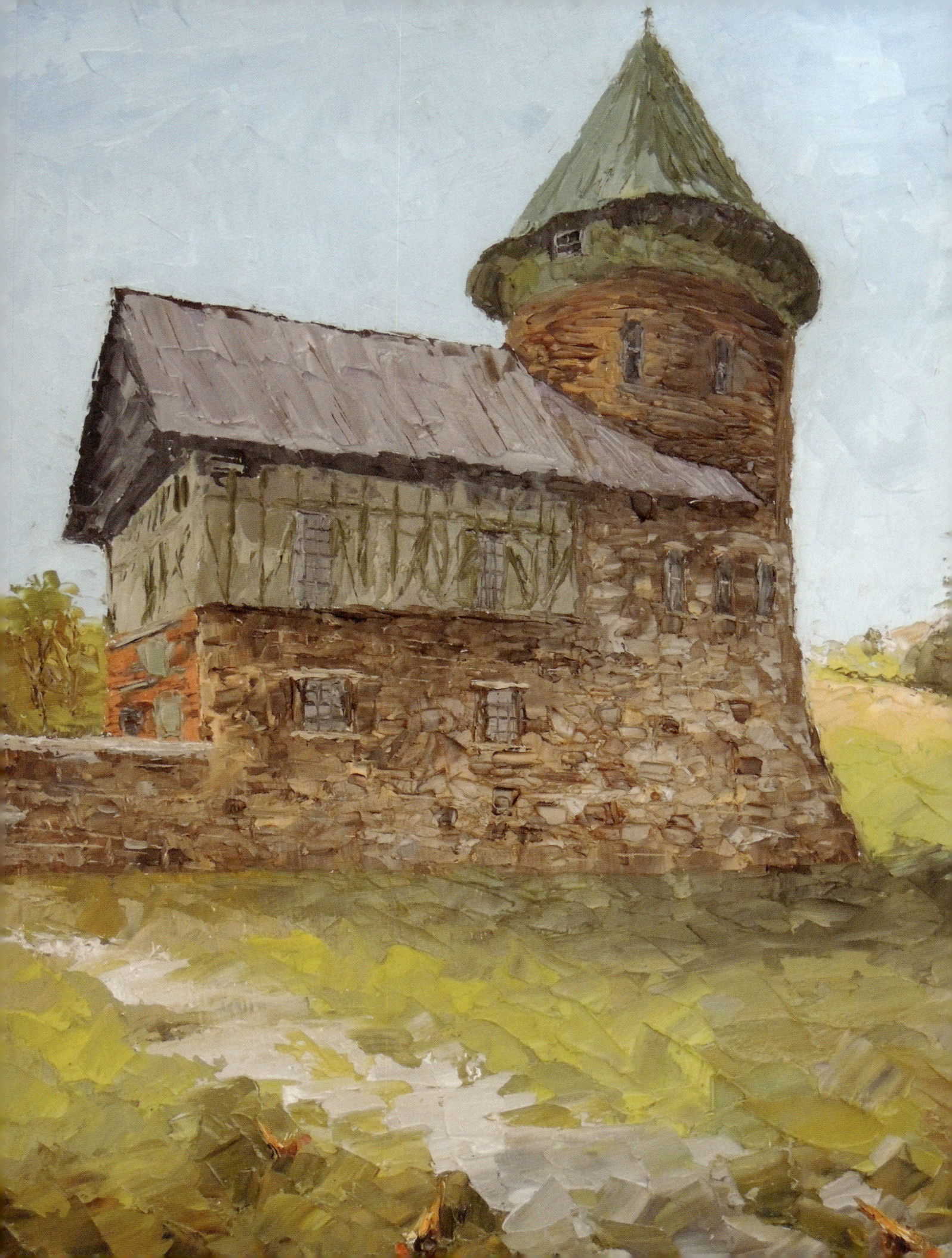

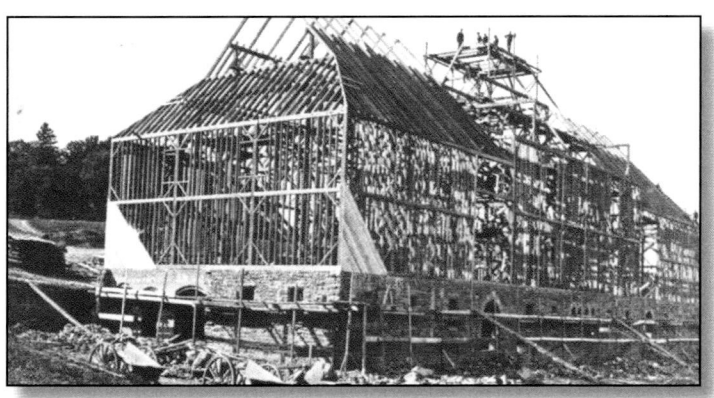

Stone barn under construction, 1888.
Courtesy of Shelburne Farms.

Each side of the barn ends in a two-story, turreted European-styled tower (featured in my painting) and the three walls enclose a two-acre courtyard, used for exercising livestock in cold Vermont winters. Although originally covered with wooden shingles (unusual since Vermont's slate was popular in that era), the hipped, gabled, and conical roofs, along with symmetrically-placed dormers and numerous ventilators and cupolas, form an irregular, ever-changing roofline, a challenge for any architect, but beautiful to behold. Gray limestone lintels and sills frame the many windows. Inside, a large tin-lined granary, a grain elevator, and a mechanical distribution system showed the Webbs' intent to make this a model farm. They planned for this barn to house livestock and crops as well as storing farm equipment.

Originally, Shelburne Farms produced corn, oats, wheat, rye, potatoes, barley, and hay – as well as raising herds of sheep and dairy cows. The barn also held a slaughterhouse, a room for storage, blacksmith and carpenter shops, a chicken house, offices for staff, a paint shop, and firefighting equipment. Today, after a $3 million renovation (1990-1993), the barn has different uses: McClure Center for School Programs and the Children's farmyard (which are pillars of the farm's educational mission), administration offices, a cheddar cheese making operation, a bakery, and a furniture maker.

Other Robert Robertson-designed barns on the farm include the impressive Coach Barn and the Breeding Barn. The Old Dairy Barn burned and the Gray Barn was demolished about 15 years ago. In 2021, the National Park Service approved a $500,000 Save America's Treasures grant to continue restorations on the 130-year-old Breeding Barn, a 44,000-square-foot building. Shelburne Farms president Alec Webb, great-grandson of the farm founders, remarked that the barn would serve as an "inspiring classroom" and a space for community events, such as the Visiting Nurse Association's 100th anniversary dinner, held in 2009. Events such as these have been held inside the barn – in the former exercise ring, where horses once walked – a space that

covers more than 31,000 square feet, almost three-quarters of an acre. Twenty-eight dormer windows at the roof line and an open central tower provide light into the massive barn. The grant, which was matched by donors, will allow Shelburne Farms to complete the $1.3 million renovation plan. Funds will be used to restore the barn's 688 original windows and to reshingle the entire exterior.

Initially, the Webbs split time between their New York City mansion and their grand home at Shelburne, which they listed as their permanent residence. Converted to a public inn in 1987, it features 24 guest rooms in the main house, four guest cottages, and a farm-to-table restaurant. And, since perhaps horse racing didn't appeal to the Webbs, golf entered the picture.

This game, ancient in Scotland, but new to America, was a fledgling sport in the late 1800s – when America's first golf course, the Oakhurst Links, was built in 1884 in White Sulphur Springs, West Virginia. Soon after that – in 1886 – golf began at the Dorset Field Club, about 80 miles south of Shelburne. When Scotsman Willie Park, Jr., twice Open champion, first visited the United States in 1895, he was hosted at New York's St. Andrews Golf Club, where he met the likes of J.J. Astor and Theodore Havermeyer, first president of the United States Golf Association. Willie also met William Webb, Lila, and their daughter and, after giving them golf lessons, he remarked, "In proportion to the male players of the game they far exceeded their English and Scottish sisters." The Webbs got hooked and hired Willie to design a course on their estate, which he did that summer – in three days – leaving its supervision to a fellow Scot, Arthur Taylor, who was the farm manager at Shelburne.

Though it was Park's first course in North America, he never listed it on his resume, preferring to keep his privately-held courses just that – private. The lessons must have paid off; when the Webbs began taking winter vacations in Florida in 1889, Lila became one of the first female golfers at the Everglades Club. The Shelburne course is gone today.

But even such a luxurious lifestyle – which included sailing on their 147-foot yacht on Lake Champlain, swimming in the oval reflecting pool, going on pheasant shoots, playing lawn tennis and croquet on immaculate grounds, and having a staff of 300 – could not prevent tragedy. After Dr. Webb developed rheumatoid arthritis, a painful condition that can cause deformity and harm to many parts of the body, he took morphine to ease the pain. Unfortunately, he became addicted and by 1910, medically challenged, he began to withdraw from business and social functions. After vacationing in Florida since the turn of the century, the Webbs built a home in Palm Beach in 1923. Dr. Webb died three years later.

After his death, Lila and the children ran the farm and

continued to entertain friends and family at their Shelburne estate. But even the Great Depression, which did affect their finances, was not enough to stop Lila from building Miradero in 1933. This opulent oceanfront vacation villa – complete with a home gymnasium – still stands in Gulf Stream, just south of Palm Beach. Lila died three years later. In 2020 her Florida estate was listed for sale at just under $14 million.

Although the New York mansion was sold in 1913, Shelburne Farms took a different path. In 1972 six great-grandchildren of Dr. and Mrs. Webb started an educational nonprofit, Shelburne Farms, dedicated to learning about a sustainable future. In 1984, Derick Webb bequeathed the farm property to the nonprofit, which uses the working farm today – including the Inn at Shelburne Farms – as its teaching campus, offering programs to educators, students, and the public. Though the colossal fortunes of the Vanderbilt railroad empires are now long gone, the nonprofit is supported by tax-deductible donations and it maintains this 1,400-acre National Historic Landmark, another priceless page in American history, for all to enjoy – on the shores of Shelburne.

MASSACHUSETTS

BERKSHIRE COUNTY

Hands to Work ... Hearts to God

This slogan identifies the community behind this round stone barn, built in Pittsfield by the Shakers, and it summarizes their philosophy, similar to that of the Trappist monks – ora et labora. The Shaking Quakers, or Shakers, were called this name – derogatorily – because they incorporated animated whirling and swirling dancing, trembling, and fainting into their religious services.

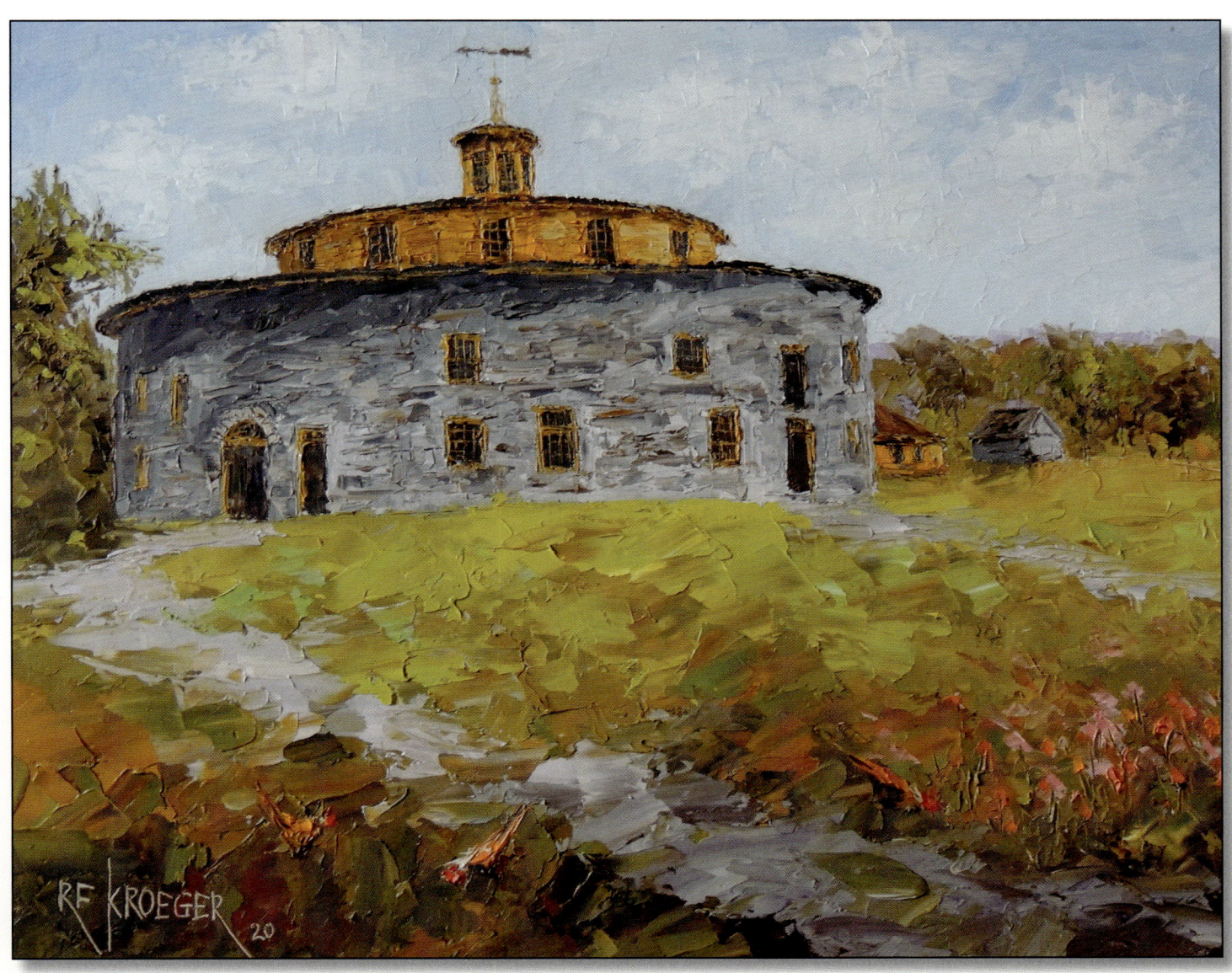

Hands to Work ... Hearts to God

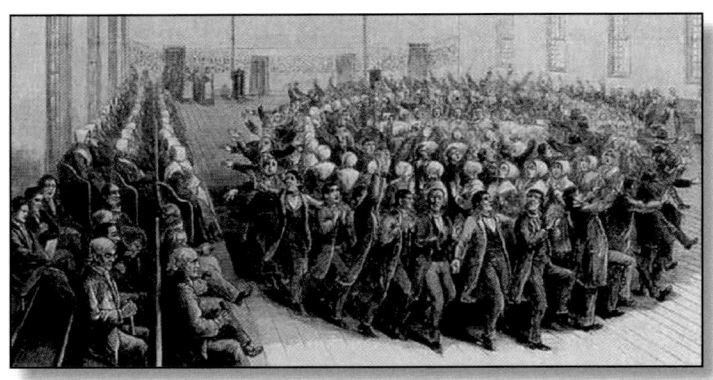

1840 engraving. Shakers dancing. National Park Service

This Protestant sect originated in England as an off-shoot of Quakerism and came to America in 1774, led by a woman, Mother Ann Lee. After she suffered the loss of her four children in Manchester, England, she and a group of eight founded a colony in Watervliet, New York, in 1776. Their pacifist religion upheld equality of gender and race and it stressed the importance of confession of sin, communal life, and celibacy, which meant that any children would have to come from outside the group. Converts had to give all their worldly goods to the commune, where they were shared by all. Despite these stringent rules, the Shakers grew. In 1787 they founded a farm in New Lebanon, about 11 miles west of Pittsfield and across the state line into New York. In 1790 the Shakers formed a colony in Pittsfield.

By the 1830s there were about 300 members in the Hancock community in Berkshire County, the third of 19 Shaker villages throughout the United States. After they had accumulated 3,000 acres of land, they built a handsome red brick dormitory, which housed more than 100. In 1826 they erected a round stone barn, farmed, and, using precise workmanship, built furniture, which became popular, evoking high quality and yet simplicity. Yet, despite the spread of the Shakers throughout New England, New York, Ohio, Indiana, and Kentucky, this round barn was the only one they ever built. Furniture was a common thread but round barns weren't.

After an earlier wooden barn burned, elders William Deming and Daniel Goodrich chose a true circular design, which they considered to be the most perfect shape. Since they originated in Manchester, they may have been aware of several round stone churches in England, which date to the 12th century and were probably inspired by Crusaders, who were impressed by the round rotunda in the Church of the Holy Sepulchre in Jerusalem. The Hancock leaders also thought on a large scale when they built this barn, which has a circumference of 270 feet and a diameter of 95 feet. They also wanted it to last and had enough funds to construct stone walls 30 inches thick. The original design provided stanchions for 52 dairy cows and a central tower 55 feet wide and 30 feet high. Despite its sound foundation, its wooden section burned down in 1864.

Undaunted, members rebuilt the barn, finishing the reconstruction by 1883, this time making improvements by adding trapdoors behind the stalls so that manure could be scraped and dropped below to wagons. To prevent combustion of hay – which may have been the cause of the fire – they built a central octagonal ventilation shaft that rises above the roof in a cupola with windows. Just below the cupola, a 12-sided clerestory, another addition, provided much needed light to the interior.

By 1850 the American Shaker population had reached an estimated 4,000 to 5,000 members but after the Civil War it began to decline. Young people (they adopted orphans) left for the world outside the community. Fueled by the industrial revolution of the late 19th century, jobs became plentiful, contributing to this urban migration, and in 1874 only 98 members were left at Hancock. By the early 1900s only 50 members remained. As their numbers declined, they began selling land and dismantling excess buildings until they stopped farming completely in 1959.

A group of local citizens, realizing the historical importance of this commune, organized a nonprofit. Shaker Community, Inc., located in Pittsfield, purchased the site, and began restoring buildings. In 1968 they rebuilt the barn, removing the original stones and replacing them as accurately as possible. Later, in 1983, the complex was added to the National Register. Interestingly, though the barn is circular on the outside, the wood frame is 14-sided in the interior. Again, even though the roof is now a clerestory design, originally it was conical.

The group now operates the 750-acre property as a museum and a working farm. In 1986 the barn got a facelift, which, as the highlight of the farm, continues to draw visitors all year round. Today there are four rings inside the barn: the innermost provides ventilation, the next ring stores hay, the third allows workers to distribute the hay to the cows, and the outermost ring is where the cows stand in their stanchions.

Hancock Shaker Village functions as a living history museum with an extensive collection of Shaker furniture, rotating exhibits, a mile-long hiking trail, and a full schedule of events, held in many of the 20 restored buildings, including this iconic stone barn. Though it was probably the first truly circular barn in America, its shape didn't motivate other farmers to follow suit. Round barns didn't interest farmers until Wisconsin's Franklin King's plans were published in farm journals in the early 1890s.

Undoubtedly the Shaker round barn attracted attention

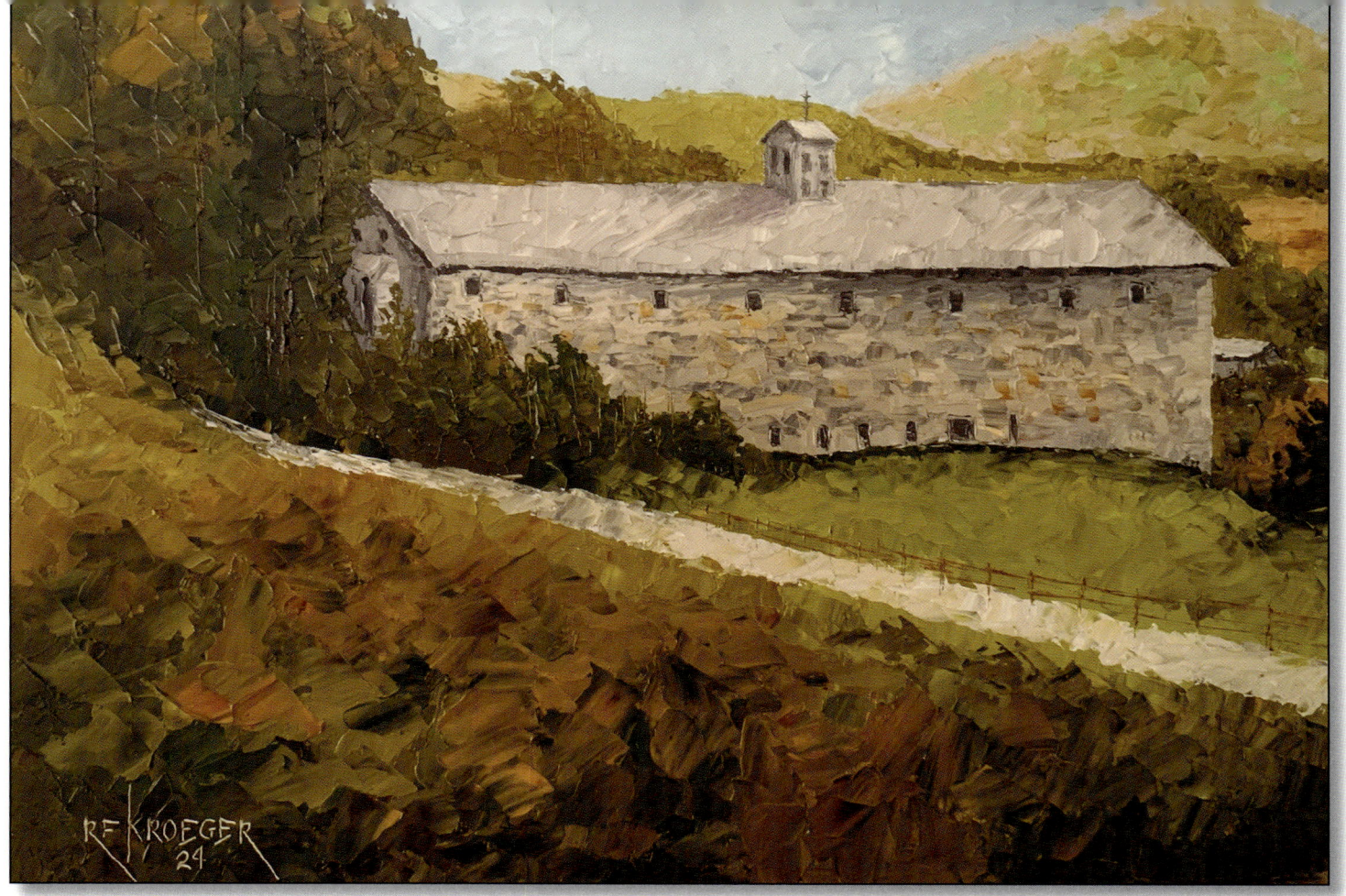

Whittaker's Wisdom

in the 19th century, but farmers may have felt – and rightly so – that such an undertaking was beyond their means. Regardless, for the past 60 years today's nonprofit organization has wisely undertaken a formidable task to preserve a memorial to a most unique religious sect. In a much smaller way, this painting and essay will remember this round stone barn, which served the commune for many years and, in a sense, symbolized its proverb, "Hands to Work … Hearts to God."

NEW YORK

COLUMBIA COUNTY

Whittaker's Wisdom

Following the death of Mother Ann Lee in 1784, who brought this Protestant faith to the colonies 10 years earlier, Father James Whittaker became the head of the organization in America. He began construction of this site in 1785, which later evolved into the center of Shaker ideology in the United States. In 1965 the Mount Lebanon site was named a National Historic Landmark, which includes its massive stone barn. The village was listed on the National Register in 1983. Additionally, in 2004 and

2006 the World Monuments Fund recognized the stone barn as one of the top 100 most significant endangered historic sites in the world.

As the Shaker community grew, it became wealthy, thanks to entrepreneurial efforts to sell garden seeds and corn brooms – and eventually wooden chairs and furniture – in the early 19th century. Such prosperity led Whittaker to envision it evolving into a model for others to follow. Buildings were constructed, farming flourished, and converts became members. By the mid-1850s, the Shakers had expanded their land at Mt. Lebanon to 6,000 acres. Around 600 people lived here in hundreds of buildings; they were divided into families of 50-100 men, women, and children. The North Family, established around 1800, served as an intermediary between the cloistered members and the outside world. The other families, the Church, Center, Second, and South stayed inside the complex.

Elder Frederick W. Evans, the North Family elder for 57 years, decided to build a new agricultural complex and to feature a gigantic stone barn as the centerpiece of the farm. In 1858 his ideas began to take shape; he hoped the village would serve as a statement that the Shakers were leaders in farming technology.

He chose Brother George Wickersham, a fellow Shaker and an experienced builder and inventor, to design the barn.

Together, they visited other massive barns, including David Leavitt's 200-foot-long Cascade Barn, three stories high, on his estate in the Berkshires. They also traveled to New Hampshire to visit existing Shaker barns, both substantial: the cow barn in Enfield (1854) and the 200-foot-long stone barn in Canterbury (1858). And no doubt the Shaker stone round barn in nearby Pittsfield helped convince them to use stone. They planned that the huge barn would replace 20 detached agricultural buildings in the village.

Wickersham completed a set of blueprints in the winter of 1858-1859. In return for his services, the North Family gave him a "case and cupboard" of their furniture. Incredibly, most of Wickersham's architectural drawings of the barn have survived, which he designed to show off the prosperity of the community, the simplicity of its lifestyle, and how barns could be made to blend in with nature. The Shakers hoped that the barn would attract new members to their celibate lifestyle and so they opened the village to the public one day a week – on Sunday, when they held a prayer service.

In an unusual move, though their members built the wooden part of the timber-framed structure, the Shakers hired an outside mason to construct the walls; it's possible they felt that no one in the family could handle such a task. Oliver P. Tanner of Lenox, Massachusetts, quarried the stone on the Shakers' farm, combining soapstone and bluestone for esthetics. Huge bluestone quoins, hand-cut, some three feet long, supported the corners. Tanner used white Berkshire marble for the windowsills and lintels and instructed his workers to add decorative touches in the pointing. Stones included marble, bluestone, limestone, and serpentine. The walls were 24 inches thick.

The gigantic barn, 200x50 feet, housed 60 dairy cows on the first level, which meant that milking cows twice a day would provide ample milk, butter and cheese for hundreds. The monitor roof had horizontal clerestory windows that stretched the entire length of the barn and included an incredible number of windows for ventilation and light. Workers built a "manure railway," designed by Evans and Wickersham, to control the smell and to sanitize the barn. Farm hands loaded manure into carts that ran on rails behind the stalls and dumped the load into a vault below, which was closed off by masonry walls and a trap door. Later, workers would compost the manure and use it as fertilizer in planting season. Completed in 1859, the barn's design was well ahead of its time. Besides functioning as a dairy barn, it allowed the Shakers to breed English Shorthorn cattle and to raise corn and grow hay. At the time, it was the largest stone barn in the United States.

As the years passed, the Shakers didn't hesitate to make improvements. When the flat monitor roof (covered with tar and 50 tons of gravel) began to leak, they replaced it in 1880 with a slate gable roof with a monstrous cupola, about the size of a small two-story cottage. In 1881 they added two masonry silos; again, this innovation was ahead of its time since silos didn't become widespread until the late 1890s. In 1901 the family replaced the original wooden floor with concrete slabs over steel I-beams and they improved the manure rail system with an overhead track system. Captivated by this stone barn, artist and author Eric Sloane put a sketch of it in his book, *Eric Sloane's An Age of Barns*.

In the 20th century, membership in the church fell and, with its decline, leaders realized that they couldn't maintain all the buildings. Accordingly, they split the village into three sections and began to sell the property. In 1929-30, the Darrow School purchased 300 acres and 40 buildings centered around the Church Family. In 1947 when the last seven remaining Shakers left, the entire village was sold. The Darrow School acquired land from the North, Center, and Second Families. The school, established in 1932, has been a college preparatory school, though, with an enrollment of only 85 in 2024, its future looks bleak. At Thanksgiving 2023, it was announced that the school would be kept open only if five million dollars could be raised. Immediately, the school appealed for help and began a campaign, which, thanks to parents, alumni, and one generous donor, raised $5.1 million by January. So, for now, the school will continue.

In 1972 when a fire destroyed the barn's wooden components, the slate roof caved in, but the massive stone walls remained, a testament to stonemason Tanner. Though the culprits weren't found, arson was suspected since the barn was

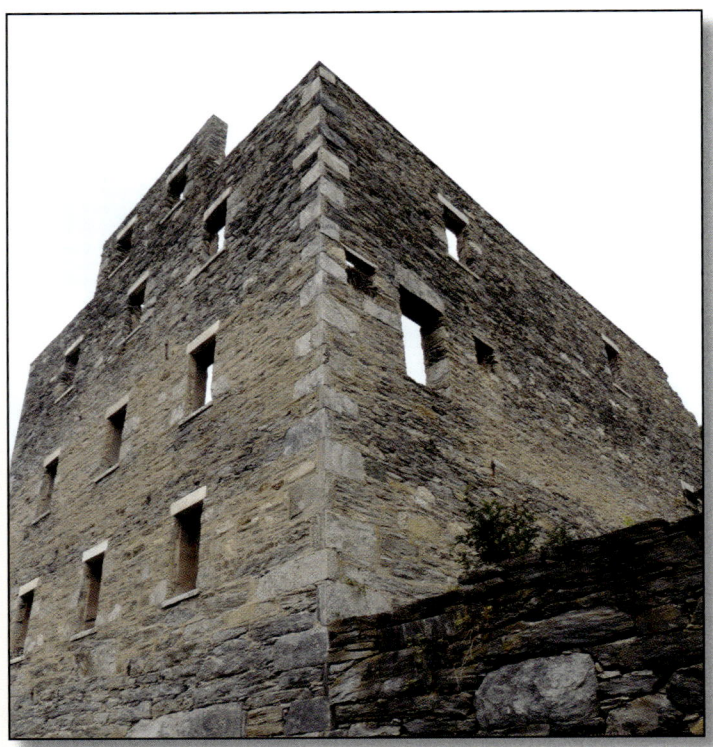

Bluestone quoins. Shaker barn, Mt. Lebanon, New York

basically vacant for decades. Thankfully, workers installed steel braces on the south side of the barn in 1984 – to prevent its collapse. Unfortunately, time caught up with the barn: part of the west wall crumpled in 2023. Regardless, the stonework continues to show the mastery of the masons: some of the stones are nearly three by six feet long, weighing hundreds of pounds.

Founded by John S. Williams, the Shaker Museum in 2004 purchased the North Family site, consisting of 11 buildings on 91 acres. But the huge barn continued to deteriorate. With a $500,000 preservation grant from the state of New York as part of a $2.75 million master plan, restoration has continued to stabilize the stone shell. Extensive cracking on the 60-foot-high west wall was repaired and other areas were tuckpointed. In 2015, for the first time in 43 years the barn was opened to the public. Visitors were allowed to freely stroll through the 8,750-square-foot space inside the colossal stone walls. However, after the 2023 damage, the museum erected a protective fence around the barn to prevent entry and possible injury to visitors.

Thanks to museum founder Williams, who began collecting items directly from the Shakers in the 1920s and 1930s, the Shaker Museum has arguably the most complete collection of Shaker furniture and memorabilia in the world – over 18,000 objects. The museum plans to conduct guided tours of the site during the summer and fall seasons, which will highlight the importance of this National Landmark and pay tribute to a religious community that designed it, built it, and used it extensively for nearly a century – the legacy and wisdom of James Whittaker.

OTSEGO COUNTY
A Treasure in Cooperstown

This magnificent stone barn, built in 1918, sits on the grounds of the Farmers' Museum in Cooperstown, a village well known for baseball's hallowed hall. The farm traces back to the era of William Cooper, though he didn't build the barn.

Born to Quaker parents in 1754 in southeastern Pennsylvania, William began working as a wheelwright and later settled with his family in Burlington, New Jersey, a predominantly Quaker town. In 1774, two years before the Declaration of Independence, he married Elizabeth Fenimore, daughter of Quaker parents. There's no record of William serving in the Revolutionary War, which began a year after his marriage. Like most Quakers, he was probably a pacifist, not favoring either side, choosing to live life quietly as battles raged.

However, after operating a store in Burlington in the early 1780s, he took advantage of the American victory, which freed up land from wealthy British nobles, who often acquired large tracts via land grants from the king. As many did, William became a land speculator and, while others weren't successful in such ventures, William was. In 1785 he purchased a parcel of 10,000 acres in upstate New York and founded the village of Otsego, selling plots in what officially became Otsego County in 1791.

William moved his family here in 1790 and, now wealthy and well known, became a county judge. Later, he served two terms in Congress, while continuing to sell acreage to land-hungry settlers, many coming from New England states. During these years he started a farm and built a mansion, which he called Otsego Hall, completed in 1799. The village's name changed to Cooperstown

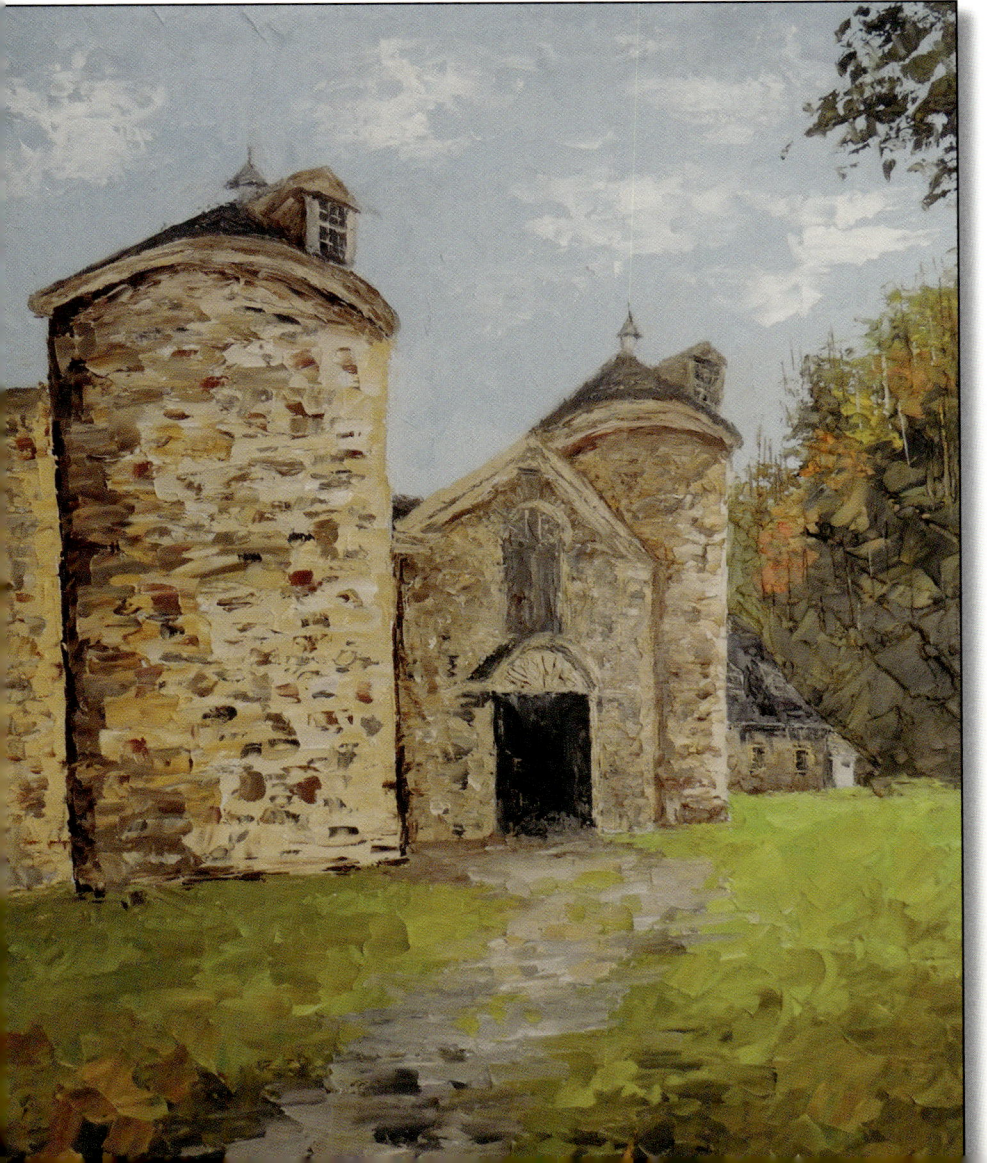

Left: *A Treasure in Cooperstown*

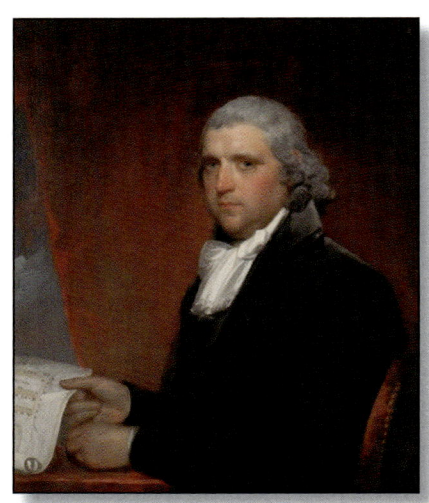

Portrait of William Cooper by Gilbert Stuart. Wikimedia Commons.

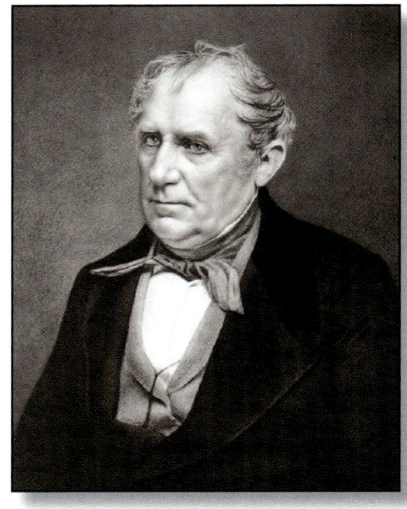

James Fenimore Cooper, 1850 photograph by Mathew Brady. WikiCommons

in 1812, three years after William died.

William and Elizabeth had 12 children, a lot of mouths to feed, indeed, but not a burden, thanks to their prosperity. They named their 11th child, James Fenimore Cooper, who was born at their home in Burlington in 1789. At 13, after being educated locally, James enrolled at Yale University, where he excelled in Latin. However, Yale expelled him for pulling dangerous pranks in his third year. Then, having always yearned for adventures at sea, he took a job on a merchant ship, the Sterling, which sailed through stormy seas – first in 1806 to England, which was at war with France, and then into Spanish waters. After 11 months of being a common seaman, James received a commission, thanks to his father's influence, as a midshipman in the U.S. Navy, where he served on three different vessels. However, when his duty failed to bring excitement, he resigned his commission in the spring of 1810. Two years later the War of 1812 began, a conflict that would have supplied James with plenty of action.

After his father passed in 1809, James and his siblings inherited not only his estate but money. Two years later, James married and he and his wife lived in West Chester County until 1813, when they moved to Cooperstown, after their first child was born. Though not famous in her own right, Susan Augusta DeLancey was the catalyst for the writing career of her husband. Often, James would read books to Susan and would complain about them. After hearing enough of his complaints, she challenged James to write his own novel, which he did in 1821. *Precaution* was a flop. Though his next novel, *The Spy*, a tale about the Revolutionary War – an ironic topic since his parents were pacifists – likewise wasn't successful, his next 31 books, including the well-known *Last of the Mohicans* and *The Deerslayer*, sold remarkably well and helped to define the young country's place in literature.

In 1826 the Coopers moved abroad, living in France, Switzerland, and Italy, where, now affluent like many expatriates, they raised their children while James continued writing. After seven years, they returned to the family estate in Cooperstown. But farming wasn't for them and three years later they sold the Fenimore farm to Samuel Nelson, a prominent lawyer and judge, who ascended from the circuit court to the state supreme court and then to the U.S. Supreme Court, where he served from 1845 until he retired in 1872. He was involved in the famous Dred Scott Decision in 1857. His law office has been preserved on this farm.

During his career as lawyer and judge, Nelson became a gentleman farmer and increased the farm to 300 acres, raising sheep, using it as a summer retreat, and renting it out. The Otsego Democrat ran a notice in 1852, advertising the rental home and farm: "To let cheap. … The house and grounds … are in perfect repair and location."

The farm changed hands again in 1876 when Ambrose Jordan Clark, son of Edward Clark, bought it. Edward, also a lawyer, co-founded the Singer Sewing Machine Company in 1851 with Isaac Merritt Singer, a penniless inventor, who granted a percentage of his patent to Clark in lieu of attorney fees. Unfortunately, Ambrose Clark died in 1881, leaving the Fenimore farm to his father, who, in turn, died a year later. The senior Clark's estate was valued at between $25 and $50 million, a huge sum in those years.

Edward Clark bequeathed the estate – along with the Dakota, a monstrous apartment building in New York City – to his namesake, his 12-year-old grandson Edward Severin Clark, the next to own the farm. Like his predecessors, Edward became a gentleman farmer, experimenting with breeding, crops, and feeding methods. He raised livestock – dairy cows, cattle, and sheep. And he built this stone barn.

Around 1916 he hired the New York City architect Frank Whiting, who had been working on the Singer building in New York City. Eventually, they became friends and Whiting moved to Cooperstown in 1932. Over the years the Clarks gave him plenty of work to do, including designing the new Baseball Hall of Fame, which opened in 1939, an idea of Edward's brother Stephen, who hoped it would attract tourism.

Whiting chose stone and gambrel roofs for the two stone silos, the giant barn, two other farm buildings, a stone creamery barn, and a cottage for the cowherd, who was in charge of 80 dairy cows. The 104x250-foot barn, nicknamed the "Cow Palace," had stanchions for all 80 cows, which represented full-time work since they required milking twice a day. Flanked by two tall stone silos, its entrance resembled the stunning Thompson round barn in Kansas, which, started in 1910, was completed in 1913, and, as an innovative design, was likely described in agricultural journals, which Whiting might have noticed. Its turreted silos also featured dormers. Inside, the roof construction was open enough for the hay fork to pass freely without interference. The stonemasonry, well maintained over the last century, shows the work of a master. Presumably found locally, the brown, beige, gray, burnt sienna fieldstones form an attractive pattern.

The creamery, the processing center for milk, was state of the art, housing pasteurization and a bottling plant on the first floor and an apartment on the second. A loading dock opened into a refrigerator room, making it easy for drivers to load milk for delivery. In preparation for wintry days, a low stone passageway provided a covered route between the barn and the creamery, regardless of snowfall. At the grand opening dinner, Clark invited 150 of his employees to witness the grandiose barn complex and, according to an article in The Otsego Farmer, he explained, "It is expected that the barn will be ready to receive the dairy by the latter part of this week." Throughout Clark's lifetime, his farm provided milk to the village; however, after he died in 1933, dairy production stopped within a few years.

The farm passed to his brother, Stephen C. Clark, who, at the time, was the director of the Singer Sewing Machine Company and an ardent art collector. Also a philanthropist, Stephen had plans to rescue Cooperstown; the bleak years of the Great Depression slashed employment in the village, which also suffered from Prohibition, which devastated the local hops industry. He paid for construction of a three-story brick building, designed by Frank Whiting, which would serve as headquarters for the Baseball Hall of Fame, which he hoped would attract tourists. His gamble paid off: the hall of fame became a mecca for millions of baseball fans. It opened in 1939.

In the same year Stephen invited the New York State Historical Association to move from Ticonderoga to the Fenimore farm and into the mansion, built by his late brother Edward in 1932. The association accepted his offer and in 2017 the historical society's name changed to the Fenimore Art Museum, located on the same land, once farmed by James Fenimore Cooper and his father. Thirdly, Stephen donated the Fenimore farm to become an outdoor showcase of rural life, which was developed around the stone barns in the early 1940s. Though the farm earned a listing on the National Register in 1980, the farm buildings were not added to the listing until 1997.

Opened to the public in 1944, this complex, called The Farmers' Museum, holds over 23,000 artifacts, including over 5,000 agricultural tools and objects, many accumulated by the Otsego County Historical Society. Two dozen buildings display collections that feature skilled workers: a blacksmith, a weaver, printers, an apothecary, and other tradesmen of the 19th century. The museum, operated by a private non-profit corporation, continues to honor the legacy of its founders, the Coopers, Nelsons, and Clarks and, hopefully as the years pass, it will continue to maintain this treasure in Cooperstown.

WAYNE COUNTY
Chiefly Cobblestone

Cobblestone barns are rare, making this one a unique piece of stone barn history. Cobblestones, though a problem for farmers in clearing fields and growing crops, were plentiful in the early days of colonization of the region beneath Lake Ontario – in New York's Wayne and Ontario counties. Glacial deposits left these smooth stones behind, rounds and ovals, some no larger than a fist which, in the

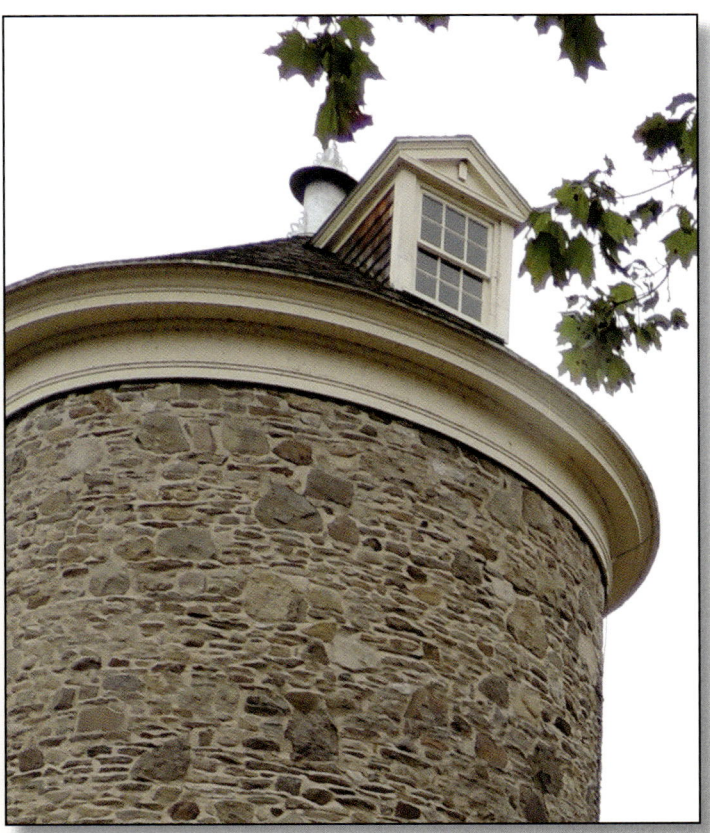

Masterful stonemasonry, Cooperstown barn, New York

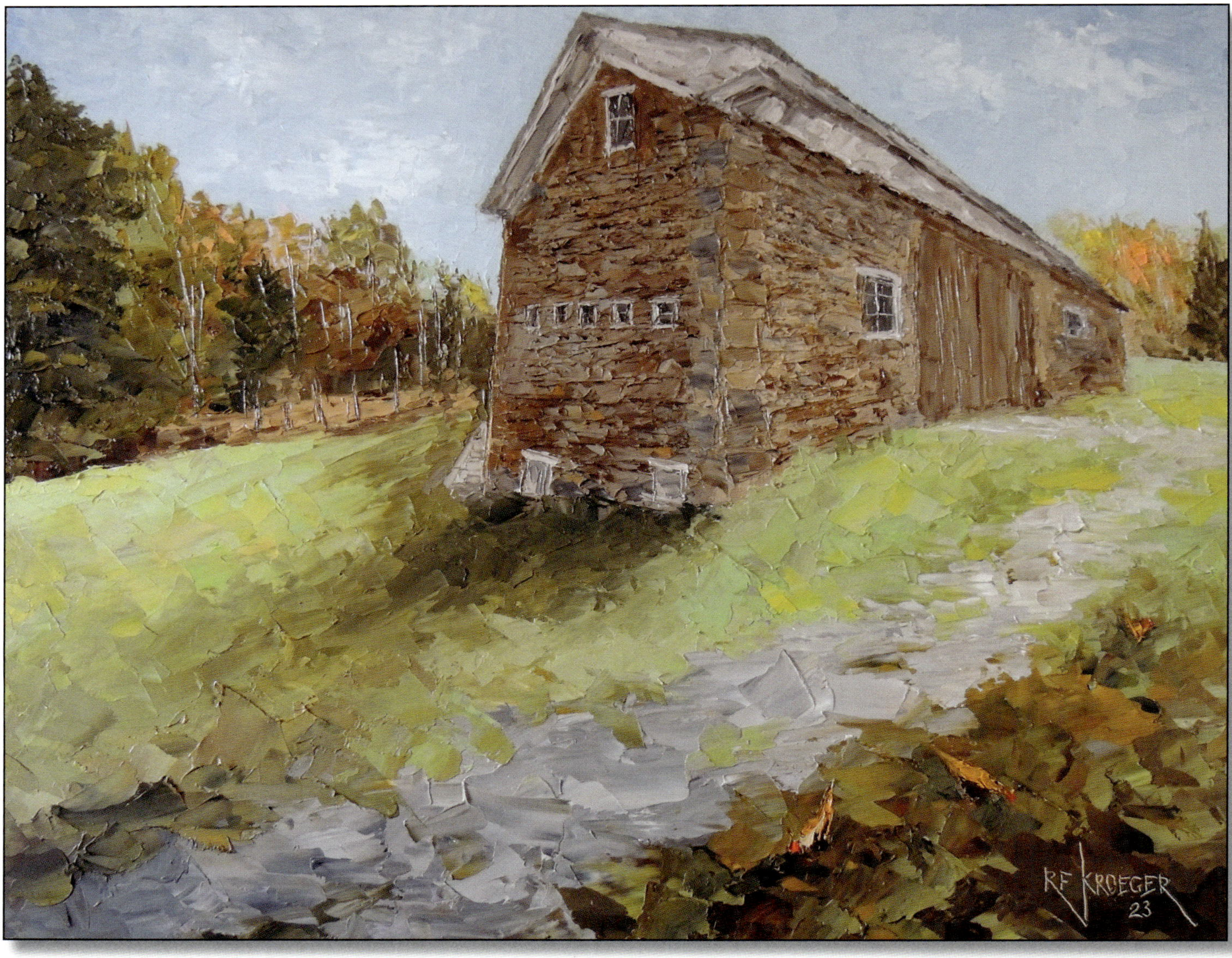

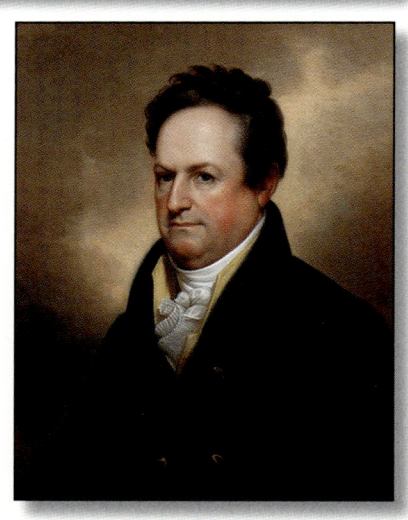

Above:
Chiefly Cobblestone

Right:
Portrait of DeWitt Clinton by Rembrandt Peale, 1812. Wikimedia Commons.

hands of skilled stonemasons, have adorned barns and houses, many of which still stand in this region today. Like premium paint in the hands of an artist, cobblestones allowed each mason to use creativity. These cobblestone-decorated buildings set themselves apart from those built with traditional wood, brick, or conventional stone.

Sue and Rich Freeman, authors of *Cobblestone Quest: Road Tours of New York's Historic Buildings*, estimate that over 700 cobblestone buildings were constructed from the 1820s to the 1860s in New York State. In fact, more than 90 percent of cobblestone buildings in the U.S. are located in upstate New York – mostly within a 75-mile radius of Rochester. The reason for this concentration traces back to the Erie Canal, dubbed sarcastically "Clinton's Folly," after New York's governor DeWitt Clinton, who played a major role in this project.

A former senator, mayor of New York City, and twice governor, Clinton served on the Erie Canal Commission from 1810 to 1824. Proponents of this canal, which would stretch 363 miles from the Hudson River in Albany to Lake Erie at Buffalo, wanted to increase commerce; opponents objected to the seven-million-dollar price tag (over $159 million today) and criticized the governor for his support. However, though he managed to get the legislature to approve the project in 1817, most residents were skeptical, leery of paying more taxes. However, by its completion in 1825, the canal changed public opinion – Clinton was now a hero. Shipping costs fell from $100 to $10 per ton on a haul from Buffalo to Albany and travel fares from huge volumes of passengers allowed the state to recoup its investment. New York City, now connected to Lake Erie, became a major seaport. And Ohio paid attention.

In 1825, Ohio was primarily an agricultural state with mostly subsistence farming, and it was the third poorest state in the Union. After witnessing the success of New York's canal, Ohio began building the Ohio-Erie canal, connecting the port of Cleveland with the Ohio River in southern Ohio and, eastwards via Lake Erie, with Buffalo. By the 1840s, Ohio was the third most prosperous state, thanks to its canal.

The canals provided jobs. Though many of the common laborers were immigrants, there was work for skilled stonemasons and stonecutters – to build bridges, aqueducts, 83 locks, and other infrastructure. After the Erie canal was completed in 1825, the demand for stonemasons declined, leaving many looking for jobs. Why these unemployed masons shifted their focus to building homes and barns out of cobblestone, instead of conventional stone or brick, is open to conjecture. Indeed, cutting and placing large stones in building a lock on a canal is much different than working with tiny cobblestones. However, a master stonemason might have viewed this opportunity as a challenge and adapted his skills to this new endeavor. Stonemasons built many beautiful fieldstone homes and barns in southeastern Pennsylvania – many still standing today – though none of their work involved cobblestones. It's probably not a coincidence that the completion of the Erie Canal was the same year – 1825 – as when cobblestone construction began in this region.

When the canal was built through Wayne County in 1820-1821, the local economy thrived and stone masons moved to the area; many from New England and Pennsylvania were attracted by advertisements for work on the canal. Those who remained – after the canal was completed – settled on farms and supplemented their income by building cobblestone structures. They would work for 50 cents to $1.25 a day and often the owner would board the mason during construction. Did they knock on doors to sell their services or were they hired, based on word-of-mouth recommendations? In *The Genesee Farmer*, March 8, 1838, a letter, written by Chester Clark, explained that he had built two or three cobblestone buildings each season (winters in western New York can last from November through April, limiting construction to six months each year). After giving specifics, he wrote, "The quality and quantity of sand with the lime is very essential … The proportion which I generally use is from five to eight bushels of sand to one of lime in the stone." He also acknowledged the attractiveness of the final product, "As for elegance and taste, everyone who has seen a cobble stone building built as it should be will acknowledge that it surpasses quarry stone or brick buildings." And he mentioned the cost, "As for the expense of building, it is cheaper than almost any other kind of building." Mr. Clark's comments give a good look at the popularity of cobblestone construction, which depended on lime. Accordingly, lime kilns dotted the region.

There's no question that cobblestone construction involves a high degree of stonemasonry in selecting and arranging the cobbles in an artistic display of craftmanship. And why were most of these buildings concentrated in the region of New York below Lake Ontario, including the counties of Monroe, Wayne, Orleans, and Ontario? Well, that's where the glaciers of 40,000 years ago left these round stones, which surfaced every spring, posing a problem for farmers. As they cleared fields before sowing crops, they'd have to separate the cobbles, often putting them in piles. Chances are good that masons had a constant supply of these for building and that farmers were delighted to get rid of them.

In his 330-page book, *Cobblestone Masonry*, published in 1966, architect Carl Schmidt describes hundreds of cobblestone buildings – mostly houses – but other buildings, including many one-room schoolhouses, cemetery receiving vaults, Quaker meeting houses and other denominational churches, hop house dryers, stores and blacksmith shops, a pumphouse, a smokehouse, a hotel and inn, and one barn. Though most were in this region of upstate New York, Schmidt identified cobblestone buildings in five other states and Canada.

Schmidt described three periods of cobblestone building; the first, 1825 to 1835, lacked the artistry of those built in later periods. Using irregular stones in uneven rows may have shown how a canal stonemason could transition from massive limestone construction to intricate detail. Stones were gathered from fields after a spring thaw and sometimes masons paid children 10 cents a day to collect stones and drop their finds into a stoneboat, a six-foot square wooden platform attached to two timbers. In the middle period, from 1835 to 1845, skill sets improved and masons became more artistic, choosing uniform stones and arranging them in even rows.

In the final era – 1845 to the 1860s – the shore of Lake Ontario served as a quarry, where locals collected rounded and water-washed cobbles, allowing masons to choose stones of a certain color and similar size and arrange them in neat rows, prompting some critics to label this as monotonous. However, there's no doubt that such work was the mark of a master stonemason, especially in Wayne County, where there are over 150 cobblestone buildings, including the circa-1824 one-room Roe schoolhouse in the town of Butler, which is probably the oldest existing cobblestone schoolhouse in

North America. There's also a blacksmith's octagonal cobblestone barn in Alloway, dating to 1832.

Eventually, the trend subsided and by the end of the Civil War, it had practically become non-existent. Why then, did cobblestone construction die out? Though the answer may remain hidden in time, the war effort took many young men into service for both sides, lowering the demand for extravagant buildings. And the war and the millions who died in it may have left a sobering effect on the general populace. Nonetheless, it's strange that such artistic stonemasonry ceased so abruptly. Interestingly, an article in a 1901 edition of the *New York Tribune* mentioned that Andrew Carnegie, who had just sold his steel empire for $480 million to J.P. Morgan, was planning on building a cobblestone barn near St. Andrews Golf Club in New York. Apparently, his plans didn't materialize.

The Morrison barn, featured in my painting, may be the only surviving rectangular cobblestone barn in this region. Another cobblestone barn, located in nearby Sodus and with a date stone of J.F. Proseus, 1849, has been dismantled.

The Morrison barn is in Marion, a town chartered in 1825 as an offshoot from Williamson, named after Colonel Williamson, who widened the road that runs by this barn. Local Marion historian Caryn Devlin related that the farm's founder could have been Reuben Adams or Micajah Harding. Orrin Hicks owned it from 1852 to 1855, when he built this barn. In 1871 Samuel Smith purchased it and later sold it to Jacob Morrison, whose name is attached to the barn, even though the farm passed through several owners since then. The current owners wish to remain private.

Today, the barn sits high on a hill overlooking miles of rolling fields and woodland, its beautiful exterior a pleasant change and a striking contrast from the steel and concrete buildings of Rochester, only 23 miles away. Recently, the farm changed hands again and the new owner reported that the walls varied in thickness from 12 to 18 inches. Courses, one after the other, spaced a few inches apart, give the uniform appearance of a brick barn. Large gray sandstone quoins have been precisely cut and lay directly on each other, fortifying the corners, which show no cracking. Further, the stonemason cherry picked the stones, selecting dark brown or black ones, almost the same size and shape. The end result is a phenomenal piece of vernacular architecture, worthy of a listing on the National Register.

Its orderly brown cobblestones suggest a late period construction and its well-cut stone quoins hint that a master stonemason built it; mortar appears intact with no visible cracks, despite the barn's sitting on a hillside. Its stonemason, whose name has been lost in time, can rest assured that his legacy has been well cared for and will always be remembered … for being chiefly cobblestone.

RHODE ISLAND

NEWPORT COUNTY

Portsmouth's Gentleman Farmer

Henry Augustus Coit Taylor, known mostly as H.A.C. Taylor, built this majestic stone barn in 1911 in Portsmouth, nine miles from Newport, a fashionable resort during the Gilded Age. The story began when Henry A.C.'s great-grandfather, Moses Taylor, a London merchant, arrived in New York City in 1836.

Moses soon became prosperous in New York and his son Jacob followed in his footsteps, entering into partnership with John Jacob Astor. In turn, his son Moses also found financial success, becoming president of City Bank (now known as Citi) in 1855 as well as owning a railroad and a canal. When he died in 1882, he left an estate valued at $40 million. Although it happens often that children of wealthy parents waste their inheritance and end up with little, this wasn't the case with Henry.

Born in 1841, Henry A.C. graduated from Columbia University and became a lawyer in New York City and, later, president of National City Bank of New York. He also had interests in steel and mining and, like his father, Henry A.C. was a railroad tycoon – with mansions in New

Below: Date Stone, Proseus Barn, 1849. Courtesy, Cobblestone Buildings in Wayne County, New York. Blogspot.com

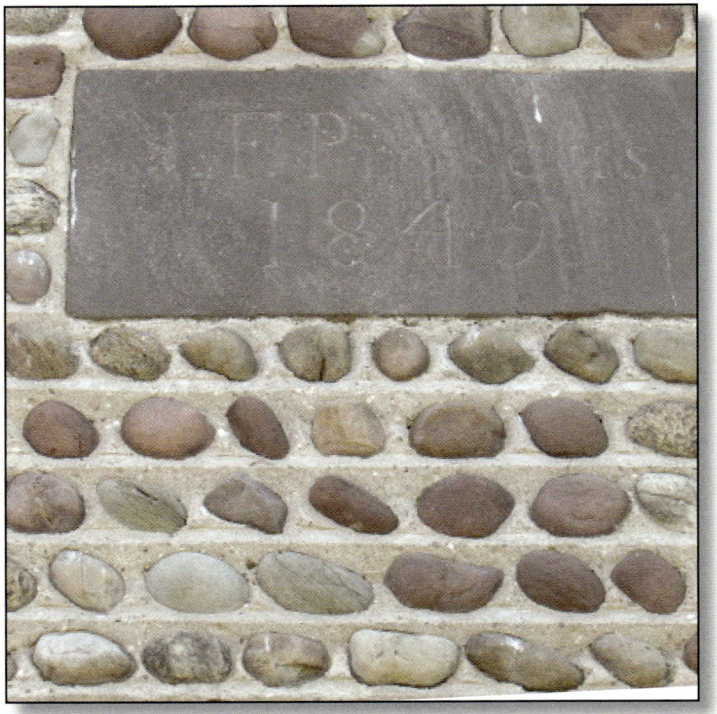

York City and the trendy ocean village of Newport, where the family would often take vacations.

However, he grew tired of the Newport scene and, wanting more privacy, he began buying farms in nearby Portsmouth, about 10 miles away. In September 1882, Halsey Coon sold his "Glen Farm," to Taylor. The farm had two farmhouses, a grist mill, two barns, corn cribs and other outbuildings, located on 111 acres. The farm was named after the scenic glen, where a stream-powered gristmill traced back to colonial times. Henry continued buying adjacent farmland and he began farming in 1885, raising Guernsey cattle in 1889. Later he switched to Clydesdales and then to Percheron horses. He entered national dairy shows and won many awards, competing with other gentlemen farmers, such as the Vanderbilts of Newport. Walls of the farm office were lined with hundreds of prize ribbons.

Like other farmers of great wealth – such as President George Washington – Taylor approached farming from a scientific basis and he wanted to showcase his efforts. In fact, he traveled to England's Isle of Guernsey to hand pick his cattle. However, when one of them, named Missy of the Glen, set a record for butterfat production, a gentleman farmer from Boston challenged that claim.

Refusing to believe that his farm hands would have been dishonest, Taylor launched a lawsuit, which, illustrating his social prominence and affluence, went all the way to the U.S. Supreme Court. When an independent year-long investigation confirmed Missy's record, the *New York Times* ran a headline in 1910 – *Champion Cow Vindicated*. Though Taylor won a judgement of $10,000, his legal fees cost $25,000, a cost offset somewhat by the increased value of Missy's calves. More importantly, his pride and reputation remained intact.

Managers kept the farm busy and productive, breeding livestock and raising enough crops to feed the 50 families who lived on the estate. A generator from the gristmill supplied electricity and other buildings showed the farm's activities: a blacksmith shop, icehouse, tool house, wagon shed, pump house, pottery shed, and animal hospital. Such a large operation required barns and, though there were some built as Taylor began buying farms, he built at least five them – which still stand today.

The wooden cow barn, built before 1902, measures 40x100 feet and contains about 4,000 square feet. Its two and a half stories feature dormers, which provide access to a hayloft. It sits on a rubblestone foundation as does the adjacent 1902-built polo barn. This barn, also a two-story wooden one,

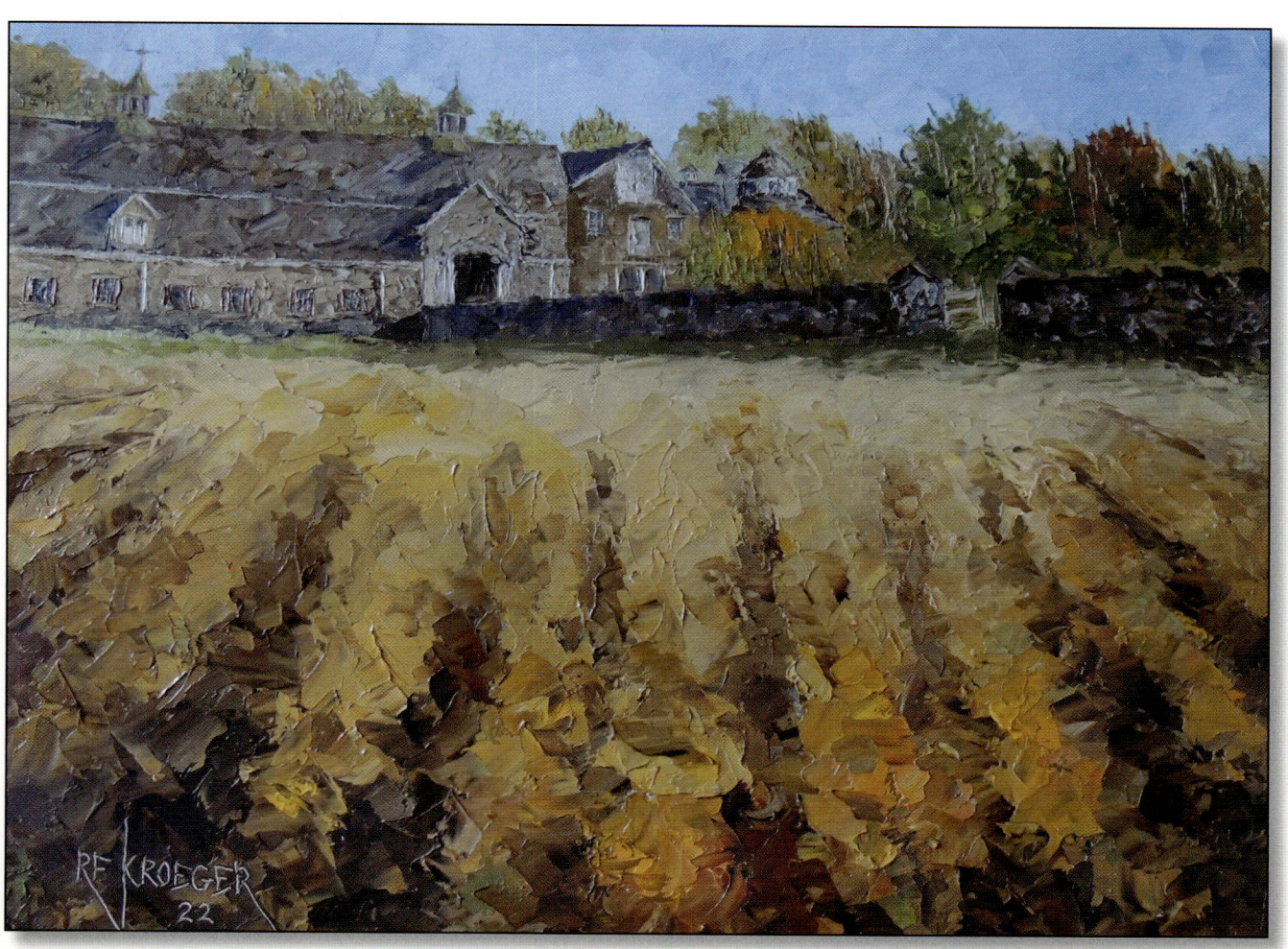

Portsmouth's Gentleman Farmer

measures 34x116 feet and has 18 horse stalls. Its gambrel roof with dormers and ventilation cupolas resembles the cow barn. However, its doors on the gable sides indicate a Dutch barn influence.

The dairy barn, built of stone in 1907, also has two and a half stories, but it's much larger than the preceding two – with over 5,100 square feet. Not only does it have a tack room and 18 stalls for horses, it also features a second-floor two-bedroom apartment. Steel beams support a partial basement and, on the north end of the barn, a stone silo connects to the barn via a covered passageway. Though brick lines the interior walls, rough-cut rubblestone covers the exterior. Brick and granite trim the lintels and sills of the barn's many windows and doors.

The bull barn, built in 1910, is another two-story stone barn, though, with about 3,500 square feet, it's smaller than the others. Inside, there are 10 stalls and, outside, a series of fenced bull paddocks are arranged with concrete posts and steel rails. Segmented arched doorways enhance the esthetics of the building.

The main stone barn, pictured in my painting and built in 1911, also has two and a half stories and, at 42x124

feet, is the largest of the barns. Rough-cut ashlar and rubblestone cover the exterior and a six-inch air space separates the brick inner wall, assuring temperature control. The dormers and cupolas mirror the design of the other barns and there is also a second-floor apartment, this one heated by an oil-fired boiler. Crenellated brick trims the granite sills and lintels of the windows. The architect designed a barn worthy of this gentleman farmer. At one time, the farm covered over 1,500 acres.

After H.A.C. died in 1921, his son Moses and his wife Edith continued to run the farm and completed Henry's mansion in 1923, designed by John Russell Pope, architect of the Jefferson Memorial and the National Gallery. They summered at the Glen Farm and, after Moses passed in 1928, Edith grew fonder of the farm. Though she remarried in 1938, she retained control of the farm, converting the main stone barn to a field hospital during World War II, though it was never used for casualties. She also repurposed a cottage into a Red Cross unit, where local ladies rolled bandages for soldiers. But, following the war, Edith began auctioning the livestock, signaling the end of farming. When she died in 1959, her son Reginald sold parcels of the farmland.

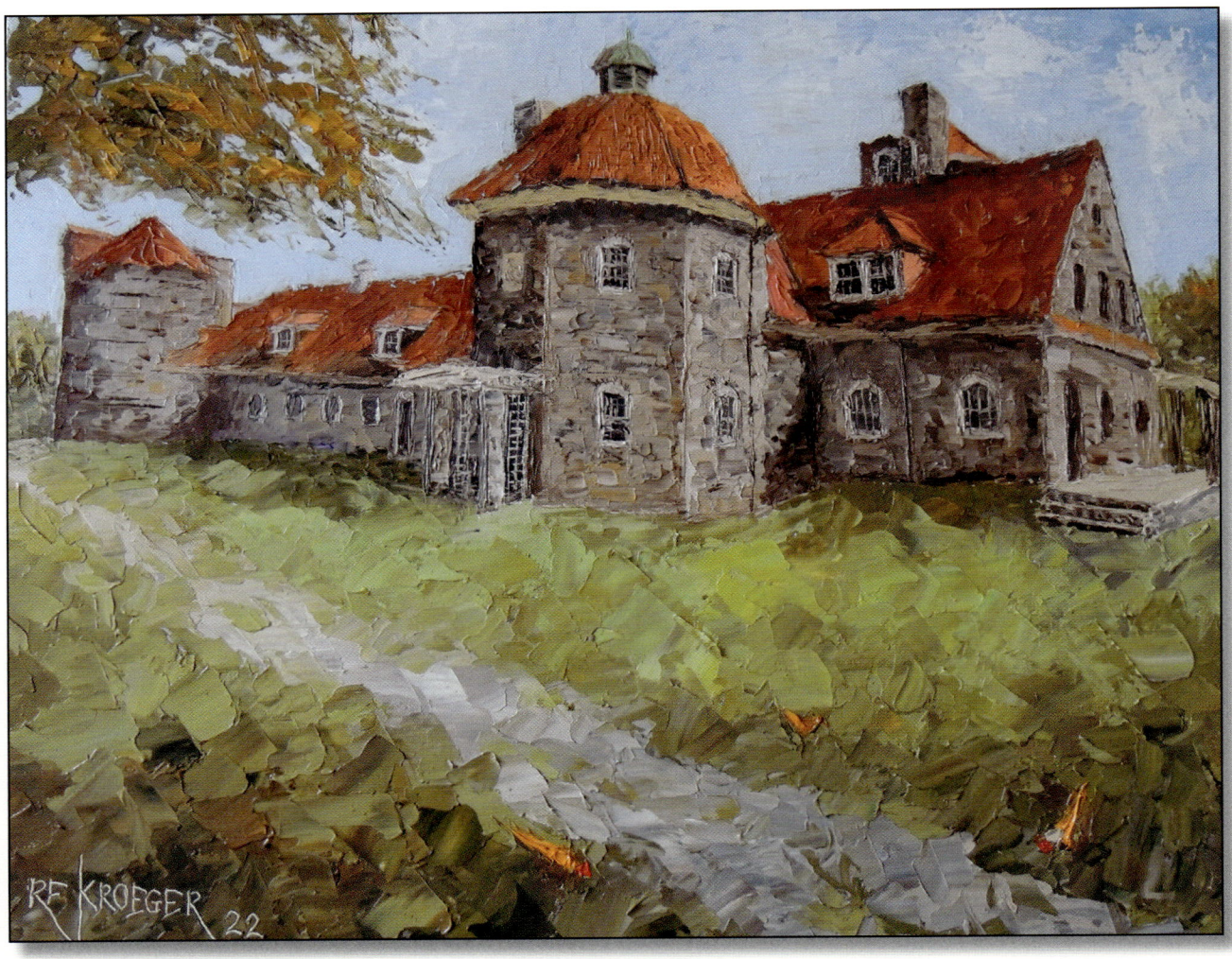

The Rubber King of Bristol

In 1973 the town of Portsmouth purchased some of the Glen farm, including Henry's stylish 1923 mansion, and started converting the land into public parks. When the last of the Taylor line, Reginald's grandson Mason Phelps, decided to sell, the town once again came through, hoping to keep the Glen Farm from being developed, and paid $3.6 million. The vote passed by a three to one margin. A year later in 1990, city officials studied ways to preserve the farm. That's when a 26-year-old Boston developer, Dan Keating, stepped in. By this time, the farm buildings and barns, without use or maintenance for decades, had deteriorated.

Keating signed a 10-year lease with the city to rehabilitate the farm. With over $600,000 of his personal funds, he replaced the plumbing, electrical, and heating systems and repaired the interiors and exteriors of the barns, installing solid brass to match the original hardware. He also constructed a polo field, home to the Newport Polo Club, the country's second oldest. The field also hosts the Newport International Polo Series. A local company operates an equestrian center, which Keating also established.

After acquiring two more parcels of adjacent land, Portsmouth now has reserved the Gardner Seveney Sports Complex for youth recreation. The city currently uses the farmhouse for its recreation department offices and has plans to develop hiking trails as well as to maintain the stone barns of Henry Augustus Coit Taylor, which, though not listed on the National Register, remain as fine tributes to the socialite financier, Portsmouth's gentleman farmer.

BRISTOL COUNTY
The Rubber King of Bristol

Colonel Samuel Pomeroy Colt, a wealthy industrialist in Bristol, built this grandiose stone barn in 1917. Although he only briefly knew him in his childhood, he was a nephew of Samuel Colt, the inventor of the famous revolver, patented in 1836, whose slogan was, "God created men. Colonel Colt made them equal." S.P. Colt's other lineage wasn't as respectable.

His mother, Theodora, was born into the DeWolf family of Bristol, which established the city as a thriving seaport in the late 18th and early 19th centuries. Her ancestor, Mark Anthony DeWolf, born in 1726 and patriarch of the family, started the DeWolf slave trading business. His son James continued in the slave trade, becoming one of the richest men in America in those years. Between 1769 and 1820 the DeWolfs transported over 11,000 Africans to the Americas. Though the United States banned this trade in 1808, the DeWolfs skirted the law by bringing slaves into Cuba, where they owned many plantations.

Even though Rhode Island was the first colony to abolish slavery in 1652, this law was largely ignored; nearby Newport was the country's leading slave-trading port. In 1774 the colony passed a law that banned importing slaves into its borders but Newport and Bristol families used their political prestige to get their candidates appointed to the customs office, which helped them to disregard this ban. Even after Rhode Island toughened this law in 1787, slavers continued to reap financial rewards. By 1800, Bristol had surpassed Newport as Rhode Island's busiest slave port.

Ironically, many of these imported slaves served in the Continental Army in several roles, including laborers and waggoners. Some fought as soldiers. Since Rhode Island, the smallest colony, had trouble meeting quotas for white men to fight in the war, Brigadier General James Mitchell Varnum suggested enlisting slaves for his 1st Rhode Island Regiment. During a four-month period in 1778 Rhode Island's Assembly allowed this, granting emancipation to those slaves who served and offering compensation to the slave owners. Though Rhode Island repealed this act, 117 slaves joined the army and won their freedom. Word spread and African-Americans continued to enlist so that by January 1778 nearly 10 percent of Washington's army consisted of former slaves.

George DeWolf, father of Theodora, took the family business to a new level and, with his skyrocketing income, was able to hire noted architect, Russell Warren in 1810 to build a $60,000 magnificent Federal-style mansion. Linden Place still stands in Bristol. S.P. Colt, born in 1852, spent some of his teenaged years – and later adulthood – in this house, now converted to a museum.

The family also entered the banking business, founding the Bank of Bristol around 1800, funding it with capital of $50,000; the DeWolf brothers were all stockholders. Along with banking, their slave business flourished – family members were stationed at every major slave auction city along the east coast. But, the whims of Mother Nature decided to end the DeWolf's fortunes.

Farmers depend on good weather for their harvests and in 1825 the weather caused George DeWolf's sugar cane crop to fail on his plantations in Cuba. Apparently, George was overextended, perhaps spending as much as he made, and he defaulted on his loans, causing hardships in Bristol. Three banks nearly collapsed when he declared bankruptcy. George couldn't pay farmers, suppliers, and others, causing financial disaster for many of the town's residents. One of the unfortunate souls was slave ship captain Isaac Manchester, who lost $80,000 and had to turn to digging clams for a living. Ah, such tragedy.

DeWolf, having angered many locals, fled from his

mansion under the veil of night. Afterwards, creditors stormed his house, taking whatever wasn't nailed down. With the family name disgraced, some DeWolfs left town. However, James DeWolf, also a slave merchant, bought George's mansion and prospered. At his death in 1837, he was one of the richest Americans.

Samuel Pomeroy Colt, son of Theodora and Christopher Colt, was born in Paterson, New Jersey, in 1852. When his family returned to Bristol in 1865, Samuel attended school there and remained there the rest of his life, determined to restore his family's name. After three years at the Massachusetts Institute of Technology, he graduated from Columbia Law School in 1876, quickly gaining entry in the bar both in New York and Rhode Island.

After initially working in politics – when he acquired the honorary rank of colonel – he served as attorney general for Rhode Island for four years. However, after being defeated for office in 1886, he switched careers and left politics. That same year he founded the Industrial Trust Company, whose members included the elite of Rhode Island's gilded age.

In 1887, aged 35, he was appointed as a receiver for the bankrupt National Rubber Company, which was based in Bristol. After reorganizing it, he changed its name to the National India Rubber Company and merged it with other companies, forming the United States Rubber Company. After another name change to Uniroyal, the company grew into the largest producer of rubber goods in the world. In 1901 Colt became its president. By 1918, the year he retired, his company employed over 20,000 workers along the east coast.

As his wealth grew, Colt began buying small farms from old Bristol families, combining them into a large farm on Poppasquash Neck. Like other gentlemen farmers in the state, he planned to showcase modern farming methods – especially in livestock breeding. A year later, Colt completed the state's largest private bridge, known as the Mill Gut bridge, a wonderful display of masterful stonemasonry, which led onto his farm. Decorated with bronze and stone statues, the bridge must have impressed the many distinguished guests who drove over it on their way to exclusive parties at Colt's casino. A bronze dog sat on a rock on the water and two bronze bulls, each over six feet tall and weighing over a ton, were placed near the entry to the estate.

Samuel installed marble gates at the entrance in 1913, which were inscribed "Private Property, Samuel P. Colt, Open to the Public." Though he spared no expense – four Rodin-sculpted statues, two large bronze bulls and two bronze colts (the family's symbol) cast in Paris, and a $30,000 entry gate modeled after the Petit Trianon at Versailles – Colt emphasized that his estate would always be open to the common person. Workers, dressed in white, would guide visitors through the barn, showing off prize cows and offering glasses of fresh milk.

By 1917 he completed the magnificent fieldstone barn and purchased a herd of Jersey cows and Berkshire hogs. They rode in specially padded railroad cars throughout the northeast to compete in county fairs. In one season his Berkshire pigs won 125 ribbons, proof that this gentleman farmer was serious about his prized livestock.

Designed by renowned Bristol architect Wallis E. Howe, a great-great-nephew of James DeWolf, the barn complex, including Colt State Park, was listed on the National Register in 1980. Two massive stone-clad silos tower over the buildings, which include a cowbarn, calf barn, dairy, maternity ward, bull pen and a central domed steel-framed hexagonal structure, which served as Colt's office. Originally, decorative red-glazed pantiles covered the roofs, adding a Spanish touch of elegance, though they were lost to a fire in the 1930s. Today, red asphalt shingles have replaced the pantiles. However, two bronze lions survived the fire and still sit on the gates in front of the barn. The Poppasquash Farms district currently contains 516 acres, the largest open space in Bristol.

Colt preferred using traditional Percheron draft horses in his fields – instead of tractors, which became available in the early 1900s. He valued these horses as much as his prize cows and sows and, if he saw the horses sweating too much while hauling wagons of hay, he would stop the haying for the day. In wintertime, as protection against the harsh wind off Narragansett Bay, the horses would wear blankets when they were used to plow snow off the roads. Though cows and hogs were housed in the stone barn complex, the Percherons were relegated to a wooden barn across the salt marsh.

Before Samuel Colt died of complications from a stroke at his beloved Linden Place, the former George DeWolf mansion in Bristol, he wisely created trusts in 1921 to provide for his two surviving sons and their families. He left the bulk of his estate to his last surviving grandchild, though he would not know who that would be. His son, Russell Colt, was allowed to live, rent-free, on the farm, provided that it would not be sold and would always be open to the public. The Industrial National Bank administered the trust.

However, Colt's sons quickly contested the will, claiming their father's mental deterioration, but they dropped this first attempt. Again, they challenged the trust in 1926, but the court upheld Colt's provisions.

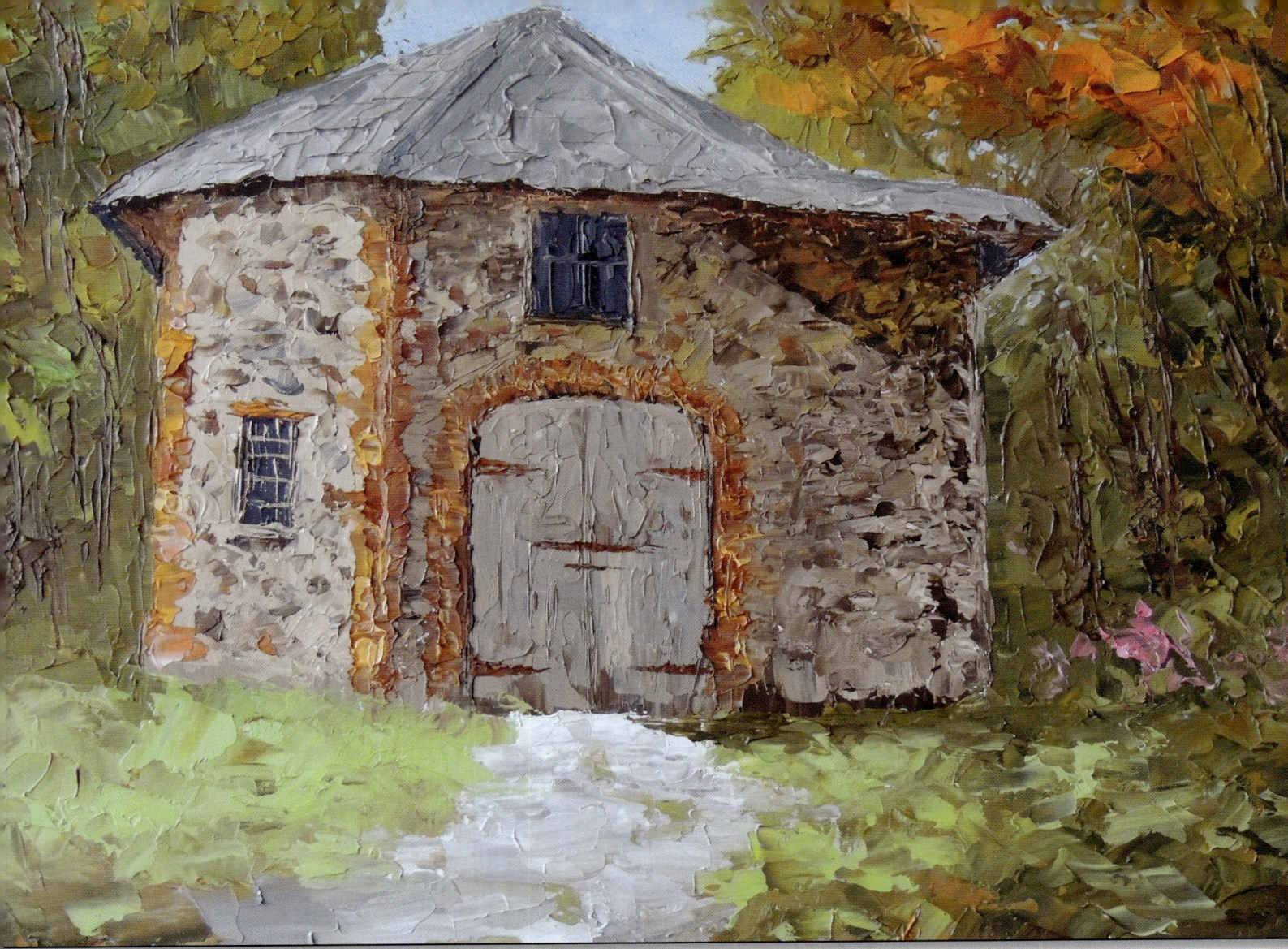

Farmin's Finest

Once again, in 1957, the heirs sued a final time, losing again. The will was never broken. Unfortunately, in this time period vandalism reared its ugly head – statues were defaced and some buildings succumbed to arson fires. A bronze dog, a favorite target of gun-toting hooligans, was eventually stolen.

Finally in 1965, the state preserved Colt's vision by acquiring the estate under the Green Acres Program, suspending payment until all the grandchildren died but one. Today, Colt State Park with its majestic vistas into Narragansett Bay is considered the gem of Rhode Island's state parks. Though the stone barn no longer provides shelter for prize Jerseys and Berkshires, it serves as offices for park employees and maintenance facilities. Summer concerts have drawn up to 10,000 visitors to grace the spacious lawns, a sight, no doubt, that would have brought a smile to "The Rubber King of Bristol."

CONNECTICUT

FAIRFIELD COUNTY

Farmin's Finest

Located in downtown Westport, this seven-sided cobble-stone barn, with its unusual octagonal roof, traces back to the late 18th century when Ebenezer Coley, a prosperous merchant in Westport, built a house for his son Michael and deeded the property to him in 1795. The Coleys were merchants, not farmers, and Michael, born in 1772, married in 1793, followed his father into business. However, three years after moving into the house, Michael incurred debts and was forced to give the house back to his father.

Ebenezer sold the house – with perhaps a wooden barn, as recorded in the National Register listing – to Mary Kent and her daughter Ann in 1799. The property – house and barn – continued in this family's hands until Paul Curtis purchased it in 1836, eventually selling to Hezekiah Allen in 1846, a resident of New York City, who may have been a real estate speculator since he sold it in the same year to Farmin Patchin.

Farmin, a stonemason and blacksmith, must have been a good businessman since he was able to afford such a house and to erect not only this cobblestone barn – sometime between 1846 and 1857 – but also another house, possibly for relatives or for rental. In 1850 he sold his smithy and blacksmithing equipment, which suggests that his masonry work was more profitable, especially since his property value nearly doubled from 1851 to 1854. However, Farmin apparently overextended himself since, in 1857, he had to mortgage his property, eventually losing it to the Sagatuck Bank, which kept it for seven years.

Why did Farmin choose such a shape? Well, according to Turpin Bannister in "The Architecture of the Octagon in New York State," (*New York History, Vol. XXVI*), there were at least 20 octagonal churches built in New York's Hudson Valley, about 100 miles away, between 1680 and 1750, which may have influenced not only Thomas Jefferson but this blacksmith as well. And, apparently initially affluent, Farmin wanted to show his good fortune to all, selecting cobblestones as his vehicle.

Cobblestone streets in Connecticut weren't rare. In fact, in 2016 the last cobblestone street in Derby – about 20 miles from Westport – was finally removed for safety reasons, after serving residents for over 200 years.

One corner of Patchin's barn was squared off, probably to fit against an attached wooden addition, which no longer exists, resulting in a combination of seven walls and an eight-sided roof. What the barn held may remain unknown, though the wooden addition hints that livestock, probably dairy cows, were housed. The barn's loft suggests hay storage. And, since Farmin sold his smithy in 1850, he may have operated as a blacksmith in the barn for only four years. The Alloway, New York, seven-sided blacksmith shop-barn looks remarkably similar to this one, even though it, like many barns, was built into a bank. Patchin's barn sits on level ground.

A nine-foot double arched door graces the entrance of the barn and twelve-over-eight windows are located irregularly on three sides. Distinctive reddish-orange brick quoins support the corners and multi-colored cobbles dot both the outside and inside of the walls. A ladder led to the loft, where hay was stored, and, in the lower level, the root cellar provided cooling for vegetables and milk – if there were dairy cows here – as well as storing ice for those who lived in Farmin's two houses. The original stonework and subsequent restoration are a tribute both to the local historical society and to Farmin's masterful masonry.

The next owner, Morris Bradley, another blacksmith – a respected and lucrative trade in those years – purchased the house and barn in 1857. After making a fortune in 1849 in the California Gold Rush, he made extensive improvements to the main house, converting the exterior to an Italianate design, an upgrade reflected in increased taxes in 1871. Morris transferred the buildings to his two daughters, one of whom, Julia, married a Wheeler. Eventually William B. Wheeler, a local dentist, owned the house and barn and willed it to his children, who, in turn, willed it to William's younger brother Lewis, a physician, who lived in the house until he died in 1958.

With no children, Dr. Wheeler left the house and barn to his housekeeper, Charlotte Darby, who lived in the house until her death in 1979. Unfortunately, she didn't maintain the barn, which had deteriorated; the roof was caving in and parts of the cobblestone walls were crumbling. Mrs. Darby's estate stipulated that the property be donated to Christ and Holy Trinity Church, which, in turn, sold it to the Westport Historical Society in 1981, creating a dilemma on what to do with the dilapidated barn – save it or scrap it. Fortunately, thanks to grants and contributions by individuals, including residents Paul Newman and Joanne Woodward, the society was able to restore the unique building, the only cobblestone barn in Connecticut. They successfully submitted the house and barn to the National Register in 1984.

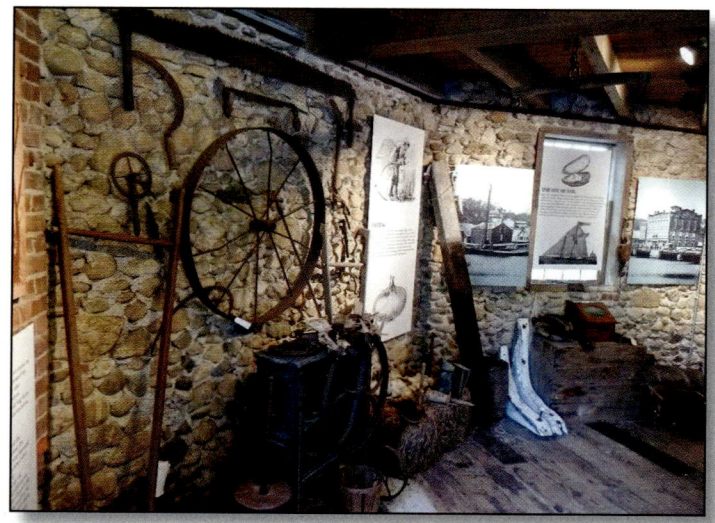

Interior of cobblestone barn. Courtesy of Westport Museum. Mike Lauterborn

Today the house serves as the headquarters of the historical society and both the house and the seven-sided barn function as museums about the history of Westport. The cobblestones, laid by Mr. Patchin over 150 years ago, still glisten when the sun hits them and they represent a bygone era and the life of a man, both stonemason and blacksmith, who built this barn, possibly his finest work.

5. MID-ATLANTIC

PENNSYLVANIA

Without question, the region of southeastern Pennsylvania can be frankly called the motherlode of stone barns in America. And despite suburban spread of housing subdivisions and industry from the adjacent megalopolis of Philadelphia, the area still maintains a bucolic flavor and its many farms and barns still preserve a way of life dating back to the 18th century. In fact, several volumes could be justified to document the thousands of stone barns here, including those in neighboring west-central New Jersey and north-central Maryland. Countless historical societies dot the little villages, townships, and cities and, thanks to many of their booklets and blogs, much is known about the history and the agricultural heritage of this land. Two books document this well. Author Robert F. Ensminger, in *The Pennsylvania Barn*, has classified these barns and has explained how farmers, leaving the "crowded conditions" of the early 19th century, took their Pennsylvania barn design with them as they migrated westwards to the fertile lands of Ohio and the rest of the Midwest, when it opened for settlement in the 1790s.

Greg Huber, in *The Historic Barns of Southeastern Pennsylvania*, has augmented Ensminger's work in describing "the hearth," a term he uses to define the area east of the Susquehanna River and south of the Blue Mountains, home to over an estimated 15,00 to 20,000 still existing barns, some wooden, some stone, and some log. While Ensminger and Huber have illustrated the many types of barns, their architecture, and their antecedents in Europe, Great Britain, and Ireland, my interest centers on the stories associated with the barns. And, to avoid making this section too large, I've limited my coverage to six counties – Berks, Bucks, Chester, Lancaster, Lehigh, and Montgomery – which provide a fair sampling of stone barns. Growth in these six counties has mushroomed from a population of several thousand people in the early 1800s to 3.5 million in 2024.

Thanks to barn tours with Greg Huber of Lehigh County and Warren Claytor of Chester County, I was able to witness this magnificent piece of Americana. And I learned that both men had lineage tracing back to England, Ireland, and Germany, countries whose immigrants settled this region. On Saturday Greg Huber, whose roots trace back to 19th century Germany, took me to see barns in four counties – Lehigh, Bucks, Berks, and Montgomery. The next day I explored Chester and Lancaster counties with Warren Claytor, an architect in Chester County who restores historic homes and barns and has a lineage steeped in local history. His ancestor Nicholas Waln sailed from England on the *Lamb*, a ship in the fleet of William Penn, the founder of Pennsylvania and Philadelphia. Their ship arrived a week before Penn's did.

Penn's ship, the *Welcome*, departed from Deal, England, on August 31, 1682, and arrived at the mouth of the Delaware River (now New Castle, Delaware) on October 27, 1682, completing the Atlantic crossing in 57 days which was slow by 17th-century standards. The voyage did not end without incident; nearly one-third of all the ship's passengers died of smallpox. On October 28, 1682, the *Welcome* anchored at Upland (now Chester, Pennsylvania) on a site chosen by Thomas Holme, Penn's surveyor general.

Warren kindly allowed me to stay in his house, built in 1764, which he has enlarged with a seamless addition. On our seven-hour tour of barns in Chester and Lancaster counties, almost everywhere I looked I saw a stone house or barn. Land conservancy has successfully stopped suburban sprawl; I didn't see a Costco, Sams, Menards, Home Depot, or Lowes! Just one quaint village after another. I wondered how this area, so close to Philadelphia and two medium-sized cities – Allentown and Bethlehem – could avoid commercialization. Warren answered my question.

As a member of two fox-hunting clubs, he explained that circa 1900 there were dozens of these clubs in this area. Fox hunts zigzag through forested land, meadows, and farm fields belonging to homeowners, farmers, all of whom love the pastoral setting of their land. Many decades ago, they began to place conservation easements in their deeds to permanently prevent the land from being commercially developed if it should be sold. Over the years, that trend has spread to thousands of homes and farms, maintaining this bucolic paradise, one of the most exceptional in the country. Conservancy groups such as Willistown Conservation Trust in Chester County continue to preserve land. And, since the National Registry lists nine of the barns we visited, I learned their stories, many of which traced back – before, during, and after – the Revolutionary War.

When English settlers first arrived in the late 17th century, thanks to William Penn's grant, they didn't need to build large barns since they had few livestock. However, as their farms grew, they soon realized that snowy and frigid winters here were much different than those in Mother England and they began to build barns, out of logs at first and then framed in wood. Stone barns came later.

Though many old barns in the "hearth" were built with limestone, one building stone, Pennsylvania bluestone, was also used. Unique to this area and found mostly in Susquehanna County, about 100 miles north of Lehigh County, the stone derives its name from its typically blue color, although variations include green, beige, and lilac – or a combination of these tints. Architects and builders prize this stone, which is strong, resists cracking, can be worked easily, and won't discolor. Another uncommon stone that still graces 18th-century barns and buildings is Pennsylvania serpentine stone. Found locally in Chester County's Brinton Quarry, the green stone is relatively soft; it ranks 3-4 on the hardness scale (where diamond ranks 10th) and, though esthetically beautiful, the stone does not weather well. It can vary in color from dark to light green and sometimes it's mottled in red, yellow, or white, resembling the skin of a serpent.

BERKS COUNTY
Gehman's Glory

At the time of the nomination for listing on the National Register in 1992, the John Gehman farm occupied 87 acres on both sides of Seisholtzville Township Road, still a dirt trail then. Though the county attempted to pave the road, it is still pastoral, but upgraded to gravel these days. The farmland, hilly with wetlands and woods, punctuated with small fields, is penetrated by a small tributary of Perkiomen Creek, which flows through this farm. Rustic worm fencing, once a common sight in this area, though now extremely rare, meandered through this farm, but has disappeared. Also known as snake fencing, worm fences have been used in America since the 1600s. Easy to build, they did not require post holes, a factor in rocky soil. The farmer simply stacked split rails on top of one another and angled each section slightly for stability. The zigzagged appearance resembled a worm or snake.

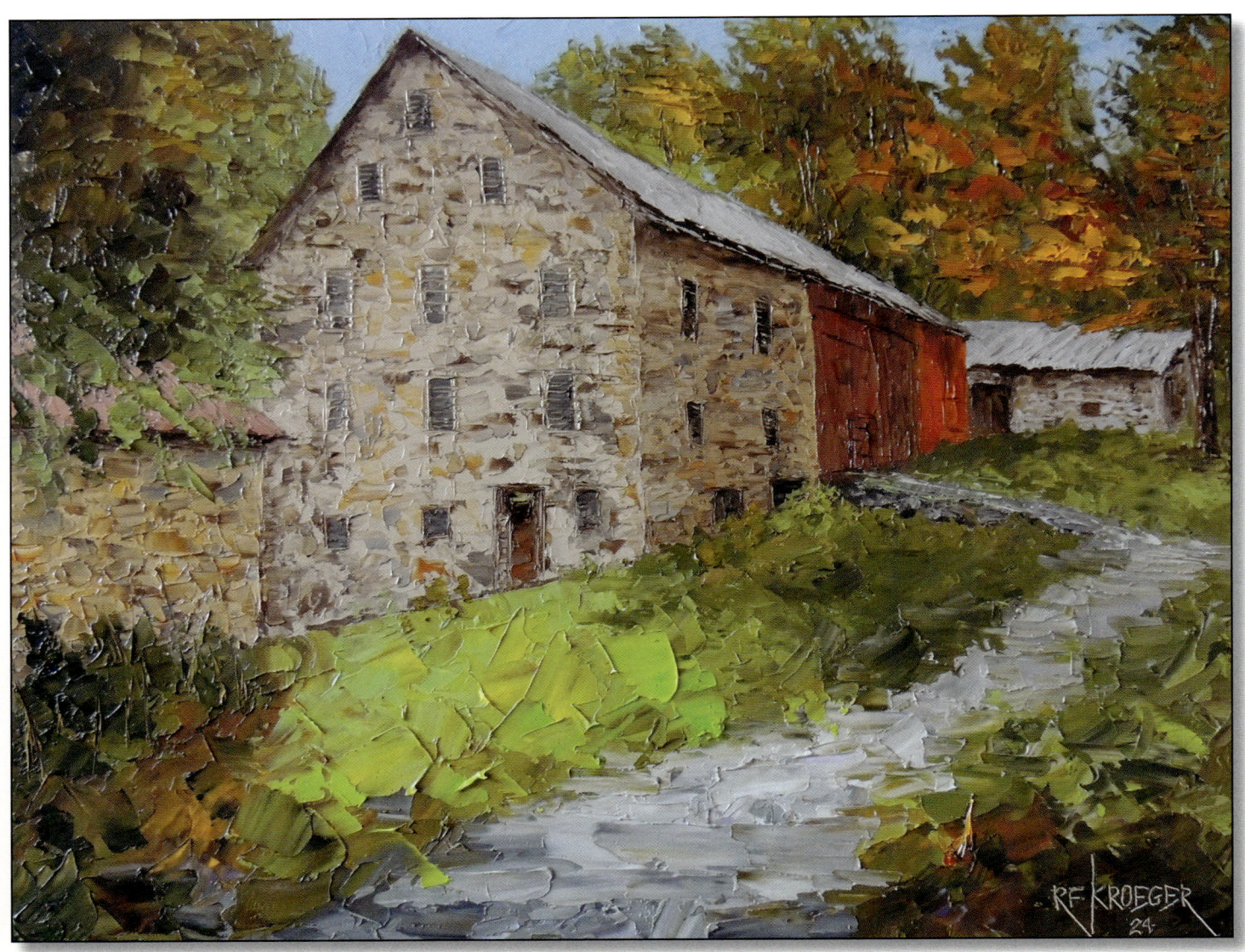

Gehman's Glory

The Gehmans originated in Switzerland, where they were peasant farmers, poor but hardworking. As their family expanded, they became congested since they, like most, rented small tracts of land from nobles. And, being Mennonites, they were persecuted. In 1734 an edict was passed to rid the land of people of this faith, according to a Gehman family history, which caused the nobles to protest, "… these Mennonites are good … we want them to farm our farms." The edict was never carried out, but the Mennonites began to leave for America. A document on the ship, the Phenix, which landed in Philadelphia on October 1, 1754, showed that 25 Mennonite families were on board, including John Gehman and others, who would form the nucleus for the Gehman's Mennonite Church.

Another Gehman family, whose ancestors settled a farm in Barto in 1792, about seven miles from Seisholtzville – where this stone barn is located – has converted part of their 190-acre dairy farm into a golf course. Butter Valley Golf Course is located on Gehman Road, which is named to honor the family. John Gehman, the eighth generation of his family to own this farm runs the golf course and works the farm. The ninth and tenth generations help.

The stone barn that's featured in this essay traces back to another Gehman family, whose three brothers emigrated from the Palatinate in the Rhine River Valley and arrived in Philadelphia in 1732. One of them, Christopher, settled in Hereford Township, where he bought a 300-acre site. Christopher's second son Johannes bought land from Andrew Maurer in 1767 and built a two- and a half-story Swiss log bank house, which, still extant, is a rare example of such a house.

Hereford Township, first settled in 1732, became incorporated in 1753 and has two properties listed on the National Register – the Gehman farm and the Hunters Mill Historic District, which includes an 18th-century mill, associated with Peter Richard, a prominent ironmaster. The large Georgian mansion typifies the costly and sophisticated architecture of wealthy families.

Johannes became a Mennonite minister, though there's no record of his activity during the Revolutionary War, which meant that, like nearly all the Mennonite and Quaker pacifists, he probably remained neutral. His son, John S., is the one who may have built this large 85-foot-long stone barn in 1806 and a two and a half-story stone farmhouse in 1810. Both are remarkable structures.

The barn, a standard Pennsylvania bank barn – as classified by historian Robert Ensminger – has two wagon floors (one of which was probably a threshing bay) and timber-framing, including hand-hewn beams, principal rafters, and staggered purlins. A weathered wooden board has documented its construction: *John S. Gehman, built 1806*. Wrought iron strap hinges on the Dutch doors and

small windows with wooden grills, now over 200 years old, provide an excellent look at early barn construction. Some of the hand-forged hinges are six feet long!

Another date stone of 1839 reflects an addition to the barn, mostly for increased storage. During the Great Depression in the 1930s, apparently looking for another source of income, the Gehmans converted the eastern half of the barn for dairy cows and added a concrete floor, cleaning gutters, and stanchions. They did another alteration in 1940, a concrete block addition, used for a milk house and chicken house.

Today, the barn's random rubble construction exemplifies the skills of master stonemasons. Huge quoins, some weighing hundreds of pounds, support the corners and offer the visitor a kaleidoscope of colors, ranging from green to rust to beige and gray. Though the barn needs maintenance – as all historic barns require – it is in excellent condition. The walls, 18 inches thick, show few signs of cracking.

Other historic buildings add to the charm of this farmstead. A stone springhouse, with a date stone of *J.G. 1847* in its upper gable, has a first-floor walk-in fireplace and a second-floor smokehouse room. The walled spring, now piped to a stream, formerly ran through the springhouse. A stone stable, one and a half stories, now converted into a garage, and a drive-through one-story carriage barn, also with stone walls, suggest that this farm was prosperous. Workers repaired carriages in the upper level. An old frame privy makes this setting essentially a living history museum.

John S. Gehman lived for a while in the Swiss log house but, with family and prosperity both increasing, he built a vernacular stone farmhouse. This two- and a half-story house, still standing, has four bays and a slate roof, another fine example of pioneer architecture. On our visit Greg and I met current owner Robert Hoffman who explained that he is currently restoring the farmhouse.

During the early 19th-century, John Gehman had an orchard, apparently productive on this hilly ground, and had an applejack distillery, built in the years before the Revolution. He hauled the liquor in large barrels in huge Conestoga wagons to market in Philadelphia, where customers paid 25 cents a gallon for his brew. This distillery was one of the first in this part of Pennsylvania.

After John died in 1869, his son Joel M. took over and continued to farm throughout his lifetime. Two more generations of Gehmans continued ownership of the farm until they sold it to Mrs. Kathleen Seagraves. She spent summers in the Swiss log and stone bank house while John and Lydia Gehman lived in the stone farmhouse. In 1961 she sold the farm to Erwin and Carol Hoffman, who wisely submitted it for a listing on the National Register in 1992. They leased some of the land to farmers who raised sheep, ideally suited to this sloped farmland. In 1996 they placed a conservation easement on the property, which prevented large-scale development. Robert told us that he has specified that the Hope Valley Community Church in nearby Red Hill will inherit the property when he passes. To show its appreciation, the church helps Robert maintain the farm.

Though this historic gem lies hidden in thick woods, it retains the charm of the 18th century when the Gehmans settled it. The rustic road, still gravel despite the county's desire to pave it, reflects a time gone by, when cows and sheep grazed, farmers rode in horse-drawn carriages, and fields of crops dotted the landscape. Despite suburban sprawl, the farm and its 87 acres resist change and continue to echo the heritage of a family that owned it for nearly 200 years, a colorful page of Pennsylvania history – Gehman's glory.

BUCKS COUNTY

Centre Bridge

This rare stone "double barn" still sits in Centre Bridge, an unincorporated community in Solebury Township, located three miles north of New Hope and 11 miles from Doylestown, the county seat. Originally named Reading's Ferry, after John Reading, a British Colonel – the ferry's owner and the first white landowner in Hunterdon County, New Jersey. Colonel Reading built this ferry across the Delaware River in the early 1700s, a business that operated for about 100 years until a wooden bridge was built in 1813. At that time, the community became known as Centre Bridge. This area, the Center Bridge Historic District, was listed on the National Register in 1985.

Richard Burgess bought land here in 1689. His son-in-law, Henry Paxson, eventually owned the land. When

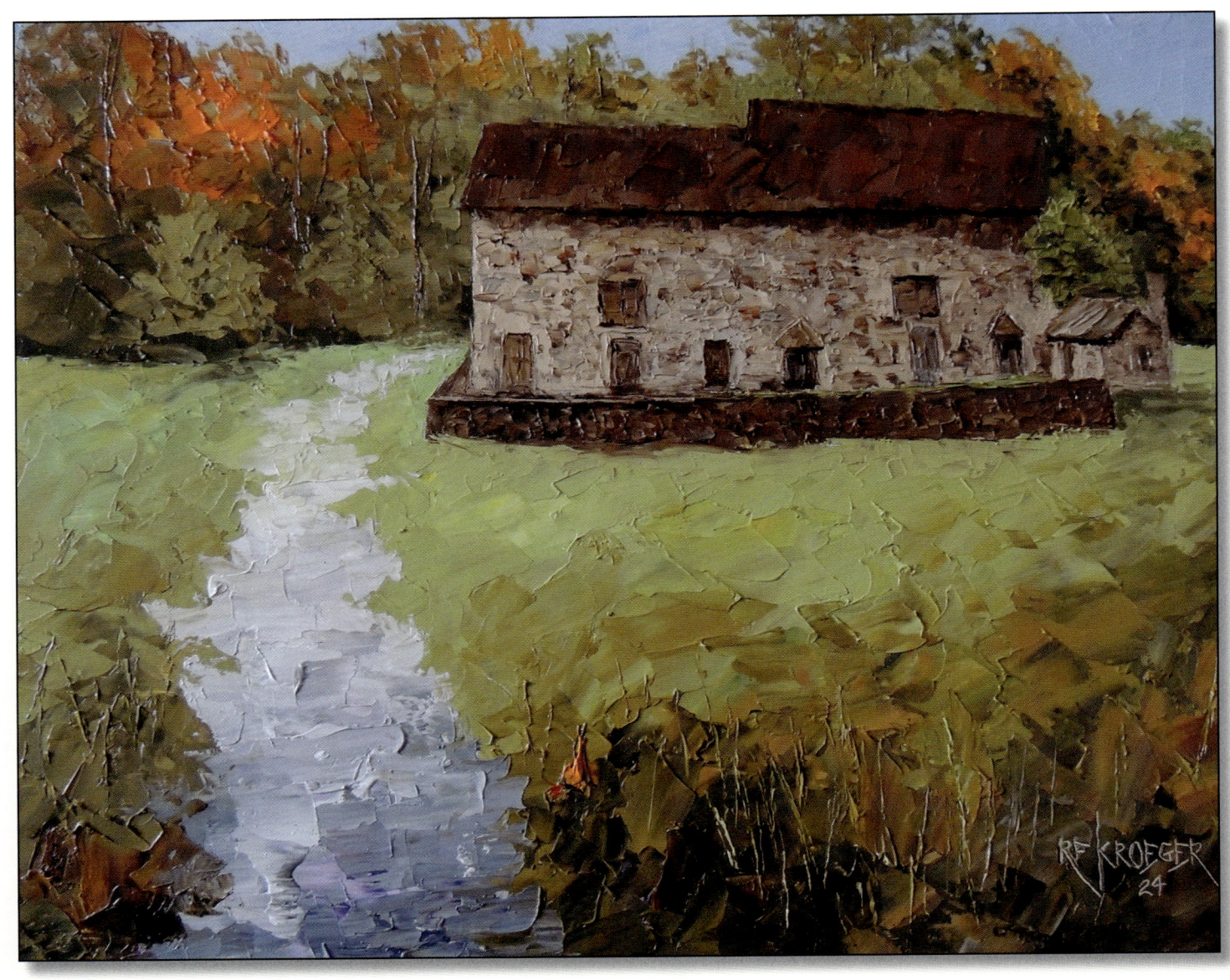

Centre Bridge

Thomas Paxson died in 1782, his son Isaiah took ownership. Earlier, in 1765, Joseph Mitchell bought land along the river, established a ferry and built an inn. He and Paxson became business partners in various ventures, including a shad fishery, which likely was profitable since every spring phenomenal numbers of shad would migrate northwards in the Delaware River. Did Paxson and Mitchell ever meet General George Washington and his army, who, according to legend, were saved by harvesting this fish?

On his large farm in Virginia, one of Washington's most successful businesses was shad fishing. Armed with this knowledge, as some claim, he took advantage of this the shad spring migration up the Schuylkill River in 1778 – to feed his starving army after a dreadful winter at nearby Valley Forge. However, as author John McPhee wrote in his book, *The Founding Fish*, this may have been unlikely. Regardless, this region around Philadelphia was a hotbed of military activity during the war and the shad may have played a significant role of one kind or another – maybe even in this village.

Isaiah Paxson built his stone house in 1785 – the date carved in stone – and may have built the first part of this "double barn" about the same time. An affluent gentleman farmer, Paxson owned a large farm in New Jersey – as well as this Bucks County farm of 200 acres. He also was a miller, a profitable business in those days, and he used his mill for grinding grain, cutting lumber, and making sashes and shutters. He also was a part owner in a New Jersey mill.

A busy entrepreneur, Isaiah also operated a cooper shop, making barrels which may have been used to transport grain and shad. He also partnered with others to build a bridge over the Delaware River, though he died before it was completed in 1814. Less than three decades later, another economic boom happened in Centre Bridge – the opening of the Delaware Canal, a waterway that allowed farmers to ship their goods easily and more efficiently than in wagons.

Paxson's estate was more than a barn; it included other stone buildings – a classic fieldstone home, smokehouse, a springhouse, and an outbuilding with a chimney, possibly a servant's quarters. Until it was purchased in 1978, the land had been in only two families since 1689.

The beautiful stonework on the first section of this barn matches that of the home, hinting that it was built about the same time – 1785. Though small – 20x30 feet – the barn's exquisite stonemasonry compensated for its modest size. Jack arches above two Dutch doors and attractive random fieldstone illustrate the work of a master stonemason. Four square ventilation windows allowed light and air flow. Wagons were led up the stone-faced earthen ramp through large barn doors.

Apparently, as his farm production increased, Isaiah needed more room and, accordingly added another stone addition sometime before he died in 1813. The new section, larger than the first, had a taller roof. However, at only 30x30 feet, the section's size and its fieldstone construction blended well with its predecessor. From a distance, the barn appears as one. A stone wall enclosed the barnyard.

After the patriarch's death, the family sold the estate to the Johnson family, which, along with other farmers in the village, benefitted from increased commerce on the Delaware Canal, opened in 1832. Unlike many other early canals, which have been replaced with asphalt roads, this one still has most of its original locks and aqueducts. Following the success of "Clinton's Folly," as New York state's Erie canal was derisively known, the Pennsylvania canal system was developed. Irish immigrants built it by hand – as they did in other states, including the Ohio-Erie Canal, which transformed Ohio from a poor state to the third best economy in the country.

One of the primary purposes of the Delaware Canal was to transport coal, lumber, cement, gravel, sand, and limestone to Philadelphia. However, the railroads soon put an end to most canal systems in the second half of the 19th century. Despite the competition, the Delaware Canal continued well into the 20th century – with tugboats that could pull several canal boats. They replaced mules, which could pull only one. The canal finally ended its service during the Great Depression which, according to the National Park Service, made it the longest-lived canal in the country. In the 1960s the state started plans to fill in the canal and pave it for a road, but locals rallied, opposing the plan, and placed the Delaware Canal on the National Register in 1974. Four years later, it became a National Historic Landmark. Today water flows in it, not far from this farmstead.

The stone barn and the farm remained in the hands of the Johnsons throughout the next 164 years – through the Civil War, two World Wars, and the Great Depression – until 1978 when the Durells purchased it and subsequently submitted the nomination for a listing on the National Register. Current owners are committed to keeping a watchful eye over the double barn, the home, and other stone buildings. They founded Burgess Lea Press, a publisher that focuses on cookbooks and donates its profits towards food-related issues, including farmland preservation, which would please not only the founders but also the current residents of the quaintly historic village of Centre Bridge.

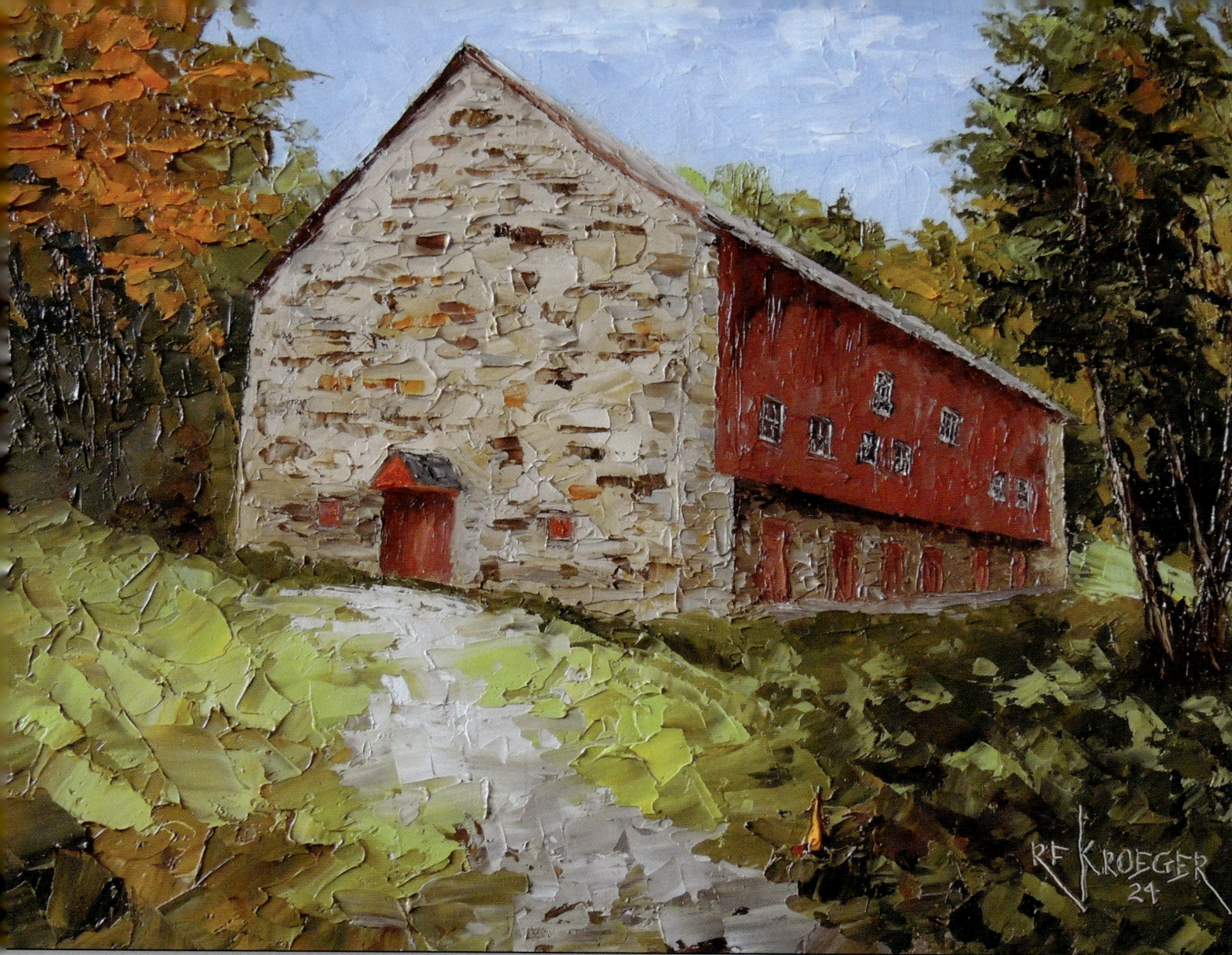

A Barn for All Reasons

A Barn for All Reasons

Abraham Funk founded Springtown in 1763 – an unincorporated community in northern Bucks County, at the intersection of Routes 212 and 412, where this barn is located. Nearby Cooks Creek drains through this agricultural limestone valley into the Delaware River, on whose banks on a snowy and sleety Christmas Day, 1776, General George Washington launched one of the riskiest battles of the Revolutionary War.

Ownership of this land was in question, even though George Wilson had established a store in Springfield Township in the 1720s, the first mine had begun operating in 1698, and a furnace was working in 1727. William Penn was known for his fairness with the Lenape tribe (including the Delawares) when he purchased their land, granted to him in 1681 by King Charles II. However, his heirs, sons John and Thomas, did not always follow their father's honorable

practices. After Penn died in 1718, his sons claimed a deed in 1737, which became known as the Walking Purchase. They based their ownership on an agreement, verbal or written, from 1686, when the Lenape promised to sell a tract of land – about 1,200,000 acres – which began at the junction of the Delaware River and the Lehigh River and extended as far as a man could walk in a day and a half. Agents for the Penns began selling this land to settlers. However, in 2004 the Delaware Nation filed suit, claiming 314 acres of this land, but lost the case, even though they appealed all the way to the U.S. Supreme Court, which refused to hear it.

One of the land investors was Caspar Wistar, a prominent Philadelphian, who purchased several hundred acres of land. He promptly sold 500 acres, presumably for a quick profit, to Quaker entrepreneur Stephen Twining, who started a farmstead, most likely with a log cabin, followed by a stone house in 1739, a date that is somewhat confirmed when

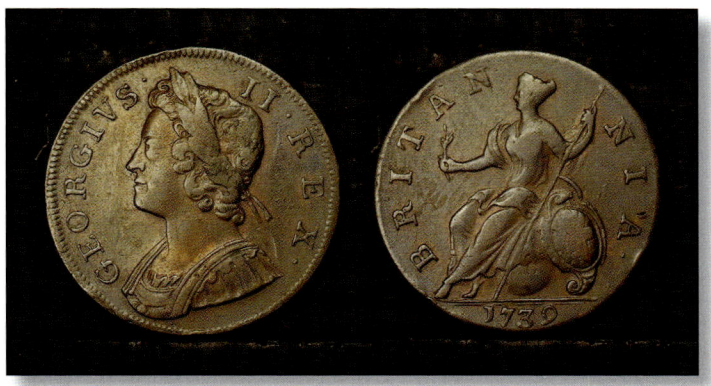

1739 King George halfpenny. Wikimedia Commons.

relatives found a 1739 King George halfpenny lodged under a windowsill.

Twining also built a grist mill downstream at the confluence of Silver and Cooks Creeks, the impetus for the village of Springtown. The mill's location near major roads was strategic; the combined path became known as the "Great Road" and by 1761, it led directly to Bethlehem and Philadelphia. Twining operated the mill until 1763, when he sold it and much of his acreage to Abraham Funk – with clear provisions regarding water rights and maintenance of the creek and mill race. Funk and his descendants continued to operate the mill for 200 years.

Three years earlier, in 1758, Twining sold his stone house and 110 acres to his son-in-law, John Chapman, a well-known surveyor who had surveyed the original Walking Purchase. By 1760 he had built several buildings, including a smokehouse, spring house, and a tannery.

In 1761 John Chapman, Sr. sold the Twining house and the 104-acre farm to Jacob Kooker, whose last name was likely an anglicized version of the German Küker. Although he also farmed, he had an entrepreneurial side since he soon applied for and was granted a tavern license. A stone mason by trade, Kooker added tavern facilities to the 1739 stone house, including a large fireplace, a sink drain, and sleeping rooms upstairs. In the 18th century, taverns were important components of colonial America. During this time, especially before, during, and after the Revolutionary War, taverns served as sites for social and political meetings.

Kooker's Tavern was located both on the busy main road leading from Bristol and Philadelphia to Bethlehem and also on the road from Quakertown to the Durham Iron Furnace and the Delaware River. In 1773 Kooker added the final section of the tavern, which remains documented in a datestone with Kooker's initials. Newspaper notices from that era showed that Kooker's Tavern was the location of public events, such as a sheriff's sales.

After Jacob passed, his heirs continued running the tavern – throughout the Revolutionary War – until his son Jacob, Jr., aged 20, inherited the farm in 1797. Successful

at farming, he also became a leader in the community, becoming a Justice of the Peace. In 1831 he was elected Director of the Poor, a position, presumably, that helped the indigent, especially the veterans of the Revolution, many of whom had suffered financially. By 1834 Jacob was serving in the State Assembly.

Soon after Jacob, Jr. died in 1844, his wife Jane's sister Elizabeth married John Eakin, who continued to run the farm and built the present barn around 1850. His skills in farming were exceptional, proving that he was affluent enough to afford a stone barn. The agricultural census of that year placed the Eakin farm in the top bracket of all 217 farms in Springfield Township.

John also entered the lime business as many farmers did in the limestone-rich valley. He operated lime quarries and had a row of lime kilns across the road from the barn. Wagons and horses, kept in the barn, could load the lime easily and transport it to area farms and to the Delaware Canal, about five miles away. His business must have prospered since he bought additional land for another quarry. In fact, the 1880 agricultural census valued the farm at $20,000, the highest in the township.

As if raising crops and livestock and running a lime business weren't enough, Eakin started a fish hatchery in the 1850s, a business that apparently meant good cash flow. He converted a walled pond, next to the stone springhouse, into the hatchery, which the 1876 Atlas of Bucks County showed in a detailed map. Silver Creek and Cooks Creek were the only two natural streams to support native brook trout.

Though John Eakin had established a prosperous farmstead and associated businesses, his descendants may not have been interested in this way of life. After Eakin died in 1882, his heirs put the farm on the market in 1883 and sold the farmstead, lime business, and fish hatchery to O.B. Fackenthal the next year.

This new owner continued to run the businesses and erected a windmill, a "wind engine to force water into his residence, tenant houses, and barn." He also expanded the farm to include dairying and he built a creamery. With rail delivery now available to markets in adjacent cities, such as Allentown, Bethlehem, and Philadelphia, milk and dairy products could be shipped easily to growing populations. Fackenthal was involved in establishing the Springtown Water Company in 1892 and he also made changes inside the tavern-house. In the process of building a straight run staircase, he found the remains of a skeleton in the chimney stack. This could have been a missing servant girl of the 18th-century tavern era. The mystery has never been solved.

Vegetables, grown on the farm, were taken by truck to Bethlehem three days a week and were also sold to a cannery in Springtown ... until it burned in 1912. The Sfrock family, who bought the farm in 1956, continued farming and hired migrant workers to pick the vegetables, allowing them to stay in Jacob Kooker's Tavern.

At the time of the listing on the National Register in 2005, prepared by then-owner Catherine Marek, there were three 18th-century buildings – the tavern-house, the springhouse, and smokehouse – as well as several 19th-century structures, including a carriage barn, smokehouse, privy, two tenant homes, ruins of a stone kitchen, and, most impressive of all, the stone barn.

Its length of 92 feet, huge for stone barn construction in the mid-1800s, testified to the prosperity of the Eakin family. Jacob's wife Jane may have been involved in financing since her will specified that daughter Elizabeth and husband John would receive "all the residue of my estate, real and personal ... during their joint lives."

Eakin built the large barn, not only for farming, but also to house wagons and horses for his busy lime business, which required frequent shipments. The two-story German bank barn, 46 feet wide, features three walls of randomly coursed fieldstone, seven original barn doors with forged hinges, but few windows, suggesting the barn was built more for wagon storage and threshing than for livestock. Colorful fieldstone – red, orange, tan, gray, green, and black – extends to the eave. The north façade features a wide bay for threshing, hinting that grain crops were raised. Metal covers the gable roof, assuring many more years for this historic barn. The stonemasonry, over 150 years old, has stood the test of time. It's been meticulously maintained and some of the mortaring is beaded.

On the ground level, six doors lead to the stables and there are several small windows for light and ventilation. Some of the stone barnyard walls remain, a remnant of history when farmers built stone walls to enclose the few livestock they kept. Inside, hewn chestnut beams rekindle memories of the years when chestnut trees were favorites of timber-framing barn builders. The destructive fungal blight, identified in 1904, destroyed between three and four billion American chestnut trees in the first half of the 20th century. By 1940 they were gone, a fact that makes this barn even more unique. The hardwood rafters, as in most stone barns, rest on the 20-inch-thick walls. Some beams have been connected with mortise and tenon joints.

When Greg Huber and I visited in May 2024, the barn appeared to be in excellent condition, but the fish pond

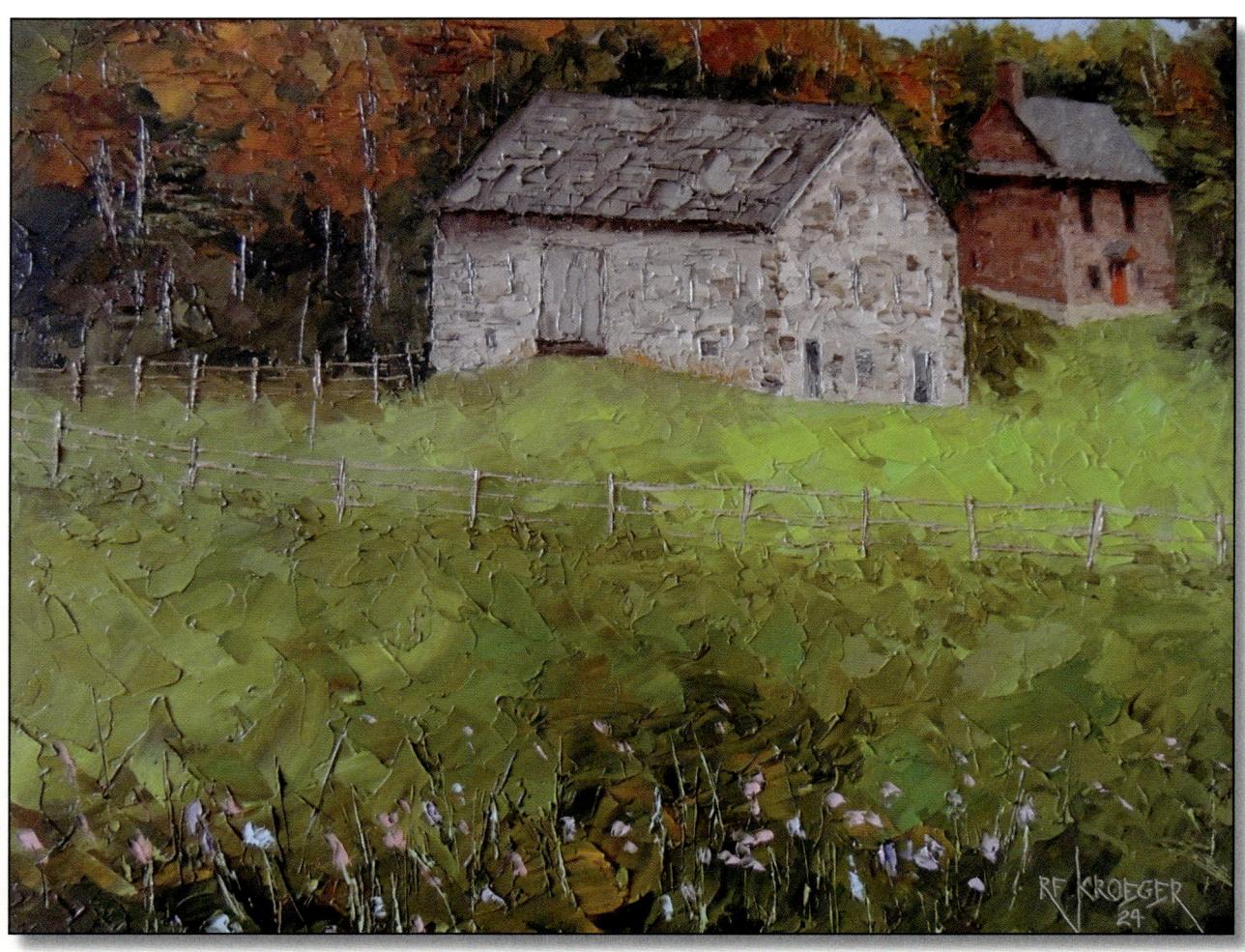

Quaker Country

and outbuildings were gone, except for a wooden privy and a small shed. Scaffolding around the 18th-century tavern showed that the owners planned to preserve this piece of history.

This barn, much like the play, *A Man for All Seasons*, the story about the heroic 16th-century martyr St. Thomas More, has had many functions over its long life – lime business, crop and hay storage, threshing grain, stabling livestock, vegetable truck farming, and dairying – which certifies it as a veritable barn for all reasons.

CHESTER COUNTY

Quaker Country

The story of this barn, possibly the oldest (stone or otherwise) in the state, traces back to the Royal County of Berkshire, now simply known as Berkshire, a ceremonial county in southeastern England. John Taylor, a Quaker, was a churchwarden and, apparently, intensely particular about his children attending religious services. On his death bed in 1677, he dictated a new will, which left his entire estate to his son John and £15 to his daughter Mary. His older children Abiah and Anne, now adults, received only a shilling. Why he excluded Anne remains a mystery but Abiah's case is clear cut.

For some reason, Abiah did not like to attend Quaker meetings. Churchwardens would address such infractions and they did so several times in Abiah's case. The position of a churchwarden, a lay person in the congregation, first appeared in English parish records of the 13th century. Eventually, these officials were elected – with the responsibility of enforcing regulations and managing church affairs. John Taylor was one of them and was probably embarrassed when his son Abiah was excommunicated in 1671. Though Abiah contested his father's will, he lost his plea. In spite of this estrangement, he married and had children. Abiah Taylor, Jr., was born in 1675.

The Quaker religion was in its infancy at this time. Founded in the 1640s by George Fox and others who saw shortcomings in the Church of England, members of this Protestant sect called themselves the Society of Friends, though they were known by most as Quakers, a derisive term given by others in reference to their belief in the biblical passage that people should "tremble at the Word of the Lord." Enraged, the hierarchy of the Church of England tried to eliminate this religion in many ways. Though Fox spent much of his life in jail, he continued preaching, as did others and, despite persecutions by the English church, Quakerism spread. By 1660 there were 50,000 followers. Many began to leave for the American colonies, where once again, they again faced discrimination. In fact, several were hanged in Puritan-dominated Massachusetts. In England, thousands of Quakers suffered decades of whippings, torture, and imprisonment.

Finally, Quakers saw a beacon of light when William Penn received a grant from the King in 1681, allowing him to start an experimental settlement in America where Quakers and other religious groups could live without persecution. In the fall of 1682 Penn and more than 100 Quakers sailed from England and founded the colony of Pennsylvania.

Abiah Taylor, Jr. emigrated to America and in 1702 he purchased 430 acres along the east branch of the Brandywine Creek in Chester County, where he built a mill on a nearby stream, which became known as Taylor's Run. Despite his father's lack of religious observance, Abiah, Jr. remained a Quaker, married a Quaker, and had children, who, likewise, kept this faith. Abiah died in 1747.

One of his children, Samuel, born in 1715, might be the one who built this stone barn in 1754. At this time, he would have been 39; his own son Abiah, named after his grandfather, was 16. He may have helped. Samuel died in 1758.

The original brick farmhouse, which has a date stone of 1724, stands above and beyond the barn in the painting. Records show that the bricks were fired from clay on the farm. In fact, this farmhouse may have replaced an earlier log home. Samuel's son Abiah Taylor, III, inherited much of his grandfather's land and continued farming throughout the 19th century.

Interestingly, a date stone of 1724 is also embedded in the stone barn, tempting some to claim this as the date when the barn was built. However, chances are that the first barn that the Taylor family erected was a log barn, typical of that era; in 1724 the region was heavily forested, and

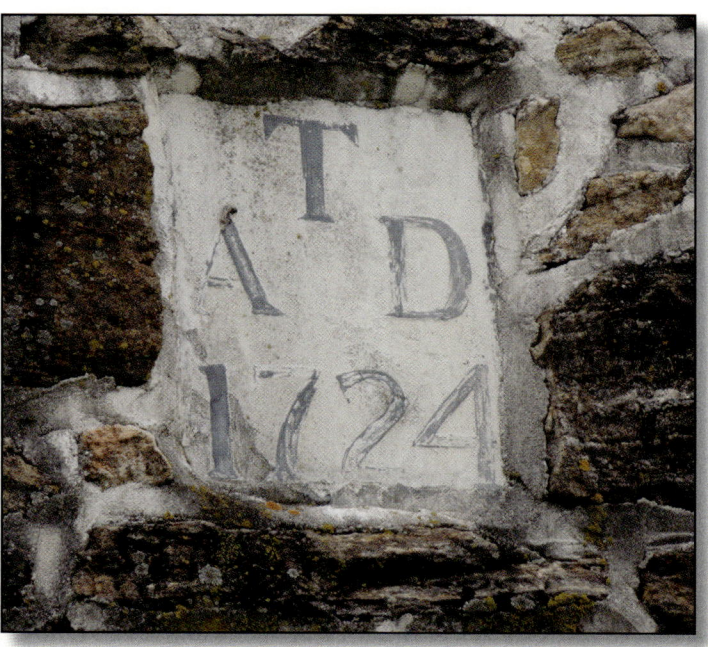

Taylor barn date stone, 1724

farming was essentially subsistence-based. Two separate analyses of the timber in the barn via dendrochronology, one by then-owner John Milner and the other by barn scholar Greg Huber, have confirmed that the trees were felled in 1753. Usually, the lumber was cut and dried for a year, which suggests the barn was built in 1754.

Adjacent to the barn and separating it from the farmhouse runs Creek Road, an early route to Birmingham Friends Meeting, where Abiah was a member. The barn reflects the family's English heritage and its Quaker attention to detail; the three-bay ground barn was designed for threshing and stabling livestock. In those days, this region of Pennsylvania was called the "breadbasket" of the colonies for its production of wheat, barley, and rye, which were likely processed at the Taylor grist mill.

The barn's stonework, random uncoursed fieldstone rubble, reflects the artistry as well as the masonry skills of the builder; the barn is a stonemason's masterpiece. Quoins, both large and small, brace the corners and 22-inch-thick walls support the rafters of the simple gable roof, which has been repaired with dimensional lumber after damage from a vicious storm in 1970. Numerous narrow ventilation slits in walls provide both light and air flow inside the small barn. Initially, the Taylors likely used the barn for threshing wheat and perhaps for housing a dairy cow or two and a few horses. Today it's maintained as a historical treasure.

As the years passed, farming in southwestern Pennsylvania changed and, by the early 1800s, cattle production was going strong: Chester County had earned the title of "fat cattle capital of the nation." The agricultural census of 1850 revealed that the Taylor farms had nearly 100 head of cattle and numerous horses, dairy cows, oxen, and hogs. However, with the advent of the railroads, crops and beef from the Midwest and western states could be shipped to eastern markets, depressing the farm industry in Pennsylvania.

At the time of the 1987 National Register listing of the Taylor-Cope Historic District, the owners of the Taylor farmhouse and barn were Eugene and Jean Gagliardi. Later architect John Milner and his wife Wynne owned the farm and restored both the 1724 brick farmhouse and the stone barn. The stonework has been meticulously tuckpointed and new lumber supports the roof. In 2016 they sold the property to Linda Thomas, who explained that the Johnstown flood and a tornado in the 1970s destroyed part of a wall, though any damage has been repaired seamlessly.

Linda purchased the farm because the Milners knew that she'd be a good caretaker of history, preserving this early page of history in Quaker country.

A Chester County Barn

In her book, *Barns of Chester County*, author Berenice Ball has classified a particular type of barn – one with conical stone piers supporting the forebay – as a "Chester County barn."

Outside of southeastern Pennsylvania and a few counties west of the Susquehanna River as well as neighboring New Jersey and Maryland, stone barns are rare and those with stone conical supports under the forebay are even more unique; they are found almost exclusively in Chester County. Robert Ensminger, in his book, *The Pennsylvania Barn*, classifies this type as a Chester County stone-posted-forebay barn and claims that such barns were built between 1800 and 1870. Though they may be occasionally found in adjacent counties, Ensminger found only one with these trademark conical supports in the Midwest – in Lafayette County, Wisconsin. The barn featured in this essay falls into this distinctive category. Though I visited this barn in springtime, thanks to a photo reference that owner Warren Claytor supplied, I chose to paint a wintry scene, an opportunity that I seldom have.

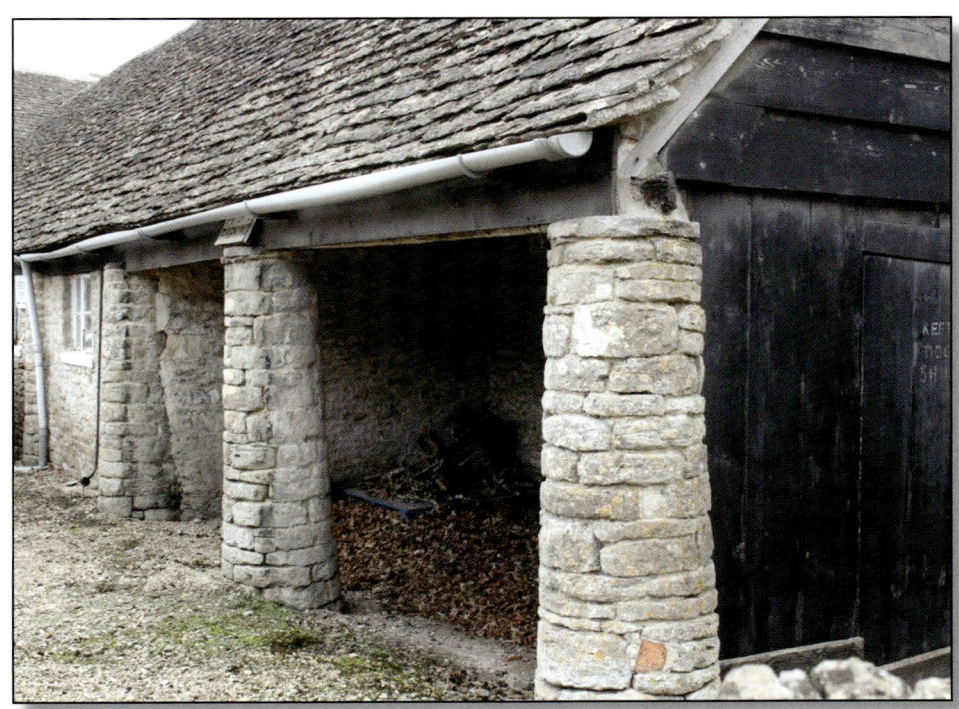

Rounded stone posts on Siddington Tithe Barn, circa 1245, Cotswolds, southwestern England. Courtesy of Ken Bonham.

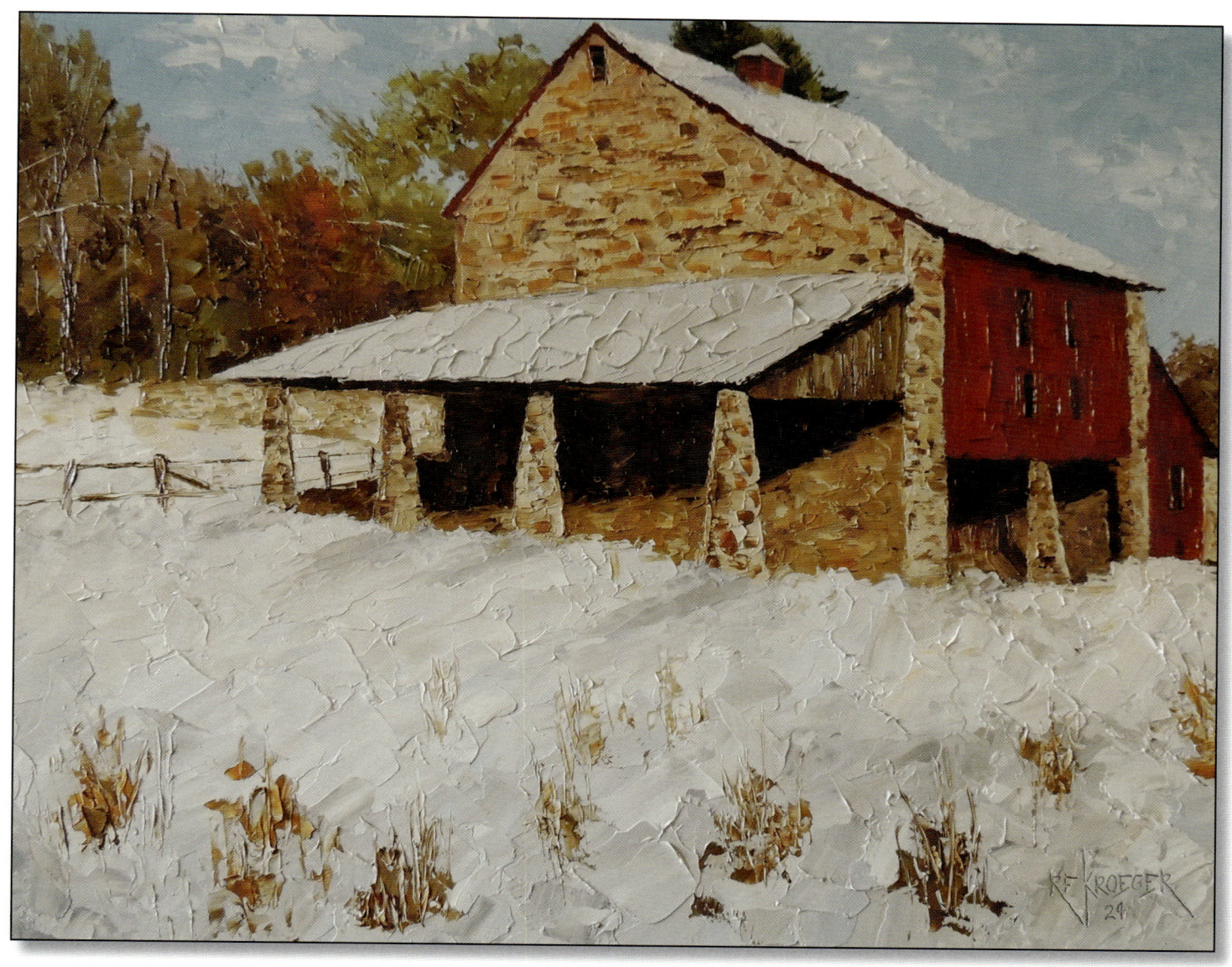

A Chester County Barn

As settlers migrated into this area in the late 17th and early 18th centuries, they initially built log barns, transitioning to stone when they became prosperous enough to afford such construction. Ensminger agrees with Berenice Ball, who claimed in her book that English Quakers, known for their industry and frugality, would often add to a barn for more storage – instead of building a new barn. As farming changed from mostly grain to include livestock in the 1790s, more space was needed for straw and hay for the animals. For this reason, they added sheds and forebays to existing barns by the mid-1700s.

The barn addition was heavy and needed support, unlike the typical German forebay, which was supported by large hand-hewn beams extending from the interior rear wall to the front wall. For some unknown reason, farmers in Chester County used conical stone piers to support the forebay, a trend that spread locally, though some barns with square stone piers or wooden beams are sprinkled throughout the region. As settlers migrated westwards and built the Pennsylvania German bank barn, they sometimes used wooden posts to support the forebay.

Stone supports were common in barns in England's West Midlands and Wales, such as the Siddington Tithe Barn, dendro-dated to 1245. According to Ken Bonham, a leading authority on England's stone barns, the pillars were rounded – rather than square with sharp edges – to avoid damage to wheels of carts that were loaded with grain and hay.

Another influence might have been staddle stones in barns of England and Wales, first appearing in the 12th century. Masons carved these mushroom-shaped structures out of stone and used them to support granaries and hay storage units – to keep vermin away. Ken Bonham, author of the online book, *A Big Book of Barns*, has documented conical stone supports in farm sheds from the 12th to 18th centuries. It's possible that English Quakers brought this tradition to Chester

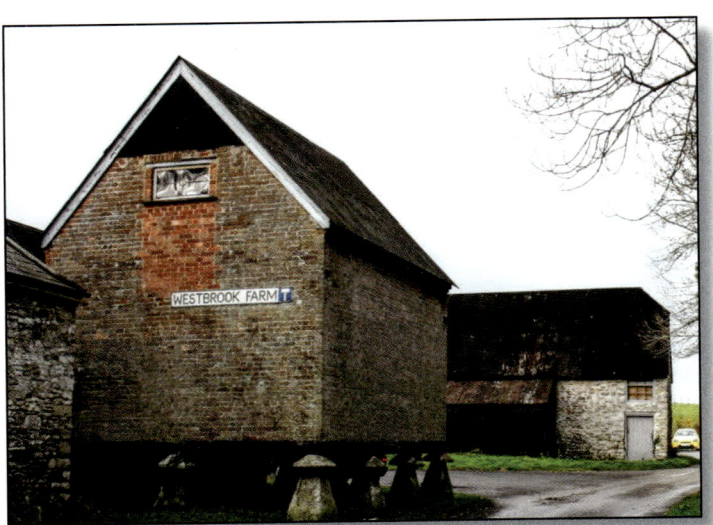

Westbrook Farm, 18th-century staddle stones under a granary. Dorset, England. Courtesy, Ken Bonham.

County, but why it didn't spread to adjacent counties remains a mystery.

Though some Chester County barns had cylindrical or square stone supports, most were conical. Tapering the cone meant that the farmer wouldn't need as much material, nor would he need as much time to construct it. Often, farmers would cover them with a whitewash of stucco, presumably to keep out water and to prevent cracking. Ball suggests that a layer of stucco would also protect livestock, but the thick hides of horses and cattle wouldn't be injured by exposed stone pebbles in the cones, which were often smooth pieces of fieldstone, found in clearing the farm's fields. Rounded posts, either cylindrical or conical, would protect wheels of carts better than posts with sharp edges. However, the stucco came with a price: it hid the beauty of the stones. Today, conical supports with exposed stonemasonry, such as in this barn, are particularly attractive, much more so than those with plastered stucco.

As years passed into the 19th century, so did the work of President Thomas Jefferson. Considered America's first architect, did Jefferson's designs have an influence on these stone-supported forebays? Jefferson was obsessed with both the octagonal shape and the work of Italian Renaissance architect Andrea Palladio, whose style incorporated Greek columns, often seen in Jeffersonian buildings, including his residences and the University of Virginia. Regardless, the conical stone piers offer a look of elegance to this type of barn.

Why were so many of these built in Chester County? Most likely it was a case of the domino effect, the same reason that so many German farmers spread their Pennsylvania barn design as they migrated westwards. The domino effect also happened in Perry County, Ohio, where four rare round barns were built within five miles of each other.

This particular farmstead has been labeled the Samuel Hall farm, according to Nagy and Goulding, authors of *Acres of Quakers*, a voluminous history of Willistown Township. The authors traced ownership back to 1723 when Samuel Levis gave 292 acres to his daughter Elizabeth and her husband William Shipley. After 10 years of ownership, the property switched owners as it did often during the next 200 years. Next was Thomas Hall and his wife Alice, who, in turn, sold the farm to their son Samuel. Apparently, Samuel and his wife Sarah owned the farm when the present-day fieldstone home was built circa 1764. But they didn't live here long.

In 1762 Isaac Garrett, a weaver, owned it and, two years later, he sold it to Samuel Garrett, a leather tanner. Trades were common occupations during colonial times and, in the case of these owners, must have provided a substantial income to afford such an impressive home. The property remained in the Garrett family until Jonathan Maris bought the farm in 1850, which was listed as only 66 acres at the time. He died of typhoid fever at 60 in 1853, when his oldest son Robert took over but, like other owners, didn't hold the property for long. County records show that a "dairy farm" was put up for sale, at public auction in October 1858. The 67 acres – 15 were "heavily timbered" – included a three-story high "commodious" stone mansion and a "new stone barn, with two floors, 60 by 50 feet, overshoot straw house, pump in the yard." Apparently, Robert Maris had built the barn by that time. Along with dairying, the farm included several outbuildings and a "thriving" apple orchard with a "variety of pears, peaches, and other fruit."

Abraham Bennett was the winning bidder, paying $5,962.94, a hefty sum in those days.

The farm's ownership continued through his family until Rebecca Bennett sold it in 1905. The farm passed to the Zirkman and Garrett families and later to about a dozen other owners throughout the 20th century.

Present owner Warren Claytor bought the 16.8-acre farm in 2002. Attracted by the historical value of the house and barn, Warren has done an outstanding job of restoring the barn, which must have been an enjoyable experience for this architect, whose work embraces restoration of historic properties, including old barns. His office location in nearby Wayne gives his firm ample opportunities to help clients maintain their historic homes and barns in this region.

When he purchased the farm, the barn's stone was covered with stucco, which he painstakingly removed to expose the handsome fieldstone, a dramatic showpiece of random uncoursed rubble. Author and master stonemason Ian Cramb would argue that this mason knew what he was doing: his work has lasted over 150 years, illustrating that an apparently random pattern has intentional structure. Warren explained that his stone mason, Vince McClatchy, tuckpointed the barn.

Built in 1870, following the lead of other Chester County barns built earlier, the 54x90-foot barn sits on level ground; a massive earthen ramp, bordered with two stone walls, leads to the upper entrance. Inside, traditional timber framing supports the roof, as do the 25-inch-thick stone walls. A rare wooden water vat, used for livestock, still stands in the upper haymow in the northeastern corner. To complement the barn's character, Warren added an extension forebay on the western side of the main gable, taking care to match the conical piers with those already existing on two other faces of the barn. On the eastern side, he converted the small shed to a tack room. Warren and his children are horseback riders. Warren served as an honorary whipper-in under legendary Huntsman, Joe Cassidy. In fact, on the Saturday before my visit he participated in a day-long father-son competition at the nearby Radnor Hunt, the oldest

continuous fox-hunting club in the country. Warren and his son Archer won first place in a race that featured the son riding while the father ran alongside.

The Claytor family has deep roots in this region. In fact, Warren is a member of the Schuykill Fishing Company, whose membership has numbered only 500 since it was founded nearly 300 years ago in 1732. Warren holds number 480; his father held 435. With such traditions, it's only fitting that Warren has taken great pains to maintain his historic farmhouse and its barn, a distinctive type found only in this county – a "Chester County barn."

The Brandywine

Chester County's Worth-Jefferis Rural Historic District, where this stone barn still stands, is described in a 134-page nomination, which earned it a listing on the National Register in 1995. This region – between the east and west branches of the Brandywine River – occupies 1,800 acres

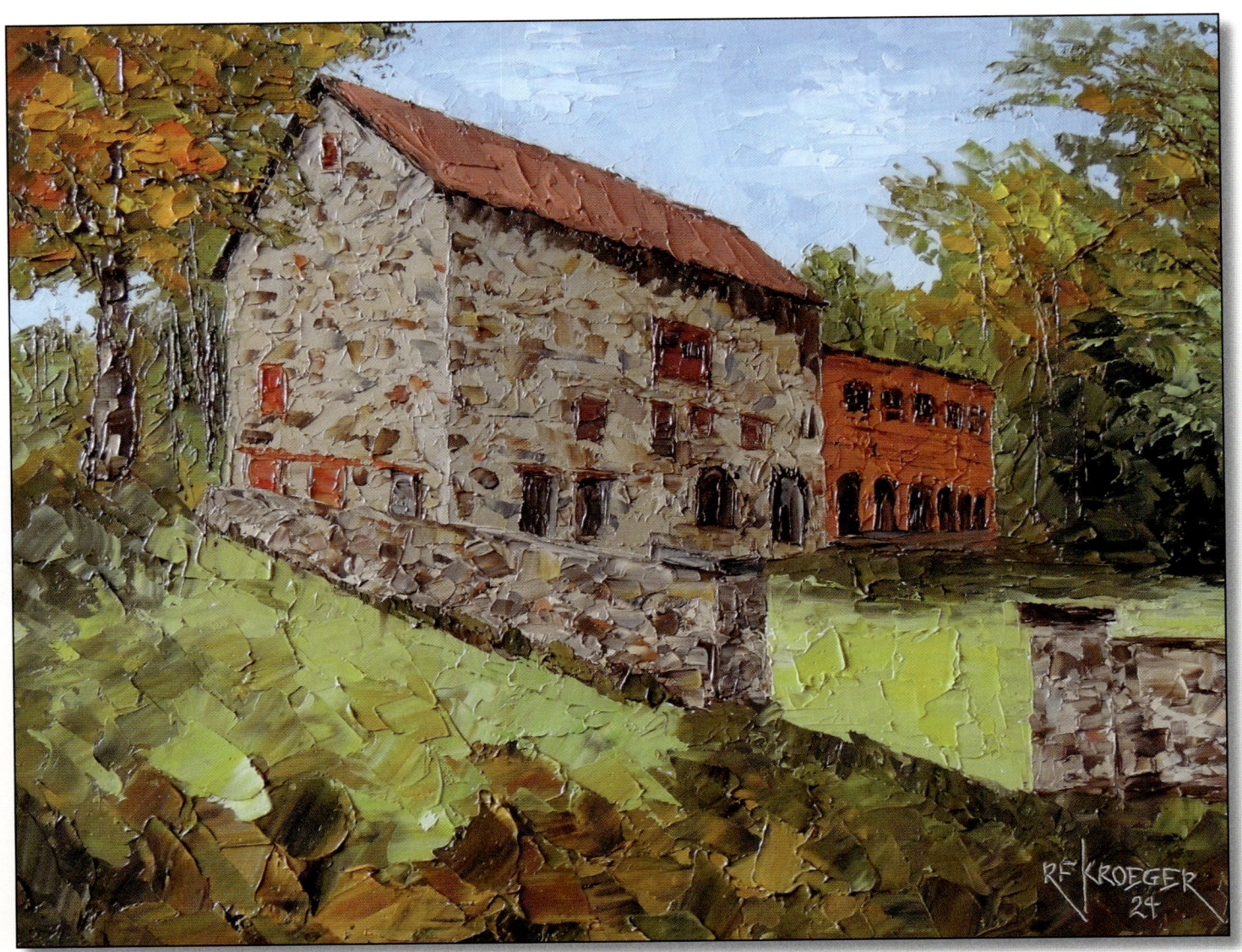

The Brandywine

in East and West Bradford Townships and includes several farms and many stone structures – nine farmhouses, ten tenant homes, five ruins, and 23 agricultural buildings such as barns, springhouses, smokehouses, and icehouses. And, since its heritage is linked to a significant battle of the Revolutionary War, when many of these buildings were standing, it's a virtual textbook of American history.

It traces back to 1686, thanks to Penn's land grant, when Thomas Holmes surveyed about 1,000 acres. Thomas Worth, who immigrated from England in 1682 and was one of the earliest settlers in the area, bought 500 acres of this tract in 1707. His Quaker family was prolific. In 1706 Robert Jefferis, the second constable of Bradford Township, bought 200 acres and soon acquired the majority of land in this historic district. Both families passed their farms down through generations and, being pacifist Quakers, remained neutral during the War.

However, that changed on September 11, 1777, when British Generals Howe and Cornwallis led 8,000 troops and pressed Emmor Jefferis, a Quaker, into service. Jefferis, owner of a tavern on a farm (now known as the Blue Rock Farmhouse) was forced to act as a guide for the British Army as it crossed the Brandywine at Jefferis Ford.

Thomas Buffington, who had acquired this land in 1709 and was likely a land speculator, sold the land to James Whitacre a year later. Whitacre settled here, established the Georgia farm, and built a stone farmhouse, still extant, in 1740, which was less than a half-mile from the east branch of the Brandywine and about three miles north of Jefferis Ford. He may have built a stone or wooden barn by that time.

The site was strategic since it was the most direct passage across the Brandywine River on the road from Baltimore to Philadelphia, home of the Continental Congress, which the British hoped to capture. Late in August 1777, a Royal Navy fleet with more than 17,000 troops landed at the northern end of Chesapeake Bay, about 50 miles southwest of Philadelphia. General William Howe led his army north, opting not to engage the Americans, an army of 20,300 soldiers, assembled by General Washington at the head of the Elk River. Instead, Howe, who had better information about the region than Washington had, decided to flank the Americans. He sent Cornwallis with his army of 9,000 north to Trimble's Ford, across the west branch of the Brandywine and through this historic district, and then eastwards to Jefferis Ford. Washington, possibly because of poor scouting, had overlooked this possibility.

A morning fog on September 11 provided cover for the British troops as they began to surround Washington's forces. However, as the British advanced, they met stiff resistance near the Old Kennett Meetinghouse, only a few miles from Chadds Ford, where Washington had planned his defense of Philadelphia. Ironically, the skirmish happened while Quakers were holding their midweek prayer service. Despite muskets and cannons firing, bullets whizzing by, bayonets and swords flashing, bodies falling, and buglers sounding, the prayers continued inside the stone building, now a National Landmark. Later, one of the Quakers wrote about the experience, "While there was much noise and confusion without, all was quiet and peaceful within." Shades of Tolstoy's *War and Peace*. From the Meetinghouse, the battle continued to the Brandywine at Chadds Ford. Now, trapped, Washington had no choice but to retreat.

Three of his divisions provided support, which allowed Washington to move his army to Chester, an escape greatly aided by a wounded 19-year-old French officer, Marquis de Lafayette, who came to fight for the Americans that summer. Estimates vary, but Washington's army lost over 1,200 men in this fight, the second longest single-day battle of the war and one that involved more troops than any other. General Howe marched his army, virtually unopposed, and captured Philadelphia on September 26, holding it until June 1778. Fortunately, the Continental Congress escaped, moving first to Lancaster for one day and then to York for nine months. Appearing before Congress after this devastating defeat, Washington, ever the optimist, said, "Despite the day's misfortune, I am pleased to announce that most of my men are in good spirits and still have the courage to fight the enemy another day." He made those remarks before the dreadful winter at Valley Forge.

After Whitacre sold the farm in 1760 to George Carter Sr. for £100, the Carter family continued ownership until 1838 when three Worth brothers – Paschall, John, and Ebenezer – purchased it. Throughout the Civil War and for the rest of the 19th century the Georgia farm remained in the Worth family. They raised crops, most likely wheat, rye, and corn and, like most other area farms, began dairying in the second half of the century. They acquired the Glen-Worth Farm and the Carter-Worth Farm and by the early 1900s the Worth family also owned the Allerton and Baldwin farms, listed in this historic district. They built the current barn sometime before 1881, which probably replaced earlier barns, made of either wood or stone.

A marble datestone in the barn, shaped in a half-moon with brick trim and located in the peak under the west side gable, with the inscription *WSS 1890*, seems to commemorate something about the barn. However, this wasn't the construction year; in Cope and Futhey's *History of Chester County*, published in 1881, a photograph clearly shows this barn on the property. It's probable that the initials may refer to someone who made changes in the barn, perhaps a 23x40 shed, located on the west flank of the barn, built shortly after the barn was completed.

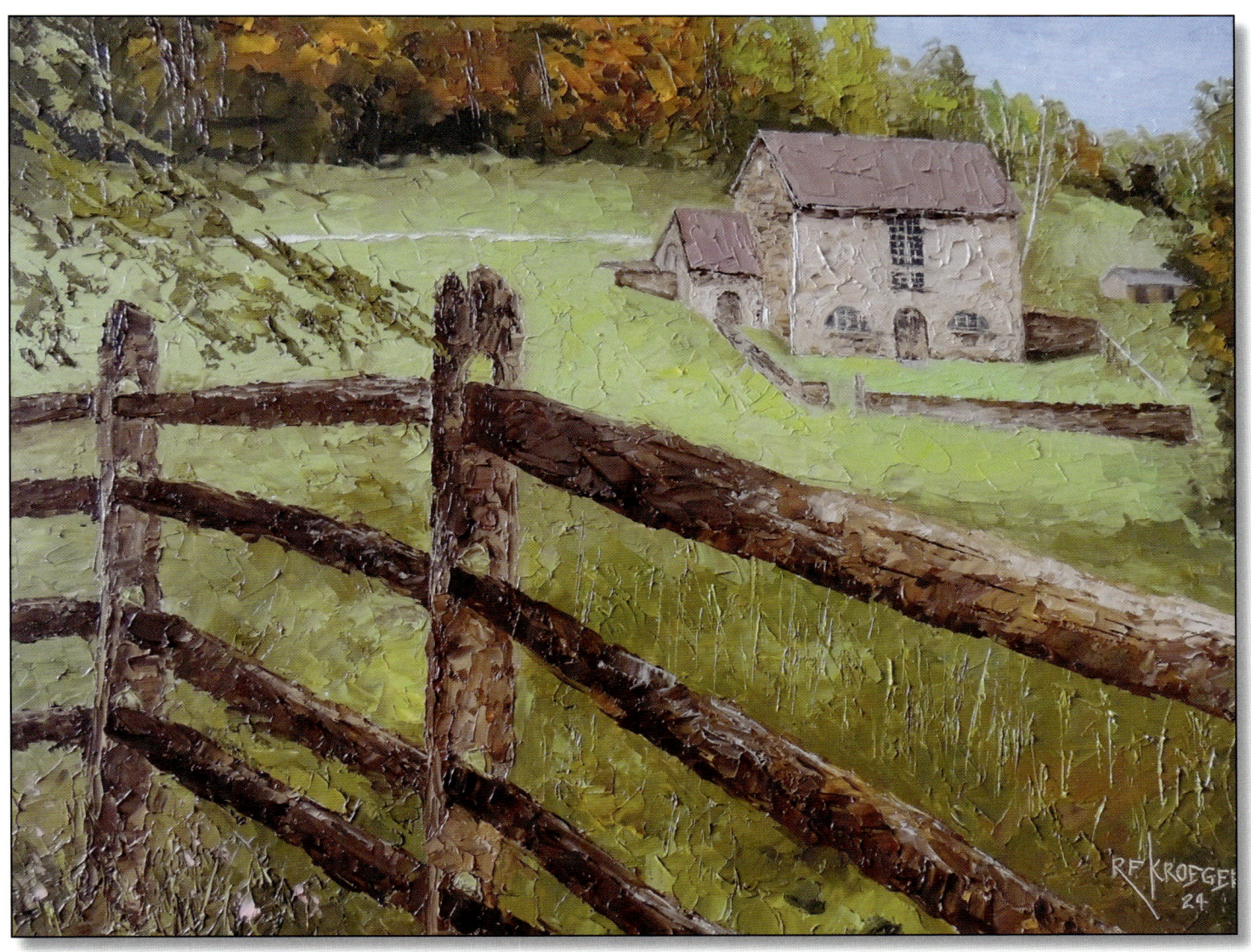

Lucky Hill Farm, 1811

The main section, 60x40 feet, of this three-story barn was probably once covered with a slate roof, though it's asphalt now. Its sawcut timbers in the floor joists and rafters hint that there was a sawmill close by or even on the property while the barn was being built. A traditional Pennsylvania bank barn, its most striking features are two stone arches and the multi-colored serpentine stonemasonry. Added in the mid-20th century, a brick extension on the east side – with six arched doors – suggested that the farm had prospered and needed more storage space. A stone barn, built in 1811, on the nearby Lucky Hill Farm features similar stone arches, which may have influenced the builder.

On the north side, a ramp allows entrance into the barn through a large sliding door. A wooden shed, once attached to the end opposite the brick extension, has been removed and replaced by a fence which leads from remnants of the stone wall that served as a boundary for the farmyard. The masterful stonework highlights the mason's skill: variegated colorful fieldstone in a random rubble arrangement, massive quoins supporting the corners, and 35-inch-thick walls. The barn would delight any masonry aficionado. Today the barn serves as storage.

According to the Oley Valley Historical Society, at the start of the Great Depression in 1931 Harry Cann purchased the Georgia Farm from the Worth family. Thirty years later, he sold it to William Laird, who held it until 1974, when Morris W. Stroud, III, purchased it and lived there. A graduate of Yale University and the University of Pennsylvania School of Medicine, Dr. Stroud specialized in internal medicine before beginning service during World War II. He served with the Pennsylvania Hospital Medical Corps in the South Pacific in the battles of New Caledonia, Bougainville, and Guadalcanal. For his heroism, he was awarded the Silver Star and the Soldier's Medal, also known as the Army Soldier's Medal for Heroism, given to a soldier who distinguishes himself by heroism not involving actual conflict with an enemy.

After the war, he chose a career of medical research at

several medical schools and was instrumental in developing diving equipment for frogmen. He also co-authored a book on heart disease. Throughout the 1960s he was a medical director at a rehabilitation hospital at Case Western University and in the next decade had a similar role at Bryn Mawr hospital in Malvern, Pennsylvania. During these years he focused on geriatric medicine and established a center, named after him, at Columbia University. Just before he died in 1990, he willed his 330-acre Georgia Farm to the Natural Lands Trust, reflecting his concern for water quality, a field he was also deeply involved in.

In 1953 an accountant, Allston Jenkins, an avid bird watcher, was concerned about Gulf Oil planning to dump oil into the marshes of the Schuykill, which would affect birdlife. He joined forces with a birding club and, together, they stopped Gulf and established what is now the John Heinz National Wildlife Refuge, the first urban refuge in the country. Next, Allston founded the Philadelphia Conservationists, a group that led to the creation of four more national wildlife sanctuaries. This eventually evolved into Natural Lands, a nonprofit that conserves land in eastern Pennsylvania and southern New Jersey.

Today, Natural Lands manages 42 nature preserves across two states and 13 counties, which includes nearly 23,300 acres. The Georgia Farm lies on this land – 571 acres are known as the Stroud Preserve, featuring six to nine miles of hiking as well as kayaking, canoeing, and seasonal hunting. Dr. Stroud also donated conservation easements to the Brandywine Conservancy, as well as granting perpetual use of this preserve to the Stroud Water Research Center, an environmental research institution, founded by Dr. Stroud's younger brother, Dick, in 1966.

These days, there are no more 18th-century English Quakers, wearing long coats, knee breeches, sturdy black shoes, and dark broad-brimmed hats, heading towards their services in stone meeting houses. Nor are there any barn raisings or farmers walking behind a horse and plow. Nor are there any buckskin-clothed colonial militia facing off against red-coated British soldiers. But something has remained the same from the days of William Penn's 17th-century land grant: water still runs clear and deep, thanks to the Stroud Preserve, through both branches of the Brandywine.

The Tile Makers

There were – and still are – many families in southeastern Pennsylvania with names that derive from the German Pfannebecker, whose two root words mean tile and baker, a trade that involved making roof tiles. The patriarch of the family line, Hendrick Pannebecker, born in Holland

in 1674, arrived in Pennsylvania and worked as an attorney and a land surveyor for William Penn, whose large land grant of 1681 included present-day Pennsylvania and Delaware. Hendrick's grandson, Matthias Pennypacker, built this barn in 1805, a date inscribed in stone in the barn's gable, along with the initials M&MP. The stone barn might have replaced a wooden one.

Matthias was born in 1742, long after William Penn arrived with colonists in 1682. Four years later, Charles Pickering, a Philadelphia merchant who had been convicted of counterfeiting in 1683, learned that mineral deposits, perhaps gold, might lie in northern Chester County. Pickering persuaded Thomas Fairman, an assistant to Thomas Holme, the first Surveyor General of Pennsylvania, to lay out a survey around this site. He finally obtained a grant from Penn for the land, which included Charlestown Village and Pickering Creek, both named after him. By purchasing land from other grantees, Pickering increased his holdings up to 5,358 acres. However, he never realized his dream of a gold strike; the mine was empty.

After Pickering died in 1701, 16 of his friends purchased tracts on this land, including 30 acres owned by Griffith Jones, who passed this land to Alexander Ross and then to James Anderson in 1713. As the first actual settler on this land, Anderson built a sawmill here in 1735 and gradually increased his farm to 51 acres, which John Custer and his son-in-law Matthias Pennypacker bought in 1774. When Custer turned the farm over completely to Matthias in 1787, the property also included a gristmill.

Along with being a farmer, Matthias was a Mennonite bishop and a well-known preacher to congregations in locations such as Phoenixville, Skippack in adjacent Montgomery County, and Germantown, one of the oldest settlements in Philadelphia. The family lived in a small home, one room upstairs and one downstairs. His son, also Matthias, was born in 1786. Although Mennonites were pacifists, Matthias, supported the colonist cause, which the British forces discovered when they came through Phoenixville in 1777.

After winning victories in the Battle of Brandywine Creek on September 11 and in the Battle of Paoli Tavern on September 20, the British continued their march towards Philadelphia, the headquarters of the Colonial Congress. As they came through the Phoenixville region, they ravaged farms owned by families that supported the revolution, which included the Pennypackers. The British ransacked the farm and destroyed the machinery in the grist mill. They advanced from here and captured Philadelphia on September 26.

Hoping to regain the city, the capital of the resurgent colonists, General Washington ordered a surprise attack at dawn on the British army in Germantown on October 4. Unfortunately, a thick fog led to confusion and an eventual defeat for the Americans. Discouraged by three successive failures, Washington led his 12,000-man army to winter quarters in December at Valley Forge, a short distance from Phoenixville and the Pennypacker Farm. Estimates claim that nearly 2,000 soldiers died during the winter – due to injuries, sickness, and problems with the food supply chain. Even though most farmers in the region were Quakers, Mennonites, or Amish, some helped the ragged army.

In *The Annals of Phoenixville and its Vicinity*, written in 1872 by the eventual governor of Pennsylvania Samuel Pennypacker, great-grandson of Matthias, the builder of this stone barn, he described how General Washington took over the family farm. "A company of horse was stationed at the residence of Matthias Pennypacker. The orchard was used as a parade ground and the barn as a magazine. The powder was kept in kegs and barrels upon the floor and the building was surrounded by a guard continually.

It is also told of this good Mennonite that he secreted a quantity of his neighbors' clothing in barrels. There was a constant picket guard through the winter, on his property, where the West Chester Road crosses the Pickering Creek."

Other families helped. Peter Pennypacker, another descendant of Hendrick, who purchased a farm in 1747, allowed Washington to use his mansion, known as Pennypacker Mills, as his headquarters – and later as a field hospital – before and after the Battle of Germantown. Located about 10 miles north of Phoenixville, the mansion remained in the Pennypacker family for eight generations until 1980, when, thanks to Mrs. S.W. Pennypacker, II, the last of the family to live in it, the mansion became an historical site, run by Montgomery County.

General Washington and his troops remained at Valley Forge until June 1778, using the time wisely for his generals to train the soldiers, many of whom were simple militia. He also chose Valley Forge to offer protection to the many colonists in the rich farmland of southeastern Pennsylvania, prime targets for British assault. His strategy

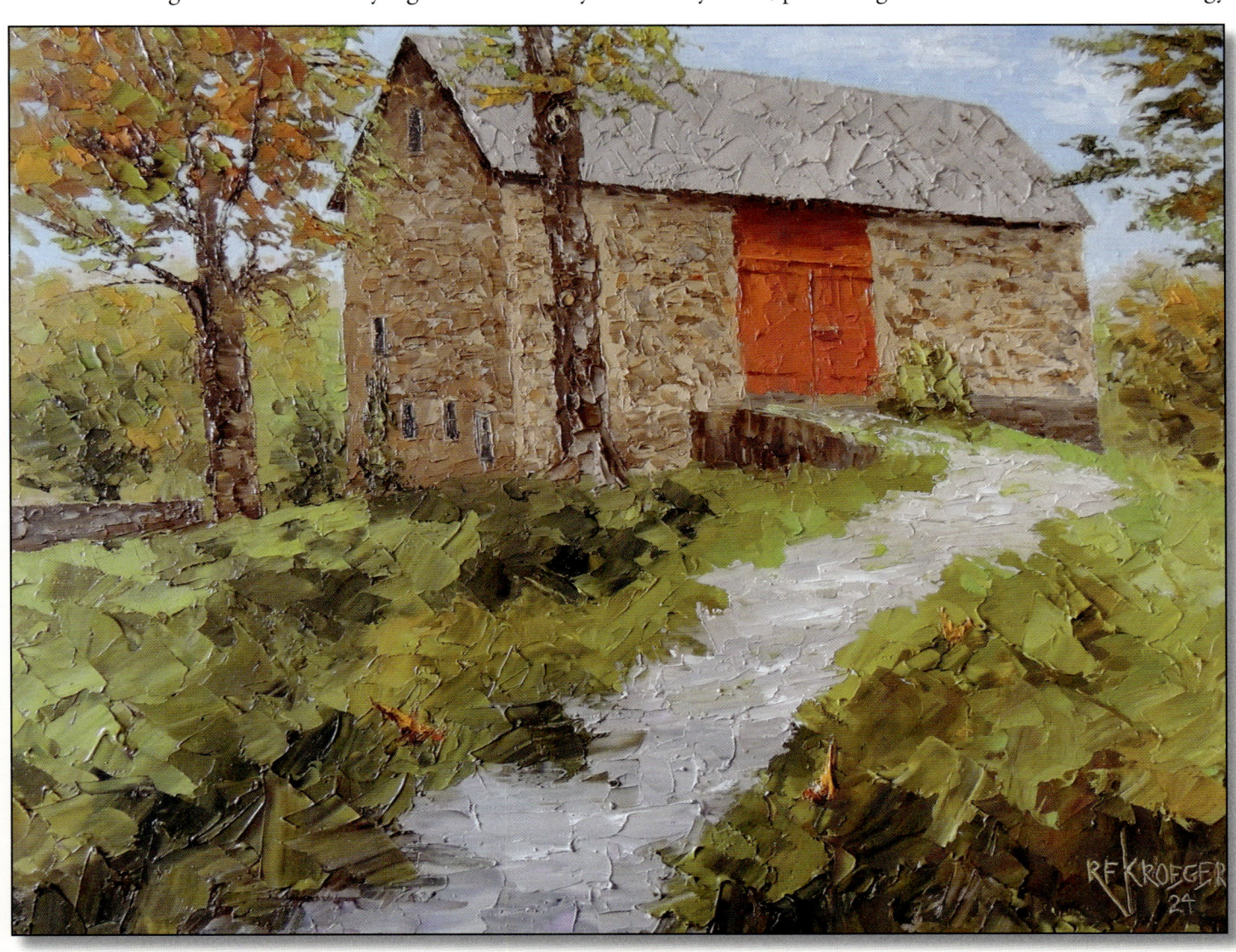

The Tile Makers

worked; by June, his army now fully recovered, he marched towards New Jersey, where, despite the 100-degree heat, the American forces claimed a modest victory in the Battle of Monmouth.

After the war, the Pennsylvania Assembly appointed Matthias as a commissioner to manage navigation of the Schuylkill River. He continued preaching and operating a grist mill and a sawmill, and he increased his acreage by acquiring nearby farms. According to the writings of Samuel Pennypacker, Matthias sent flour and money to people in Philadelphia when a plague of yellow fever devastated the city in 1793. After he died in 1808, his large funeral drew visitors from five counties. His son Matthias continued farming and he enlarged the farmhouse, building an addition in 1830.

The stone barn built by Matthias and presumably by his son – who was nearly 20 years old in 1805 – was a large one, measuring 40x60 feet. It still sits proudly on a slight bank and its stonework, an attractive and colorful random rubble, has been maintained well. Large quoins support the corners and a metal roof ensures longevity.

Though the grist mill had deteriorated and was torn down in 1885 by yet another Matthias – Dr. Matthias J. Pennypacker – the barn survived. The farm, also known as Tinker Dam Farm (after dams that were essentially piles of loose stones built into the rivers), was reduced in acreage to six acres over the years and passed out of family hands during the Great Depression in 1934. In 1977 owner Lawrence Drake submitted a detailed history of the estate, a nomination that earned the Tinker Dam Farm a listing on the National Register. This recognition cemented the heritage of the Pennypackers, the Dutch tile makers, and their contributions to early America.

Elijah's Exquisite Example

Located in Schuylkill Township and not far from the Tinker Dam Farm, is a farmhouse, whose initial section was built circa 1770. Elijah Funk Pennypacker was born here in 1804. His father Joseph, likely a descendant of the patriarch Hendrick Pannebecker, was also born on this farmstead, currently known as White Horse Farm. Joseph was presumably the farmer who built this stone barn circa 1810. Though it was his father's, Elijah made the barn famous, thanks, in part, to an underground tunnel that led from the farmhouse to the barn, a clever way to hide runaway slaves if bounty hunters arrived to search the house.

Though Elijah probably helped run the farm with his father, he had other interests. After his education in New Jersey, he worked as a surveyor, which involved real estate work – along with surveying the Pennsylvania railroad

system. At 27, he served as a state representative in the Pennsylvania legislature, which lasted from 1831 to 1836. During these years he worked closely with Thaddeus Stevens, a lawyer from Gettysburg who was a fierce abolitionist. Stevens later was elected to Congress in 1848 and again in 1858. His influence may have convinced Elijah to end his political career in 1836 – in favor of helping slaves escape to Canada. By 1840 his estate, White Horse Farm, had become an official station on the Underground Railroad.

Pennsylvania, founded by Quakers, was well known for its anti-slavery stance. In 1780 Pennsylvania passed a law that phased out slavery within its borders. However, other areas of the north still prospered by importing slaves; in Bristol, Rhode Island, the first colony to abolish slavery in 1652, the DeWolf family transported over 11,000 Africans to the Americas between 1769 and 1820. Ten years later, Great Britain passed legislation outlawing slavery in all its colonies, prompting many slaves to try to escape from the cotton and tobacco plantations of the South. Word spread that most northerners sympathized with their plight and were willing to help.

When he began his political career in 1831, Elijah married a Quaker, Sarah Coates, who persuaded him to join the Society of Friends. When Sarah died in 1841, Elijah married another Quaker, Hannah Adamson. Though Elijah and Sarah had no children, Hannah had plenty – nine, enough to fill the house on White Horse Road. By this time, Elijah had become well-known for harboring fugitives, and he became active in the American Anti-Slavery Society, founded in Philadelphia in 1833. Kindhearted beyond belief, he also reached out to the downtrodden Irish, whose population was decimated by the potato famine in the late 1840s.

Slaves, often traveling at night, in darkness lit by the moon, approached White Horse Farm from three routes, typically moving along the shores of Chesapeake Bay and then through Delaware, Maryland, and adjacent counties in southeastern Pennsylvania. From his station, Elijah would help them reach cities, including Philadelphia, Norristown, Quakertown, and Reading, from where they would continue their journey northwards. Sometimes he would transport the slaves directly. None were captured under his care. His work was well known, vaulting him into the positions of president of both the Chester County and Pennsylvania abolitionist societies.

When, under pressure from southern states, the government passed the Fugitive Slave Act in September 1850, harboring escaped slaves became a federal crime, punishable by a fine of $1,000 and a prison sentence of six months. In addition, the convicted was liable to pay $1,000 to the slave

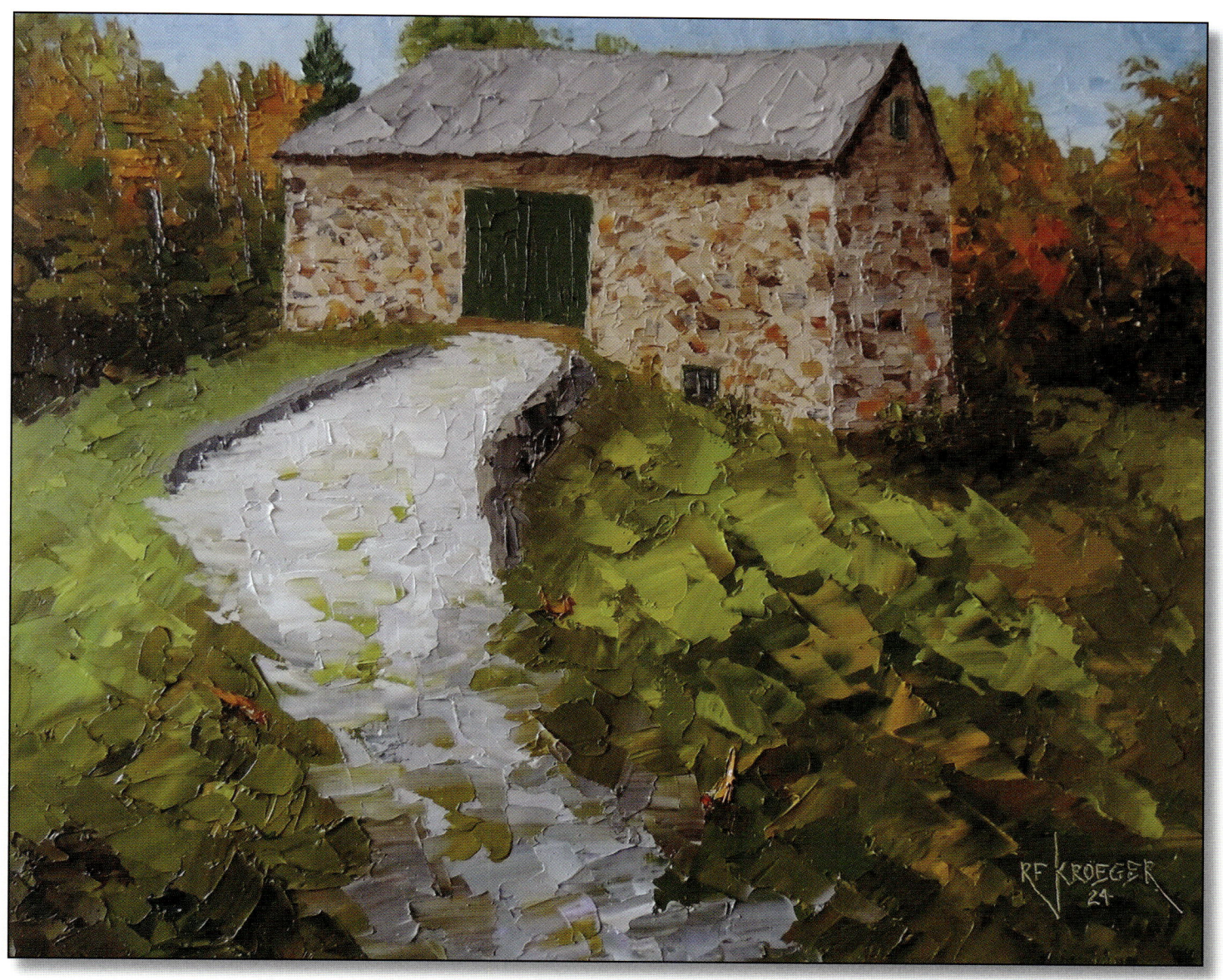

Elijah's Exquisite Example

owner. Though some northern states – such as Wisconsin and Vermont – passed legislation to skirt this law, slaves had to travel to Canada for complete freedom, no easy feat in wintertime. Helping slaves escape became much more difficult and dangerous: bloodhounds, reward notices posted in taverns, and watches set up at river crossings. Slave owners had motivation – slaves were valuable commodities, traded in markets in cities such as Richmond, Virginia, Savannah, Georgia, Charleston, South Carolina, and New Orleans, the largest of them all. Prices of slaves varied with gender, condition, and age but often would range in tens of thousands of dollars in today's currency. Still, Elijah lost none to bounty hunters.

At times he would transport women and children, hidden in a wagon, the men walking alongside, most likely disguised. Instead of crossing the bridge over the Schuylkill River – where bounty hunters waited on the opposite end – they would often have to ford the river near Fitzwater

Station. Though he successfully helped hundreds to escape, Elijah was particularly proud of having reunited a husband and wife, who had been separated for years, as many were when auctioned to the highest bidder.

After the Civil War, Elijah continued farming and resumed his political career, becoming a member of the Prohibition Party. He ran for state treasurer in 1875 but was defeated. Along with farming, he also entered the insurance business, founding the Pennsylvania Mutual Fire Insurance Company. He died in 1888 and was buried in the Schuylkill Friends Meeting Cemetery.

Though the White Horse Farm passed out of family hands, new owners were able to maintain the property through two world wars and the Great Depression. In 1986 Mr. and Mrs. Joe Thomson, owners at that time, successfully submitted the nomination for a listing on the National Register. Most recently, in November 2022, the farm sold again.

The barn, built circa 1810 – when Elijah was a young boy – sits 80 feet from the house and is timber-framed with mortise and tenon joints, held together with wooden pegs. I decided to paint the stone barn as it might have looked when it was built, which meant not including a two-story addition that was likely built in 1915, during the same time as major remodeling was done to the farmhouse. I also chose to expose the colorful fieldstone, which has since been covered with white stucco. Stone walls, which support the banked entrance, are still present.

On the rear side, three stable doors are paired with a small window. A fourth entrance on the south end used to feature a double door with an entry into a wagon shed. The two-story, shed-roofed addition that now attaches to the north wall houses a stone room on the first floor and a wood-framed room on the second floor. A modern (1983) garage roll-up door has replaced the original double door.

Over 200 years old, the barn has witnessed its share of history, much of it, thanks to the courageous and selfless acts of Elijah Pennypacker. Another abolitionist and fellow Quaker, well-known Massachusetts poet John Greenleaf Whittier said of Elijah, "In mind, body, and brave championship of the cause of freedom, he was one of the most remarkable men I ever knew." Yes, he set a standard for all Americans – a simply exquisite example of humanitarianism.

Seventeen Children

This farmstead in Chester County is yet another example that illustrates a family changing its name to Pennypacker. But it began, not with a Pennypacker or Pennebecker, but with Zachariah Rice, who was born in Bavaria in 1731, emigrated from Germany, sailed on the *Edinburgh*, and arrived in Philadelphia in 1751. A millwright, carpenter, and farmer, he joined the Pikeland Company, a cooperative settlement, and began farming. Chances are that he also worked in a nearby mill since a millwright, though often self-taught, was usually also skilled in engineering and carpentry and knew how to run a mill.

He married Abigail Hartman, also a German immigrant, who sailed from Rotterdam on the *Royal Union* with her parents in the summer of 1750. Many died on these trans-Atlantic voyages and one passenger on this ship, Gottlieb Mittelberger, recorded his observations, "During the journey the ship is full of pitiful signs of

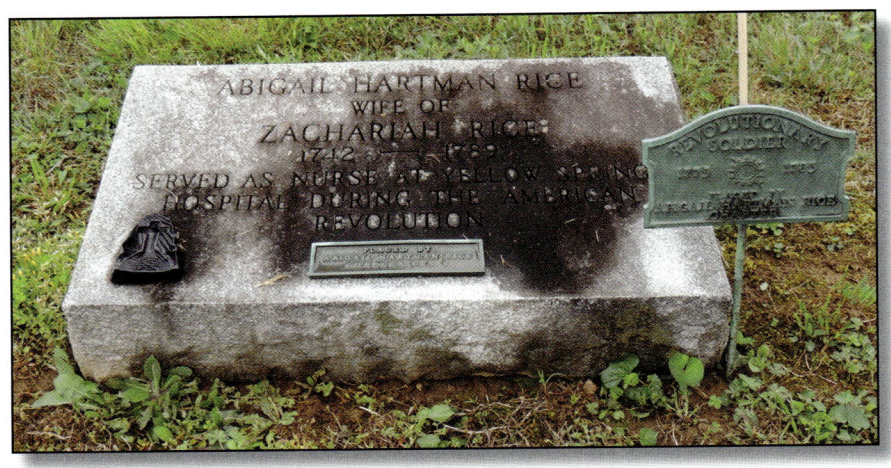

Grave marker of Abigail Rice, 1789, St. Peter's Cemetery, Pikeland Township, Chester County

distress – smells, fumes, horrors, vomiting, headaches, heat, constipation, boils, scurvy, cancer, and similar afflictions… add to all that shortage of food, hunger, thirst, frost, heat, dampness, fear, misery, vexation, and lamentation as well as other troubles." Abigail was only seven when she arrived in Philadelphia. At 16, she married Zachariah in a ceremony conducted by the reverend Henry Muhlenberg, the father of the North American Lutheran church. Two years later she delivered her first child, whom they named John. From 1760 to 1774, Abigail delivered a baby each year – with the exception of 1766. Seventeen of her 21 children survived to adulthood. Her gravestone read, "Some have children, some have none, here lies the mother of twenty-one." Unfortunately, when I visited her gravesite, this original tombstone was missing.

In 1767, with eight children and a wife nearly continually pregnant, Zachariah received a 205-acre parcel of land from Abigail's father Johannes Hartman, who purchased lots as many did in the Pikeland community. Zachariah built the first part of the still-extant stone farmhouse and a rudimentary stone barn as well, though only the house is documented with this date. According to the tax record of 1798, his farm had 180 acres and his barn, half log and half stone, was narrow – 48x21 feet. Chances are that this was a ground level barn, which later owners modified and enlarged. Zachariah also had a grist mill, which helped support his growing family. In 1785 he modified the mill to process clover, which was becoming an important soil additive in the late 1700s in Pennsylvania.

Most farmers in this region grew crops of corn and grain – wheat, alfalfa, rye, hemp, and flax. However, repetitive planting led to soil depletion, which farmers tried to neutralize by adding lime, gypsum and eventually red clover, which helped tremendously. Clover also provided high-protein hay, which was used for livestock feeding, apparently popular since its seed quickly became an important export in southeastern Pennsylvania; newspapers in the 1780s advertised "Lancaster County red clover seed." The 1810 census stated the county had 12 water-powered clover mills and that the county's clover seed production was a phenomenal 4,900 bushels. In fact, the street where the Rice farm is located was named Clover Mill Road.

In 1776, the year that the colonies united against Great Britain, Zachariah was 45, Abigail was 34, and their children numbered at least 15. With this responsibility, Zachariah probably did not serve in the Revolutionary army, though some records suggest that he enlisted in the militia – as a carpenter, engineer, and millwright. Another source claimed that he also owned a tavern. Regardless, the family led a colorful and busy life but, unlike many of their Mennonite, Amish, and Quaker neighbors, the Rice family supported the revolution.

In time, battles crept closer to Clover Mill Road. On September 11, 1777, the British defeated the forces of General Washington at the Battle of Brandywine Creek, about 15 miles from the Rice farm. Five days later, British general Howe decided to attack the weakened American army, but a torrential downpour lasting two days, likely a nor'easter storm, made combat nearly impossible in what's known as the Battle of the Clouds. According to the Rice family bible, Washington stopped at the farm, where Abigail and her children gave them drinks. That

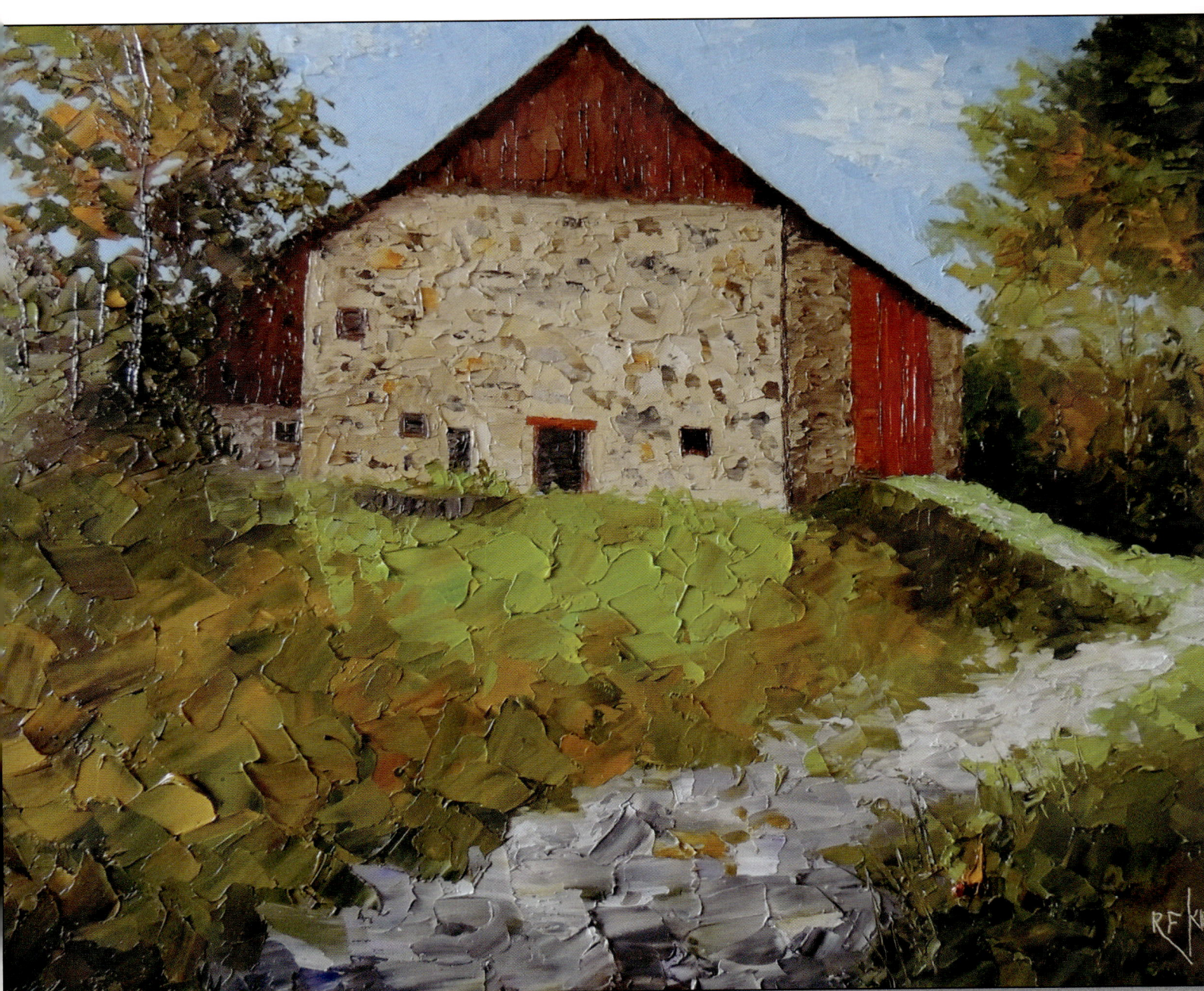

Seventeen Children

night General Anthony Wayne's army camped on the Rice farm.

Washington retreated and ordered General Wayne to remain behind to slow the advance of the British army. Wayne followed orders but was surprised by a silent attack on the night of September 20, which was another victory for the British, a battle described as the Paoli Massacre. Six days later, the British captured Philadelphia, headquarters of the Continental Congress. Washington made one final attempt on October 4 to retake the city – in the Battle of Germantown, about 28 miles from the Rice farm – but, hindered by a thick fog, he once again lost the battle and suffered heavy losses. With his army weary and discouraged, he settled in Valley Forge to regroup for the winter.

In his later writings General Washington described his thoughts about Valley Forge, "To see men without clothes to cover their nakedness, without blankets to lay on, without shoes by which their marches might be traced by the blood on their feet, and almost as often without provisions as with; marching through frost and snow and at Christmas taking up their winter quarters within a day's march of the enemy, without a house or hut to cover them till they could be built, and submitting to it without a murmur is a mark of patience and obedience which in my opinion can scarce be paralleled."

With many of the 12,000 soldiers injured, malnourished, and exhausted, disease became rampant – typhus, typhoid fever, dysentery, pneumonia and perhaps malaria. Less common were tuberculosis, smallpox, and influenza, which also took their toll. Logistical problems led to a shortage of food, which caused scurvy. Medical care, by today's standards, was primitive. Sterility was nonexistent. Antibiotics, intravenous medications, and life-saving surgical techniques weren't available and the resulting death rate was high – between 1,800 and 2,000 men died, while General Washington watched in horror. In his journal, Rhode Island colonel Israel Angell described his soldiers as "poor naked souls destitute of money and every necessity of life."

After petitioning Congress many times, finally on January 3, 1778, Washington received approval to build a hospital in Yellow Springs, about 10 miles from Valley Forge. Zachariah Rice, a carpenter, millwright and engineer, apparently played a major role in constructing it, only a mile from the family farm. A plaque honors him at the ruins – now only fieldstone walls – of the Yellow Springs hospital, the only one commissioned by Congress during the Revolutionary War.

Yellow Springs was first named by the Lenape and Iroquois Indians for the water's rich iron, magnesium, and sulfur content and healing properties. Over the years,

colonists discovered its medicinal value and began visiting the mineral springs. Doctors in Philadelphia sent patients there, hoping for cures, and one physician, Dr. Samuel Kennedy, bought the springs in 1774.

General Washington knew about these springs since his army had camped there after the Battle of Brandywine and thought, after witnessing his army being decimated by disease, that the village would be a good spot for a hospital. Generously, Dr. Kennedy loaned a portion of his land for the hospital. Construction on the hospital, named Washington Hall, an ample sized one at 106 by 36 feet with three stories, began in March and was completed in August. In May, General Washington visited the sick soldiers and talked with each one. By August over 1,300 soldiers had been treated by doctors and nurses, one of whom was Abigail Rice.

In 1777, John, the oldest Rice child, was 18 and several of the others were teenagers, old enough to run a household and perform chores on the farm. Abigail must have felt that she could leave the farm in good hands and walk a mile to the hospital, where she would work as a nurse. She may have started her visits while Zachariah was building the hospital, and, according to writings of her descendants, she "came on her errands of mercy, carrying foods and delicacies to the sick and wounded soldiers." Other wives did the same.

By and large, pioneer women were relegated to taking care of the house, bearing children, and raising them … and not much more. Abigail and the other volunteer nurses stepped outside of the traditional role of the colonial wife, but they weren't totally happy. Dr. Bodo Otto, the hospital's director, wrote a letter to Congress, complaining of lack of supplies and also listing the grievances of the nurses. He wrote that the nurses "refuse serving any longer, as they have received no pay." His letter worked; Washington convinced Congress that the hospital had to have supplies and had to pay the nurses. By the end of the war in 1783, some nurses were paid more than enlisted soldiers.

With disease so prevalent in the hospital, nurses and doctors risked their lives in treating the sick and, unfortunately, some fell ill. One of the unlucky ones was Abigail, who contracted typhoid fever. Complications of the disease made life difficult even though she was in her early 40s and obviously healthy enough to raise a large family and walk two miles daily to work at the hospital. She bore her last child, Benjamin, in 1785. Four years later she died. There's a plaque honoring her at Valley Forge and at St. Peter's Cemetery, thanks to the Abigail Hartman Rice chapter of the Daughters of the American Revolution. Sitting next to Abigail's gravestone is a granite marker for her father, Johannes Hartman, who died in 1787.

But that wasn't the only problem for her husband. A year after Abigail died, the Rice farm went into foreclosure. Although America was regarded as the land of opportunity by European immigrants in the 18th and 19th centuries, it was also the land of opportunity for land speculators: some succeeded, some failed, and some were just plain dishonest. One glaring example of a land speculator was Robert Morris, a founding father, signer of the Declaration of Independence, and the financial genius behind the American Revolution. After the war, he joined partners in land speculation, borrowing money for millions of acres, hoping to sell lots quickly. But sales didn't materialize and he went bankrupt, spending over three years in a debtor's prison. No public ceremonies marked his passing.

Another example of greed and deception involved Andrew Allen, a prominent Philadelphia merchant and a member of the Continental Congress. He bought 17,000 acres of the Pikeland tract from Samuel Hoare, a London merchant who purchased the property in 1750, originally patented by William Penn in 1681. Hoare carried the mortgage on the sale to Allen, who, in turn, divided the parcel into lots of 200 and 300 acres, one of which Johannes Hartman bought and gave to his son-in-law Zachariah. However, Allen kept the money and did not register the land, making the deeds worthless, unbeknown to Hartman and Rice. After the Revolutionary War began, Allen fled to Trenton and asked General Howe for protection. But, when the war ended, civil courts were established and Sheriff Ezekial Howard was given writs, dated August 26, 1789, to begin foreclosure on the Hoare-Allen mortgage, and to begin the sale of the farm. Rice wasn't the only victim; 114 other families in Pikeland Township forfeited their land as well.

After losing his farmhouse, his stone and log barn, and his clover mill, Zachariah, now 60 years old, left the county in search of cheaper land. With his 17 children, their belongings packed in Conestoga wagons, he headed about 100 miles west to Juniata County, where he purchased a small farm, which he paid off in 1801, receiving clear title. He also donated an acre and a half for a Lutheran church, which he helped build between 1794 and 1797. At the age of 80, he died in 1811 and was buried in a cemetery next to his church.

At the sheriff's sale of the Rice farm in 1790, Gabriel Shuler was the highest bidder, though not much is known about his ownership. At some point, Gabriel transferred or sold the farm to William Shuller, whose name is recorded in the 1798 tax record. At the time, the barn was listed as being part stone and part logs and measuring 48x21 feet, a narrow barn, typical of early stone barns. He also owned a grist mill, 24x21 feet, possibly built by Zachariah.

In 1801 Shuller sold to John Pennebecker, who began the next chapter of this farm. John died two years later, but his son Joseph took over, farming and running the clover mill until 1814. His cousin James continued to operate the farm until 1826 when he died and his son George took the reins. At some point – probably between 1831 and 1832 when George expanded the farmhouse – he rebuilt the stone and log barn into its present configuration. George also Americanized his name to Pennypacker as well as switching from grain farming to dairying. A relative, Joseph Tustin, continued to farm, which, with the arrival of the railroad, meant increased prosperity. Now farmers could ship butter, eggs, cheese, milk, and vegetables to markets in nearby Philadelphia. By the early 1900s their herd of 30 dairy cows was producing 800 pounds of milk each day. The farm left family hands in 1912 when a group of fox hunting enthusiasts bought it.

Fox hunting, traditionally a sport of the upper class, originated in England in the Middle Ages when horsemen, led by hounds, sought to kill foxes that raided their farms, eating chickens and small farm animals. It evolved into a sport in elite circles, which involved wearing formal jackets, usually black or red, and black hats. When the hounds finally cornered the fox, the hunt ended. In 2005 the United Kingdom banned this tradition.

The website of a group that raises funds for the Chester County Hospital Foundation proclaims that "Every Chester County day begins with a fox hunt." Unfortunately, because of inclement weather, the 2022 hunt was cancelled. However, the Kimberton Hunt Club, established in 1870, is alive and well and holds fox hunts twice weekly in autumn in Kimberton and Chester Springs, the location of the Rice and Pennypacker farmstead. Current law requires that, once the hunt is finished, riders must shoot the fox, rather than allowing the hounds to destroy it.

After the fox hunters sold the farm in 1927, it passed through two owners until Harvey and Alice Mandell purchased it in the 1980s. Historically inclined, the Mandells successfully submitted the farmstead for a listing on the National Register in 1986, which nomination included valuable historical information on the Rice and Pennypacker families. Today it's owned by the Natural Lands Trust, a nonprofit that preserves farmland and nature preserves. The trust leases the farm to Gail O'Neill, who has operated a horse boarding and training facility with her daughter Emily for over 30 years. Gail said that Harry Mandell made wine in the lower level of the barn, giving it yet another function.

The large double decker stone barn, 55x85 feet, was built well before 1849, when it was listed in a sales notice. Did Zachariah Rice built the original structure in the 1770s and did one of the Pennebeckers increase its size? Some queries will never be answered.

Built into a bank, it is a traditional Pennsylvania barn with stalls for horses beneath the forebay and inside the ground level. Gail currently boards 11 horses and offers lessons on sprawling pastureland that surrounds the barn, stretching to distant woodland. A small stone carriage barn across the street was formerly part of this farm. Both stone barns exhibit exquisite stonemasonry; Serpentine fieldstones of red, tan, orange, and dark blue are arranged randomly in an esthetically pleasing pattern. But, unlike the iconic conical piers of Chester County barns, four square stone columns support the forebay of this one, making it unusual as well. The 20-inch-thick stone walls support the rafters.

Today, the farmstead, called Fox Meadow Farm, shows excellent maintenance. As its 300th birthday approaches, the buildings serve as a memory of both the Rice and the Pennypacker families, who witnessed the early years of America, including the Revolutionary War, the War of 1812, and the Civil War. It also reminds us that land speculation flourished in those days, often prompting heartaches and causing difficulties – such as when Zachariah Rice lost his wife and then his farm, forcing him to leave and march 100 miles away for a new start … with 17 children.

LANCASTER COUNTY
Windom Mill

This farmstead with its stone barn and stunning stone mill is located in Manor Township – on land purchased by Samuel Herr in 1769, not far from the West Branch of the Little Conestoga River. In his book, *Mills of Lancaster County*, author Donald Kautz has documented three other attractive stone mills along this branch as well

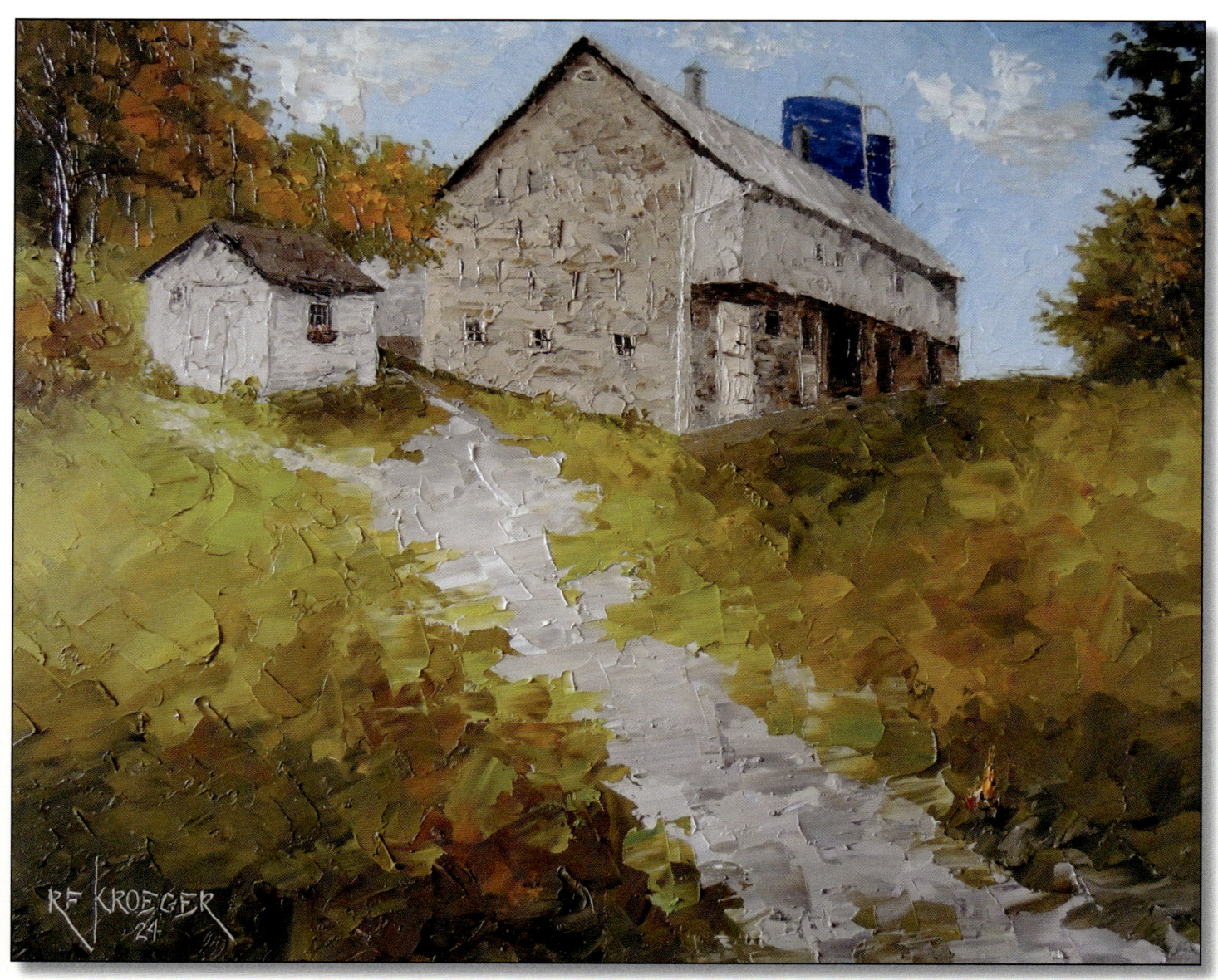

Windom Mill

as 45 historic mills in the Conestoga River watershed. Samuel was a descendant of Reverend Hans Herr, one of the early settlers in this region. His father, also a Samuel, was born, circa 1686, on a farm in the Kraichgau region of Württemburg, then part of the Holy Roman Empire, a part of Europe that amalgamated into Germany in 1871.

Warren and I arrived on a Sunday in May, well ahead of schedule, and met Doug Rohrer, whose parents Ken and Cheryl own the farm. After attending church services, the owners arrived later, graciously understanding our unexpected early arrival. They were looking forward to showing us their farmstead, essentially a living museum of 19th-century Pennsylvania farm life.

According to a history of Manor Township, published in 1883, the township was the "wealthiest and most populous" township of Lancaster County. Bordered by the Susquehanna River on the west and the Conestoga Creek on the south, it was an area rich in limestone, sandstone, and water. Three major waterways, Pequea Creek, Chickies Creek, and the Conestoga Creek traversed the region and flowed into the Susquehanna River. The land was fertile and, thanks to the many German, English, and Swiss immigrant farmers, it would become the "breadbasket of pre-Revolutionary America." In the early 18th century, Lancaster County led the state in wheat production. The golden age of Pennsylvania agriculture, led by the counties in the southeastern section of the state, lasted from 1790 through the 1840s.

Taking advantage of William Penn's offer of land and freedom from religious persecution, many of the immigrants were Mennonites, a sect that traces to Menno Simon, a contemporary of Martin Luther. Simple and religion-oriented peasant farmers, they came to the colonies to start a new life, one free from military service. However, unlike the farm fields of their homeland, this new land was heavily forested, which meant that they had to clear the timber before they could plant crops and establish orchards. Farmers quickly realized that the limestone-rich soil was productive and they built stone kilns, used to extract lime from limestone – commonplace by 1750. Farmers also saw the benefits of growing red clover to replenish the soil.

They raised wheat, barley, flax, and hemp, though their most lucrative crop eventually became tobacco, which was a popular export to Great Britain and Europe. Livestock were not raised for their meat since wild game was plentiful in the 18th century.

With the harvests of such crops and with abundant sources of water, grist mills sprang up throughout the area. By 1779, Samuel Herr's farm had a grist mill and a sawmill.

The miller's stone house was built earlier, in 1763. Other families followed in building mills in Manor Township: Christian Burkholder, Jacob Goodman, Rudolph Herr, Christian Herr, John Keller, Christian Kauffman, Jacob Kauffman, and Yost Musser. Almost all these families were pacifist Mennonites and did not support either the British nor American side during the Revolutionary War. They were content to continue farming and raise their families as the war raged around them, even though occasionally their farms would be requisitioned for supplies by either side. Whether the Herrs participated in the war, though unlikely, remains unknown.

This typical early 19th-century Pennsylvania stone barn was constructed in 1800 (or perhaps was enlarged from one built earlier) – mostly likely by Samuel Herr, who would have been around 50 at the time. His son-in-law Jacob Kauffman, apparently also a prosperous farmer, built a large flour and feed mill in 1810 – after an earlier mill had burned. Though not much is known about the early barn builders, the masons who built this mill staged a contest to see which one could form the most perfect corner. The one who built the southeastern corner won the $10 prize. He marked the cornerstone with a number – 307 feet above sea level. Apparently, he was a perfectionist.

About the same time, Kauffman built a tavern, which became a Conestoga Wagon stop on Blue Rock Road, a busy route to the Susquehanna River. By all accounts, business was good for Jacob, a fact substantiated by the 1815 tax records, which listed the farm as one of the most valuable in Manor Township. By 1810 the mill had doubled as a post office. What happened after that remains a mystery. In 1825, John Landis, another Mennonite, bought the farm in a sheriff's sale.

Landis, born in 1786 into a prominent family of Manor Township, continued to maintain the farm buildings, the mill, and the tavern. In 1839 he served as a county commissioner. Though he passed in 1870, his descendants took over the farm and added to its diversification by using the mill as a creamery and a cider mill. By 1900 the farmstead was a busy place. Ken told us that this mill, a solid stone building with 30-inch-thick walls, became a "drive through" for apple cider. Farmers would park their wagons next to the mill, drop off a load of apples, and wait until the apples were crushed into cider, when they'd open a spigot to fill their barrels. Long lines would form at harvest time. Sometimes, Ken explained, schoolboys would stop by after school to see if any juice was left over, which they happily consumed – the cider had fermented. Ah, school days.

The large, 100x40-foot barn has been enlarged over the years, though the additions don't detract from its beauty. The mason used limestone in a random rubble pattern, harvesting the stone from a quarry 300 yards away. Huge quoins support the corners, narrow ventilation slits provide light and airflow, and the randomly arranged cream and gray limestone paints an attractive picture, proving that this was the work of a master stonemason. Inside, the 22-inch-thick stone walls brace the rafters and show little signs of cracking. Hand-hewn beams, 50 feet long, are strong enough to hold up the forebay without posting. Ken said that the chestnut lumber was floated down the Susquehanna River and that the early owners cut four owl holes in the barn, as insurance against damage from vermin.

In 1894 the family used the barn as a creamery and in 1899 it became a post office. The Landis family held onto the farm until 1948, when Nelson and Sylvia Landis sold 106 acres to Grant and Fannie Noll. When her husband passed, Fannie wanted the farm to go to people she knew personally and offered it to Paul Rohrer, Ken's father. However, Paul had recently bought a dairy farm in 1951, not far away, and declined Fannie's offer, not wanting to overextend himself. Later she offered it to him again, but he passed. So, in 1965 Fannie found another buyer and, when the financing fell through at closing, frustrated, she approached Paul for a third time and said, "You will buy my farm." He agreed.

As the years flew by, Paul's sons leased the farm. Ken and his wife Cheryl purchased it in 1992 and entered it on the National Register in 1994, a listing that includes the 18th-century farmhouse, the stone barn, and several other 19th-century buildings – two tobacco barns, an icehouse, a pig pen, a milk house, and a carriage barn, which has been converted into a garage. The grist mill, miller's house, and tavern, all built in 1810, are also listed. A quarter mile of the original millrace is still visible, as are ruins of a family graveyard. On a more modern note, Ken told us that he bought the two blue Harvestore silos in 1969. And, unlike many historic barns, the three levels of this one still are utilized: Ken and his son farm about 470 acres, raising rye, alfalfa, soybeans, corn, barley, and hay. A newer barn houses Holstein cattle.

The tavern, once a stop on a covered wagon route, has been converted into a dwelling, where Doug and his family live, and the mill has been repurposed into a carpenter's workshop as well as a venue for hosting events. That so many historic buildings, including the 1780 farmhouse, have survived as a close-knit group for nearly 250 years reflects the maintenance given by many generations of owners, including the current ones. Eventually, Doug will be the third generation of Rohrers to own this historic farm. The stone farmhouse, the tavern, and the miller's house, as well as the stone barn and stone mill, are fine examples of highly skilled carpenters and stonemasons of two centuries ago. Thanks to Rohrers and to the many former owners of this farmstead, Windom Mill is alive and well and, with proper care, will last for many more years.

LEHIGH COUNTY
The Liberty Bell

Southeastern Pennsylvania has hundreds of stone barns, many located in farms that date to the 18th century, a time when colonial settlers were beginning to tire of Mother England and her oppressive taxation. On July 4, 1776, in nearby Philadelphia, delegates from the 13 colonies agreed on a famous document, The Declaration of Independence, which summed up their thoughts and included the words, "that they are endowed by their creator with certain unalienable rights, that among these are life, liberty and the pursuit of happiness." One of these rights, liberty, was probably the highlight of the life of a minister, Abraham Blumer, who lived in a farmhouse near these stone barns in Lehigh County. Ministers often farmed in the 18th century and it's possible that Blumer used both of these two stone barns.

The county lineage traces back to the Lenni Lenape tribes, who were present when the first settlers arrived. They paid homage to the Indians with the word, Lehigh, which is derived from Lechaweki, the name for a river that winds through most of the county.

Initially, it was part of Bucks County, one of the three counties established by Penn's grant in 1682. German immigrants came in 1715, as recorded in a datestone at the Swamp Church in Lower Milford. The Swiss and English followed, all seeking liberty, land ownership, and freedom of religion. Thanks to advertisements in Germany in 1730, more immigrants arrived, taking advantage of fertile farmland. Slowly, the Indians moved westwards and by 1773 Lehigh County had grown: over 37,000 residents, nearly 9,000 acres of grain cropland, and 886 farmers. One of the immigrants, Abraham Blumer, a Protestant minister, settled near a farm that was established in 1744 in South Whitehall Township, an area heavily populated by Germans of the Lutheran religion. One of them, Lorenze Guth, donated 50 acres of his farm in 1752 to build a church and school for the Jordan Reformed Church, which is the church where Reverend Blumer first preached when he arrived in 1771.

Blumer was born in Switzerland in 1736 into a long line of church people, including his own father, likewise a Lutheran minister. Though Abraham was only 10 when his father died, he continued in the family's religious tradition and was ordained in 1756. A year later he took a job as military chaplain to a Swiss regiment, serving the King of Sardinia, where he remained for 10 years. Unlike the pacifist Quakers and Mennonites, the Lutherans supported the military. Three of Blumer's brothers died in service in Switzerland and another died on his voyage to America.

A year after Blumer arrived in Lehigh County he married and worked in four congregations. He and Susanna raised four children, one of whom, Henry, married Sarah Mickley, whose father helped rescue the Liberty Bell. When war broke out, Abraham supported the colonial cause and eventually became chaplain to the Northampton County Militia.

In September 1777 Washington's army had suffered several defeats, allowing the British to march unopposed toward the colonial capital. Locals became concerned that the army would capture the huge bells of the state house and other bells from churches and melt them down to make munitions, including cannons. To prevent this, two men, Frederick Leaser and John Jacob Mickley smuggled 11 bells out of Philadelphia, a monumental task since the Liberty Bell alone weighted over 2,000 pounds. They disguised them in hay and manure in wagons and transported them in a caravan, likely pulled by horses and oxen, and were escorted under the command of Colonel Thomas Polk and 200 militia of North Carolina and Virginia. When Leaser and Mickley arrived with the valuable shipment in Allentown, Reverend Blumer allowed the bells to be hidden under the floorboards of his church, which had been used as a hospital for wounded American troops. Figuring that the British would never guess to look for the bells in a church, Blumer kept them there for nearly a year. It's easy to visualize him delivering a sermon with the congregation listening intently, knowing that the precious bells of liberty were hidden beneath them.

In 1962, a museum was built inside the church to display items relating to the Liberty Bell, patriotism, and local history. It also contained a full-sized replica of the bell – one of 55 cast in France in the 1950s for a savings bond drive – as well as Zion's Reformed Church bell, cast in 1769. Unfortunately, due to declining and aging membership, the congregation voted to put the church up for sale in late 2022. Sadly, the museum closed permanently in April 2023.

However, the story of the Liberty Bell began much earlier. In 1746 the statehouse in Philadelphia was completed and was at the time the most magnificent public building of Colonial America. Four years later, as some historians believe, locals began making plans to commemorate the 50th anniversary of William Penn's 1701 Charter of Privileges, which granted legislative powers to the Assembly. Accordingly, the Pennsylvania Assembly ordered a bell from London's Whitechapel foundry, which cost £150, a large sum in 1750. The bell arrived in Philadelphia on September 1, 1752.

In March of the following year, they rang the bell to test the sound, but it cracked. Rather than scrap the bell, officials hired two "ingenious workmen," Pass and Snow, to recast the bell, which they did by adding more copper to the mix. Their repair bill cost £36 and stated that the bell weighed 2,081 pounds. In 1754, they tested the sound again, but it didn't sound good; so they ordered a new bell from Whitechapel. The Assembly agreed to pay for the new bell but decided to keep the one repaired by Pass and Snow and installed it in the state house steeple. The new bell was hung in a cupola on the state house roof, near the clock, and was rung to announce local time. The Pass and Snow bell was rung only for special events.

In 1757 it was rung to announce a meeting of the Assembly for the purpose of sending Benjamin Franklin to England to address colonial complaints. It was rung several more times, leading up to the Revolutionary War: in 1771 it rang for the Assembly to ask the king for a repeal of taxes on tea, in 1775 to announce the battles of Lexington and Concord, and in July 1776 to herald the first public reading of the Declaration on Independence. Today, each state capitol displays a replica of the Liberty Bell, thanks to a government initiative to sell U.S. savings bonds.

The bells were kept in Blumer's church until June 1778, when the Liberty Bell was returned to Philadelphia but not hung, since the steeple was too rotten. It was stored for seven years. In 1787 it rang again to announce the ratification of the Constitution. A bronze plaque, located at the entrance of the church that hid the bell, commemorates both Lorenz Guth for his donation of land and Abraham Blumer for his patriotism in moving and safeguarding the bells. Blumer retired from preaching in 1801 and died in 1822.

When Greg Huber and I visited in May 2024, Frank Scattene, project manager for the Jeras Corporation, kindly opened the barn and answered questions. He explained that Reverend Blumer lived in the farmhouse in the distance (a stuccoed stone house shown in this painting) and likely used this barn, which has been well maintained. Its wooden shake roof, rarely seen today

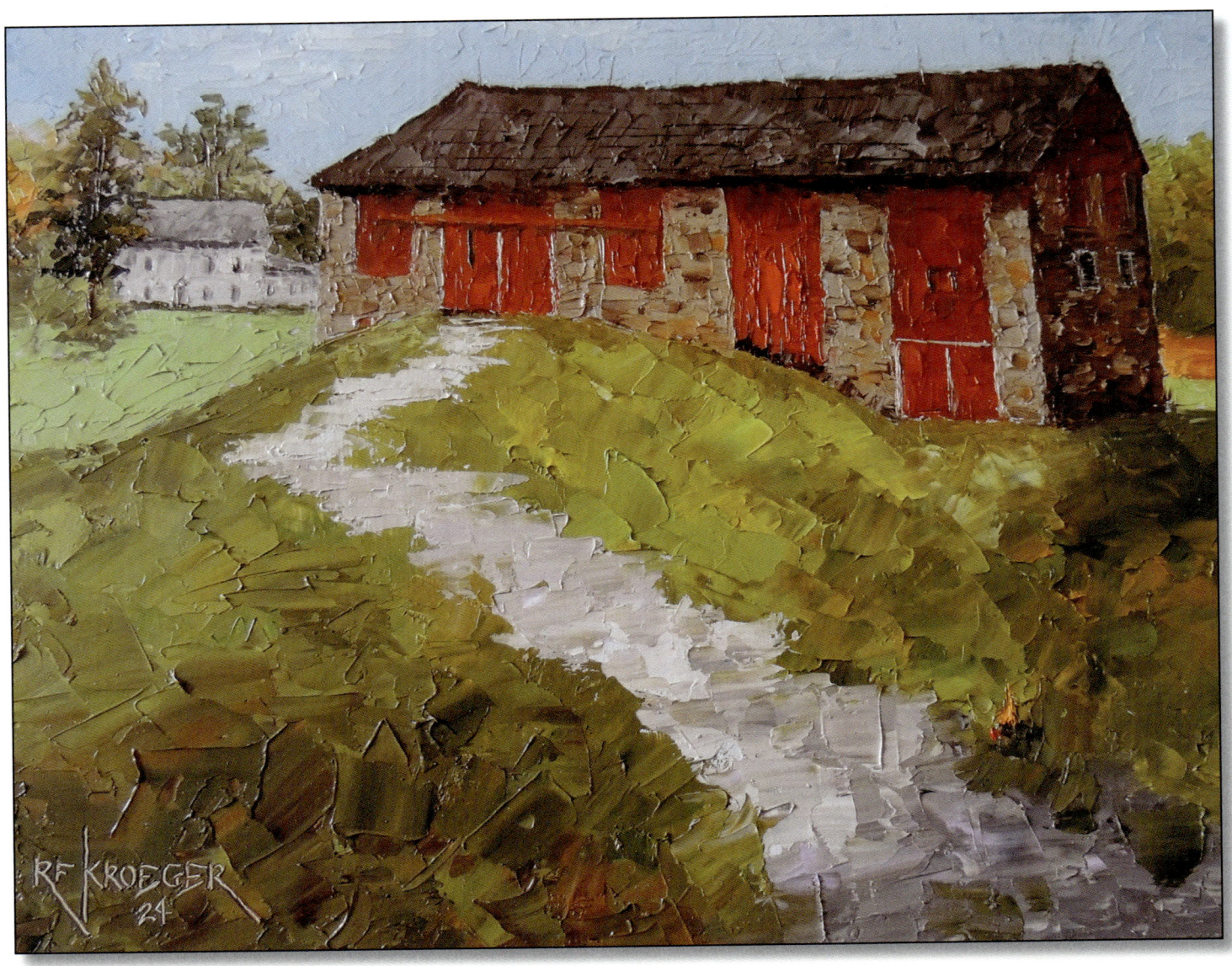

Jeras-Blumer Barn

in such large barns, still keeps rainwater out and its asymmetrical shape classifies the barn as a Sweitzer. The magnificent, variegated fieldstone walls, 18 inches thick, still support the principal rafter system. Thanks to beaded tuckpointing, the master stonemason's handiwork continues to display his high level of skill. The Jeras family, owners, use the barn for storage.

Though Blumer also lived on Iron Bridge Road, about a mile from this second barn, he likely knew the owners, the Troxell family, who bought the land in 1743. After farming there for over a century, they sold it to the Minnich family in 1854, who owned it until the early 1900s, when the Bronstein family took over.

And what a barn it is! Its five distinctive stone arches make this barn rare. In fact, this is one of only two of its type that has been found in Lehigh County. Whereas most Pennsylvania barns have cantilevered forebays, supported by horizontal wooden beams or vertical posts of wood or stone, this one goes a step further in making

the barn a remarkable showpiece of artistic craftmanship. The stone arches, perhaps built as a way to display the farmer's wealth, exhibit exquisite stonemasonry, not only from an esthetic perspective but a technical one. Massive quoins support the corners and there is no evidence of cracking, another feather in the stonemason's cap since his masonry, verified by a date stone of 1806, has lasted nearly 220 years. The Jeras family has shown their commitment to preserving the barn by adding a metal roof.

The next part of this story begins with Jesse B. Bronstein, whose descendants still own these barns, the 1744 Troxell house, the oldest building in the county, and possibly more land than anyone else in South Whitehall Township. Bronstein and fellow chemist F.B. Holmes discovered a process to produce a stable nitrostarch while they were working at DuPont's Eastern Laboratory in Gibbstown, New Jersey. An entrepreneur at heart, Bronstein left DuPont and founded the Non-Freezing Powder

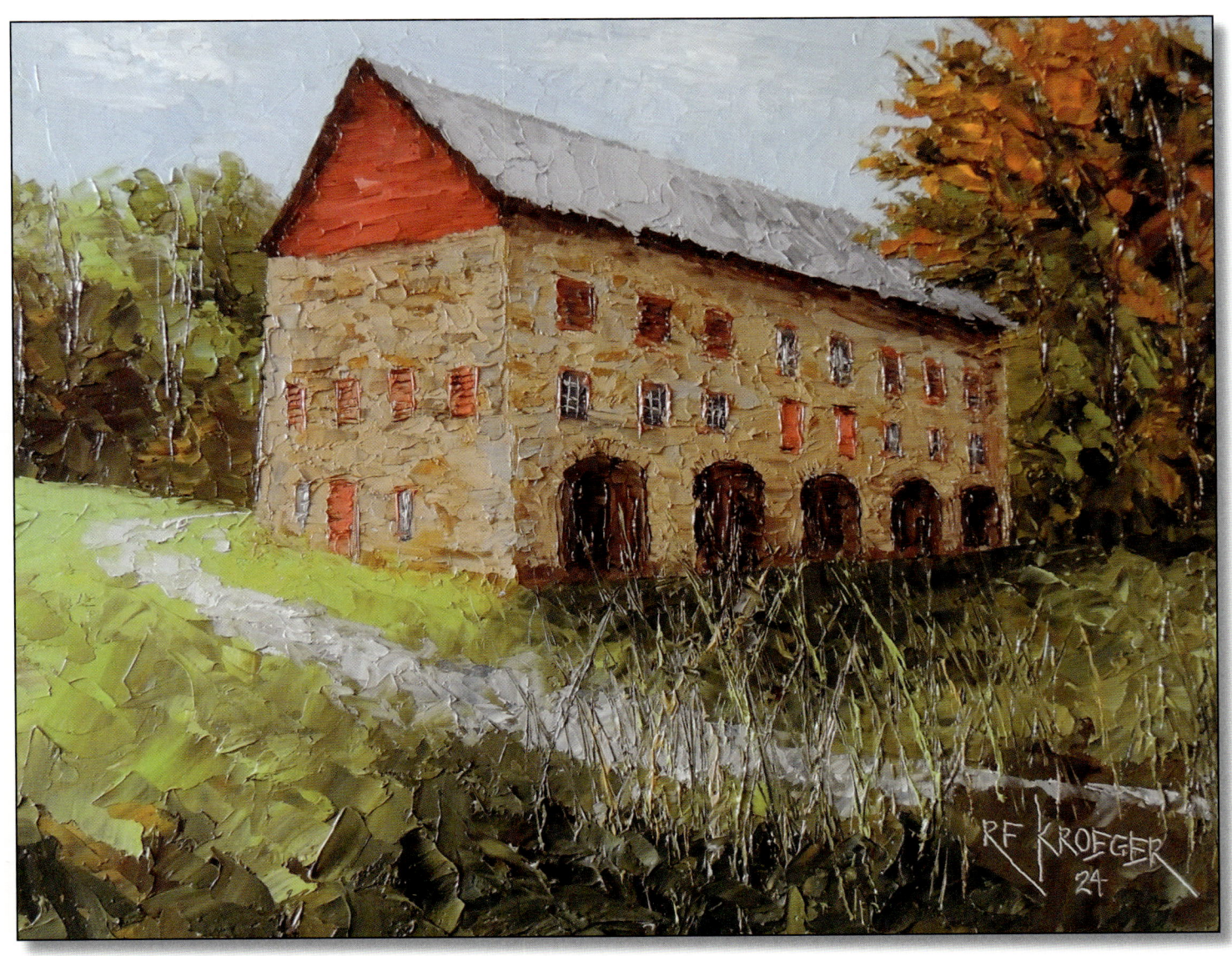

Jeras-Troxell Barn

Company in 1905 in New Jersey. After a fire, the company moved to Allentown and began producing explosive powder both in their facility in Lehigh County and at a site in California. Bronstein served as president of the company, which sold their products not only to the military during two world wars but also to companies that built roads and train lines through the country. It became known as the Trojan Powder Company. Jesse B. Bronstein, Jr., who joined the company in 1937 and became its president in 1961, continued his executive role after the firm was acquired by Commercial Solvents Corporation in 1967.

In the early years, in order to protect locals from possible explosions at the Allentown plant, Jesse bought adjacent farms, many that included historic buildings such as the Troxell house, the Blumer barn, and the Troxell barn with its stunning stone arches. After the sale of the factory to the CSC company in 1967, the family formed the Jeras Corporation and retained extensive acreage, which they lease to area farmers. The company maintains these stone barns, which remain historic icons, though they don't have an agricultural function.

Each letter in the name of the Jeras Corporation signifies an original family member, such as the company founder, Jesse B. Bronstein. One of the family's descendants and vice president of the company, Elizabeth Koontz, in an article, published in 2021, was quoted, "I am pretty old now. The J's and S's and A's in the name Jeras are all at rest in the Grandview Cemetery." Thanks to her family, the barns have been meticulously maintained and will continue to honor the memory of Reverend Abraham Blumer's patriotic deed of securing one of America's treasures – the Liberty Bell.

MONTGOMERY COUNTY

Heckler's Heritage

The date of 1761, carved into a wooden lintel over the wagon bay entrance to this stone barn, authenticates the year of its construction, showing that it's one of the oldest stone barns in Pennsylvania. Twenty years earlier, Lower Salford Township was established; its four villages, Harleysville, Lederach, Mainland and Vernfield, have distinctive Germanic roots.

Even earlier – in 1718 – one such German, a Mennonite, Hans Reiff, purchased 270 acres of land from David Powell, a surveyor and land speculator, according to a history of the township, written in the 1880s by James Y. Heckler. Since the area was large, Reiff, acting with consent of his neighbors, asked Philadelphia County officials to establish Lower Salford Township. Most of these immigrants came from northern Europe – Germany, Switzerland, and Holland – and most spoke and wrote in German or a close variation. That changed in the 1850s when the state ruled that all teaching in public schools must be conducted in English. Until that time, locals taught their children in German, mostly in one-room schoolhouses. For many, the transition to English was difficult and slow – with some residents continuing to speak Pennsylvania Dutch well into the 1900s.

As the township grew throughout the 18th and 19th century, villages were established, often centered around a tavern or inn. Though farming was the main occupation, businesses in towns included tinsmiths, harness and leather workers, weavers, and carriage-makers. Grist mills sprang up along streams, which also powered sawmills for cutting trees into lumber. Masons used abundant stone from local quarries to build houses, barns, and outbuildings, many of which have survived over 250 years later, including this stone barn.

Hans built two log cabins, one of which may have been situated on the present Heckler Plains location. Though archaeology students have excavated around the Heckler house, looking for signs of this cabin, they found only pottery shards. In 1746 Hans sold some outbuildings and a tract of 243 acres for £280 to Peter

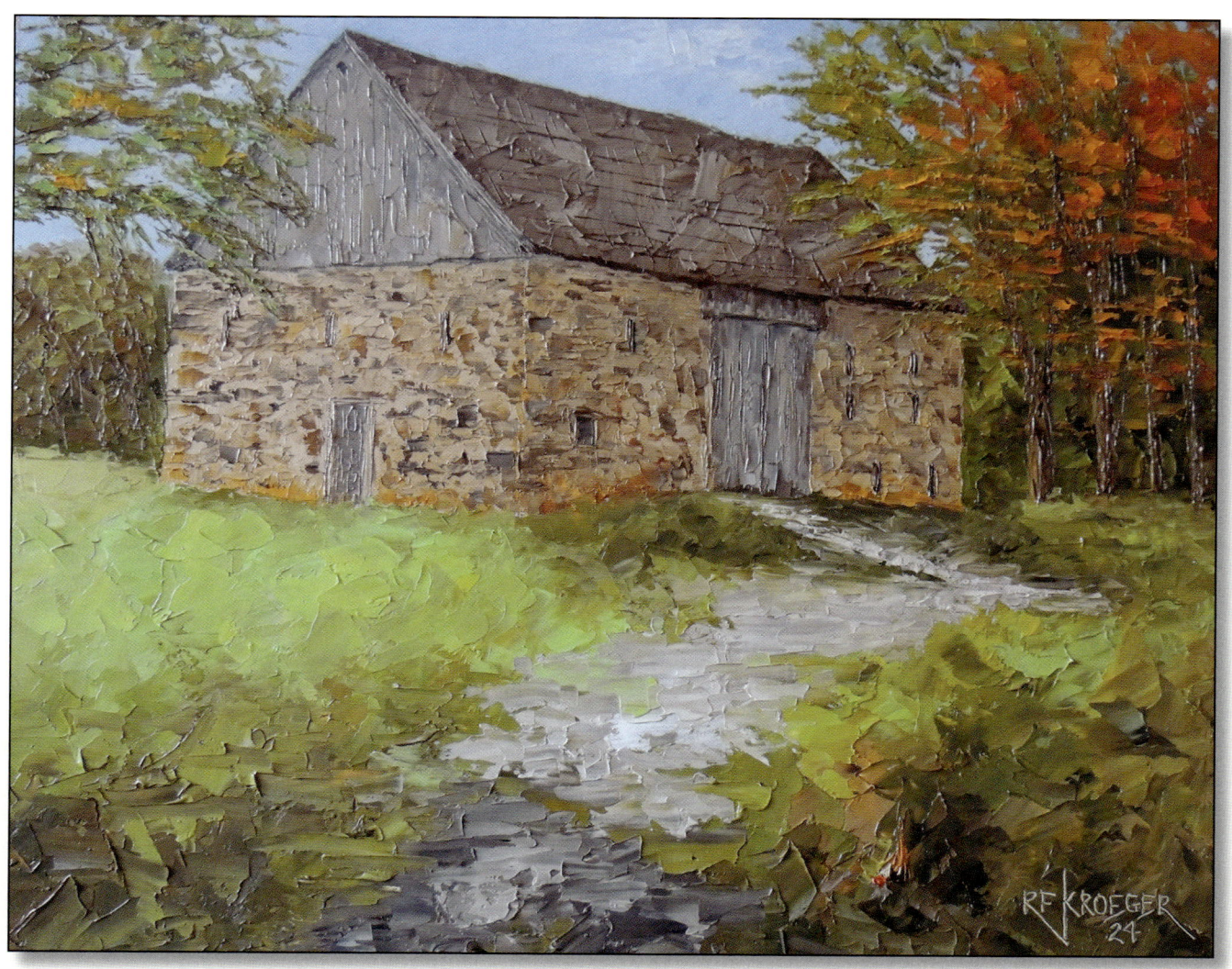

Heckler's Heritage

Freed, who may have been his son-in-law. Peter built this barn in 1761.

Unlike the traditional bank barn, this one, a Rhine Bottom type, was built with its threshing floor on the ground level between the livestock stalls. According to barn scholar Greg Huber, this barn is one of Pennsylvania's most outstanding and it may be the earliest ground barn in this region that is in essentially original condition. Hay and grain were stored on the level above the stables that are in the end bays. Wisely, the mason included ventilation slits, 18 inches long, on all walls, so necessary for livestock and hay storage. Original roof timbers rest on sturdy stone walls, 18 inches thick. Thanks to the local historical societies, a new, period-authentic, wooden shake roof has added even more charm. The stonework, an attractive arrangement of random rubble courses of local limestone, Pennsylvania stone, and Serpentine stone, was the work of a master stonemason. Fieldstones were likely quarried nearby or found in the fields after winter's freeze and spring's frost. Well-formed quoins support the corners and most of the original timber framing remains. Antique farm implements hang from the walls, an educational display for adults and children. Near the peak of an eave, a diamond-shaped owl hole remains – a swelmeloche, an old-fashioned way to get rid of mice and rats, always a threat to stored grain. Our host Don Orcutt commented on seeing owls in the barn. But no mice. Hmmmm.

At 56x34 feet, the barn was large enough for a small farm, enough to sustain the Freed family. In 1785 Peter sold the farm to his son-in-law George Heckler, another Mennonite, for £2,000, which he paid in installments.

George, whose name was originally spelled Hechler, was born in Retchweiler, Lower Alsace, a region bordering present-day France and Germany. He immigrated to the colonies in 1754, riding on the vessel *Neptune* – as an indentured servant, as did many who were unable to pay for their own passage. He worked for three years for John Stoner of North Coventry Township, Chester County, until his debt was satisfied, and then worked for him for seven more years. In 1764 he married Christina Freed.

Nine years later, enraged and over-taxed colonists dumped tea in Boston Harbor. On April 19, a day after Paul Revere's famous ride, the Revolutionary War began with the battles of Lexington and Concord. During these turbulent years, the Hecklers continued farming, though their involvement in the war was unlikely since their Quaker religion – a freedom established by William Penn in his 1701 *Charter of Privileges* – vehemently opposed war. During the War, about three dozen Mennonites fought with the British and others took up arms with the patriots. The church excommunicated both groups.

The Heckler land was heavily wooded, but a section of 40 acres was low and level, overgrown with bushes, berries, and briers, commonly called Hecklers Plain, which contained about 500 fruit trees, mostly apple and peach. Taking advantage of these trees, George decided to augment his income by building a distillery in 1795, making applejack liquor and peach brandy. This came only a year after General Anthony Wayne defeated the Indians in the Battle of Fallen Timbers in the Ohio Country, leading to settlement in the western half of present-day Ohio. Many from the eastern seaboard headed west, seeking less crowded land.

However, the Hecklers remained and branched out into other fields as well, showing their entrepreneurial spirit, using the apples for apple butter and for making a drink called cider oil, well-liked in colonial times. They raised bees, sold honey, and produced a liquor from honeycomb, called metheglin, a drink that had been popular in England for centuries. Other colonists were just as creative, brewing sassafras, birch, and spruce into beers and boiling roots and herbs to pair with pumpkin and apples, sweetened with maple syrup and molasses.

The family also raised sheep and harvested the wool, which women spun into yarn and men wove into cloth. Another business venture, tied closely to their family name, was dressing flax, which involved hetcheling or hackling, the process of separating coarse and fine fibers by pulling the flax through graduated heckling combs, rakes composed of various sizes of nails. After heckling and spinning, the flax was ready to be woven into linen. The German name Hechler means one who hackles flax. They also raised cattle and vegetables, taking their produce on horseback to markets in Philadelphia.

When George Heckler died in 1816, he gave the farm to his two sons Abraham and David, who held the property together until they divided it in 1839. David's part included the farmhouse, stone barn, and summer kitchen. After David's passing, his son George P. Heckler took over, keeping it in family hands until 1926, when it was sold to settle the widow Angeline's estate. Three years later the Hubickys, Ilko and Paracia, bought the farm and owned it until they died, when their son Paul became owner. In 1974 Paul sold the historic 35-acre farm – including the farmhouse and stone barn – to Lower Salford Township for $82,500 – with the provision that he be allowed to live on the property. He died in 1984.

Since that time, the 16,000 residents of this township have proved that they are fine stewards of history by periodically reliving pioneer days as well as by restoring and developing the grounds into a playground, ball fields, a bike path, a nature trail and a pavilion for local sports teams and family reunions. Thanks to the many volunteers in the Lower Salford Historical Society and Heckler Plains Folklife Society, children and adults can watch re-enactors performing ancient tasks such as hetcheling flax, candle dipping, redware pottery making, tin smithing and tin punching – common in colonial times – and fractur, the art of creating a Pennsylvania German document in calligraphy, illuminated with designs. Folklife Society members also demonstrate scherenschnitte, an artform, stemming from a German word, meaning scissor cuts. This tradition, which involves cutting intricate designs out of paper, traces back to the 18th-century German immigrants who settled here.

The Folklife Society members also maintain a four-square Pennsylvania German herb and vegetable garden at the farmstead and offer an annual herb festival each spring. They hold a colonial craft festival each August and host a Christmas Carol sing-along around a bonfire. Along with preserving these age-old traditions, they maintain both the farmhouse and the stone barn, which always entails significant expense. Yes, thanks to them, Heckler's heritage is alive and well.

A Proud Peg

When Greg and I visited the Heckler stone barn, I noticed something unusual – a window frame connected with wooden pegs. Though I've visited hundreds, if not thousands, of old barns in Ohio, Indiana, Kentucky, Michigan, and many other states, I've never seen this. I figured its individuality deserved a painting, even though

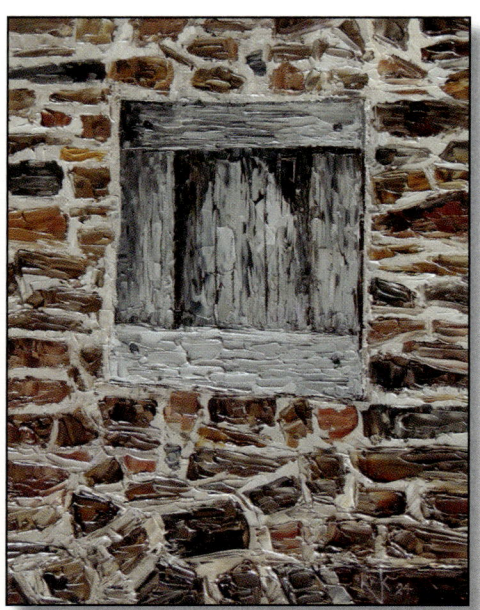

A Proud Peg

Greg mentioned that such pegs in window frames weren't uncommon in southeastern Pennsylvania. Neither are stone barns, though they're rarities elsewhere, I thought.

Prior to 1800 metal nails were expensive: it took time and skill for a blacksmith to forge a nail. For timber-framing barn builders, the mortise and tenon joint was an ancient technique, developed in the old countries of Europe. To connect the joint, the builder would carve a peg out of green wood to fit tightly into a hole that he drilled in the wood. With moisture and time, the peg would swell slightly, forming an airtight connection. In old American barns, these wooden joints have lasted over 200 years in some cases and in medieval stone barns in Britain the joints have lasted many hundreds of years.

In the colonies before the American revolution, England supplied the nails. But, when the war began, England stopped shipments, making nails a scarce commodity. In many villages, settlers would burn down old houses to recover valuable nails.

After the war in 1795, a Massachusetts entrepreneur named Jacob Perkins invented the cut-nail. He built a nail producing factory in Amesbury, which became a successful business, and was used elsewhere, despite his patent. The process involves cutting a nail from a sheet of raw iron. Such nails, often found in old barns, have flat heads and a cylindrical shaft, much different from the mass-produced common penny nail of today – with its rounded head and shaft. Perkins continued to invent things – including mechanical refrigeration in 1834 – and he received 40 patents in the United States and England.

However, although cut nails were available in the early 1800s in the young country, barn builders continued to use the traditional joint and its wooden peg. Eventually, cut nails became less expensive and were used in various applications in barns and homes. But old ways die slow deaths and the mortise and tenon joint and its wooden nail can still be seen in some transitional barns built in the early 20th century. And, in historic barns in southeastern Pennsylvania and adjacent states, if one pays attention, he might see a wooden window frame with a proud peg.

The Distillers

This farmstead, with its stunning stone barn, traces back to 1761 and Adam Hoffman, a miller and one of the first German immigrants to settle in the Welsh-Quaker region of Gwynedd, established by William Penn in 1698. Today, it's known as Upper Gwynedd Township.

In 1763 Hoffman sold the 150-acre farm to fellow German Johannes Kneip, a name that derives from the Middle High German knip, a cobbler's knife, which likely connotes that family members were shoemakers. The name was later anglicized to Knipe. Joseph, their sixth son, was born in 1766 on a farm that abuts the northeastern side of what would become his future home.

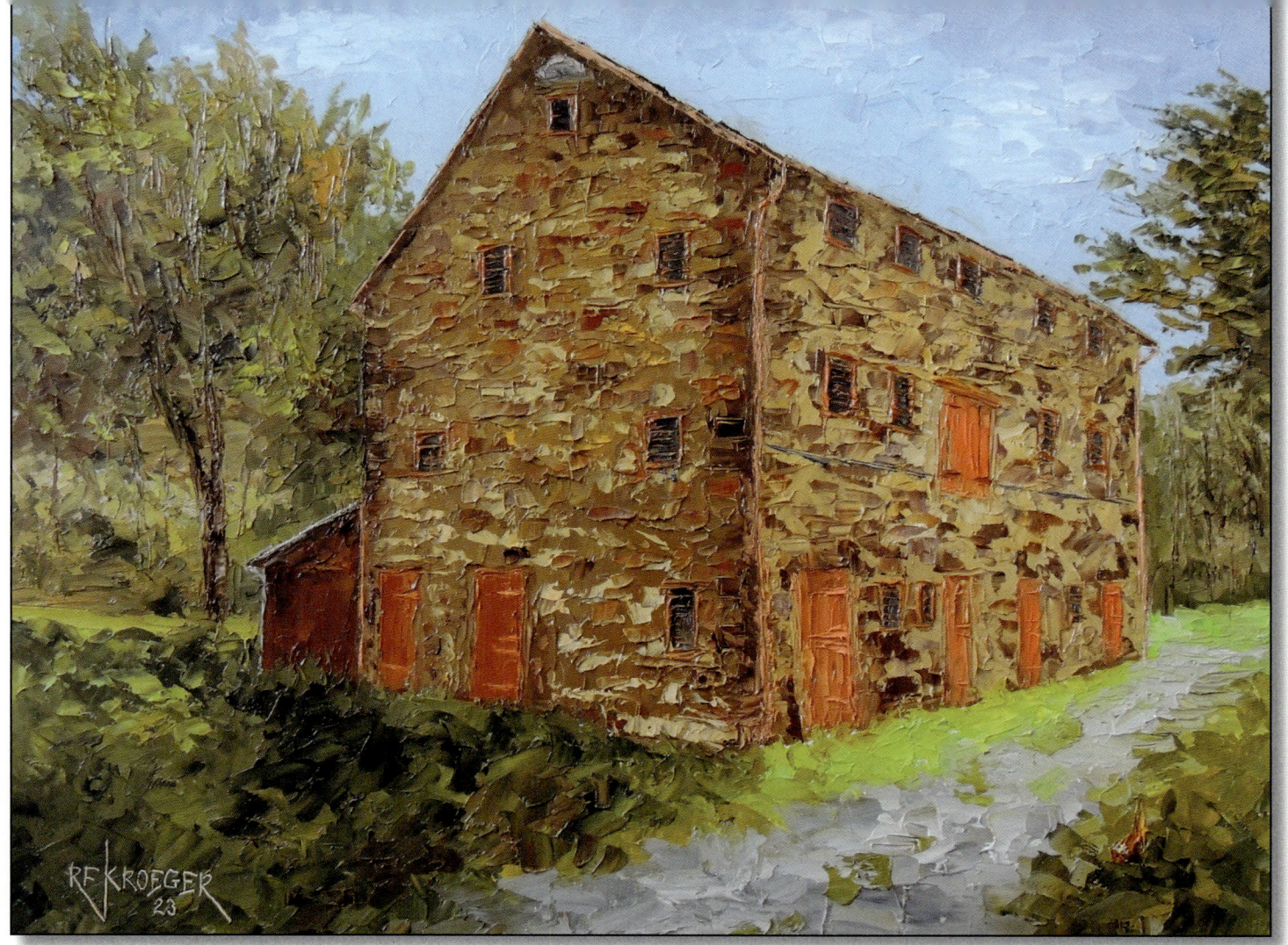

The Distillers

When, at 23, he married Anna in 1789, they lived on their parents' farm and began to have children. Within two years, they moved away, bought a tract of 30 acres from Daniel and Barbara Hemsher, and established the current farm, where Joseph raised crops and livestock. The family grew to include six children. In 1793 he purchased more land, 43 acres in two parcels from his brother Christian. At the time, the township tax assessor's records showed that Joseph's holdings included the 73-acre farm, two horses, two cows, and a still. This was the first of many references to his distilling, a business that tax records showed that his brothers David and Christian were also involved in. How much income the whiskey enterprise provided for the Knipes is not known, but it must have been profitable since many farmers had been engaged in it for years, if not decades.

Pennsylvanians like to claim that American whiskey was born in their state. Germans, Scots, Welsh, English, and Irish immigrants arrived in Pennsylvania in the 17th century, and most were farmers. Nearly all planted rye, which grew well in the rocky limestone soil, and being frugal, they didn't waste anything, including excess grain, which they used to brew beer and later whiskey. Distilling whiskey spread southward and westward over the years, where farmers began using corn, creating bourbon whiskey. Pennsylvanians stuck with rye.

After the Revolution, the young government had serious debt and began exploring ways to reduce this debt since there was no personal or corporate income tax at the time. Such taxation wouldn't be introduced until 1909. However, in 1791 politicians passed a bill that taxed liquor production, which was universally unpopular, especially in Pennsylvania, where farmers usually sold their product through bartering. Buying with cash was rare. Many, especially the small farmers, refused to pay this tax, making the job of collecting this tax difficult. In fact, 700 men showed their displeasure in 1794 by torching the Pennsylvania home of a one of these tax collectors, a wealthy landowner. Perhaps the memory of the Boston Tea Party, only 20 years earlier, was still fresh in their minds.

In response, President George Washington sent 13,000 troops to quell this rebellion; the leaders of it were tried, convicted, and sentenced to death, though

Washington eventually pardoned them. It was a good thing he did since he, himself, a prosperous farmer of over 5,000 acres, had begun distilling. After his first trial production was successful, he built a larger distillery, one with five copper pot stills. This new operation produced 4,500 gallons of whiskey in 1798 and almost 11,000 gallons in 1799 – with a profit in that year of $1,858, making the distillery Washington's most lucrative business. The whiskey tax, virtually impossible to collect, was repealed in 1802.

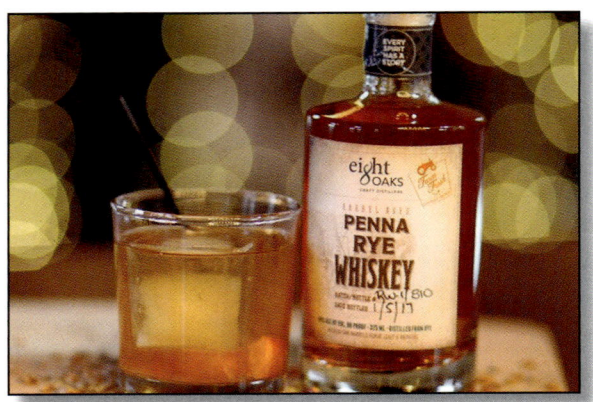

Pennsylvania Rye Whiskey, courtesy of Eight Oaks Distillery, New Tripoli, Pennsylvania.

In 1795, Joseph Knipe acquired more land, enlarging his farm to roughly 100 acres, a size that lasted for the next 56 years. In 1808, Joseph, apparently prosperous, built this massive stone barn, the year verified by a date stone in the top center of the southern gable. By this time, the Knipe family included six children, ranging in age from three to 19. Their family continued to thrive as children grew up and moved away throughout the early 1800s … until his wife died in 1837, an event that seemed to devastate Joseph. For the next few years, he lived with other relatives, leaving his son Joseph, Jr. in charge of the farm. But, by 1840 Joseph, now 74, had returned to the farm and in the following year he sold it to 28-year-old Adam Moore for a sum of $4,561, equivalent to about $160,000, a bargain in today's real estate market of Montgomery County.

By 1877, Adam Moore, his wife Ann, and their four children had expanded their farm to 108 acres and obviously were doing well. According to agricultural census records, their farm was one of the largest and most productive in the township. Along with raising crops – wheat, rye, oats, potatoes, corn, and hay, Moore had started a dairy business, which, like many in the region, had prospered during the Civil War years. He also produced eggs, poultry, and hogs as well as grapes and apples from his orchards. By June 1880, thanks to railroads, the Moores began shipping milk to butter and cheese factories. At this time, according to the farm census, the 67-year-old Adam lived with his wife and his bachelor son Daniel but rented the farm to his younger brother, 27-year-old Joseph K., who lived nearby.

Oddly, Adam did not want to sell or bequeath his sons with the farm. In 1884, shortly before turning 71, he wrote in his will that the farm be sold in a public auction within a year of his death, which came six months later.

It's unlikely that the auction was held publicly since Daniel and Joseph's brother-in-law John Shaw were the purchasers. They owned the farm for the next 12 years.

In 1897 Oliver Evans bought the farm, held it for a few years, and sold it in a public sale in 1902 to a Philadelphia woman, Mary Rupp of Germantown. Though the deed was in her name, her two bachelor brothers George and Ernest were the actual buyers of the property and had formed a tightly knit group of five siblings, who had lost their German immigrant parents "by disease and accident" in 1879. At that time, they were teenagers, which motivated their 70-year-old grandmother, Eva Babette Metzger Rupp, to relocate from Germany to care for her orphaned grandchildren. She remained the head of that household even after the children reached adulthood. According to a descendant, when they moved to the farm in 1902, Eva was in her nineties and was crippled with arthritis. She died there in 1906.

The Philadelphia Rupps decided to gentrify the farmhouse, adding a new front porch with gray fieldstone pillars and they renamed the property, Cedar View Farm. These city dwellers also tried farming, experimenting with asparagus, celery, and an orchard of over 1,000 fruit trees. Another descendant remembered that they cut ice blocks from a pond for storage in a stone icehouse, which also served as a springhouse and smokehouse and still existed at the time of the listing on the National Register in 2003.

Despite their urban roots, they continued farming through the difficult years of the 1920s and into the Great Depression until Ernest became ill, when the family's days of farming ended. When Mary, at 94, died in 1962, the family gifted the farm to three nieces. After one of them passed away in 1968, the two survivors established a family corporation, Mary M. Rupp, Inc., which remains the owner and has leased the land to tenant farmers throughout the years. Mrs. Grace Mucarella, a descendant, responded to my inquiry and explained in a hand-written letter that the barn "is perfectly preserved."

Ever since Pennsylvania passed reforms in 2011 that allowed distillers to offer tours, samples, and sales on-site, the number of craft distilleries increased dramatically. Today, there are several that use rye to make whiskey and offer tastings in Montgomery County, a heritage

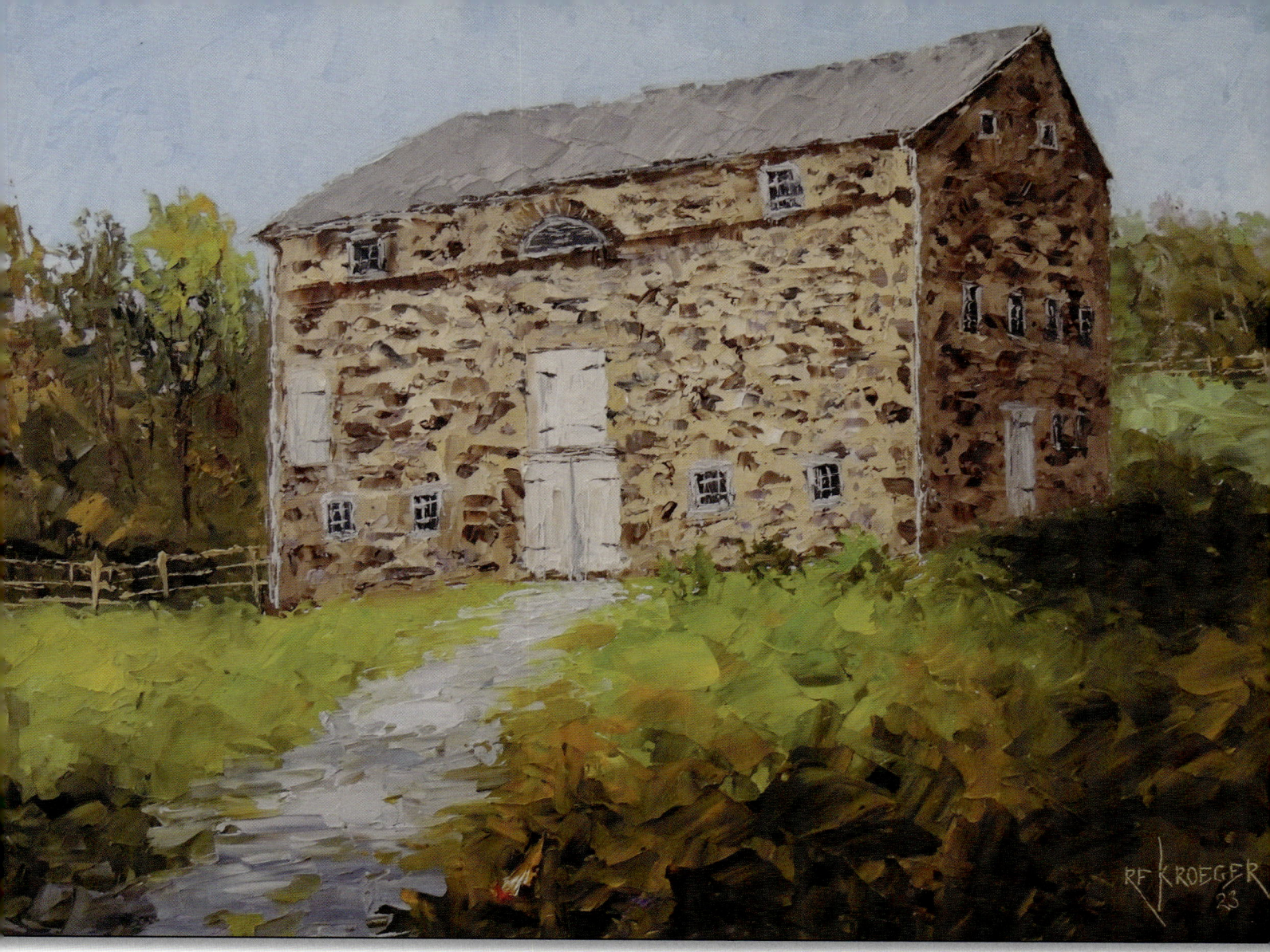

Patriotism Personified

that has been rekindled from 1790s. And, thanks to the Rupps, who have owned and maintained this impressive stone barn since 1902, it remains as a testament to the 19th-century Moore family farmers, and to Joseph Knipe, its builder and one of the early distillers of Pennsylvania rye whiskey.

NEW JERSEY

MERCER COUNTY

Patriotism Personified

It's appropriate that this farmstead and its striking stone barn are located in Mercer County, which is named for Brigadier General Hugh Mercer, a surgeon who not only died in the Battle of Princeton in 1777 and served with George Washington in the French and Indian War but also fought with the Jacobites at the Battle of Culloden in Scotland in 1746. Three months earlier, John Witherspoon,

an outspoken Scottish Presbyterian minister who opposed the Jacobite cause, was imprisoned in Doune Castle, following the Jacobite victory in the Battle of Falkirk Muir. Witherspoon founded the estate where this stone barn is located.

After the fall of Bonnie Prince Charlie and his highlanders at the Battle of Culloden, Witherspoon continued his prominent rise in church circles and, in 1766 he was offered the presidency of the College of New Jersey, which has evolved into Princeton University. Richard Stockton, whose wealthy father John had donated land for the college when it moved from Newark to Princeton, invited Witherspoon. Though, at the urging of his wife, Witherspoon initially turned down the invitation, he accepted it later, emigrated to America with his wife Elizabeth and five children, and moved to Princeton in 1768.

The primary purpose of the College of New Jersey, founded in 1746, was to educate men for the Protestant clergy. In 1768 Reverend Witherspoon became its sixth president, following five Congregational and Presbyterian ministers, and lived in the President's House at the college, now a National Landmark. When he arrived, the school had weak instruction, was saddled in debt, and had a mediocre library, which he augmented with 300 of his personal books. He also began reconstructing the curriculum, basing it on what was used at the University of Edinburgh and at other Scottish universities. His efforts at broadening the scope of studies paid off; one of Witherspoon's students, James Madison, became the fourth U.S. president and others rose to prominence in political and judicial circles. He also toughened up the admission criteria, hoping to compete with other institutions, such as Yale (1701) and Harvard (1636). At the sesquicentennial celebration in 1896, the name changed to Princeton University. His term as president lasted until 1794.

In 1774 Witherspoon began supporting the colonies' movement towards independence and was elected to the Continental Congress, where he was appointed congressional chaplain. Besides signing the Declaration of Independence, in his time in Congress he served on over 100 committees, helped organize the executive departments, and contributed to the Articles of Confederation.

During the war, as the British approached Princeton, Witherspoon closed and evacuated the college, which the army ravaged, destroying many of his papers and personal notes. However, after his surprise victory at Trenton, General Washington tricked the British and marched towards Princeton in January 1977. After winning this battle, Washington retreated to Morristown.

Though he lived in the president's house, in 1773 Witherspoon established an estate – only one mile from Nassau Hall on the college campus. He named it Tusculum, after the Roman town of the same name, where the orator and writer Cicero lived in a country villa. The stone house he had built included 5,000 square feet – with a study, kitchen, parlor, drawing room and two bedrooms. Although at first he rented the Georgian style home and allowed tenants to have a small garden, he preferred to farm the greater acreage himself, experimenting with various crops, much like George Washington did in his Virginia farmstead.

In 1779 Witherspoon decided to live in his estate at Tusculum, two years before the Battle of Yorktown, which led to the American victory. He continued running the college but towards the end of his presidency, his health declined, in part because of eye injuries, causing him to be blind by 1792. A year earlier, at 68, he remarried, this time to a 24-year-old widow, with whom he had two more children. He died in 1794.

Soon after he passed, a sales notice provided a good picture of his farming: "Beautiful farm called Tusculum … containing 238 acres of land … a kitchen garden enclosed by a dry laid wall, orchards, meadows, workable land and pastures … five horses for working and carriage; 2 beef cattle, 4 milk cows … 26 sheep or ewes, 14 pigs … The harvest yields substantial income from 14 or 15 acres of rye, 16 or 17 acres of oats, 20 acres of corn, 10 or 11 acres of buckwheat, one acre of flax, 1 acre of potatoes, 30 to 40 tons of hay."

His widow Anne sold the estate in 1796, which then went through a succession of owners until Richard Stockton purchased Tusculum in 1815. His father, also a Richard, was a signer of the Declaration of Independence and also influential in bringing Witherspoon to Princeton. One of his son Richard's nine children, Samuel Witham Stockton, inherited the estate upon the death of Richard in 1826. At the time Samuel was 25 years old and unmarried. Why he was chosen out of nine remains a question. His older brother Robert was a naval officer at the time.

Samuel did marry in 1833 and his wife Mary had two children, the second one arriving shortly after Samuel's untimely and mysterious death in 1836. He may have already built this stone barn by then or that honor may go to his older brother Robert, who assumed control of the estate after Samuel died.

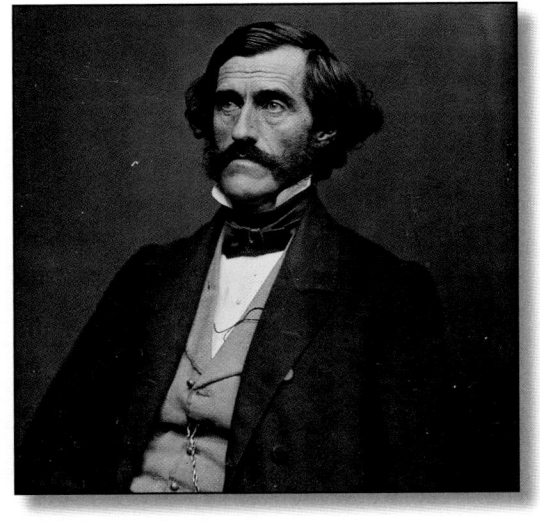

Commodore Robert F. Stockton, circa 1835. WikiCommons

Shortly after he turned 16, Robert dropped out of school to join the Navy at the outbreak of the War of 1812. He was appointed a midshipman, served with distinction, earned the nickname "Fighting Bob," and was promoted to lieutenant. After the war, he continued his naval career on the *Erie*, which cruised in the Mediterranean, where he became an ardent opponent of flogging. In fact, when he took command of the *Alligator* in 1821, he threw the ship's flogging lash overboard. Thirty years later, as a U.S. senator, he would sponsor a bill to abolish flogging in the Navy.

A sailor at heart, Stockton, while in command of the *Alligator*, became the first Navy officer to fight slavery when he negotiated a treaty with an African war lord to establish the country of Liberia as a haven for freed American enslaved people. It became Africa's first and oldest modern republic. Stockton also captured slave ships, including several off the coast of Spanish-controlled Cuba, where, if unable to apprehend the slavers at sea, he would lead his crew to track them down onshore.

After these heroics and after 14 years at sea, the Navy granted Robert an extended leave to attend to his holdings in New Jersey and the Tellurium Gold Mine in Virginia, which he operated and eventually purchased in 1848.

Robert resumed his Navy duty in 1838, this time as a captain, sailing in the European region. Though offered the position of Secretary of the Navy by President Tyler in 1841, he declined, perhaps feeling it would not be as exciting as being at sea. Four years later, under orders from President Tyler, he sailed on the *USS Princeton*, the country's first steam-powered ship-of-war, one that Stockton encouraged the Navy to build. His ship headed to Texas with an offer to Mexico from Congress to annex the land.

After this negotiation, Stockton returned to the President, warning him of a looming war with Mexico. After hearing that, the president sent him to the coast of California, where Stockton took over command of the Pacific fleet – with a combined force of about 3,000 sailors in three frigates, a naval warship, and four sloops. Arriving in December 1846, off the coast of Monterey, he came to the rescue of Brigadier General Stephen Kearny, wounded himself and in charge of 60 weary dragoons, whom the Mexican-Californio army had surrounded. After rescuing the trapped army, Stockton joined forces with General Kearney and John Fremont's California Battalion, and they defeated the Mexicans, forcing the Treaty of Cahuenga, which ended the fighting and won California for the United States. Stockton served as the second military governor of the new territory.

In the 1850s, Robert appointed his son, John Potter Stockton, to be in charge of tenant farming at Tusculum. During this decade, the Stocktons sold the estate, which went through several hands before Edward Jewell bought it in 1857, holding on to it for nearly 30 years. A dentist, Dr. Pardoe, bought it and lived there until he sold it to the Pardee family in 1924.

The Pardees occupied Tusculum for most of the 20th century and wisely set aside 20 acres for historic preservation. Mrs. Ario Pardee submitted a nomination for a listing on the National Register, which was approved in 1978.

The listing included the stone barn, as well as other stone buildings dating to the 1790s – a springhouse, icehouse, and farmhouse. The barn and farmhouse – along with nearby Nassau Hall, the oldest (1756) building at Princeton University – were built with argillite, a light brown sandstone quarried locally.

The barn, described by some as one of the 10 most interesting buildings in New Jersey, dates to the 1830s. Regardless of whether the builder was Samuel or Robert Stockton, the exquisite stonemasonry showed that their finances could afford to hire a master stonemason. Sitting into a slight bank, the three-story barn contains elements of Dutch, English, and German design, rarely seen in stone barns. In years past, it served its farmers well – for livestock and crop storage as well as for threshing grain. It could hold as many as 50 cattle.

According to Greg Huber, the barn has several rare features. At the top of the front wall and just below the windows, there's a stone ledge, which is seldom seen on front walls of stone barns. Other unique aspects of this barn are the five Dutch bays and two rare king posts on the upper floor, making this essentially a Dutch derivative barn. Why the barn builder, likely familiar with all three types of barns, combined Dutch, English, and German designs is unknown. Some mysteries will remain unsolved.

Measuring 45x57 feet, its size was unusually large for a stone barn in the 1830s. Threshing was done on the upper level, hay was stored in the mow, and livestock were housed on the ground level. Though the forebay is gone today, there's evidence that it originally stretched across the entire south wall of the barn, a traditional German-Swiss characteristic. Openings on all four sides, now covered with window frames and panes, were likely louvered openings for ventilation when the barn was built. Massive Dutch doors rise above the bank on the north side.

The mason may have been familiar with Nassau Hall, built in 1756 for the college and only a mile from the barn. In fact, its beauty may have swayed him into using the same stone – argillite – and into incorporating decorative keystone arches on both the north and south façades. The large dressed dark brown quoins and the randomly coursed stone, its colors artistically mixed, show that he was a highly skilled stonemason.

Thomas and Avril Moore purchased Tusculum and its 82 acres in 1996, when it was in significant deterioration. They closed the gaps in the roof of the farmhouse, replaced support beams, and repaired floors, eaten by powderpost beetles. In 2006 they sold 35 acres to Princeton Township for a greenbelt to preserve the native landscape and in 2007 they put the property up for sale with a price tag of $12 million. With no takers, they continued to live on the estate.

Six years later in 2013, they again listed the house, this time for $6.5 million. When that didn't attract buyers, the realty company put it up for auction in November, which did result in a sale – for $5.5 million to Meredith Asplundh and Tim Gardner. Historical preservationists, they hosted an event in 2022 that benefitted Crossroads of the American Revolution, a nonprofit that focuses on early American history in this region.

This barn painting and essay help to relive the memories of the array of influential early Americans, including Reverend John Witherspoon and his son James who died in the Battle of Germantown, Richard Stockton, another signer of the Declaration of Independence, whose son Richard purchased Tusculum, and his son Robert, a Navy officer, who fought against slavery and helped win California for the young United States. In those early years, America grew and prospered, thanks to their courage and guidance, which can be summed up in two words: patriotism personified.

Crossing the Delaware

Rarely does an old stone barn sit on the grounds of a national landmark, much less than one that changed the course of American history. Military historians have called Washington and his army crossing the Delaware the first "turning point of the American Revolution." The ferry master, who owned this farm, played a pivotal part in this crossing.

In Titusville, New Jersey, and on the banks of the Delaware River across from Pennsylvania, Garrett Johnson built a timber framed, clapboard-sided house on his 490-acre plantation around 1740. Several years later – in 1748 – he began operating a ferry service across the river, which became known as the Johnson Ferry.

About 30 years later, the colonies rebelled against England, formed a Continental Congress, and appointed

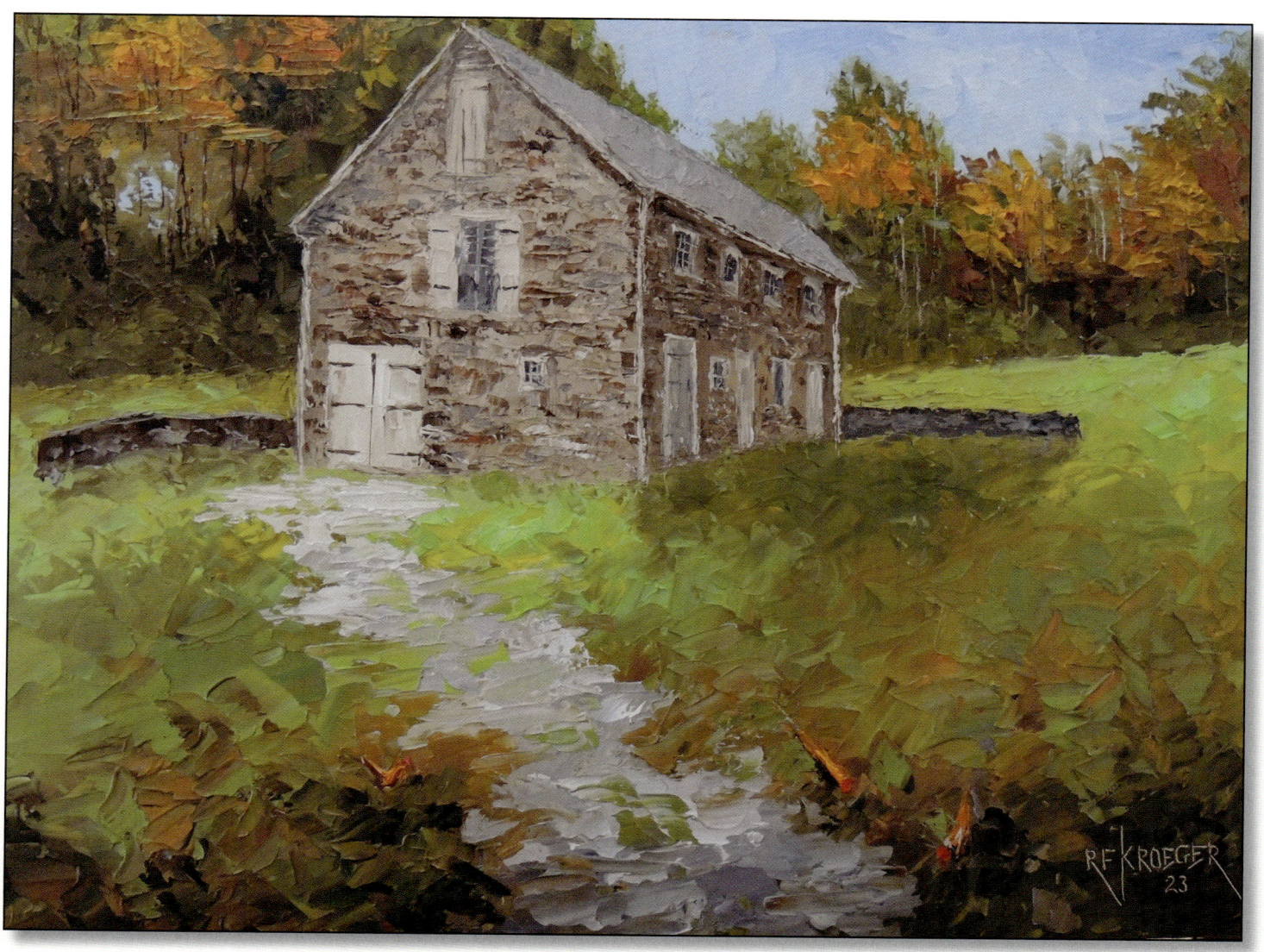

Crossing the Delaware

Virginia farmer George Washington as commander of the army. Ironically, many years earlier Britain made a huge mistake when it refused to give an officer's commission to Washington, despite his valiant service in the French and Indian War. After this snub, Washington was happy to lead the colonists, though he got off to a rocky start.

In August 1776, the same month that delegates signed the Declaration of Independence, the British and their Hessian allies (conscripted from present-day Germany) invaded New York, defeated the Americans in the Battle of Long Island, and drove them out of Manhattan. They pursued Washington's army that retreated across the Delaware River into Pennsylvania. Luckily, the British could not find boats to cross and, instead, went into winter quarters, leaving Hessian troops in Trenton, New Jersey. It was cold that December.

Morale was low in the fledgling militia and Washington faced another problem: the enlistments of most of his soldiers were due to expire at the end of December, when they would be free to return to their homes. The general knew something needed to turn the tide and devised a plan – to attack the British – mostly Hessians – across the river in Trenton. It was Christmas day and it was frigid … and maybe it was Washington's last chance to keep a ragged and starving army together. "I am determined, as the night is favorable, to cross the River, and make the attack upon Trenton in the Morning," Washington wrote. Others weren't so sure the general's plan would succeed. John Greenwood, Fifer, 15th Massachusetts Regiment, wrote in his diary, "We had to wait for the rest and so began to pull down the fences and made fires to warm ourselves, for the storm was increasing rapidly. After a while it rained, hailed, snowed, and froze, and at the same time blew a perfect hurricane."

So, hoping to use the element of surprise, Washington led his troops that Christmas afternoon across the river in long ferry boats, loaded with men, horses, and cannons. However, the weather didn't cooperate. A storm developed around midnight, making the ice-clogged river even more difficult to cross – sleet, hail, and snow came with a fury. Colonel Henry Knox, Continental Artillery, recorded his thoughts, "… the army… passed the river on Christmas night, with almost infinite difficulty. … The floating ice in the river made the labor almost incredible. However perseverance accomplished what at first seemed impossible…. The night was cold and stormy; it hailed with great violence…."

For nearly 10 hours, Washington and 2,400 soldiers of the Continental Army crossed in boats and ferries, landing at Johnson's Ferry, then owned by James Slack, who may have provided them with shelter and food in his house. Once in New Jersey at nearly 4 a.m., the troops marched – some without shoes – towards Trenton, a nine-mile journey in the snow. Finally arriving in Trenton at daybreak, they attacked the Hessians, taking them by complete surprise, overrunning the town, and killing their commander. They soon surrendered. The battle lasted an hour and a half. The Americans had killed or wounded 100 Hessians and took 900 prisoners, along with their weapons and artillery. Their own losses were small – two dead and five wounded, including future president James Monroe, who was shot in his shoulder.

Though Washington wanted to continue to battle the British at Princeton, once he learned that some of his troops failed to cross the Delaware, coupled with continued bad weather, he re-crossed the river once again. He marched the Hessian prisoners into Philadelphia, sparking news of the victory throughout the colonies and giving Washington and his officers renewed hope.

Upon returning to Johnson's Landing, Washington crossed the Delaware yet again, this time marching to Trenton for a minor victory and then onto Princeton for yet another win. These successes made other countries, France, Holland, and Spain – no friends of England – suspect that perhaps the colonists might succeed. Thanks to support from France, they did.

After the war, Abraham Harvey, a wealthy Quaker farmer from across the river in Bucks County, built this stone barn, circa 1786-1788. The fieldstone English bank barn replaced an earlier one, a Dutch frame barn, built around 1740 by Garrett Johnson, the ferry operator. Later, Moses Harvey, Abraham's son, lived here and ran the ferry business. After Samuel Thomlinson purchased the farm in 1801, it passed through several owners until the state of New Jersey bought it in 1922.

Mercer County, where this stone barn sits, takes its name from another patriot, Brigadier General Hugh Mercer, who led the troops with Washington across the icy river that Christmas night. Born in Scotland in 1726, Mercer, a seasoned teenager in 1745, became a physician, joining the Jacobites and Bonnie Prince Charlie as an assistant surgeon. He served in the Battle of Culloden, the last gasp of the Scottish highlanders and a terrible loss for them. English soldiers hunted down Prince Charlie's supporters, killing as many as they could, forcing Hugh Mercer to flee to America in 1747. He settled in Pennsylvania and practiced medicine for eight years.

During the Battle of Princeton on January 3, Mercer's brigade of 350 battled a superior British force and, as his horse was shot, he fell to the ground and was ordered to surrender. Instead, he drew his sword and, though outnumbered badly, began to fight the same army that he had fought against 30 years earlier at Culloden. He was bayoneted seven times and left for dead by soldiers who thought he was Washington. Still with a bayonet impaled in him, Mercer refused to leave his men, inspiring them and General Washington to rally the troops to victory. Mercer died nine days later.

Attractive fieldstone walls suggest that a master stonemason built this barn, using fieldstones that had been gathered over a 40-year period of clearing woods for cropland. Typically, each spring the Johnson and Harvey families would use a sled to move the rocks from the fields over to the fence lines, stockpiling them for future building projects. Built into a steep hillside, the barn's lower end features an upper-level haymow and a Dutch door on the ground level. However, the original barn has been altered over the years.

Thanks to Nancy Ceperley Deal, historian at the Johnson Ferry House, and Ralph Dowdell, volunteer at the barn who maintained an 18th-century carpentry display inside the barn for years, the changes have been documented. During the Great Depression, workers, likely the Civilian Conservation Corps, converted the barn into a visitor center. This project involved adding bathrooms and removing the third floor. Workers also repaired mortaring around the fieldstones, which they left in place, testifying to the skill of the master stonemason, who built this barn. The mason likely would have used stones from the family stockpile, although stone outcroppings near tributaries of the Delaware River may have provided larger rocks for the quoins.

Inside, a swing beam, hand-hewn and likely repurposed from the earlier Dutch barn, runs the entire length of the barn. Log rafters, flattened only on the ends, rest directly on the 16-inch stone walls, a feature seen in many stone barns that eliminates the need for traditional timber framing. There are no center supporting posts. The size of the barn, 40x27 feet, has also fluctuated over the years – as have doors and windows.

The back of the barn featured an unusual ramp to a large – 16x18-foot – barn door. From about 20 feet away, it proceeded along the back wall, rising about seven feet during a 30-foot run, before turning abruptly to the left. Ralph commented on this unique design, which was discovered in a 1920s-era aerial photo, "I would feel uneasy about trying to negotiate a pair of oxen around that sharp turn, high in the air, knowing that oxen don't back up well."

The 18th-century farmers likely raised grain for threshing and hay for feed, and had a few milk cows, evidenced by a milking room and a trap door where hay dropped down to animal stalls. But, with a relatively small sized barn, the families most likely produced only enough food for themselves, selling minimally, and may have had other occupations to supplement their income.

Today, the barn and farmhouse-tavern serve as venues for public events, including educational meetings and lectures. Ralph's woodworking shop on the lower level has been removed; now it's used for storage. To demonstrate the historic crossing, Washington Crossing State Park displays a full-scale 40-foot-long authentic reproduction of the ferry barge, originally designed and built by Nancy's father, Mike Carter. After it weathered beyond repair, Mike's son Thomas built a new one, displayed in the photograph.

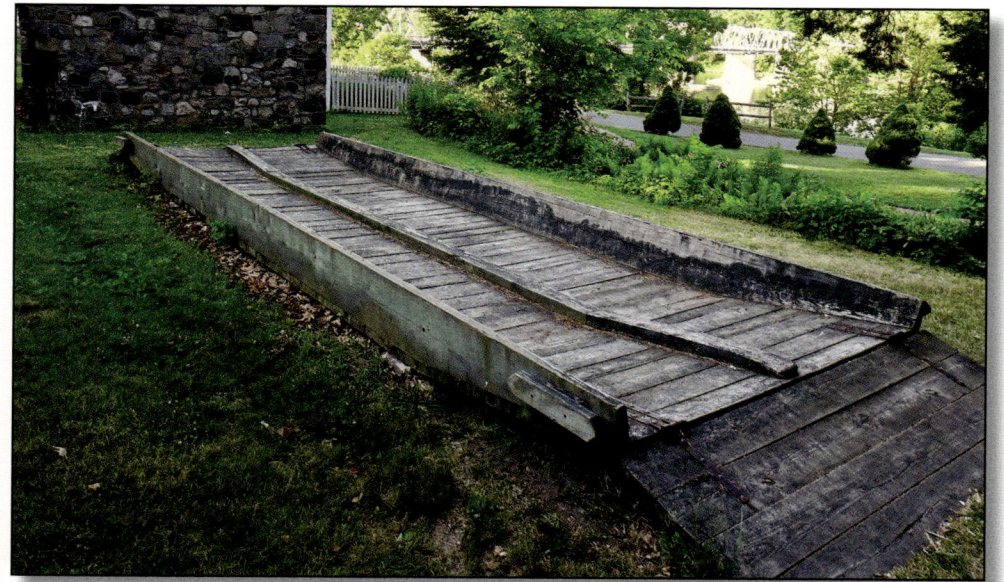

The New Jersey Division of Parks and Forestry maintains this historic site, which is supported by the Washington Crossing Park Association, a nonprofit of locals that works to preserve the history of the famous crossing, occasionally staging reenactments. Washington's Crossing was named a National Landmark area in 1961 and was listed on the National Register in 1966. On the Pennsylvania side of the Delaware, a well-maintained state park of 478 acres preserves history, as well. Samuel McConkey operated the ferry business on the Pennsylvania side in 1776.

Replica Ferry Barge, Washington's Crossing the Delaware, courtesy of Washington Crossing State Park

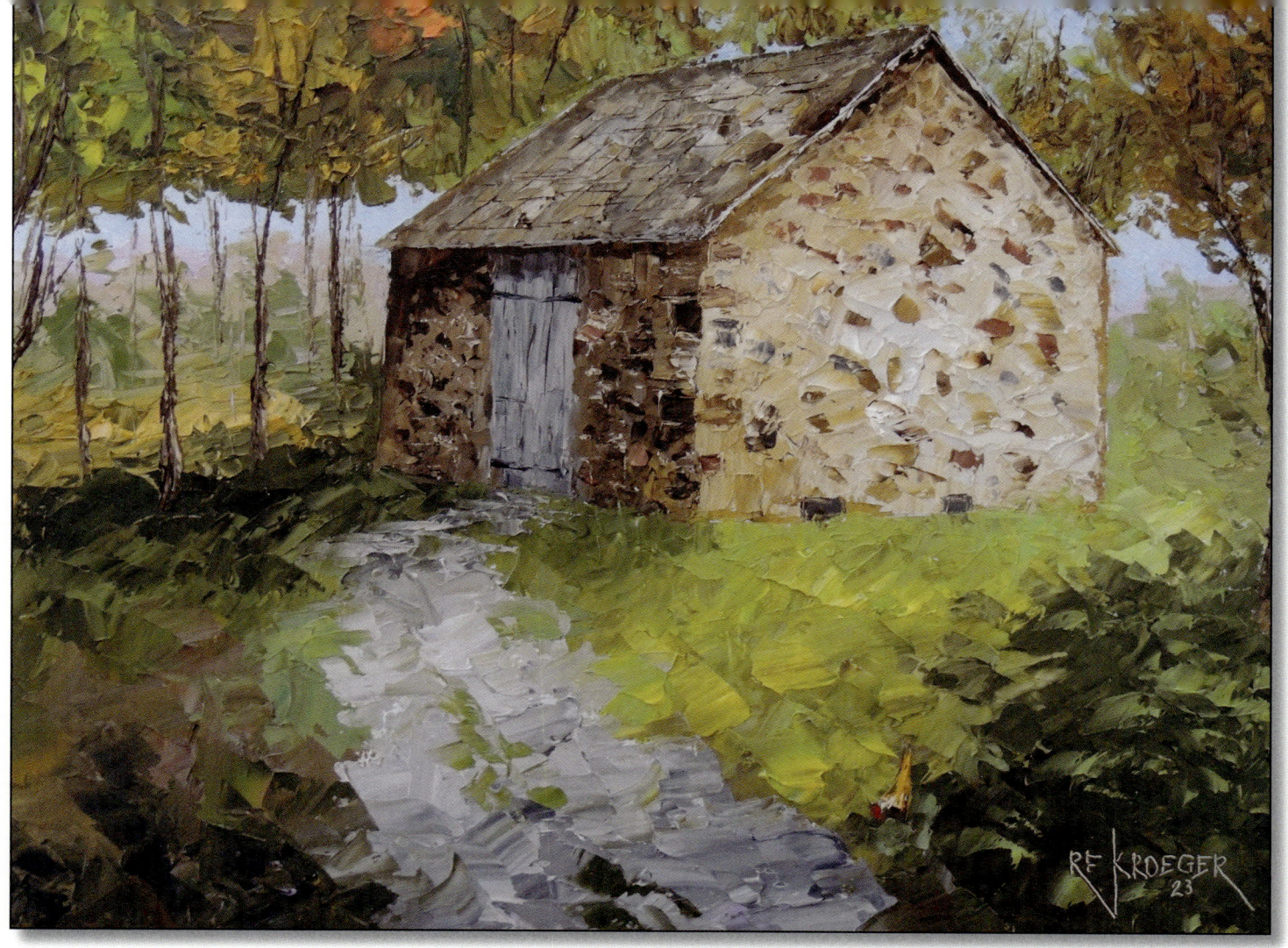

The Kilns of New Castle County

Though the barn did not witness the famous crossing by generals Washington and Mercer and their armies, it still stands on the ground where these heroic men staged a comeback from earlier defeats and continued the quest for American independence, a gift that all should be grateful for.

DELAWARE

NEW CASTLE COUNTY

The Kilns of New Castle County

This colorful fieldstone barn, a small garden variety of the English three-bay style, dates to 1809 and lies within the Eastburn-Jeanes Lime Kilns Historic District, which was listed on the National Register in 1977. At the time of the listing, the barn, together with eight lime kilns, two abandoned quarries, and various other stone buildings illustrated a unique local industry – the production of lime, used both as fertilizer and in the mixture of mortar for stone construction.

David Eastburn, born in Bucks County, Pennsylvania, in 1773, three years before the Declaration of Independence, was the 10th of 11 children in a Quaker family. In 1801

he married Elizabeth Jeanes and eventually they moved to New Castle County, Delaware, where they began farming on Paper Mill Road. David was likely the one who built this stone barn, probably using stone from a nearby quarry, which might have been on his own property.

Like many Eastburns, David and his wife had many children. Fourteen of them. Joseph, their first child, was born in 1802, before the family moved to Delaware. As a teenager, he helped his father in a secondary business in burning lime, an important ingredient in mortar mixes. In time, they also sold lime for use as an inorganic fertilizer. However, like most farmers, their primary job was to farm enough to support their family.

The other part of this story is Abel Jeanes, the brother of Elizabeth, who was also born in Pennsylvania – in 1795. The youngest of 12 children, he, too, moved to Delaware and bought a farm along Pike Creek. Around 1816 Abel formed a partnership with his brother-in-law David to quarry limestone and burn lime. The business, though small, provided income to supplement their farming.

When David died unexpectedly in 1824, at only 51, his oldest child Joseph was 22 and his youngest was only six days old. And, though he passed early, he had acquired substantial land for future Eastburn generations. As often happened in the 19th century when the patriarch died, the widow and her children kept the farm going. In this case, Joseph also continued running the lime business with his uncle Abel.

Apparently, as farmers in the area expanded their acreage and used more fertilizer, demand for lime grew, mushrooming the Eastburn-Jeanes enterprise into a full-time business. Reflecting such prosperity, Abel Jeanes built a massive stone barn in 1832, which unfortunately burned in the early 1940s, leaving only a stone skeleton. The huge barn was large enough to house his livestock, including 12 yoke of oxen and 38 horses. Why so many? Abel and Joseph needed animals to transport their growing lime production. As word spread, they began delivering their product to sites further away – as far south as Middletown and as far north as Lancaster, Pennsylvania, a distance of about 40 miles, which took considerable time when traveling with a team of horses or hauling a heavy wagon load with oxen.

By the 1840s, they employed dozens of workers, 14 working for Eastburn and about 30 working for Jeanes, keeping the kilns burning all day long, quarrying stone and timber, and delivering goods to market. Seven kilns operated on the Eastburn farm and about a dozen on Abel's farm, a

stone's throw across the street. As their business expanded, they built more structures, all made from local limestone, including a shed for storing wagons, a springhouse, and a wheelwright's shop, where workers repaired and maintained wagon wheels, analogous to the automotive repair shops a hundred years later. Some buildings still stand.

Today, several of these kilns can be seen on the side of Pike Creek Road, formerly only a dirt trail but now covered with asphalt. Each kiln stands anywhere from 15 to 23 feet high, its beehive shape built into the slope of a hillside, which protected the fire from wind and, located roadside, made loading the wagons an efficient process. Built by masons, the stacked limestone proved to be an ideal material for kilns. In 1816, records showed that the annual production was 95,000 bushels of quarried limestone for the Eastburn-Jeanes company. Each kiln could produce 300 bushels of lime every 24 hours. They kept the kilns burning year round.

Workers, employed by Abel and Joseph, used sledges, hand drills, and possibly black powder charges to quarry rocks, which they broke into stones smaller than 10 cubic inches. They also cut timber, lots of it, to keep the kiln fires burning. Every six to eight hours, workers would use

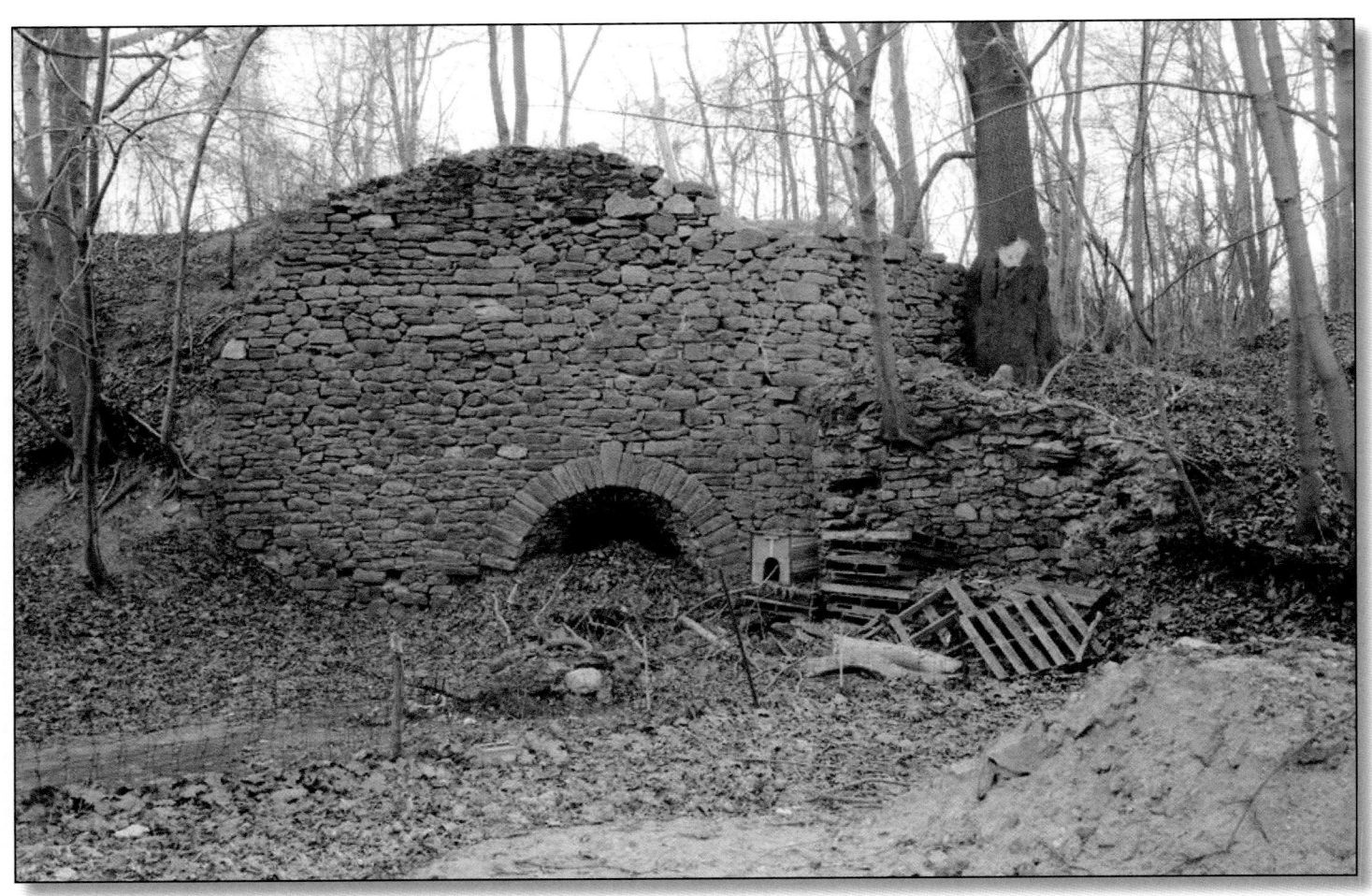

Eastburn Lime Kiln, circa 1900. Wikimedia Commons.

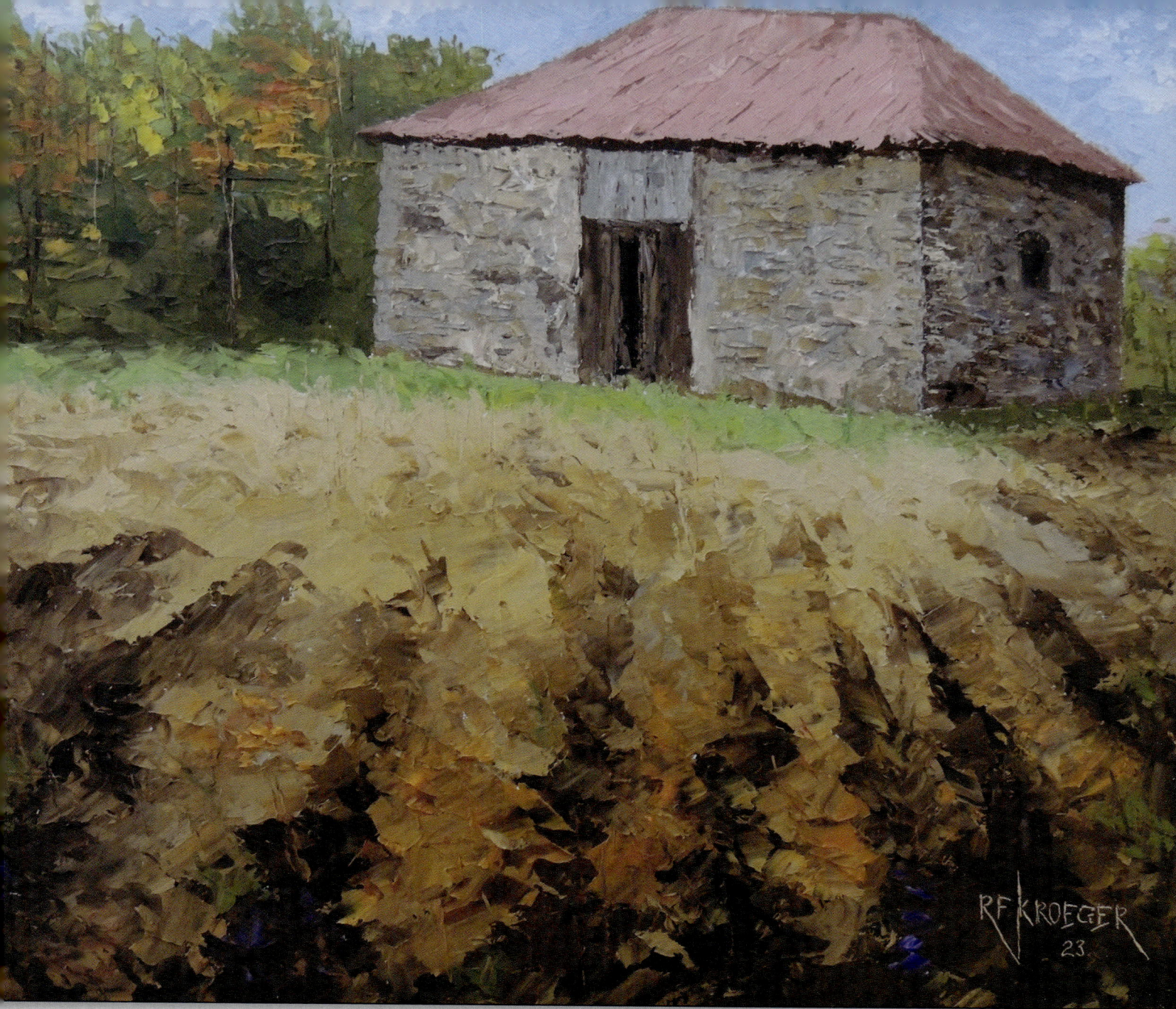

The Battle That Saved Washington

a long hook-shaped rake to remove the burnt lime from below the iron grate. The work lasted all day and night, seven days a week. They built more kilns as they needed them. Business was good and continued throughout the 19th century.

Apparently, the lime business agreed with Abel and Joseph so well that they far exceeded the average male life expectancy of 44. Abel, 85, died in 1880 and Joseph, 80, died in 1882. His son, also Joseph, born in 1847, continued running the business, though it began to slow down in the 1890s. Eventually, the Eastburn-Jeanes business could not compete with larger and more efficient lime-producing operations elsewhere, which sold lime products for less money. By 1900 Joseph shut down the kilns.

Though lime kilns were numerous throughout the early 19th century in the eastern United States, most have disappeared, making way for industry and housing developments. However, this attractive stone barn survives, thanks in part to its mortar, a product of the kilns of New Castle County.

MARYLAND

FREDERICK COUNTY
The Battle That Saved Washington

It's unknown whether the French Vincendières family started their slave plantation on Saint-Domingue (present-day Haiti) before or after the French Revolution, a rebellion which gained momentum with the storming of the Bastille in 1789. Another factor that might have led the family to flee to Maryland was the Haitian Revolution that began in 1791 and lasted until 1804, when the colony of Saint-Domingue gained its independence from France. It was the largest slave uprising since Spartacus' revolt against the Roman Republic, 1,900 years earlier.

Fearing the loss of their plantation, the family either sold their land or simply left the island, one that was rich in sugar and coffee and, by 1760, the most profitable colony in the Americas. In 1793 the Vincendières began slowly to acquire tracts of farmland that would become a 748-acre plantation in Frederick County. They left Saint-Domingue with 12 African slaves, the most that Maryland law allowed them to bring. However, most likely through private sales or auctions, they purchased more and soon their plantation had second largest number of slaves in the entire county. The family called their estate L'Hermitage, a French word for the dwelling of a hermit – an odd name, since there were mostly enslaved people on the farm, and no hermits. By 1800, Victoire Vincendière, a female, was the legal head of the plantation, which was home to 108 people. Ninety of the 108 were enslaved; indeed, the family was lucky their workforce didn't revolt. In those days having a stone barn and a large number of slaves showed the landowner's wealth. Victoire built the barn around 1798.

Records show that they were cruel to the slaves. In June of 1798, a Polish diplomat, Julian Niemcewicz, traveling by coach, recorded his impressions as he passed the farm, "One can see on the home farm instruments of torture, stocks, wooden horses, whips, etc. Two or three negroes crippled with torture have brought legal action ..." And, since the farm had over 700 acres, many laborers were needed to work it. However, perhaps farming did not agree with Victoire.

For unknown reasons, by 1816 she began selling sections of the farm. By 1829 the household had shrunk to 11, including four freed slaves and the number of the enslaved laborers had dropped from 90 to 48. She sold the farm to John Brien, a wealthy landowner in Frederick and Washington counties, for $24,025, more than 10 times its value in 1798. Victoire Vincendière moved to a townhouse in Frederick, Maryland, where she lived until she passed in 1854.

Over the years, the farm traded hands until it was purchased by Charles E. Trail in 1852, who likely considered it an investment since he never farmed it himself,

only rented it to tenant farmers. One of those was David Best. Though they never owned the farm, the family farmed it until National Park Service acquired it in 1993. It was added to the National Register in 1975.

Born in 1804 in Adams County, Pennsylvania, David married Ann Mary Lentz of Frederick County in 1831 and remained in the county, working on the Trail farm in 1852 and, like the Vincendière family, using slave labor. Though they had four children, including two sons, Best needed slaves to work the large farm. In fact, he used some of his slaves as collateral for loans and he sold some just before the outbreak of the Civil War. Maryland, though a Union state, did not abolish slavery until late in 1864. In the years leading up to the war, the Best family had a modest farm income, based on 12 horses, 9 cows, 3 cattle, 20 sheep, and 40 hogs. David also ran a blacksmith shop. His family's life was about to change, however, when the Confederate Army approached.

On September 9, 1862, the Confederate Army, after camping on the farm, gave David Best a four-dollar payment for a cord of wood. While camped there, and unbeknown to Best, General Robert E. Lee issued his Special Order 191. As Confederate troops departed, they burned the B&O Railroad bridge over the Monocacy River, a 58-mile tributary of the Potomac. Days later, the Union Army camped on the Best farm and one of the soldiers in Company F, 27th Indiana Volunteer Infantry, discovered Lee's orders in an envelope with two cigars, which the general had misplaced.

The soldier dutifully passed Lee's notes, which outlined his army's movements, up the chain of command, all the way to the top – to Union General George B. McClellan. Upon reading Lee's plans, which detailed his route, McClellan held up the envelope and exclaimed, "Here is a paper with which, if I cannot whip Bobby Lee, I will be willing to go home." It's not known if he smoked the cigars.

Two years later the farm was once again the stage for another episode in the war. On July 9, 1864, the Best Farm was center stage during the Battle of Monocacy. This would be the final Confederate effort to take war into the North and to occupy Washington, which would be a huge blow to Lincoln's chances for reelection. In the "The Battle That Saved Washington," Confederate forces, led by Lt. Gen. Jubal A. Early faced a smaller Union army, commanded by Maj. Gen. Lew Wallace.

When the two sides collided on the fields of the Best farm, it's possible, like the neighboring Worthington family, John Best – who, by then, had taken over farming from his dad – and his enslaved laborers were busy harvesting crops or hiding livestock and horses. At 8:30 a.m. the battle began. Confederates set up artillery and their sharpshooters hid in a frame barn that the Bests had recently built. When Union troops began shooting, the barn caught fire, destroying grain, hay, and farm equipment. Though the Confederates won the day, the delay was costly, giving General Grant time to send reinforcements to protect Washington. In less than a year later, the war had ended.

Despite the losses during the Civil War and having yet another frame barn burn down, John Best continued to excel in farming, producing wheat, corn, oats, wool, potatoes, butter, milk, orchard products, hay, and clover seed. In June 1869, he hosted an exhibition of mowing machines for the Frederick County Agricultural Society and later became a leading proponent of dairy farming. The family continued to be leaders in farming well into the 20th century. The National Park Service acquired the Best Farm in 1993.

The park service has maintained this historic stone barn well, a rare one that not only has a hipped roof but dates to the 18th century. And, unlike the traditional Pennsylvania German forebay bank barn, prevalent in Maryland at the time, it's a simple three-bay English threshing barn. Its two doors on either side could be opened, allowing wind flow to separate the chaff. Unfortunately, without cupolas and only two windows on either end, it lacked light and ventilation, suggesting that this was a small farm operation at the time. Inside, there are no vertical posts, although originally there were probably partitions for the livestock, hay, and grain. Rafters rest directly on the massive 23-inch-thick walls. At 30x61 feet, with walls 20 feet high, the barn was expensive to construct, a showpiece of an affluent farmer. It's possible that enslaved labor helped build it.

The stonework was well done. Limestone, either quarried, gathered from farm fields, or harvested from creek beds or bluffs, was laid in a random rubble pattern – with mortar that appears to be mostly original. Another highly unusual feature are stone projections, about the size of a footprint, that protrude from the corners on all sides, except the south, where a structure had been added (now gone). These may have been used for scaffolding, but it's more likely they were tie bars for a planned addition … or they might have been "through stones," long reinforcing stones that would extend from the outer wall to the inner wall,

seen typically in stone barns in England. Regardless, the stonemason was experienced.

The metal hipped roof is also unusual. Most barns had simple gable roofs in the 18th century or, especially in Pennsylvania, the asymmetrical Sweitzer types. Another attractive touch is the rust-colored brick arch, capping each window on the ends, a highly decorative feature. It's likely the workers fired the bricks on site – as George Washington did when he built his 16-sided barn on his estate in Virginia in 1794.

In 2006 the Monocacy National Battlefield Cultural Resource Division conducted a Historic Structure Assessment Report of the barn, which recommended some repair. They strengthened the roof by adding framing, did some tuckpointing to the walls, and removed a concrete apron that was poured while the farm was privately owned. During a study of the farm in 2002, archaeologists discovered several previously unrecorded structures, including an addition to the barn, a privy, a cistern, and an icehouse. The 25x35-foot addition, also of mortared stone, was probably built in the early to mid-19th century. It may have served as a milkhouse since the Best family began dairying. Analysis indicated it was damaged by fire.

Though its construction date is unknown, the 6x7-foot privy, lined with dry-laid stone, probably dates to the 1790s since it resembles other 18th-century privies found in the area. And having a bathroom was a high priority. The cistern, constructed with bricks, was likely built later and collected rainwater for drinking. According to those who lived on the farm, both the cistern and privy were used until the 1950s when indoor plumbing was installed in the main house.

Today, the National Park Service owns over 1,600 acres of this land, which includes not only the Best Farm but others as well: the Thomas Farm, the Lewis Farm, the Baker Farm, the Worthington Farm, as well as the Gambrill Mill, a three-story limestone flour mill that the Union army turned into a makeshift field hospital even though it was under continuous fire during the battle. The park service leases the fields out to local farmers to maintain the agricultural appearance of the landscape.

Though the stone barn doesn't hold hay nor wheat nor livestock today, it's well cared for by the National Park Service and sits as a reminder of refugees from the French Revolution, their enslaved workers, and the "Battle That Saved Washington."

MONTGOMERY COUNTY

Seneca Sandstone

This beautiful barn was built with Seneca red sandstone, also known as redstone. Formed in the Late Triassic age, 230 to 210 million years ago, the stone is geologically known today as a Poolesville Member of Manassas Sandstone. Masons prized it for its easy cutting, durability, and bright rust color, the result of its iron oxide content. This stone, though malleable when first quarried, becomes hard with time and can resist damage from the elements, much like marble and granite. An unknown stonemason built the barn sometime between the 1790s and the early 1800s.

Not much is known about William Young, who founded the farm and built this barn, though there's a record that he sold it to Martin Fisher in 1824. His son, Joseph R. Fisher, apparently scratched his initials, JRF, into a redstone block. Next, the Donaldsons owned it in the Great Depression years and into the 1940s and replaced the roof with metal. They may also have repaired some of the mortar with Portland cement, according to the date 10-5-44, etched into the mortar, which had to be removed during renovations in 2009. Portland cement is rigid, unlike lime mortar, and leads to cracking in stonework.

In 1999 owner Herman Greenberg donated this 418-acre farm to the Maryland-National Capital Park and Planning Commission for equestrian purposes, an appropriate gift since the barn was built to house horses. Today it's part of the Woodstock Equestrian Park, 872 acres of rolling farmland and forest, 16 miles of equestrian and

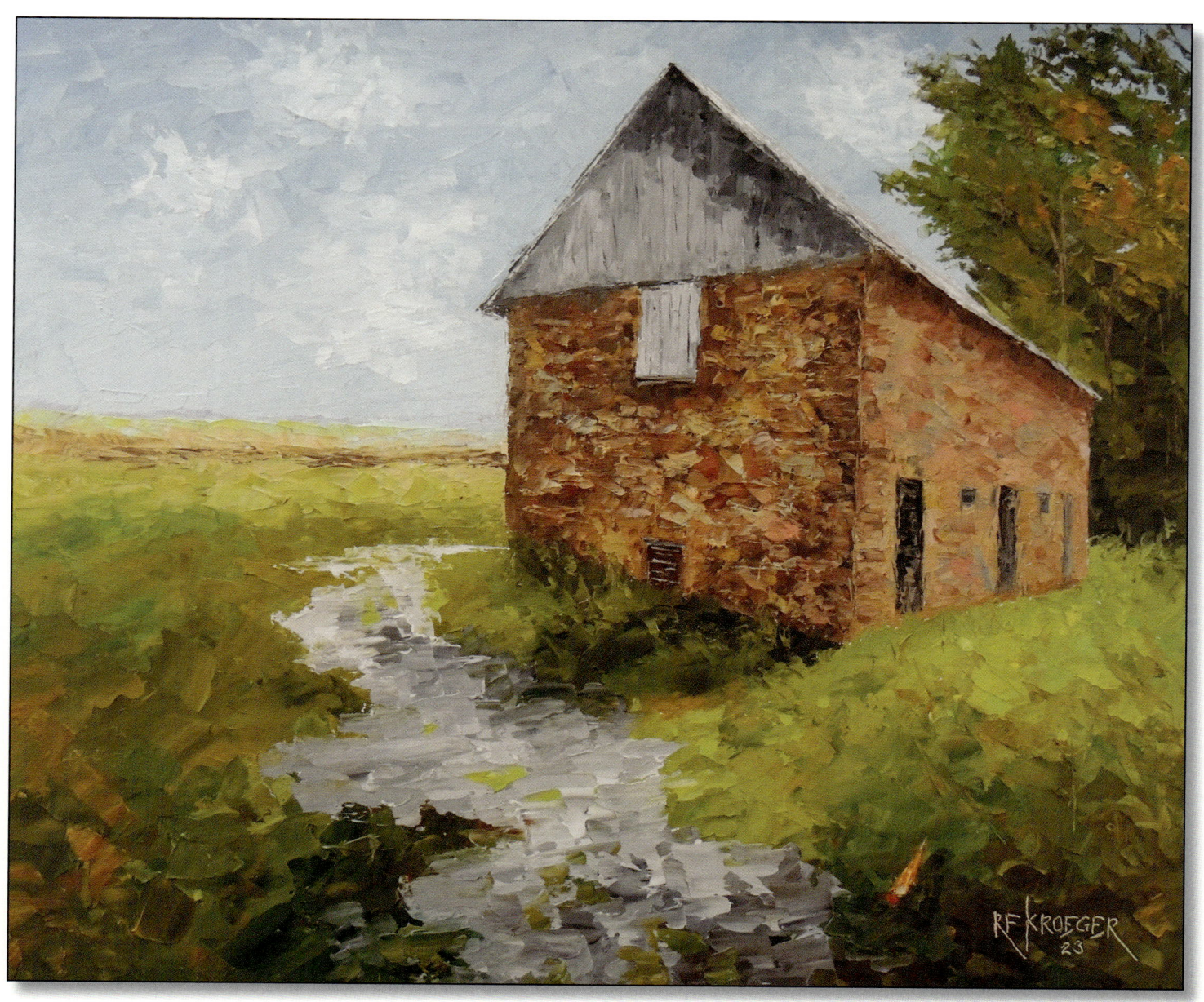

Seneca Sandstone

hiking trails, and three horse-friendly bridges.

Redstone occurred often throughout the region – in outcroppings, bluffs, and creek beds, notably the Seneca Creek, a 5.8-mile-long stream that flows through Montgomery County and drains into the Potomac River. Historic descriptions of the creek called it "the most powerful consistent stream in the county," which made it ideal for mills. In fact, Montgomery County had 44 of them by 1800. Perhaps the oldest was at Seneca Ford, near the mouth of Seneca Creek, already productive by 1732. Settlers used them for grinding wheat and grain, sawing wood, powering bellows in forges, and making wool cloth. In 1850, Montgomery County records listed 51 mills: 25 grist, six flour, 15 saw, one bone, two clover, one paper, and one sumac.

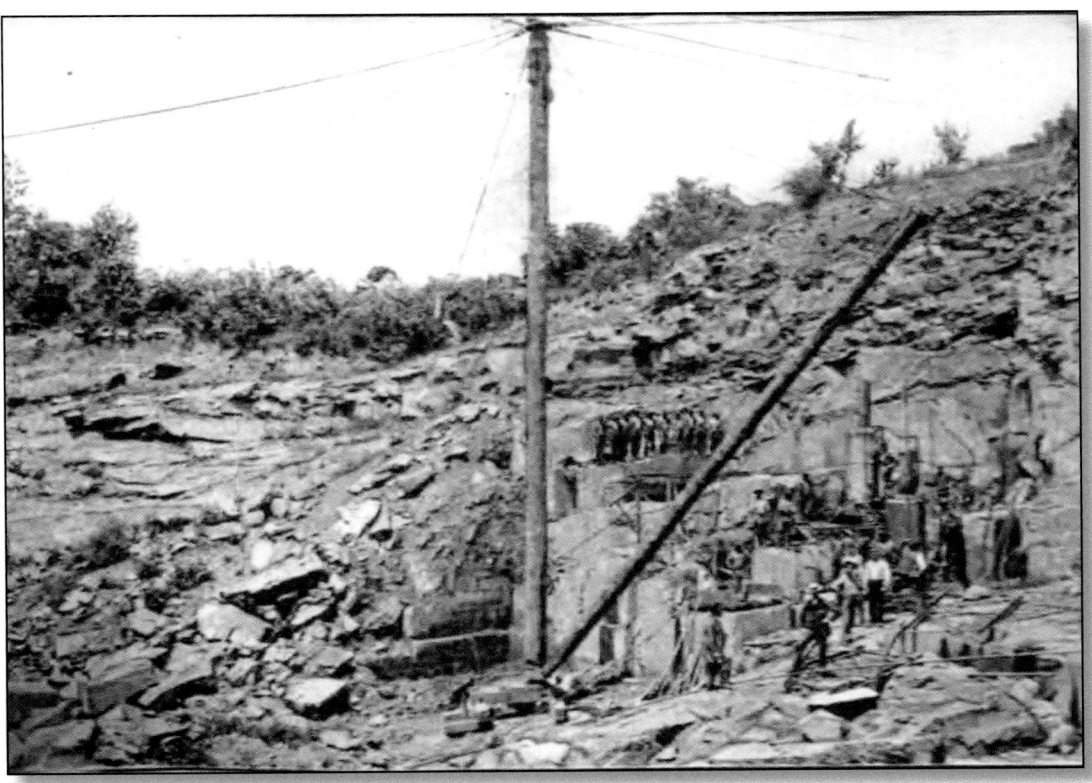

Seneca Quarry, circa 1898. Wikimedia Commons.

Listed on the National Register in 1978, the Seneca Historic District features 3,850 acres of federal, state, and county parkland and farmland, featuring 15 historic buildings, including smokehouses, springhouses, corn cribs, tobacco barns, and slave quarters. Red sandstone fences border farms, whose barns often have been painted red – to match their redstone foundations.

Though, at first, farmers gathered their own stone, in time, quarries sprang up and became prosperous businesses, supplying stonemasons and employing many quarrymen and stonecutters. Quarries on Seneca Creek first appeared in 1785. A year earlier, the Potomac Company, whose early proponents were George Washington and two others, had been incorporated to extend navigation upstream on the Potomac River ... and eventually open travel west to the Ohio River, Washington's dream. Seneca Quarry, one of the first and just west of the mouth of Seneca Creek, was listed on the National Register in 1973.

Though brush and trees have now surrounded the quarry and the ruins of the Seneca Stonecutting Mill, in its heyday the quarry was thriving. It supplied stone for homes and barns in the 1780s and also for the Potomac Company's construction of the Patowmack Canal in the early 1800s. And it was the source of stone for the building of the Chesapeake and Ohio Canal, which replaced the Patowmack Canal and began operating in 1831. After the canal was operational, redstone from the quarry was transported to Washington for houses in in the historic Dupont Circle and Adams Morgan area. When the Smithsonian awarded a contract to build its "Castle," (now its administration building), the directors chose Maryland redstone, less expensive than marble and just as attractive. Its young architect – not yet 30 – James Renwick Jr., traveled to Seneca Quarry to select the stone. He built the iconic, Romanesque style, multi-turreted building from 1847 to 1855 – a prime example of this reddish-brown sandstone.

Water from the nearby canal was also diverted to power machinery to cut, smooth, and finish the rough blocks. The Chesapeake and Ohio Canal, though it served for decades to transport Maryland's redstone, never fulfilled Washington's quest to reach the Ohio River at Pittsburgh, though it did stretch 185 miles, ending in Cumberland, Maryland. The quarry closed in 1901 when the remaining stone had deteriorated too much to be useful.

When Greenberg donated the stone barn and surrounding 418 acres in 1999, the barn was in danger

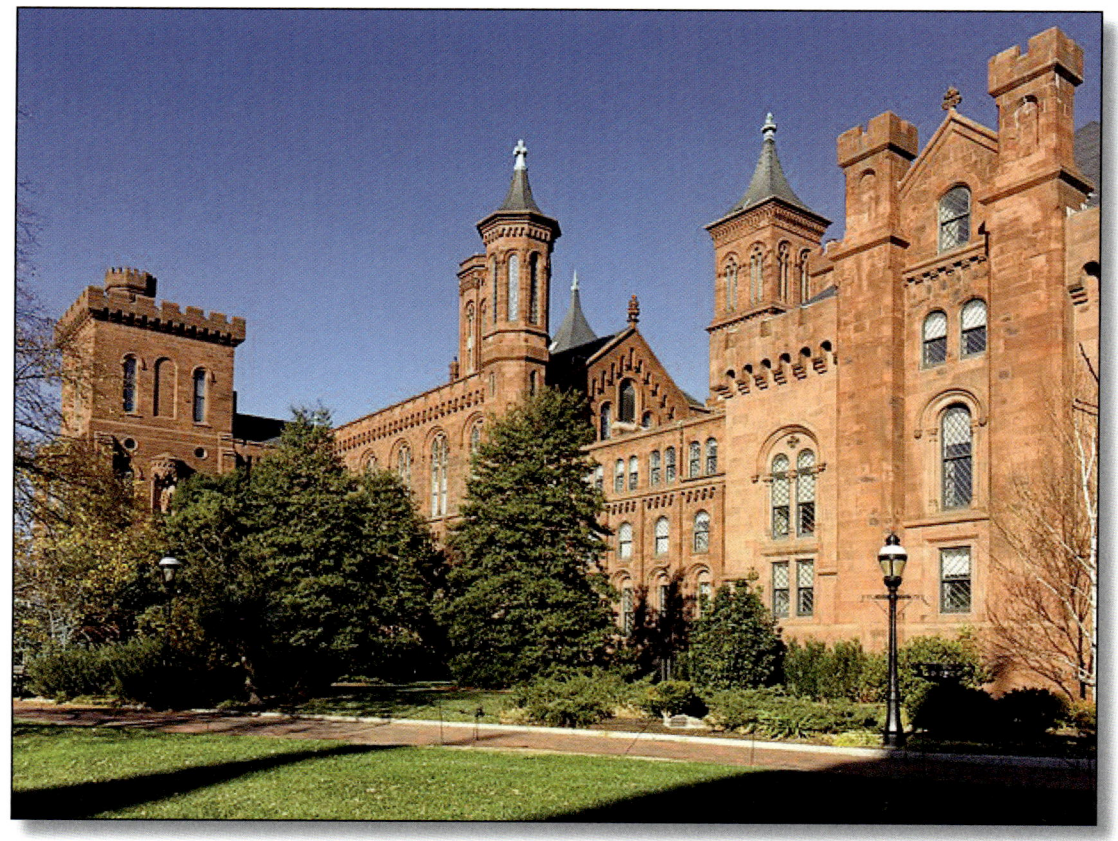

Smithsonian "Castle" Wikimedia Commons, P. Hughes

added to replace what had deteriorated around the windows and doors. Wisely, they graded the ground around the barn to divert water from the foundation.

This small two-story barn, only 22x40 feet, was probably used for horses, prompting some to call it a stable, although it qualified to be labeled a barn since it housed livestock and hay. In the barn, prior to renovations, stone lintels capped the three doors and windows, which had stone sills. Originally, the windows had wooden bars placed horizontally across them. On one end is a small opening for a haymow, although there

of collapsing. In a 2003 site assessment, the report described the barn as "extremely deteriorated, structurally unstable, and potentially dangerous." That was putting it mildly. The roof was broken in spots, allowing water to penetrate and rot the timbers, windows and doors were collapsing, and sections of the stone walls were tilting. Fortunately, staff in the Park Development Division decided the barn was worth saving. And, thanks to funding from the State of Maryland's Department of Natural Resources and the Department of Parks' Restoration of Historic Structures Capital Improvement Program, they were able to hire the Oak Grove Restoration Company. The rehab began in 2009.

The company set up scaffolding and began rebuilding the stone walls, using redstone. Half of the walls were dismantled and rebuilt. Workers removed the Portland cement mortar and installed a new concrete foundation. They added a new metal roof and, inside, restored the wooden loft floor, where hay was stored. New wood was

are no large barn doors, suggesting that wagons never entered, only animals, including perhaps a cow or two. Unlike the Pennsylvania German bank barn, this one resembled a three-bay English barn, though it probably was not used for threshing and, with only a few windows and no cupolas for ventilation, it probably did not house many animals, who need both light and ventilation. The stonemasonry repairs have been done well – large corner quoins and a random coursed redstone were the trademarks of early masons in this area.

Today the barn sits on the side of a gently sloping hill in hundreds of acres in Woodstock Equestrian Park. Hikers and riders can enjoy Nature's pristine beauty – nearby, a small creek flows among hardwoods, as it did over 200 years ago when this barn was built. Thanks to the park district of Montgomery County, it has been preserved, an ancient monument, remembering the families who lived here and the stone that covers its walls – Seneca sandstone.

6. MID-SOUTH

WEST VIRGINIA

JEFFERSON COUNTY

Survival

York Hill Farm, where this 200-year-old stone barn still stands, is located in Shenandoah Junction, in the eastern panhandle of the state, only nine miles from Harpers Ferry, where abolitionist John Brown staged his famous raid on October 16, 1859, the ominous preface to the Civil War.

Over a century earlier in 1719 a rich British noble, Thomas Fairfax, 6th Lord Fairfax of Cameron, then only 26, inherited the vast Culpeper family estates in Virginia's Northern Neck, a land grant dating to 1649 and totaling about 5.3 million acres in the Shenandoah and South Branch Potomac valleys. In order to sustain an aristocratic lifestyle, including the maintenance of Leeds Castle, where he was born in England, he needed income from his colonial holdings and began selling plots and renting them, conducting his business through an agent. Thomas first traveled to Virginia to inspect his property around 1735 and by 1738 he had established roughly 30 farms near present-day Burlington, about 75 miles west of Shenandoah Junction.

In 1748 he met a young George Washington, a distant relative of the Yorkshire Fairfax family, who must have impressed him, even though George was educated in the colonies since his father had died and the family couldn't afford to send George to England for an education, as was the custom for wealthy Virginia planters. Lord Fairfax hired the 16-year-old to survey his lands,

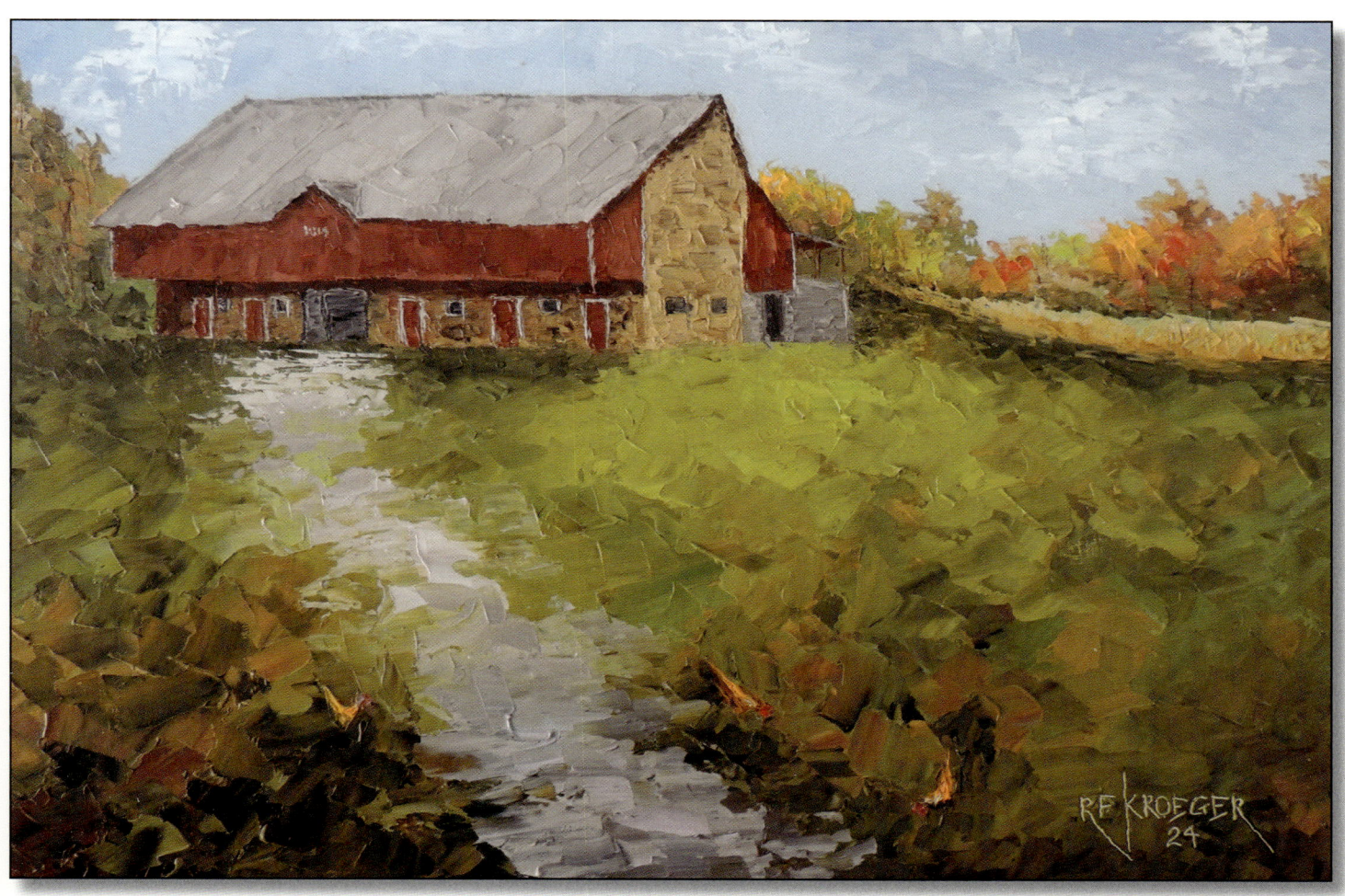

Survival

Washington's first job, and they became friends. Though he was loyal to the Crown during the Revolutionary War, Fairfax's close ties to Washington spared him, although the Virginia Act of 1779 eliminated his title. Two months after the American victory at Yorktown, the 88-year-old Fairfax died.

In April 1750, Lord Fairfax sold a 360-acre tract of land to Samuel Darke, who had probably settled here earlier, building a log house on the farm, where this stone barn still stands. In 1762 Colonel James Henricks bought the farm for £370, his rank of colonel possibly stemming from his service in the French and Indian War or perhaps his time in the Virginia Militia during the Revolutionary War, when, beginning in 1776, he served in Captain William Morgan's Company. There's also a record of John Hendricks, Esq., who served in "1777 under Capt. Nicewanger in Frederick County state of Virginia." This entry may refer to James' son. Regardless, the Henricks were true patriots.

When James fell ill, he wrote his will in January 1795, which divided his 360-acre farm among his children, an extensive document that mentions orchards several times, "stones at the corner of my son James' orchard." Though most farms in Virginia in the 18th century were mainly tobacco oriented, wheat had become the cash crop in the second half of the century and orchards also played a role in agriculture. As early as the first half of the 18th century, sales and leases of farmland required them, often specifying 100 apple trees be planted and, in some cases, even more fruit trees of the tenant's choosing.

However, in those years, wheat, rye, and oats were kings. In fact, the states of Virginia, Pennsylvania, and Maryland led the nation in flour production. Grist mills and whiskey stills lined streams and farms. Nearby in Maryland's Frederick County there were plenty of them: as many as 80 gristmills and 300 to 400 stills. By 1810, the much smaller Jefferson County had 31 mills along its waterways, which had become preferred routes of transportation since the region was still heavily forested and the roads were crude. And, the Potomac River, only five miles from Shenandoah Junction, was a primary artery for moving farm goods. In 1785 the Potomack Navigation Company was officially incorporated.

In July 1795, not long after James' death, his son John Hendricks, who inherited the southeastern third of the 360-acre tract, advertised his farm for sale: "A Valuable Plantation … lying about 3 miles from Shepherd's Town … well fenced, a good dwelling house, barn, apple orchard, meadow, good water." In March of the following year, after selling some of the acreage to his brother, John sold the remaining 98 acres of his

inheritance to Martin Myers of nearby Washington County, Maryland. Apparently, Myers was a land speculator since he sold the farm a year later to Jacob Snyder, also of Washington County – for £800.

Jacob bought the farm for his son John, who was listed in the 1798 tax assessment for Berkeley County, Virginia (Jefferson County was created from a part of this county in 1801). Being a considerate father, Jacob sold the farm in 1802 to his son John Snyder for £100, well below what he paid for it only a few years earlier.

John Snyder had big plans. To begin with, he built the stone barn in 1812, probably to replace an earlier frame barn. Why did he choose stone? Well, according to a genealogy records, John Snyder was born in December 1770, in Lancaster County, Pennsylvania, and, though of English descent, was probably exposed to the many German and Swiss stone barns of that region, only about 125 miles away from Shenandoah Junction. Tax records show that in 1816 John was assessed for his 100 acres as well as another adjoining tract of 91 acres. He added more in 1816 with the purchase of 76 acres on the farm's southern boundary, bringing the total to 267 acres.

The barn, a typical Pennsylvania German bank barn with forebay, exhibits extensive hand-hewn timber throughout. The bank leads up to the threshing floor, formerly used for separating grain, likely wheat, rye, and oats, though it's now used for storage and weddings. Under the forebay extension, doors lead into where livestock were housed and, above, a dormer protrudes from the roof. Nine vertical slits supply light and ventilation on each of the end walls, both stone to peak, and two louvers, situated at the bottom, provide additional ventilation.

The stonework is magnificent, the trademark of a master stonemason. Large limestone blocks have been arranged in random uncoursed rows with no visible cracking. A door, cut into stone, opens into a small storage shed, added on the left side of the front end.

A census listing for 1820 showed that not only was Snyder's farmland increasing but his family was, too. By this time, John was supporting a wife and six children, who were beginning to marry and start their own families. Accordingly, in the 1830s John began selling his land to his sons so that, as his father did before him, they could have their own farms. The census record in 1850 showed that John Snyder, Sr., aged 80, was living at his home with some of his family. Eight years later, just before the Civil War began, John died and provided in his will, written in 1849, that his son John Snyder, Jr. would have "my mansion-house and the land attached thereto, (being about 183 acres) at the price of 50 dollars per acre."

At the time of his death – at 88 more than double the average life expectancy – his personal estate inventory showed that he had been a prosperous farmer in both grain and apples, like most of the region's farmers. However, the Civil War was about to engulf Virginia and the southern states that had left the Union. Throughout the war, Jefferson County was occupied nearly constantly – by both sides – since the B&O Railroad line was an important Union supply route. Allegiance shifted many times from North to South, even after West Virginia was established as a Union state in 1863. Despite this, the county furnished the Confederacy with five infantry companies and four calvary companies. Many joined other commands, essentially taking most of the young men, which left farming up to the women. In fact, shortly after John Brown's raid on Harpers Ferry in 1859, Henry M. Snyder, about 23, signed up as a private in the 2nd Regiment, Virginia Infantry, a group known as the Letcher Riflemen.

In October 1864, Union General Philip Sheridan's "Valley Campaign" devastated the farms throughout the Shenandoah Valley. That autumn – after a summer's harvest – Sheridan sent a report to General Grant, "I have destroyed over 2,000 barns filled with wheat." It's likely that the Snyders weren't spared, but their stone barn survived, perhaps because the soldiers didn't think they could burn it. Unfortunately, a month later, Henry, now a full-fledged Confederate soldier and at home on sick leave at York Hill Farm, was killed by carpet baggers.

By 1870 the next Snyder owner of the farm was Jacob, who, with his wife Susan, raised seven children, as listed on the census of that year. It was a time of transition for farmers in this area since wheat and other grains, raised in Ohio and other parts of the Midwest, could be shipped via railroads to eastern markets and priced far less than that of eastern farms. So, adapting to this challenge, area farmers shifted their focus to apples and other fruit trees. The 1913 agricultural records of Jefferson County stated that 4,385 acres had been planted in orchards compared to only 40 acres in 1876. By the end of the 19th century, there were five commercial orchards located in Jefferson County. The Snyders made this change, too, adapting their farm from grain and livestock to apple storage. The 1910 census listed Jacob's occupation as a "fruit man" and "fruit grower." He died in 1915.

His wife Lizzie inherited the farm but, also aged, she passed away in 1919. Her will specified inheritance to their children and in 1921, the children agreed to sell the farm, now 145 acres, to both Ferdinand and Maria Snyder. Within four years, the farm, which had been called the Snyder Farm, became known as the York Hill Farm, possibly referring to their orchards of York apples.

However, the 1920s, while "roaring" for most cities in America, were bleak ones for agriculture, thanks to depressed prices of produce and farmland. Many farmers, overzealous in the heydays of World War I, when they supplied most of Europe as well as our country's war effort, lost their farms to banks during the 1920s. This trend worsened in the next decade with the Great Depression. In 1939 the Snyders were no exception; after trying to repay debts by leasing 35 acres of wheat, they declared bankruptcy. Nan Wilson bought the farm in a sheriff's sale and five years later in 1944 she sold the 135-acre farm to a partnership of Milton Burr, Samuel J. Hockensmith, and Robert A. Hockensmith.

In 1951 Robert Hockensmith purchased Burr's interest in the farm and acquired land, bringing the total to 174 acres. Two years later, Robert Hockensmith's wife Pauline purchased Samuel Hockensmith's interest, making them the sole owners. Part of the acreage provided direct access to the east-bound B&O Railroad, making it easy to ship apples. At the time, they had purchased an apple evaporator for cutting and drying apples on a commercial basis and they also changed the stone barn, converting it from a former livestock-and-grain barn to one for apples. After the owners lined and enclosed the animal stalls, the barn's lower level could now be used for cold storage. On the upper level, they reinforced the floor with concrete and steel I-beams so that it was strong enough to hold large crates of apples. Originally used for mostly tobacco and wheat, the farm had adapted.

In 1958 Mary Frances Hockensmith, daughter of Robert and Pauline, married Jerry Hockman, who was an orchard man himself, president of the Twin Ridge Orchard Company. In 1989, following their divorce, Jerry Hockman conveyed their jointly-owned property to his ex-wife. Then in 1997, her mother Pauline Hockensmith conveyed what remained in her ownership of the 135-acre Snyder farm to her daughters Mary Frances Hockman and Margaret Anne Saunders. The Twin Ridge Orchard Company is the parent-company of the York Hill Orchard & Farm. Mary submitted the farm for the listing on the National Register in 2006. The next year Jefferson County recognized the farm as a local landmark. These days, West Virginia ranks 10th in the country in apple production, thanks to its orchards in the eastern panhandle.

Mary's son Gordon took over operations of the farm in 2007 and added a new function for the barn – weddings. The York Hill Farm Facebook page shows many photos of happily married couples, dating to 2018, though COVID apparently put an end to this; the last wedding entry was in January, 2020.

Today, in addition to the barn, two other stone buildings survive – a stone smokehouse and a stone springhouse. The original farmhouse, with log sections dating to the 18th century and stone additions of the early 1880s, is also included in the National Register nomination, as is the family cemetery of the Henricks and Snyders. Indeed, York Hill Farm remains a testament to settlers of nearly 300 years ago, people who witnessed the three wars of America, two world wars, as well as the grim years of the Great Depression. The stone barn, built over 200 years ago, has changed its function, illustrating that fact that adaptation is essential for "survival."

VIRGINIA

FLUVANNA COUNTY
Beautiful Bremo

John Hartwell Cocke built this impressive stone barn in 1820 on a plantation he inherited in central Virginia, not far from the James River. Marc Wagner of the Virginia Department of Historic Resources described it as the state's most exquisite stone barn. Although the barn has been restored, I based the painting on a circa 1930 photograph taken by Frances Benjamin Johnston, who documented historic buildings during the 1920s and through the Great Depression, working on a grant from the Carnegie Corporation for the Carnegie Survey of the Architecture of the South. Over 7,000 of her photographs are stored in the Library of Congress.

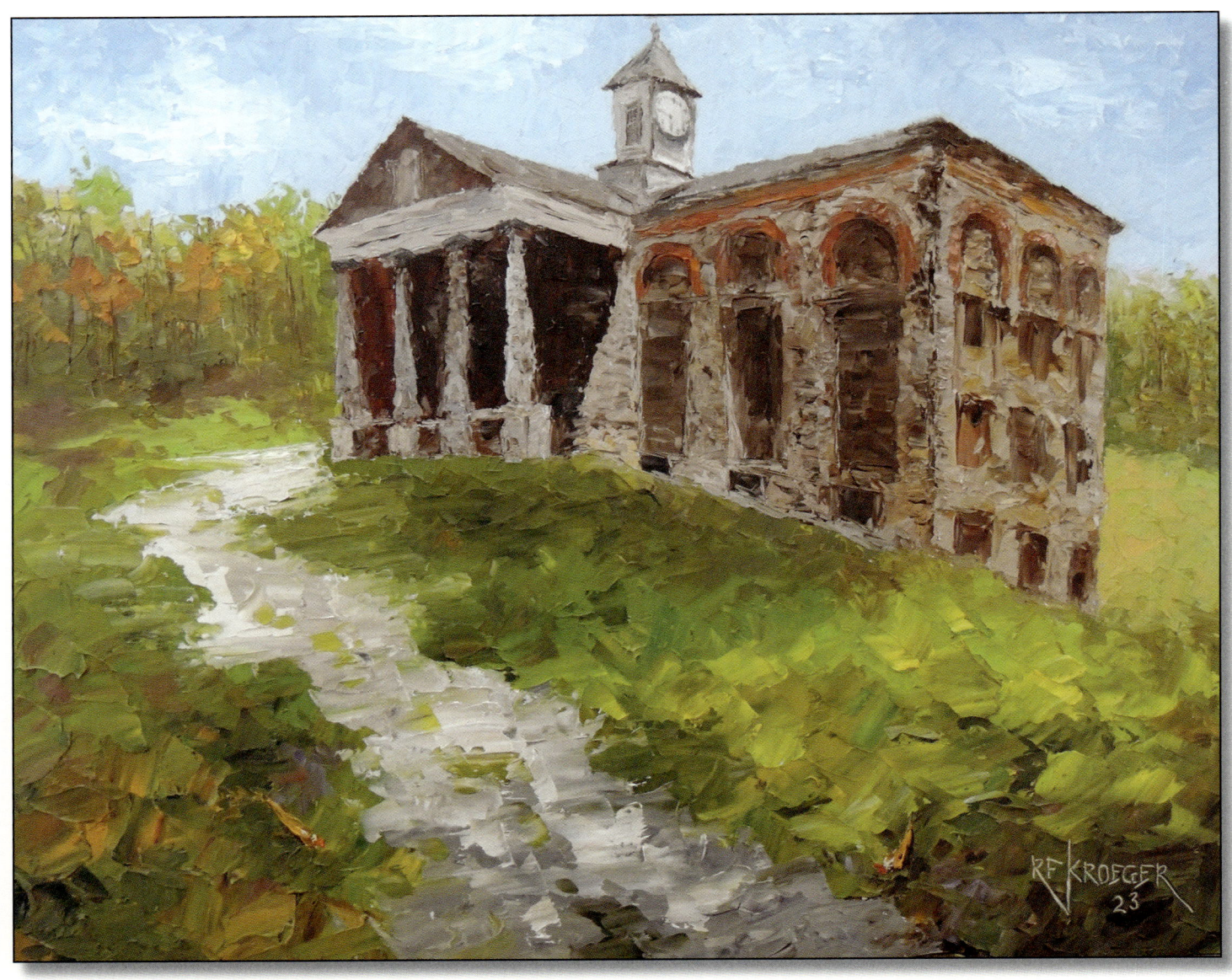

Beautiful Bremo

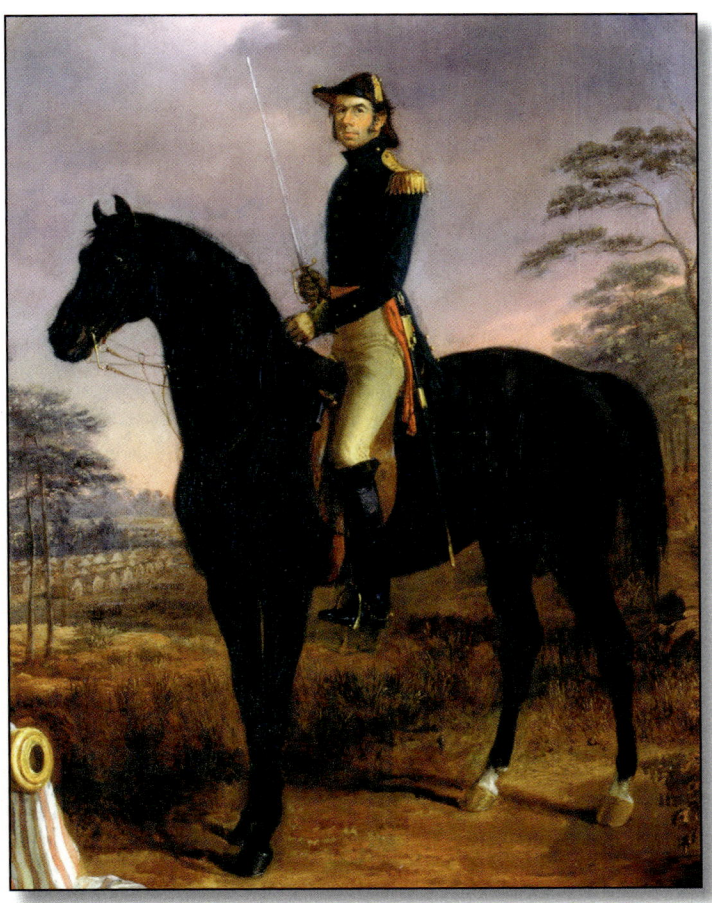

John Hartwell Cocke, circa 1814. Wikimedia Commons.

Cocke named the estate Bremo – after his ancestral home in Braemore, an area in northeastern Scotland in the Caithness region. The family moved to England in the 16th century and Richard Cocke, born in 1597, emigrated to Virginia in 1627, only 20 years after English settlers landed at Jamestown, about 100 miles eastwards on the James River. Though it struggled, Jamestown became the first permanent English settlement in North America. In 17th-century Virginia the Cockes were among a handful of the wealthiest and most powerful families; among their descendants were George Washington, Thomas Jefferson, and Robert E. Lee. Cocke descendants settled in Henrico and Surry County, where John Hartwell Cocke was born in 1780.

Thanks to a land grant from King George I in 1725, the Cockes received a large tract of land in Fluvanna County, where they arrived on a ship filled with slaves, who helped build a hunting lodge. John Hartwell Cocke, whose parents had died when he was 10, inherited over 5,500 acres in Surry and Fulvanna counties when he reached 21 in 1801. Earlier, another Virginia gentleman planter, Thomas Jefferson, likewise inherited his father's vast estate when he turned 21 – in 1764. Cocke and Jefferson would become friends, leading to Jefferson's influence on the design of this barn and the mansion.

John graduated from the College of William and Mary in 1799, where, as a student, he resolved to free the slaves he would inherit but, upon further reflection, he concluded that, intellectually, they were not ready for independence. He also met his future wife in college, Anne Barraud, whom he married in 1802. They lived initially on the family estate in Surry County, but taking advantage of his inheritance, they moved to the Bremo plantation in central Virginia, near the James River and 25 miles south of Monticello, where Thomas Jefferson had been planning and building his famous mansion since 1769. Upon arrival, they lived in the stone ancestral hunting lodge until a few years later when John built a modest home and, presumably, a wooden barn. They subsequently raised six children.

Coming from a line of British officers, John entered the War of 1812 as a captain and, in 18 months, finished his service as a brigadier general. However, like Washington, he was more interested in farming and resigned his commission in 1829, preferring to experiment with agriculture.

By the time his wife Anne died in 1816, John had begun plans for a mansion and other farm buildings, commensurate with his stature as a wealthy Virginia planter. He took advice from a Richmond architect named Conneley and from his friend Thomas Jefferson, who had finished his second term as president. In fact, he hired one of Jefferson's joiners, John Neilson, who, as a master carpenter, drew up plans for the elaborate Bremo mansion and its stunning stone barn. Cocke incorporated Jefferson's architectural ideas, which were based on the work and writings of the 16th-century Italian architect of the Renaissance, Andrea Palladio, whom many regard as one of the most influential architects in history. Jefferson, known as the father of American architecture, sent plans, formulated while he served as ambassador to France in years 1785-1789, for a college, which evolved into the University of Virginia. He also worked on his beloved Monticello, which he eventually finished in 1809. Master carpenter John Neilson worked on both buildings for Jefferson from 1804 to 1809, when he began work on the Montpelier estate of James Madison, president for two terms, beginning in 1809.

Though little is known about builders of early stone barns, Neilson, born in Ireland, continued to work on the University of Virginia buildings, including two pavilions, seven dormitories, the rotunda, and a theater. He died a wealthy man with a considerable estate in Charlottesville.

Though the original plans of the Bremo mansion and barn were destroyed in a fire in 1894, architectural experts identified the style of the buildings as Palladian, which meant that Jefferson, himself, probably played a role in the plans. Although Cocke built the barn with stone, he used brick for his five-section mansion, perhaps feeling that brick would give it a more refined look and that stone would be more rustic, appropriate for a farm building. After a few years, Cocke changed the roof – from a flat one that leaked – to a hipped one. He designed the house with many architectural features loved by Jefferson: the Tuscan order in the portico, high ceilings, bed alcoves, and narrow staircases.

Cocke followed the same design in the barn, which features four stone Tuscan pillars under a portico in the front entry and a tall central cupola with a large clock. Brick arched veneers decorate the outside walls, which were built with numerous windows and doors. The stonemason, who remains unknown, was a master of his craft. Random courses of multi-colored limestone impart an esthetic appearance, a reflection on Cocke's aristocratic standing in 1820, which is when the mansion and barn were completed.

Now, the owner of one of the finest plantations in Virginia, Cocke must have felt the need to develop scientific methods of farming. He founded the Agricultural Society of Albemarle and tried terracing, using marl and manure, cultivating silkworms, and experimenting with forms of pest control. He wrote more than 10 essays and letters, which were published in the *American Farmer,* a journal established in 1819 in Baltimore. He also published his ideas in the *Cultivator* and the *Southern Planter*. Concerned about the expense of transporting farm goods to market via horse- or oxen-pulled wagons, he promoted construction of a canal system.

After his wife died in 1816, John's life changed and he experienced a conversion to evangelical Christianity. He became an outspoken opponent of alcohol and tobacco, which he felt had depleted the soil, and, though he owned slaves (89 in 1816, 107 in 1830, and 135 by 1860), he claimed to be against slavery. Hoping to recolonize slaves from America back to Africa, he helped establish a colony in Liberia and later bought a cotton farm in Alabama, where he planned to educate and prepare slaves for their journey. However, out of the 82 slaves reported on that farm in the 1860 Alabama census, only 14 met his criteria for the return voyage, which disappointed him so much that he concluded that slavery was of divine origin and that God had intended these Africans to remain slaves. However, during his tenure at Bremo, he illegally educated his slaves and built a board and batten chapel for them, which still exists. Five years later in 1821, he married Louisa Holmes, a

Norfolk widow, whose views on Christianity mirrored her husband's.

At the onset of the Civil War in 1860, now aged 80, he supported the southern cause. Although John was too old to serve, Philip, one of his sons, became a brigadier general in the Confederate Army. During the war, the wife of General Robert E. Lee lived in the Cocke mansion at Bremo, even though it was 80 miles from her home in Richmond. Anna could travel relatively easily on the James River and the Kanawha Canal to Bremo, which did not suffer the wartime shortages that afflicted Richmond. Her husband, General Lee, also visited the estate in 1865, the same year that Union forces raided Bremo. After the war on August 1, 1865, Cocke took the amnesty oath, as a condition for a presidential pardon, required since his property exceeded the value of $20,000. He died a year later and is buried in the family cemetery.

Bremo continued in family hands when, in 1905, a daughter, Clara Cocke, married Forney Johnston, son of Joseph F. Johnston, two-term governor of Alabama. Their son, also a lawyer and a graduate of Princeton University and Harvard Law School, Joseph Fortney Johnston, was born the next year. As a lawyer, he worked in his father's law firm in Birmingham and continued to take care of Bremo, a 10-hour drive away. Like the Cocke ancestors, he served in the military, working in the legal department at the Pentagon in Washington. He rose to the rank of lieutenant colonel and was awarded the Legion of Merit. A life member of the Fluvanna County Historical Society, he submitted the Bremo Plantation for inclusion in the National Register in 1969. Two years later it became a National Historic Landmark. He died, at 97, in 2003.

His son, Joseph F. Johnston, Jr., an attorney like his father and grandfather, died in 2023. According to the Princeton Alumni Weekly, he and his wife moved to Virginia in 1978, and spent time at the family's ancestral farm at Bremo on the upper James River. During this time – in 2019 – a restoration company, Alexander Nicholson, performed much needed work on the mansion, including a new roof and drainage gutter system, adding skylights, rebuilding chimneys, and renovating interior woodwork. It took five carpenters nine months to finish.

Today, the Bremo Plantation – with its Jeffersonian mansion and barn, is owned by the Bremo Trust, which maintains the 750-acre estate, including the brick mansion, the stone barn, a stone-and-brick milkhouse, two slave quarters and a slave chapel, all built under the supervision of General Cocke. Bremo Trees, a family-owned

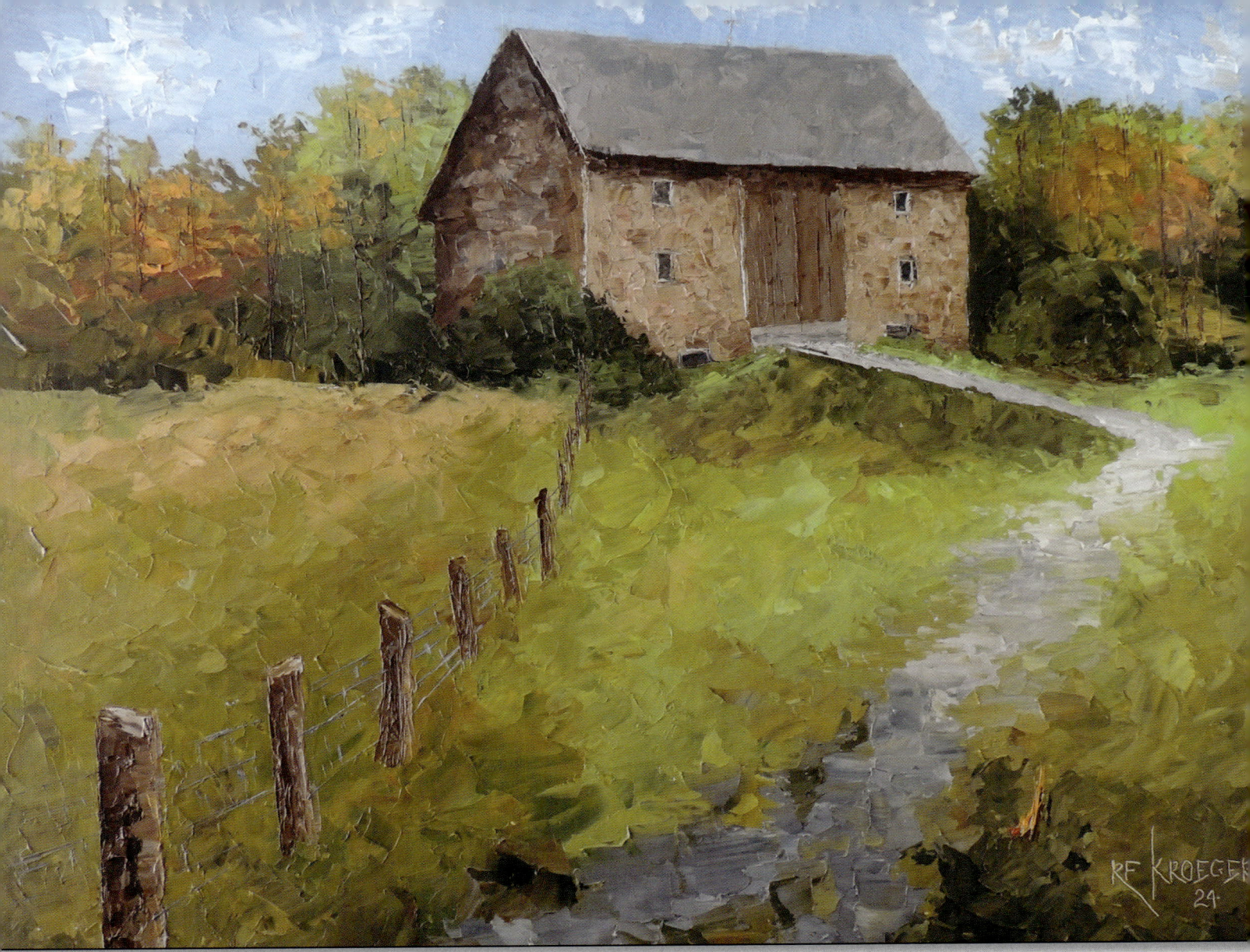

Children of the Mist

wholesale nursery, occupies 250 acres of the plantation and grows and sells over 100 varieties of broadleaf trees, evergreens, and shrubs, as their website describes.

Looking back to the plantation's beginning in 1725 with the family's stone hunting lodge and during the three hundred years of the Cocke family's resilience during many wars, droughts, and depressions, General John Hartwell Cocke, without any doubt, would be more than pleased with the preservation of his beautiful Bremo.

LOUDON COUNTY

Children of the Mist

This handsome stone barn has deep roots, tracing from the MacGregor clans in Scotland to the British colony of Virginia. Thomas Gregg founded the Silver Linden Farm in 1744 and built this stone barn a year later, which makes

it possibly the oldest existing stone barn in the country. His wife Hannah and he were farmers as were their three sons – Thomas, John, and William. They trace back originally to Scotland; Gregg is a derivation of Gregor and MacGregor.

This highland clan, one of the first to play the bagpipes in the early 17th century, descended from royal blood. Initially, they held lands in three glens, Orchy, Glenlochy, and Glenstrae, though they were no friends of the Campbells. When Robert the Bruce, a Campbell supporter, granted the clan lands in MacGregor territory, the MacGregors eventually were restricted to Glenstrae. To survive, they resorted to poaching and cattle rustling, often doing battle with the Campbells.

In one of their wars with another clan, the MacGregors irritated King James VI so much that he proscribed their name on a royal warrant in 1603, effectively giving them a choice to drop their surname or be punished by death. Resisting this order, the clan retreated deeper into the highlands, where bloodhounds tracked them. They became known as "Children of the Mist" and their women were stripped, branded, whipped, and marched through town streets. Anyone who killed a MacGregor would not be prosecuted; rather he or she would be rewarded. Though the proscription was lifted when the clan fought for the crown against Cromwell circa 1650, William of Orange reinstated it in 1693. The MacGregors became outlaws.

Perhaps their most famous one was Rob Roy MacGregor, born in 1671, who had to take his mother's maiden name, Campbell, to survive. Later, he became a Scottish folk hero, and, though captured and imprisoned, he was later released. Rob Roy, unlike many MacGregors, died a natural death in 1734. Sir Water Scott published his book, *Rob Roy*, in 1817 and other writers and movie directors followed. Persecution of the MacGregors did not end until 1774, 30 years after Thomas Gregg founded his Virginia farm.

However, Thomas did not emigrate from Scotland, but rather from Northern Ireland. In order to bolster the Protestant population here, King James "encouraged" Scots to move here in the early 1600s. Many did; sometimes entire communities left their homeland. Among them were the MacGregors and Greggs. Thomas Gregg, Sr., was born in Coleraine, Northern Ireland, and died in 1698 in Loudon County, Virginia. His son, Thomas Gregg, Jr., founded this farm.

The barn originally had four walls of stone, though at some point there was an addition, presumably for more storage space, on the back wall, which is now wooden.

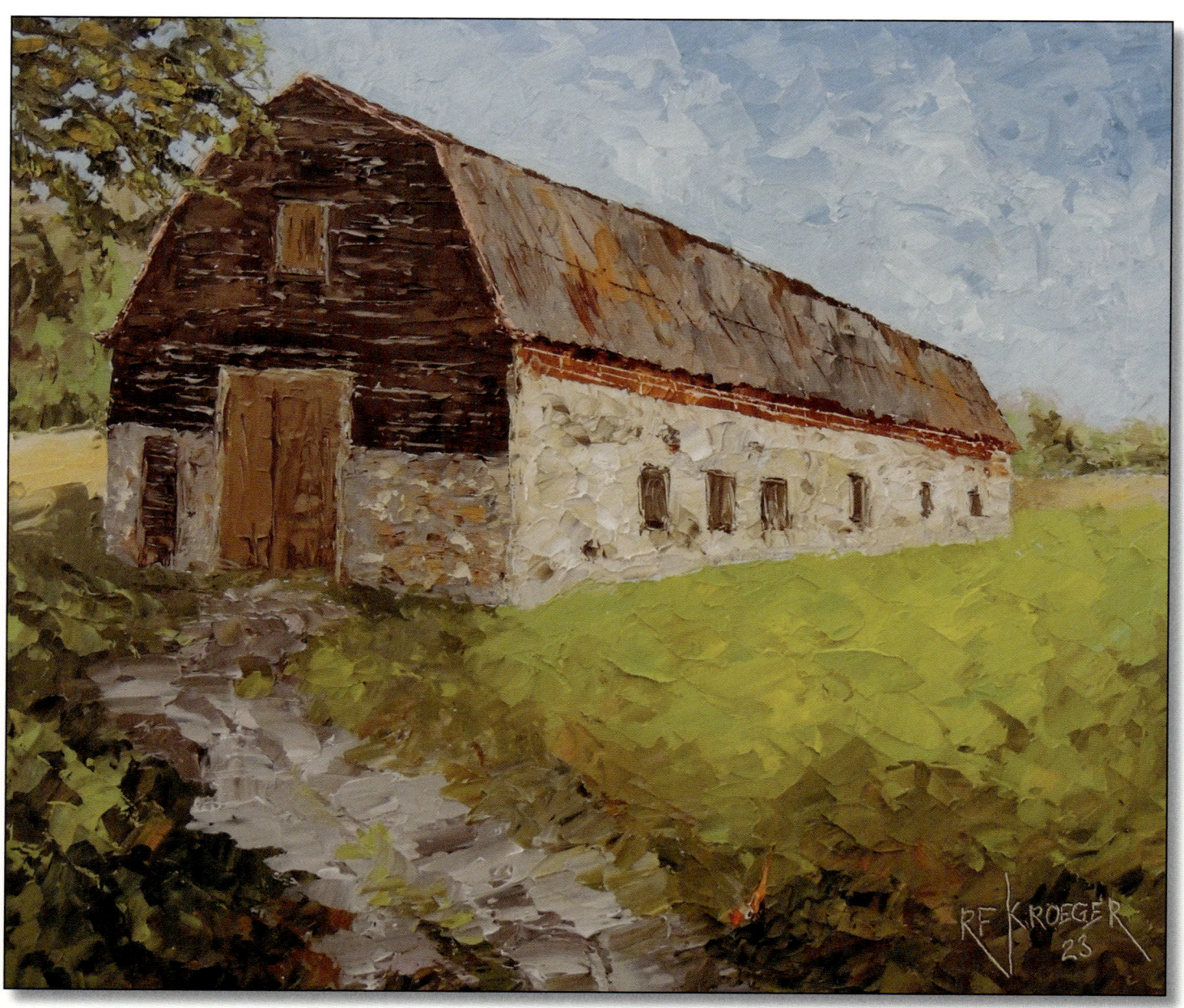

Tennessee Magic

Its modest size – 34x55 feet – hints that the farm was self-sustaining, and it also shows the work of a master stonemason, who likely gathered the stone from the farm field. The multi-colored fieldstone is dazzling. Stone walls measure two and a half feet thick. It was made to last.

The Gregg family owned the farm and barn for 120 years; since then, there have been six owners, including the Hall family who purchased it in 2018. Now known as Sylvanside Farm, the owners continue the farming tradition – raising Clydesdales and Devon milk cows. According to Terri Hall, the family stages weddings and events in both a large post-and-beam barn and the smaller stone barn, giving the barns a new purpose and honoring the memory of a persecuted clan that wouldn't yield to a king's condemnation. Long live the MacGregors and the Greggs and their heritage of Children of the Mist!

TENNESSEE

MEIGS COUNTY

Tennessee Magic

Meigs County, where this impressive stone barn still stands, lies in southeastern Tennessee, about halfway between Chattanooga and Knoxville and 12 miles north of Cleveland, an industrial city in adjacent Bradley County. Meigs County is primarily agricultural – with a population of only 13,000, less than a third of the city of Cleveland. And, it was named after Colonel Return Jonathan Meigs, Sr., a Revolutionary War officer from Connecticut, who was one of the founders of Ohio, establishing Marietta in 1788. Thirteen years later, President Thomas Jefferson appointed him to become the U.S. Indian agent to the Cherokee Nation, where he became a trusted friend of the tribe. With pressure to find lands for immigrants, the Hiwassee Treaty of 1819 gave the area north of Cleveland to the United States, opening up the region for settlement. Colonel Meigs continued to serve as Indian agent until he died in 1823, his death attributed to pneumonia contracted from sleeping outdoors in a tent; in an act of kindness, he gave his own living quarters to a visiting Indian chief. In the photo, he holds a presentation sword for his heroism in the Meigs Raid in 1777, when he led his regiment of 220 men in 13 whaleboats across Long Island Sound to attack the British fleet at night. His troops succeeded in burning 12 ships and taking 90 prisoners without losing a single man.

Officially established in 1836, the county quickly became agricultural; by 1850 nearly 600 farms had been founded. However, farming wasn't the only game in town.

In 1843 a prospector, searching for gold, discovered copper near Potato Creek in nearby Polk County, the birthplace of the barn's first owner, S.B. Rhymer. Copper mining began in 1847 and, by the end of 1853, 11 mines were operating.

Unfortunately, the Civil War put a damper on

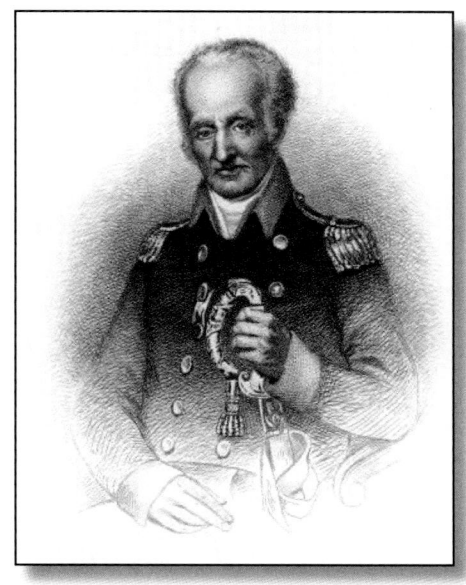

Drawing of Colonel Meigs with presentation sword. Wikimedia Commons.

Cleveland's copper production. Though the region sympathized with the Union, Tennessee became a Confederate state, despite locals trying to split the state at a convention in 1861. To show their support for the North, they placed a Union flag in the courthouse square in April 1861, where it remained until the Confederates removed it a year later. The Burra Burra Copper Company, named after the famous Australian mine of the period, had consolidated three other copper mines in 1860 and began operating under the direction of a young German engineer, Julius Raht. However, when the Confederate Army took over the mine, they began using the copper for their ammunition and Julius Raht fled to Cincinnati. When the Union army won the town, they closed the mines. And, amidst artillery fire from both armies, Cleveland and much of Bradley County was left in ruins.

After the war ended, Raht returned and reopened the copper mine in 1866, restoring some prosperity to the town. Although it suffered financial collapse in the late 1870s, Burra Burra had produced 24 million pounds of copper by 1878. The mine, along with other industries in the area, such as the Hardwick Stove Company, Cleveland Woolen Mills, Cleveland Hosiery Mills, and Cleveland Chair Company helped the region to recover more quickly than the rest of the post-Civil War South. By 1890 these factories saved Cleveland's economy, supporting nine physicians, 12 attorneys, 11 general stores, 14 grocery stores, three drug stores, three hardware stores, six butcher shops, two hatmakers, two hotels, a shoe store, and, most importantly, seven saloons.

At the start of this industrial revolution, Stephen Bradford Rymer was born on October 22, 1879, in Polk County. As he grew up, he witnessed the growth

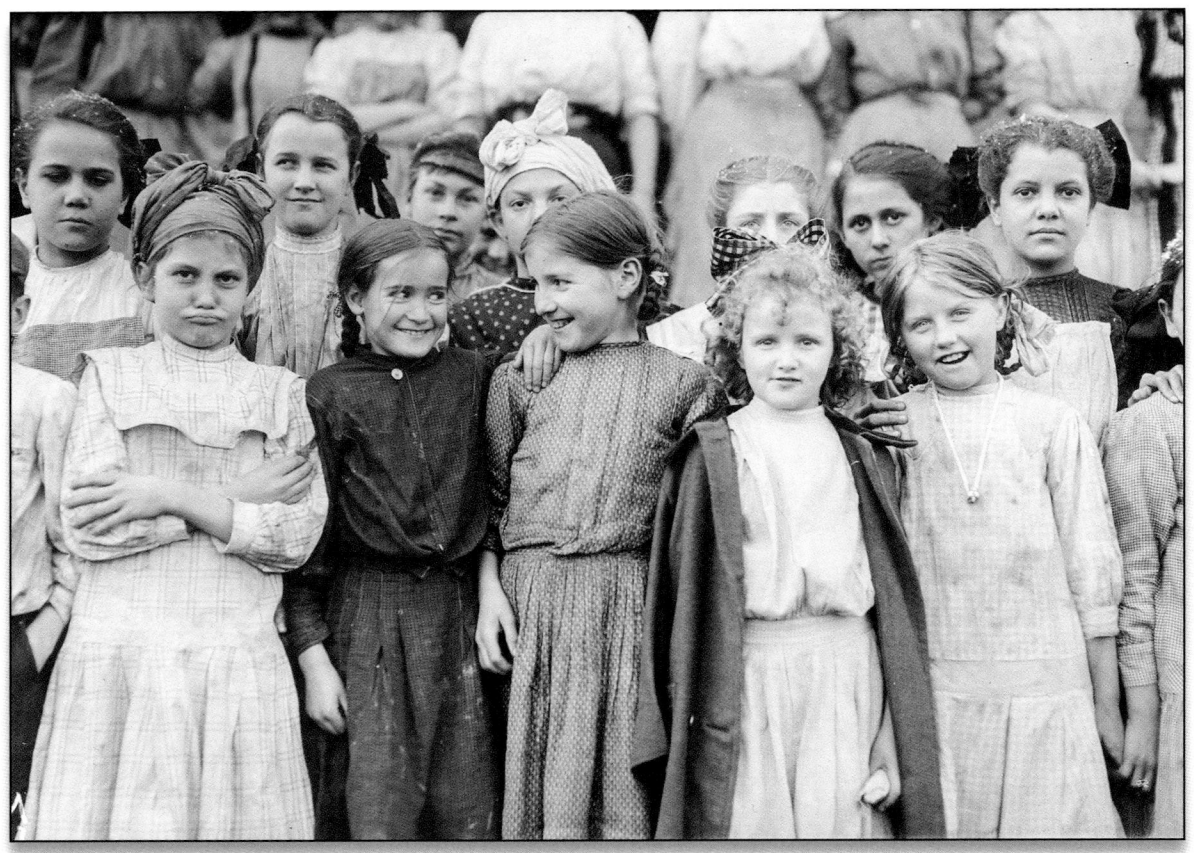

Child workers from Cleveland's Hosiery Mills, 1910. Wikimedia Commons. Lewis Hine

of companies and factories, perhaps instilling in him a sense of entrepreneurship. In his youth, he learned the value of hard work in jobs of logging and sawmilling in the Polk County mountains. At 23, he married his wife Clara in 1902 and moved hundreds of miles away to start a homestead in Oklahoma. But, apparently, either unhappy with the wilderness of the western plains or homesick for Tennessee, they returned two years later, settling in Cleveland. By then, his entrepreneurial side had taken over; he founded the Cleveland Coal and Feed Company and the Cleveland Builders Supply Company. The 25-year-old was just beginning.

In 1916 he founded the Dixie Foundry, a company that would become his golden egg. By the 1920s the company's stoves and ranges were known nationwide and Rhymer had become wealthy. Perhaps wanting to return to the life of a farmer that he experienced in 1902, he bought farms, three of them. According to his daughter Zola, who wrote a book about him, "He bought the first farm near Charleston for a hobby, which he greatly enjoyed." The one near Georgetown, where this stone barn still stands, "… consisted of bluegrass pasture for the Herefords." Though he was actively engaged in growing his company, Rhymer was the classic gentleman farmer and, according to Zola, he received a phone call everyday at 6:30 a.m. for many years from his tenant farmers to discuss weather and the day's farmwork.

The barn he built was extraordinary, not only considering when it was built – 1930, the beginning of the Great Depression – but also for its size, its stone, and two of its features. Inside, two stone walls run the entire length of the barn, creating a central corridor, something seldom seen in any kind of barn. Doors to individual stalls open into this central passageway. Outside, just underneath the eaves of the metal gambrel roof, a horizontal banded lattice spans the entire length of the barn, a brilliant design for ventilation and also extremely rare. Six windows, unevenly placed, provide light. Hay is stored in the second-floor loft.

Four-hundred-and-sixty-eight miles away in St. Louis, Missouri, John Ringen, a German immigrant, started a tin shop in the 1850s. His business evolved into a partnership with another German, selling housewares, washing machines, and cooking stoves – to make "quick meals," as they called them. With some mergers, this enterprise turned into the American Stove Company in 1901, which sold the first oven temperature control device in 1914. In 1929 it used the name, Magic Chef, for some of its products. The brand was so successful that the company changed to the name of Magic Chef, too.

Meanwhile, back in Cleveland – once known as the stove capital of the United States – J. Bradford Rhymer, who had guided his company through the dark years of the Great Depression and the anxious years of World War II, had retired in January 1950, becoming chairman of the board. His son, S. Bradford Rymer, Jr., took the helm and continued to grow the business, changing the name to Dixie Products. In 1958, Cleveland's little stove company purchased Magic Chef, which made it the 249th largest industrial company in the nation. Later, Maytag bought it for $740 million. In turn, Whirlpool acquired Maytag in 2006 but retained the Magic Chef brand. The company still employs nearly 3,000 workers in Cleveland.

However, the younger Rhymer didn't have a passion for farming and sold the stone barn and the farm to W.H Lonas in 1953, who actively farmed and used the barn. Enamored with its history and unique design, he listed it on the National Register in 1982. Today's current owners have taken good care of it, as it heads towards the century mark.

Meigs County, though saddened by the great Cherokee exodus in the 1838 Trail of Tears and devastated by the cannons of the Civil War, has rebounded, though most of it has maintained its rural farming roots. The Rhymer stone barn, a monument to a local entrepreneur-turned-industrialist, still stands in this Appalachian valley, a reminder of what was once a little bit of "Tennessee Magic."

GEORGIA

CHEROKEE COUNTY
Cryptic Coggins

Thanks to a local history group, this stone barns still stands, an impressive and rare example of unusual barn architecture and a sad, but important piece of American history. The barn is located about 40 miles north of Atlanta in Canton, the county seat and a city of nearly 23,000, whose population has tripled in 20 years as

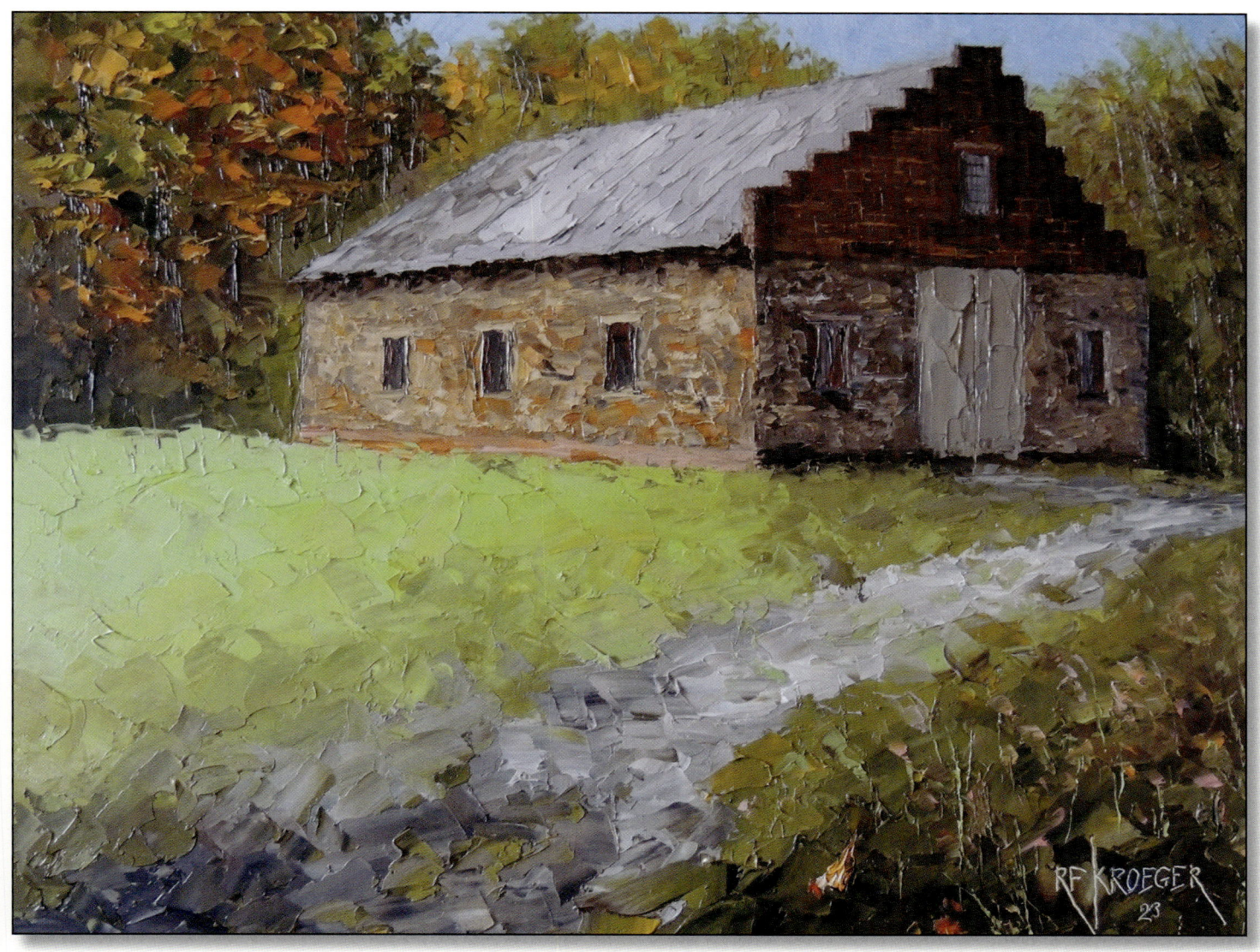

Cryptic Coggins

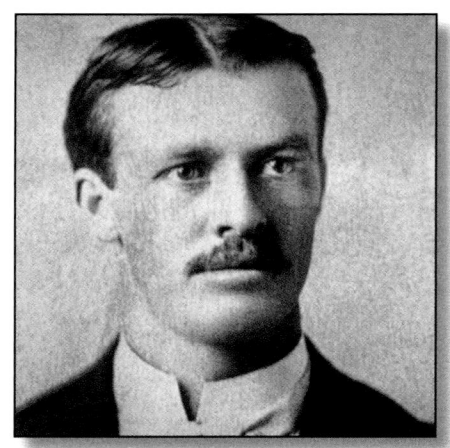

A young Gus Coggins, circa 1890s. Courtesy of History Cherokee.

Atlanta's growth inches northwards. Though it was originally on lands of the Cherokee Nation, the state of Georgia claimed the land after gold was discovered in the area in 1828. Later in 1834, the town changed its name from Etowah to Canton.

One of its residents, Augustus (Gus) Lee Coggins was born in 1868 into a family, whose father owned a gold mine and a livery stable, which young Gus eventually took over. Growing up in a socially prominent family, he became so well known that the town elected the 25-year-old as its sheriff in 1893. A few months later, he married Daisy Ryman at her family mansion in Nashville, Tennessee, over 200 miles from Canton.

The Ryman family, whose wealth came from owning a steamboat line on the Cumberland River, was a step up from the Coggins clan. Yes, Gus was climbing the social ladder. Daisy bore a son and a daughter within five years. During the 1890s and early 1900s, Gus expanded his livery business and began buying and selling mules and horses, traveling to Tennessee, Missouri, and other states to acquire stock, which he sold in Atlanta, where his brother Rol was manager. In 1915 the *Atlanta Constitution* posted an ad, "Full Trainload of Mules Arrive." The ad copy continued, "Coggins & Bros. Have Received Largest Shipment of Mare Mules Ever Brought to City – On Sale Monday." Of course, by 1915 the automobile, thanks to Henry Ford and his inexpensive Model-T, was offering an alternative to the horse and mule. Farm tractors would follow.

By the mid-1890s, Gus Coggins leased a 350-acre farm from Major Wallace Campbell, Jr. and began raising crops and livestock. Coggins purchased the farm in 1903, calling it Crescent Farm – after the crescent-shaped path of the nearby Etowah River. He used the farm to breed mules and horses – standardbreds for harness racing.

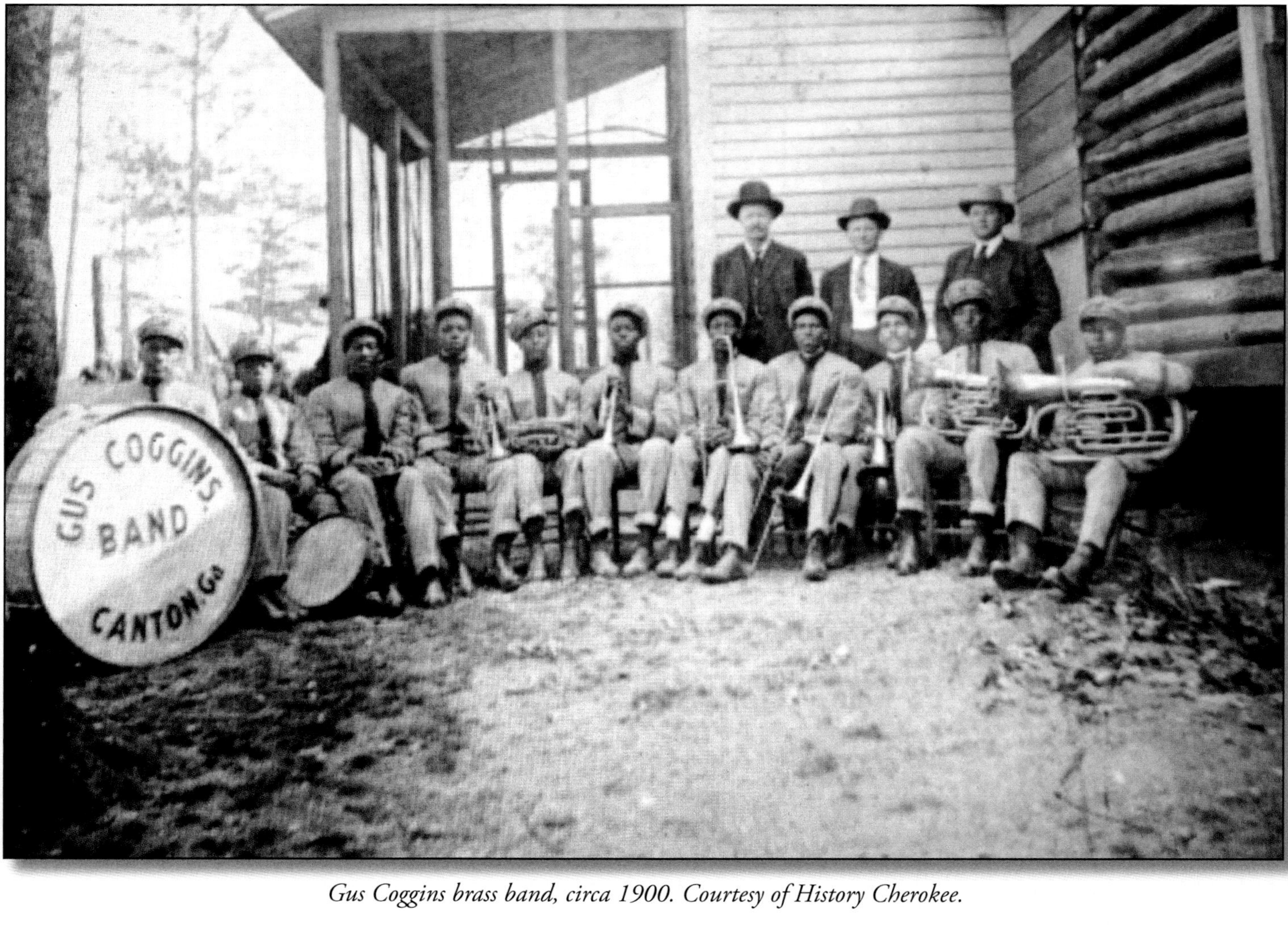

Gus Coggins brass band, circa 1900. Courtesy of History Cherokee.

He also raised turkeys, pure-bred Jersey cattle, guineas, hogs, sheep, peacocks, and dogs. With plenty of acreage, Coggins also farmed corn, cotton, molasses cane, and hay – mostly for feed for his cattle, mules, and horses, for which he built a one-mile racing track. To care for his large farm, he needed labor – lots of it – and he hired as many as 75 African Americans, which he may have done to save money since their wages were below those of whites. He wasn't the only farmer to take advantage of such low-cost labor; many others did the same. However, this angered a significant few, who saw this as a loss of employment for themselves and their families. At one time, there were 50 tenant houses on Crescent Farm. To entertain guests, Coggins outfitted a brass band – The Gus Coggins Band, a group of 11 black musicians. He also had a pet monkey and a bear. In addition to a wooden barn for racehorses, the farmstead had a cotton gin, a smokehouse, and a blacksmith shop. The Crescent Farm brimmed with activity. But trouble was brewing.

Vigilante groups of dissatisfied whites, who called themselves "night riders," threatened farm owners and merchants who hired blacks and tried to persuade cities and villages in northern Georgia to become "sundown towns." The vigilantes would tolerate daytime visits by blacks but they wanted them gone by sundown. If not satisfied, they'd ride on their horses at night, setting fire to homes and businesses that didn't comply. They succeeded in enforcing their demands in adjacent Forsyth County. In fact, Gus Coggins hired some of Forsyth's black fugitives, likely infuriating the night riders even more. The persecution soon spread into Cherokee County; according to Federal Census records the county lost 23 percent of its black population between 1910 and 1920, the largest drop in its history.

In 1900 one of his barns mysteriously burned, possibly done by night riders in retaliation for Coggins refusing to comply with their "sundown" rules. The fire killed cattle and a valuable racehorse, along with harvested crops, a loss of $3,000, only partially covered by insurance. This might have prompted Gus to consider a fail-safe structure, which he did in 1906, building this stone barn, using rocks quarried on the banks of the Etowah River.

Though the work isn't typical of a master stonemason – the rough irregular rubble masonry lacks defined quoins – the barn is one of only a few with a stepped parapet roof. The iconic Alamo of Texas fame, originally a mission built by the Spanish in 1718, shows a similar stepped roofline, though it was not part of the building until 1849. This type of a roof façade traces back to battlements in ancient castles and then into buildings throughout European countries. Often called

corbiesteps – after the Scottish word, corbie, meaning a crow – this architecture is extremely unusual in American homes, buildings, and barns. According to architectural historian Robert Gamble, now a volunteer with History Cherokee, wooden stepped parapet fronts were often seen in commercial mule barns, which used to be part of smalltown America. What motivated Coggins to use such an expensive and elaborate design remains unknown. Did he see a picture of it somewhere? Did he want his stone barn to have a little flair? Did he hire an architect to suggest brickwork on the top half of the gable ends, which was much easier than using stone for the parapets? Regardless of his motivation, the barn's roofline puts it in a class by itself.

Inside, as with many stone barns, the rafters rest on 26-inch thick walls, which are exposed stone. Three windows on each side, bordered by concrete sills and lintels, provided adequate ventilation and enough light for the horses. Hay was stored on the second floor. And, though not huge, the barn's 3,000 square feet were enough to house a modest collection of Coggins's valuable racehorses.

In 1913 another unsolved fire claimed a Coggins wooden barn, reputed to be the largest in northern Georgia at the time. However, despite the worry of arson, business continued to grow for the Coggins brothers. Frank owned the Coggins Marble Factory, Gus owned Crescent Farm, and brother Rol, who married Daisy's sister, managed their horse and mule brokerage at a stockyard in Atlanta. Gus also rose in the eyes of Canton residents – after his term of being sheriff, he founded the Bank of Cherokee in 1913, becoming its president and principal shareholder. He also took his prized standardbreds to run in races throughout the South. One of his horses, Abbedale, born in 1917, became a Grand Circuit champion and was inducted into the national Harness Racing Hall of Fame. He sired six 2:00 pacers. This horse also illustrated the passion for harness racing – and perhaps gambling – that Gus Coggins had.

More tragedy struck in December 1915, when two of Coggins wooden barns burned to the ground, killing more than 160 head of livestock, 16 thousand bushels of corn, tons of hay, and farm equipment, a loss of $75,000, the equivalent of over $2 million today. Did Coggins hire someone to burn his barns to collect insurance money? Not likely; the same night a tenant house was set on fire and the next night four more houses and barns were burned in the eastern region of the county. No, this was likely the work of night riders, whose members had organized into a group a month earlier, becoming another chapter of the Ku Klux Klan. It's probable that they would have set fire to the barn housing valuable standardbreds, too, were it not for its stone construction. Undeterred, Goggins bought other farms in the region. His empire thrived despite the continual threat of arson.

Unfortunately, Daisy wanted no part of these surroundings and, at some point, moved back to her family's mansion in Nashville, where she raised their two children. Was she concerned about the night riders? Was she disillusioned about her handsome husband and his obsession with horse racing and gambling? She did allow the children to visit Gus, but only at Christmas and during the summer. Their visits were newsworthy enough to be recorded in the local newspaper. But she stayed in Nashville. They lived apart; divorces were frowned upon in those days.

However, years later and after her mother passed in March of 1926 Daisy Coggins decided to move back to Canton. The family mansion in Nashville was now an empty home and one that was beginning to deteriorate, along with the surrounding neighborhood. So, Daisy moved into the fashionable Edgewater Hall, and lived there with her estranged husband, though their time together would not last long – about seven months.

World War I was a boon to American agriculture. With the war in Europe raging, farmwork declined there, giving American farmers the opportunity to supply Europeans with livestock and produce. This excess production raised – and sometimes tripled – agricultural prices, not only of crops but land, as well. Farmers borrowed money, bought more farmland, and kept up with the overseas demand. Unfortunately, during the early 1920s, European farms recovered more quickly than anticipated, leaving American farmers with excess goods, lowering the price of those goods, and creating an agriculture depression, followed by the Great Depression of the 1930s. Many lost their farms to banks.

However, the Coggins mule and horse business flourished during this time. In December 1914, the French government paid Gus and his brother Rol a check for $80,000 for their shipment of 500 horses for the French army. The next month the French signed a contract for half a million dollars for 4,000 horses, which prompted Gus and Rol to hunt for new stock throughout the South. However, German U-Boats began sinking transport ships, making it difficult for the Coggins to move their horses to France. Prices plummeted and by the end of the war in 1918, the brothers were stuck with excess livestock. Despite this, their finances were still healthy; after a 1917 fire consumed the Victorian home where Coggins lived, he was able to build a grandiose mansion, called Edgewater Hall, which he finished in 1922.

Two years later in 1924 Gus sold one of his racehorses, Mag Abbe, for $10,000, a huge sum for a horse in those days. Apparently, newspaper headlines focused on his successes, but did they know about his losses? With any race, there are expenses: insurance, travel, and employee food and lodging. And there's also the betting. Gamblers love to mention their wins but are reluctant to broadcast their losses. The chinks in his armor were beginning to show.

Oddly enough, a mule barn on the Crescent Farm burned in the early 1920s. Was this the work of the Klan or of Gus, hoping to claim the insurance payout for his loss? Prices for mules and horses suffered after European farms recovered at the end of World War I and the automobile and farm tractors were beginning to spell the end of farm work for horses. But Gus Coggins was admired in his town and no records have revealed him as a convicted arsonist.

In fact, he was so respected that many residents of Canton invested with him directly. According to exhaustive research by Wheeler and Cowart in their 36-page paper, *Who Was the Real Gus Coggins?: Social Struggle and Criminal Mystery in Cherokee County, 1912–1927*, published in a 2013 issue of *The Georgia Historical Quarterly*, Coggins was a good salesman and trusted by many. Since there were no pensions, 401K retirement programs or Social Security payments in those days, people looked for vehicles to rely upon during their golden years. Word spread that Gus Coggins was a safe vehicle. Apparently, he'd solicit with the pitch, "The bank will give you six (percent interest), but I'll give you eight." It worked; by 1926 when he went bankrupt, over 100 individuals had invested over $750,000 with him, much of it being their entire life savings.

Thanks again to research by Wheeler and Cowart, in February 1924 Coggins swapped 100 shares of stock in his Bank of Cherokee with Paul Jones of Jones Mercantile for 100 shares of stock in his Canton Cotton Mills, the largest employer in the city. Gus, without changing ownership of the stock, used it as collateral in his own bank, taking out $20,000, clearly bank fraud. Coggins needed cash and got it anyway he could.

About this time, Florida and coastal Georgia were experiencing a massive real estate boom. Northeasterners, tired of cold winters, decided to build or buy a home or apartment in the warm South. But real estate valuations, just like a roller coaster, go up and come down. By the mid-1920s, investors speculated on land, started banks, and used deposits to fund developments. But, when the investors couldn't sell lots quickly enough, the real estate bubble burst, land prices plunged, and banks, one after another, failed. It wasn't the first time for this sad story;

Robert Morris, signer of the Declaration on Independence and the financial genius behind the American Revolution, became a land speculator after the War ended, but failed badly in this venture.

In 1926 150 banks in Georgia and Florida crashed, including the Manly-Anthony bank chain, which took down the Bank of Ball Ground, not far from Canton. Newspapers ran ads to calm the public panic, including one that listed the assets of the Bank of Cherokee as having $400,000, as verified by its president Gus Coggins. But by the autumn of 1926 Coggins knew his bank was failing and he took measures to raise cash by selling an ice plant, a building in town, and 550 acres of farmland to well-known moonshiner John Henry Hardin for over $27,000. He also took a note from an Atlanta bank for $62,000. On November 6 Coggins skipped town, leaving behind a bank that didn't open that morning. Over 100 investors along with Daisy and her children were shocked. Where did Gus go? He never returned until a few months before he died nearly three decades later.

Soon after he left town, the federal court issued an involuntary order for bankruptcy – on November 10, the same day that Coggins, flush with cash, paid $25,000 to clear his debt to the Harper Mule Company in Illinois. Apparently, Gus was interested in returning to the mule selling business. He traveled and lived further west – in Montana and perhaps Texas – though no records exist about whether he had success in stock raising. In 1926 he was only 58 years old – at the peak of a financial career for most in this industry. Since he didn't appear in either the 1930 or 1940 census, he may have changed his name to avoid creditors. Did his passion for horse racing and gambling make him go through his pile of cash, much of it owed to the locals in Canton? But now alone, living in a little house and without a wife or children, he finished his final years far away from Georgia – in Wray, Colorado – where he contracted leukemia in 1952 at the age of 81. That same year he traveled to live with his sister in Canton, where he died a few months later. His sister hosted a funeral for him in her home in Canton but it's unknown how many attended. He's buried next to his parents in Canton's Riverview Cemetery.

In 1927 bankruptcy proceedings began to liquidate his assets, beginning with his farms. Jones Mercantile Company got the Crescent Farm, its stone barn, and Edgewater Hall. During the late 1960s the Cherokee County Board of Education purchased the stone barn and the surrounding 30 acres with a plan to build an elementary school. But, in 1987, the board donated the barn and a half acre to the Cherokee County Historical Society, which developed a plan to renovate the barn, then covered by vines, though the stone walls remained intact.

In 2020 the historical society adopted a new name for its center, History Cherokee, which includes the county historical society. As the owner of the barn, a national treasure and justly listed on the National Register, it now uses the restored barn as an event center and wedding venue. Its exposed stone walls, showing century-old rustic masonry, polished floors, and its remarkable corbie-stepped roof, have become a charming place to hold a wedding or other event, which book quickly.

The elegant 9,935-square-foot Edgewater Hall, the Coggins palatial residence from 1922 to 1926, passed through several hands before the Cherokee Federal Savings Banks purchased it from the Pope family in 1986 and converted it to their corporate headquarters. In December 2022, it was being leased by the Wellstar Health System and was listed with a realtor for $3.2 million – as an income producing commercial property.

The life of Augustus Lee Coggins is intertwined with his stone barn and poses questions that may never be answered. Did night riders burn his other barns? Did he burn one of them in the 1920s to collect insurance money? Why did he and Daisy live apart for most of their married life? Why did he take money for investments from so many who entrusted him with their life savings and then run away? How did he live the final 23 years of his life out west? Yes, Gus Coggins is somewhat of an unsolved riddle, but regardless of whether such questions will ever be answered, he left behind a legacy of this unique stone barn, one of a kind just like his cryptic life.

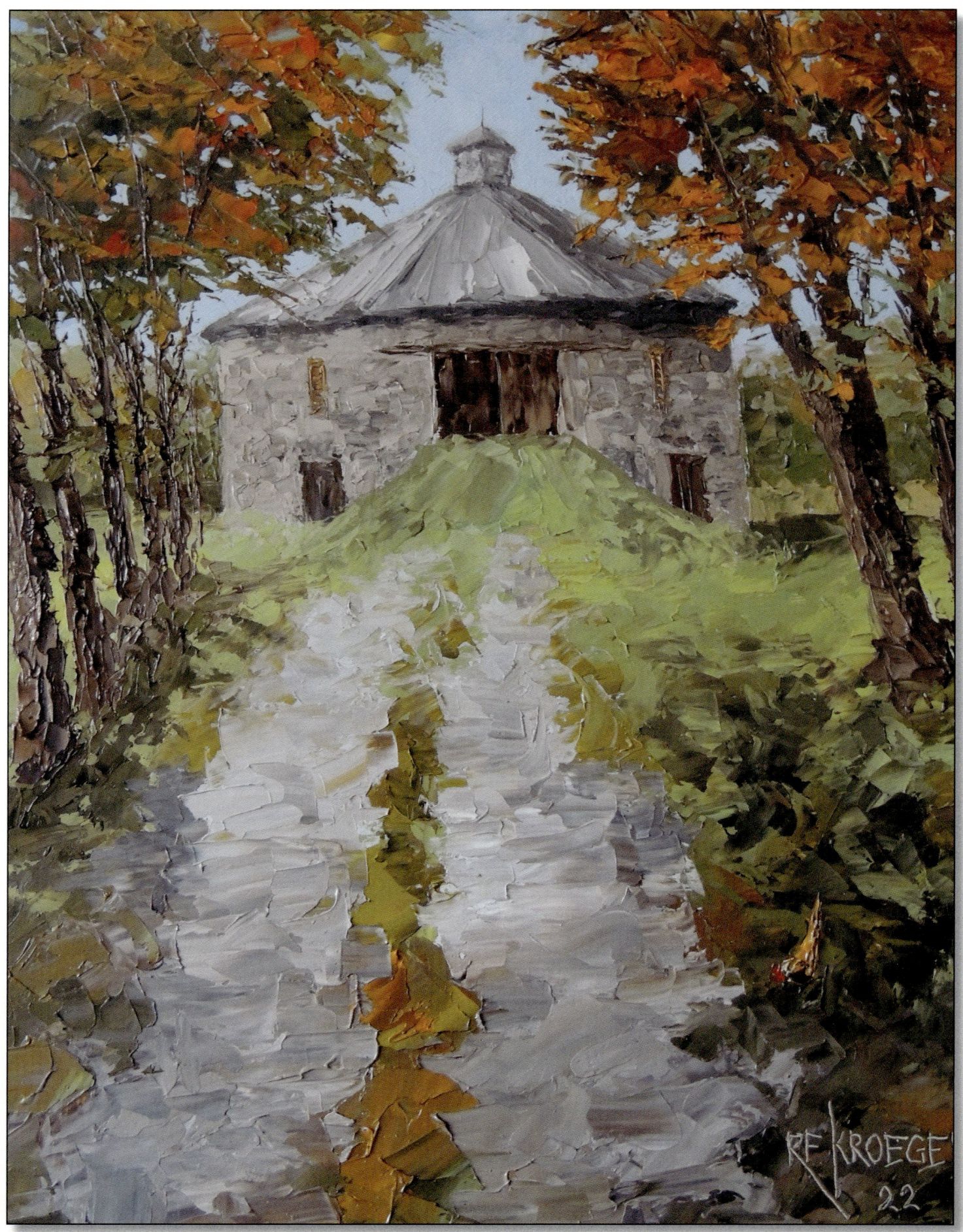

Rarest of the Rare

6. MIDWEST

OHIO

CLARK COUNTY
Rarest of the Rare

This octagonal stone barn is almost one of a kind. In fact, I had to search far and wide before I found another – the Gilmore barn in Missouri, a three-story limestone octagonal bank barn, built in 1899. Restored smartly, it serves as an event center for the community. In 1994 it made the National Register of Historic Places. Another stone octagonal barn was built in 1939 for the Sheridan, Wyoming, County Fair, thanks to President Franklin Roosevelt's New Deal Program. Today it houses livestock in pens beneath seating that can hold up to 420 – for viewing presentations. That makes this Ohio barn a rare bird!

Several years ago Bob McClure, son of the owner, Marjorie McClure, took some time out of his farming schedule to show me not only his barn but several others close by, including a wooden octagonal. Ohio's wet spring had delayed planting.

Mrs. McClure bought the barn in 2010 in a farm auction from Glenn Murphy, not because of the unique barn but because of the 64 acres of prime cropland that came with it. The stone barn was a bonus, but it was a mess. Bob explained that they filled 40 dumpsters with trash from the barn and disposed of 300 old tires in the clean-up. He also installed new shutters and a front door.

Bob didn't know much about the history of the barn, though a local farmer, Joe Shank, owned it at one time, along with the wooden octagonal barn a few miles away. McClure's barn was probably built around 1900 in a time when many polygonal barns were built, though much later than another Ohio icon, the octagonal brick one-room schoolhouse in Sinking Spring, Highland County, which was built in 1831. Octagonal buildings weren't common.

The irony of the round barn, outlined in an 1853 publication, *A Home for All*, was that this type of barn enclosed the most space per lineal wall of all shapes, leading one to think that it would be less expensive to build than a rectangular one. The reality, eventually discovered, was that it was more difficult for the carpenter to build and construction cost more than a barn of traditional shape. The author, Orson Fowler, felt that the octagonal barn design, easier to construct than a circular one, also provided more space than one with square corners. More experts and writers, notably Elliot Stewart of New York, editor of the monthly *Buffalo Livestock Journal*, acclaimed the design of the octagonal barn, encouraging farmers to consider this design. These publications planted the seed for such barns and, indeed, some farmers began building octagonal barns in the 1870s and 1880s.

Though this barn sits on level ground – overlooking the tillable 64 acres – the farmer built an earthen bank that leads to the main entrance; he anchored it on both sides with stone walls. This gave the barn two levels. On a rear side, a large wooden door opens to the hay-mow on the second floor and four sets of doors open on the lower level, two of them Dutch doors. Some of the major beams are hand-hewn; stalls for livestock remain intact.

The stonemasonry is superb. Cut and dressed limestone, alternating between yellow ochre and gray, has been laid in coursed rows. Large gray quoins support the corners. Now, standing for over a century, the stonework shows no cracking, hinting that the mason used the correct mixture of mortar. Stonemasons can leave their mark that withstands all kinds of weather, even snowy and cold Ohio winters. Perched on top, the decorative octagonal cupola is still in good shape, though it serves only for ventilation. Perhaps one reason for the barn's durability is that it has only five small windows, hinting that this may have been used for beef cattle and sheep, which can handle most winters outdoors.

Overall, this barn, maintained well by the McClures, is not only an Ohio gem, but a national treasure and deserves a listing in the National Register of Historic Places. After all, it's the rarest of the rare.

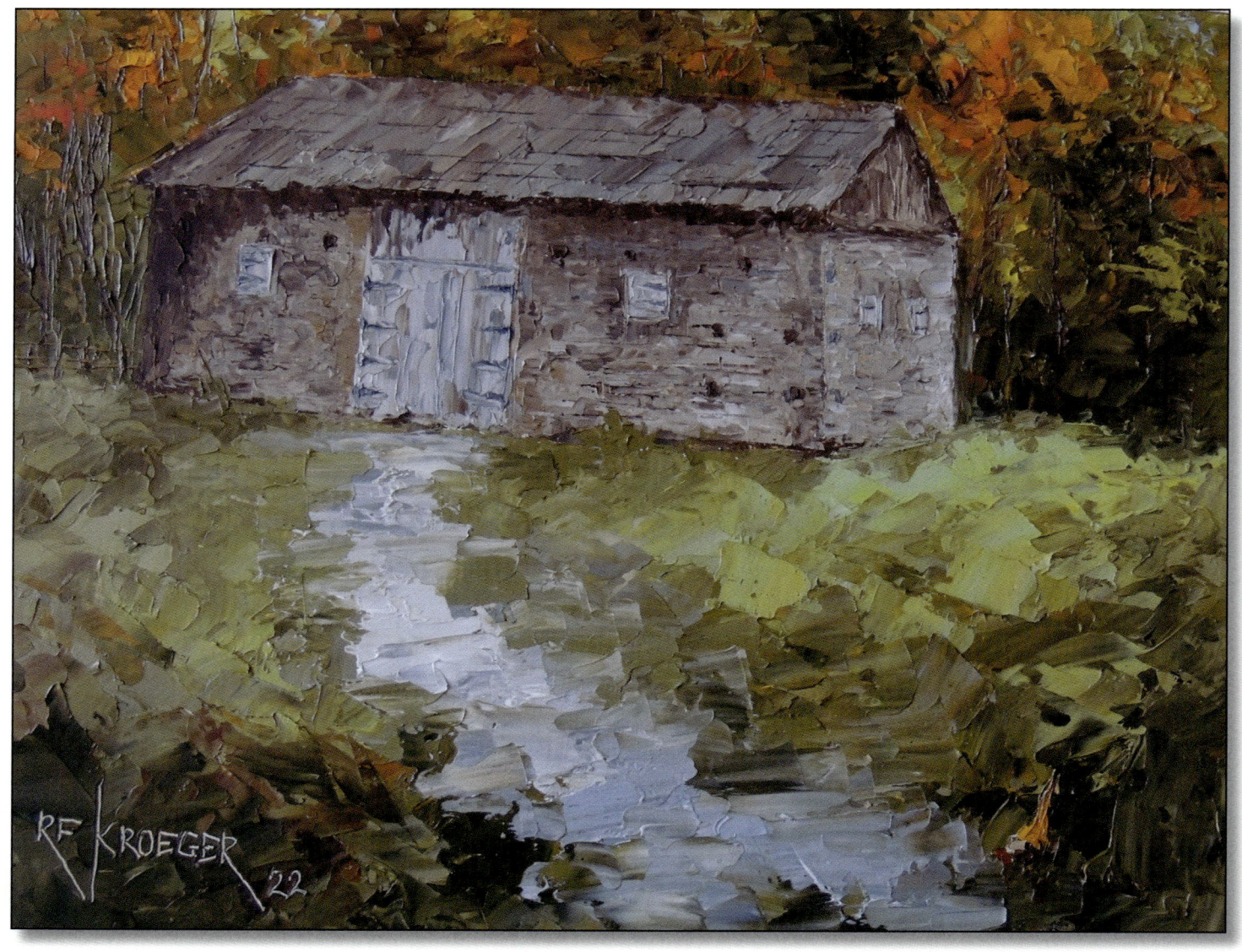

Drake's Dazzling Delight

HAMILTON

Drake's Dazzling Delight

Yes, this stone barn deserves the adjective, dazzling, in every sense of the word. It's one of America's rare architectural marvels built with creek stone rubble masonry. The Drake barn is also remarkable for its age, which is circa 1800, three years before Ohio statehood. And its story is equally fascinating. Since the owners wish privacy, their names and the location of the barn will not be disclosed.

William Drake II was born in Scotch Plains, New Jersey in 1757. His family originated in Devonshire, England, and may be related to the family of Sir Francis Drake, the famous 16th-century English explorer, who circumnavigated the world from 1577 to 1580. The next year he bought Devon's Buckland Abbey, which includes a massive medieval stone barn, built by the Cistercians in 1278. Francis Drake helped defeat the Spanish Armada in 1588 and he planned to attack the Spanish once again in Panama in 1595, but

fever broke out on his ship and he died. After his passing, since he had no children, the estate passed to his brother Thomas Drake, and it remained in the Drake family until 1946 when the National Trust bought it. The Cistercians – known as "white monks" due to their undyed habits – were a branch of the Benedictine Order, following strict routines. They believed in the importance of a life of austerity, prayer and manual labor.

William Drake served in the militia during the Revolutionary War and, afterwards, married Anna Turril in 1781. With other relatives (including Isaac), he left Pittsburgh and traveled down the Ohio River on a flat boat. In 1790 they settled in Losantiville (Columbia-Tusculum area), which was later renamed Cincinnati. Having considerable wealth, they purchased 500 acres – at one dollar per acre – in what is now a northeastern suburb of Cincinnati, in 1800. Though William lived in Losantiville till 1802, he likely built a temporary log home to live in while he built the stone barn. His relative Isaac was relatively poor and moved to Kentucky.

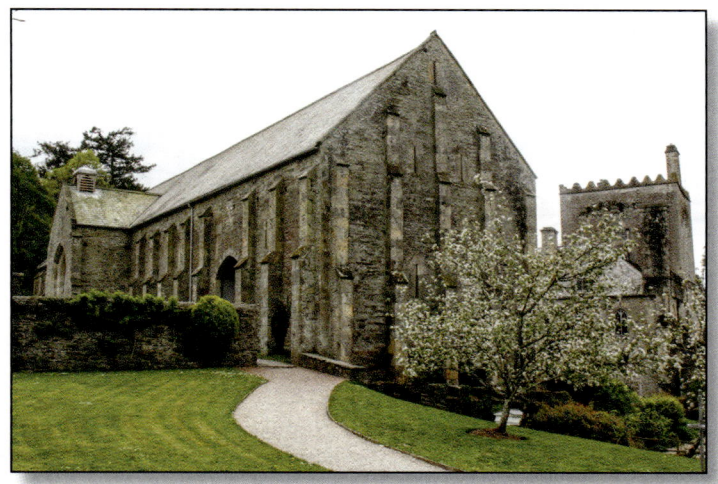

The Great Barn, Buckland Abbey, Devon. Courtesy of Ken Bonham

Though Isaac's son Daniel, born in 1785, had minimal schooling, he had learned to read by age seven and, apparently a bright child, he mentored in 1800 under Dr. William Goforth, one of Cincinnati's first physicians. By 1805 Goforth granted the young Drake a formal certificate, the first diploma to practice medicine issued west of the Appalachian Mountains. He opened a practice in Kentucky but returned to Cincinnati in 1807.

Dr. Drake played a major role in establishing the Medical College of Ohio in 1819, which eventually became the University of Cincinnati College of Medicine, considered the oldest medical college west of the Allegheny Mountains. Besides practicing medicine, he had a strong interest in natural history and published a book in 1815, *Natural and Statistical View, or Picture of Cincinnati and the Miami County*. Not only did his book describe the dinosaur bones found in Kentucky's Big Bone Lick ("most of them gigantic"), but it devoted a chapter to the mounds built by Native Americans, including one altered by General Anthony Wayne in 1794 to fashion a sentinel. Fountain Square, the center of downtown Cincinnati, now covers the site of these mounds. To honor his contributions, the University of Cincinnati's Daniel Drake Center for Post-Acute Care is named after him.

Meanwhile, William Drake also built a stone house, whose masonry is slightly more finished than that of the barn and was probably completed before 1810. Massive, rough-cut hand-hewn beams, still exposed in the basement, point to the early 1800s. Today, thanks to a litany of historically minded owners, the stone house has been incorporated into a larger home, preserving its stone walls and hearth. William and Anna had nine children, including four sons, ages 9 to 21, who probably helped build the barn. Since the stonemasonry is more polished on the house, it's likely that Drake hired a stonemason for that job.

For the barn, however, the family probably used limestone and shale rubble from adjacent creeks, which still flow through the region and abound in shelves of slate, shale, granite, and other rocks, ideal for building walls. In fact, a creek less than a mile from the barn features a 40-foot-high exposed bank of shale. Though corners of the barn are neatly cut quoins, suggesting solid stonemasonry skills of the barn builder, the majority of the stones have irregular shapes, hinting that a short construction time was more important than esthetics. Small openings, spaced randomly but about three to four feet apart, dot all four sides of the barn and appear to be weep holes, but they're not: they don't penetrate the interior. Chances are that the holes were used to support scaffolding as the barn was being built.

Interestingly, about eight miles away is another stone barn, likely used as a carriage barn for horses, with the same randomly coursed rubble creek limestone. However, this one, located on the exclusive Peterloon Estate, was built over a century later. It sits at the foot of the driveway, leading to John Emery's mansion, one with 36 rooms, 21 bathrooms, and 19 fireplaces, finished in 1930.

Drake's barn's interior beams came as another surprise, one that shows the efficiency and ingenuity of the builder.

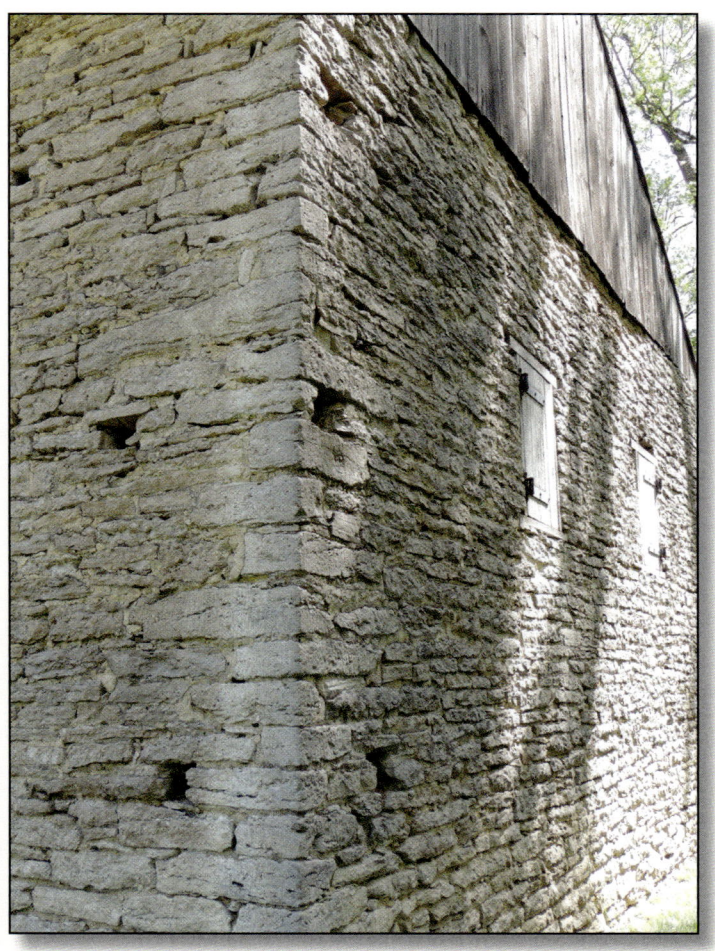

Scaffolding holes, Drake barn, Hamilton County 2021.

Designed as a timber-framed three-bay English threshing barn, this one veers from tradition in lacking not only a post and beam-supported roof but also mortise and tenon joints, almost universally used in barns of this age. However, to avoid constructing these time-consuming joints, the builder cleverly placed the hand-hewn beams directly on top of and into the 18-inch-thick stone walls. Two hundred years later, they're still in place. (Architectural planning of mortise and tenon joints in a timber-framed barn involves precise measurements, skill, and time, especially in the scribe rule method, generally used at this time.)

And, to avoid using vertical posts to support the roof – which take up room – the principal rafters also rest on the stone walls. Originally, these were probably wooden logs with bark still on them but planed on one side to support the roof. Current rafters appear to be sawmill-cut. There were probably sawmills in this area by 1800.

Also interesting is that the barn apparently has not shifted, a common problem with old buildings. Though a geologist could tell if the barn sits on top of bedrock – as is the case for the Kindelberger barn (65 feet of solid flint rock) – there's no visible evidence that it's been raised. Its small size – 28 by 52 feet with a 15-foot height – may be another reason for its stability.

Since the Drake family farmed hundreds of acres, they may have constructed one or more larger wooden barns to handle the workload. This stone barn would support only a modest farm and this hints that the family may have had other income. Nearby, about 20 feet from the barn, is a circular cement slab, possibly the footprint of a former silo.

Over the centuries, the estate of 500 acres split up and the farm passed out of family hands. When former owners, who purchased it in 2007 and sold it in 2024, considered moving here, they wanted a home with country charm, not a modern gargantuan edifice, and they passed on several homes for sale. But, at their first glance at the barn, they were hooked, "We bought it the day we saw it." The original stone house was a bonus. For a historical preservationist, this was heaven.

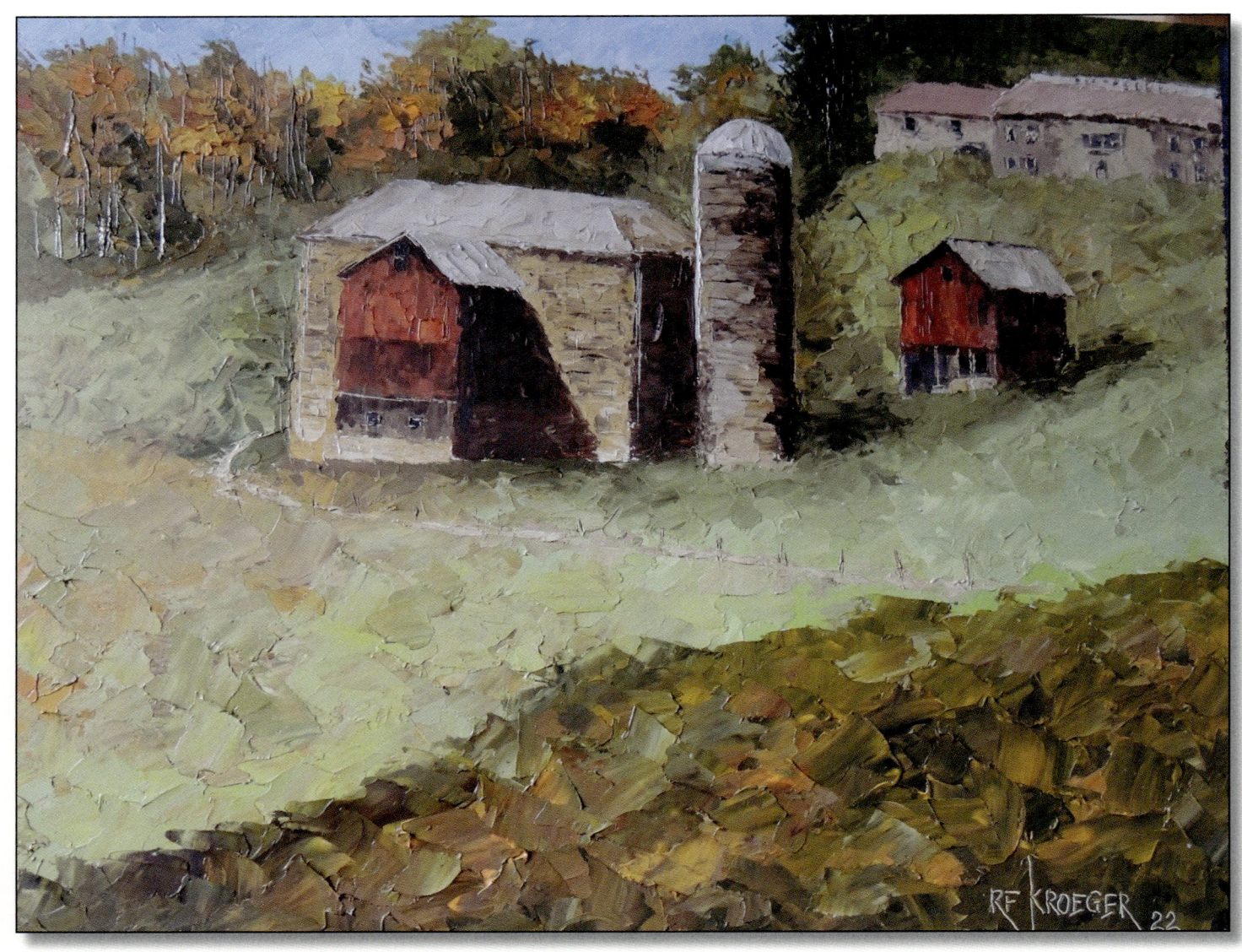

Kindelberger New

Previous owners had replaced the wooden barn doors and windows, being careful to keep the gray weathered appearance. But, according to one owner, the asphalt-shingled roof had to go. So, they replaced it with wood shakes, most probably what William Drake used two centuries ago – as well as what almost all barn builders used in the early 19th century. For a privately-owned old barn to get a wooden replacement roof is quite an honor. No longer a farm, the three acres, a small remnant of the 500-acre William Drake estate, serve as a comfortable residence and, nearby, the barn continues to dazzle and delight all that understand the historical significance of one of America's architectural treasures.

MONROE COUNTY
Kindelberger New

To drive the narrow, winding roads of Monroe County is like riding a roller coaster. There's nothing flat here. In fact, they call this part of Ohio "Little Switzerland;" the school district is officially The Switzerland of Ohio Local School District. From an artist's perspective, this lively terrain isn't boring, especially compared to flat topography. A beautiful scene pops up nearly everywhere. And one of those scenes is the stone barn at the farm of Marjorie and Gary Baumberger. I call it "Kindelberger New," as opposed to "Kindelberger Old," which was the original barn built by these Ohio pioneers in 1855.

Barns and farms that pass from one or two generations are fairly common, but one that has passed to the fifth generation – Marge – merits a rare rating. In fact, their daughter Beverly, the sixth generation, may own this farm someday. But let's go back to the beginning.

The Kindelberger family emigrated here from Bavaria, as many Germans and Swiss did in that era, a time of unrest, hardships, and war. The family – Frederick, Sr., his wife Margartha, a daughter and a son, Frederick, Jr. – arrived in America in 1838. Eight years later, they paid $950 for a farm and its 80 acres from John Lapp who was the original pioneer, having started the farm in 1831. The deed was registered at the Ohio Company Land Office in Marietta, which dates to 1788, the first in the Ohio Country. The land office still exists, and it's the oldest building in Ohio. President Andrew Jackson signed the Kindelberger's deed – the presidential signature was required for all land deeds during his presidency.

Frederick was a stone mason, as well as being a farmer, and used his skills to build the "old" barn's stone foundation, which still bears *FK 1855*, etched in stone inside the barn, though the rest of the barn is wooden. The family farmed the hilly land and eventually acquired 200 acres. His son,

Frederick, Jr., only 11 years old when the family purchased the farm, learned stonework from his father. In 1860 he married a woman from neighboring Belmont County and, shortly after their marriage, they moved in with the groom's parents and joined them in farming. Later and after the birth of their fourth child, Frederick decided his family needed a larger home. And, having learned stonemasonry from his father, he wanted the home to last. In the same year – 1872 – that he purchased the farm from his father for $2,400, he built the house, using stone quarried on the farm. He insulated the tin roof with sawdust and he used sand under the floor, making it soundproof, warmer in winter, and nearly fireproof. Clever man. The sandstone block home still sits on a hilltop next to a road, appropriately named German Ridge Road.

Although the farm already had three small barns, Frederick decided to build a larger one and, one day, while drilling for water, he found a perfect site – a flat spot on 65 feet of flint bedrock and next to a slope. Frederick and his father cut huge blocks of sandstone from a quarry on their property about a quarter mile away. William, his young son, and daughter Mary hauled these huge pieces – via horse and wagon – to the building site. That in itself was an accomplishment. Yes, two Kindelberger teenagers contributed to this masterpiece.

Though he used his own masonry skills to shape and dress each piece exactly, he also hired local stonemasons. They sculpted blocks, four to seven feet long and 25 inches thick at the bottom, which gradually decreased in size to the top, where they measured 12 inches wide. This gradual tapering required the use of an off-square guide to give each stone the proper shape. The stones, 150 years later, look as if they were placed yesterday. What an incredible piece of architecture, reminiscent of Roman aqueducts, which, mortarless, still stand throughout Europe!

Each block had a dimple, centered, where ends of giant tongs could grab the block, allowing it to be hoisted. Kindelberger thought so much of these tongs that he sculpted one into a date stone. The barn hasn't budged and, barring a massive earthquake, it should stay put for centuries to come. They finished the barn in 1886.

The third part of this process was to place the sandstone blocks into position, each of which weighed hundreds of pounds (the heaviest weighed over a ton). Now, for the lower levels, that wasn't too difficult. But how about the higher levels? There are approximately 20 rows of stones in the barn, from top to bottom, stretching about 35-feet high. To protect the workers, the central part of the roof, measuring 15x30 feet, was in place before the community barn raising. Although the event was a traditional German-Swiss festivity, involving food, drink, and song, Frederick paid stone masons and carpenters two dollars a day for their

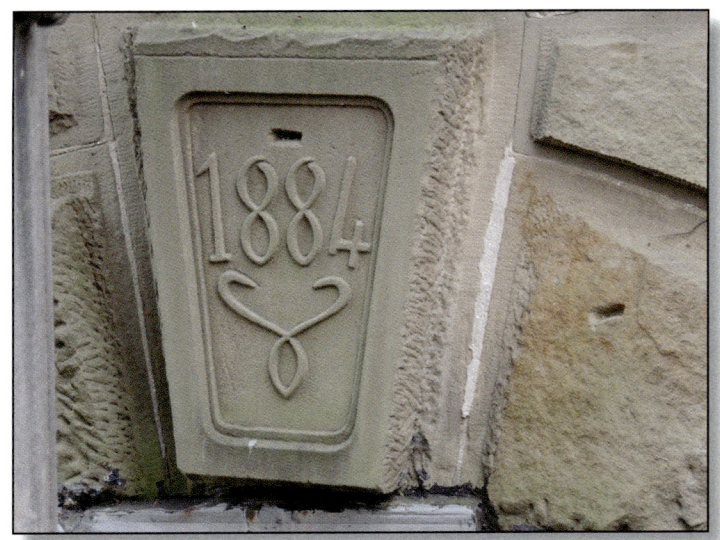

Date stone and tongs, Kindelberger barn, 2023.

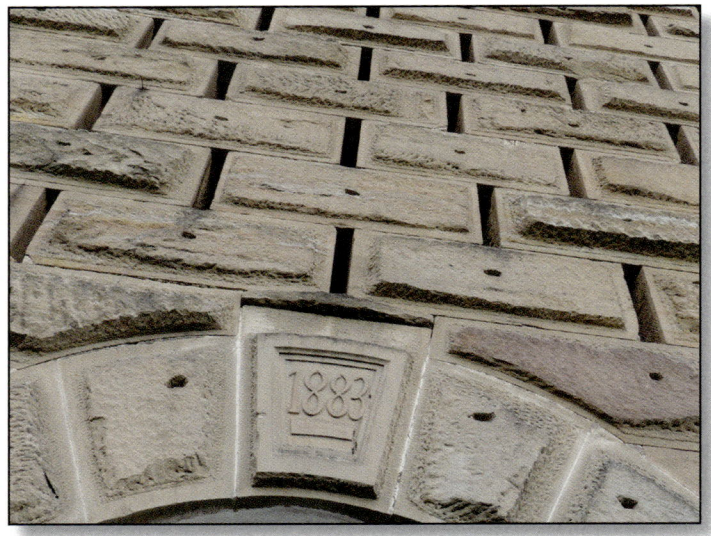

Date stone, dimples, and ventilation slits, Kindelberger barn 2023.

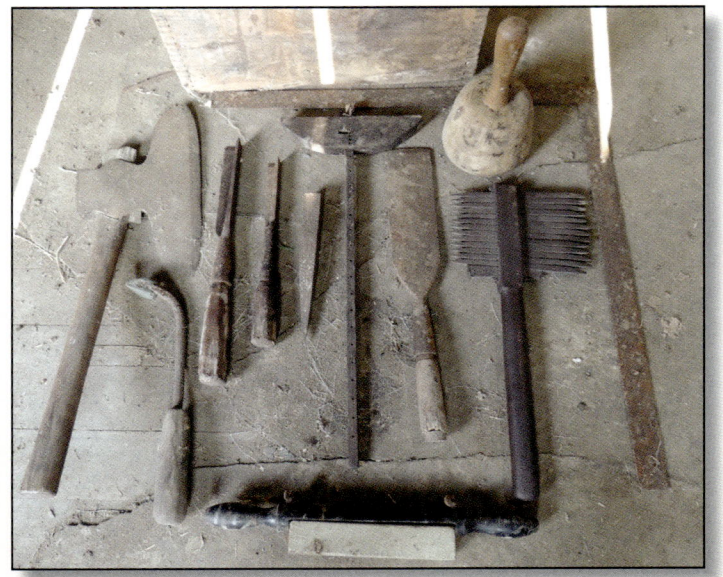

Stonemason's tools, Crandall on the right, Kindelberger barn 2023.

help. According to a 1945 newspaper report in *The Spirit of Democracy*, published in nearby Woodsfield, 60 workers raised the barn, using a 40-foot-long hickory log as a boom and pulleys to raise the blocks, secured by tongs, into position. They held pikes to support the walls. Imagine these men – and the two teenagers – sweating and using every ounce of strength. No modern cranes in those days. Just manual labor, German ingenuity, and two teenagers, as the newspaper reported, "the husky youngsters, furnishing the hoisting power with muscle and brawn."

As he had done with his stone house, he insulated the roof with sawdust, but this time he used slate to cover the hipped roof and its flat central section, a bit unusual for a barn roof. Inside the three-level bank barn, four 45-foot hand-hewn beams, each 12-inches square, support the rafters and roof in traditional timber-framing. Wagons could enter the second level of the barn on the hillside and unload hay and grain, which were stored in the mow and granary. They built the floors to last – half-hewn lumber, six inches thick, laid side by side.

The lowest level housed livestock, stanchions and a dairy. Originally a windmill on the roof was used to power small equipment inside the barn. A concrete silo came later. Spaces left between the blocks provided light and ventilation, shown in the photo.

The farm passed to the next generation of Kindelbergers in 1906 when "Junior" sold it to his son, William, who, in the 1940s, lived with his daughter and her husband, Marjorie's grandfather, J.D. Caldwell, who was next in line to buy the farm. J.D. was a renaissance man. He had imagination and thirst for knowledge. A beekeeper and a horticulturalist, he planted walnut trees on the farm in the early 20th century. Along with farming the land, he developed hybrid corn and raised honey. And he lived a long time, selling the farm to Marjorie and her husband Gary Baumberger, whose roots also go back a long way in this county. Gary's great grandparents owned a home that had the date prominently displayed in the slate roof, commonly done in the late 1800s in eastern Ohio. He grew up a farmer. Today, his repurposed double log pen home has become a family museum.

One day after they bought the farm in 1976, while rummaging through the barn, Marge and Gary discovered the tools that "Junior" and his dad used to cut, shape, and move the sandstone blocks. One of them, a crandall, had a long handle with serrated metal teeth on one end and probably weighed ten pounds. As I held it – with some difficulty – I tried to imagine those sturdy stonemasons carefully shaping each piece, being careful not to chisel off too much stone. Scattered on a hillside near the barn are some stone blocks that didn't cooperate: so, they were rejected.

Gary took me on a tour of the barn, which could serve as Monroe County's historical museum: stonemason's tools, an old wooden sled, an old wooden wagon, and a ladder made from hand-cut wood, all from two centuries ago. He also showed me a 20-foot brine trough, hand-hewn from a log that these early settlers used to preserve meat by placing it in salted water.

Though several years ago Gary and Marjorie worked the farm industriously, they've slowed down. After decades of dairy and cattle farming, they've cut back to raising chickens (buyers stop by every day to pick up eggs), a dozen dairy goats, and a few beef cattle. Gary tends to the chickens and a few beef cattle and Marge still milks the goats. Kindelberger farming continues.

Gary no longer raises hay, which may sound easy, but it's not. When he was engaged in this only a few years ago, on the first day he cut the hay. On the next, he'd pick it up in a "chopper" that blew it into a wagon, which Gary would unhitch and take to the silo. This continued until the silo was full. But, if there was more hay on the land, Gary would cut it, allow it to cure in the field, rake it into round bales, and then haul it to the barn for storage until winter

feeding. Whew! They've also constructed a beautiful rental cabin, resembling the lodge at Yellowstone, which can be rented by the day or by the week. It's quiet and only about 300 yards from the stone barn. Information is available at stonebarnfarm.net.

In 1980 the National Register listed this unusual barn and the stone house, an honor the family deserves not only because of unique architecture but also because the stone work has stood the test of time, monuments to master stonemason Frederick Kindelberger, Jr., Marge's great-great grandfather. Ohio is lucky to still have this spectacular stone barn, which it will have for many more years to come.

KENTUCKY

CAMPBELL COUNTY
Camp Springs

Tucked away in a deep ravine along Four Mile Road in rural Campbell County, Camp Springs, an unincorporated community, represents a 19th-century settlement

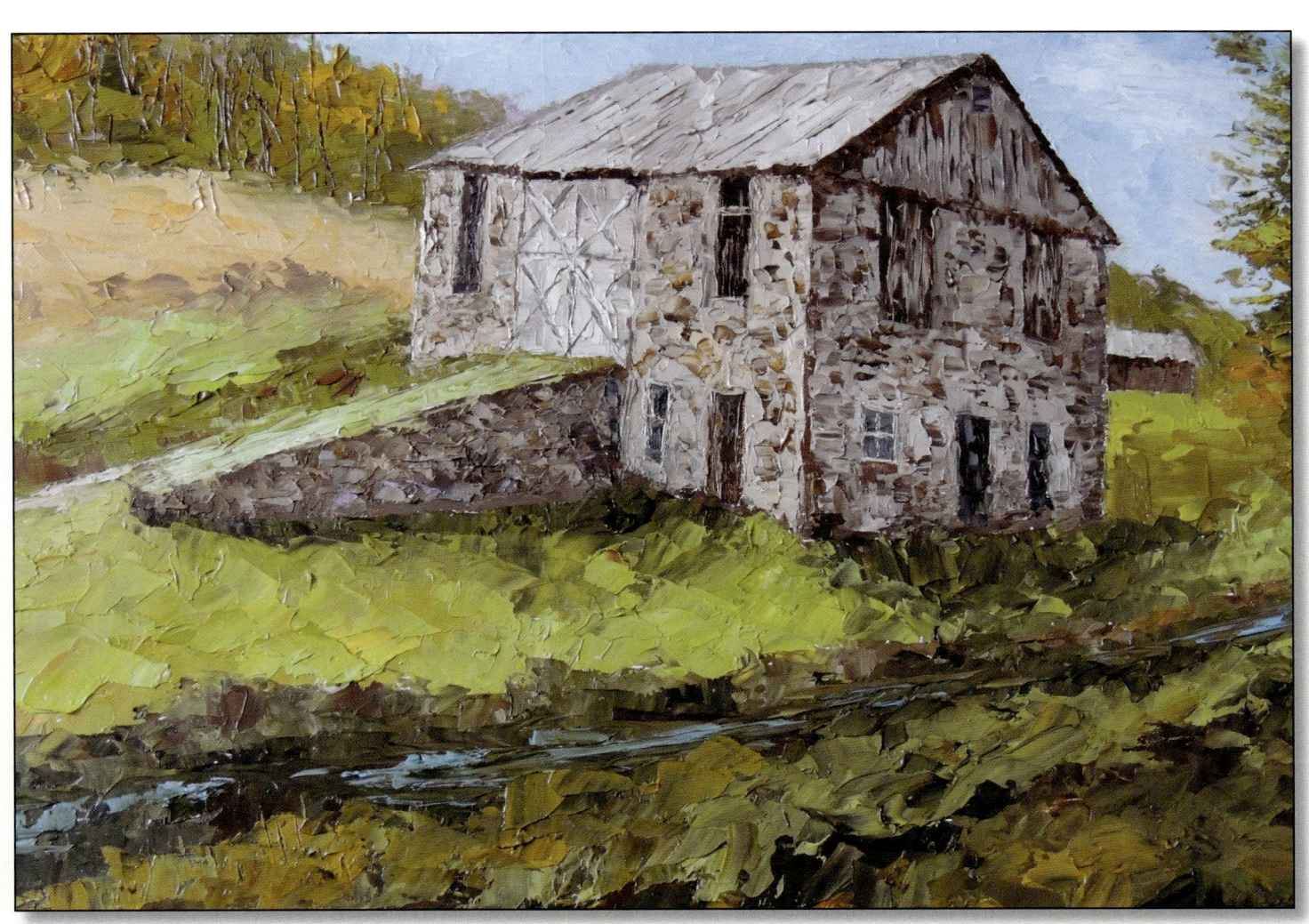

Camp Springs

of German immigrants. Many of them, stonemasons, built multiple, still existing, limestone rubble buildings, 27 of which have been listed on the National Register since 1979 – including this stone barn.

Whereas many Germans arrived in Philadelphia, others took ships that sailed to the port of New Orleans, where passengers boarded riverboats, transporting them up the Mississippi, then onto the Ohio River, before finally settling in Camp Springs, about a dozen miles from the public landing in Cincinnati. The first Germans arrived here in the 1840s. In time, their friends and relatives followed.

Though the hills and valleys weren't ideal for crop farming, the newcomers made the best of the situation by planting vineyards, not a difficult transition from farming since they came from the Rhineland in southwestern Germany, one of the country's most productive wine regions. Though the industry faded after a destructive blight in the 1880s, two wineries have recently re-opened – Camp Springs Winery and Stonebrook Winery.

The stonemasons also took advantage of the landscape, turning its limestone rubble – found in creeks and fields – into many handsome stone buildings, many of which still stand – over 150 years later. One of them (though originally made of logs), built in 1845, is the oldest Catholic church in Campbell County. St. Joseph's church, now brick, has renovated its stone school into a more modern facility.

About 12 stone buildings on the National Register listing stand next to Four Mile Road and one of them, the Camp Springs House, originally served as a stage-coach stop, an inn, and a tavern. Built for William Uthe by the Ort brothers in 1866, the three-and-a half-story stone structure now serves as a bed and breakfast. Others, including the stone Kort Grocery, built by Peter Kort in 1880, and the Isadore Baumann House, built in 1854, command attention on this same road.

Another unique piece of Camp Springs is a stone smokehouse. Apparently, these German stonemasons were intent on building structures for posterity and chose readily available stone over wood or brick. Three of these round rubble stone smokehouses, capped with a charming conical roof, still survive; one is close to the main road.

In 1855 about 60 Germans from Camp Springs and Cincinnati, left on a steamboat and headed for the Kansas Territory, which had just opened for settlement – with offers of cheap land. They arrived in Kansas City, Missouri, in March and the settlers selected a site on the south side of the Kansas River, near the mouth of McDowell's Creek. Although under the impression that the entire journey would be on a river boat, they had

to cross land on the final segment of their trip; so, they bought covered wagons and marched. Since many were admirers of Kentucky's Henry Clay, they named their town "Ashland," after Clay's mansion. However, some of the group became discouraged with life on the prairie and returned home. Others remained, built log cabins and barns and eventually more durable buildings, using the abundant limestone. Many stone barns in the Flint Hills of Kansas still stand.

Though German stonemasons built many stone barns in Camp Springs, only one survives today. Andrew Ritter purchased this small farm from H.J. Bell and built this stone barn in 1883 – as well as supervising the stone foundations of other local barns. Though small (23x28 feet), this bank barn deviated from the traditional German designs of the Sweitzers and forebays of south-eastern Pennsylvania. It's simply a two-level barn and timber-framed – with livestock housed below and crops and hay stored on the main floor. Hand-hewn ladders lead to the hayfork track. Joseph Blenke, a friend of the Ritters, did the framing.

Along with the barn, the National Register listing includes a stone chicken house and a stone smokehouse (10x10 feet), located on the north side of the farmhouse. This represents the only observed example in the area where an outbuilding is connected to a farmhouse, more common in New England, where wintry conditions warranted such attachments. The smokehouse has a vaulted cellar below, containing a springhouse, where butter and milk were stored. A wooden framed barn, possibly built circa 1900, sits higher on the bank, above the stone barn, hinting that Ritter had become prosperous enough to build yet another barn.

Besides being preserved in this painting and essay, Camp Springs was featured on KET (Kentucky Education Television) in 2003 in a short documentary, which was saved in YouTube format. What the video fails to show is the adventure of driving down Four Mile Road, swerving left and right and up and down the hills, mirroring Ohio's Monroe County.

Unfortunately, the Camp Springs barn is located on private property and not accessible to the public. Perhaps someday it will be included on an annual tour of the stone buildings, sponsored by the local community. Regardless, only 12 miles from the bustling metropolis of Cincinnati, Camp Springs is quintessential Americana, an interesting look into the past at the art and the skills of German stonemasons. Their buildings, including the Andrew Ritter stone barn, continue to stand, resisting the ravages of time.

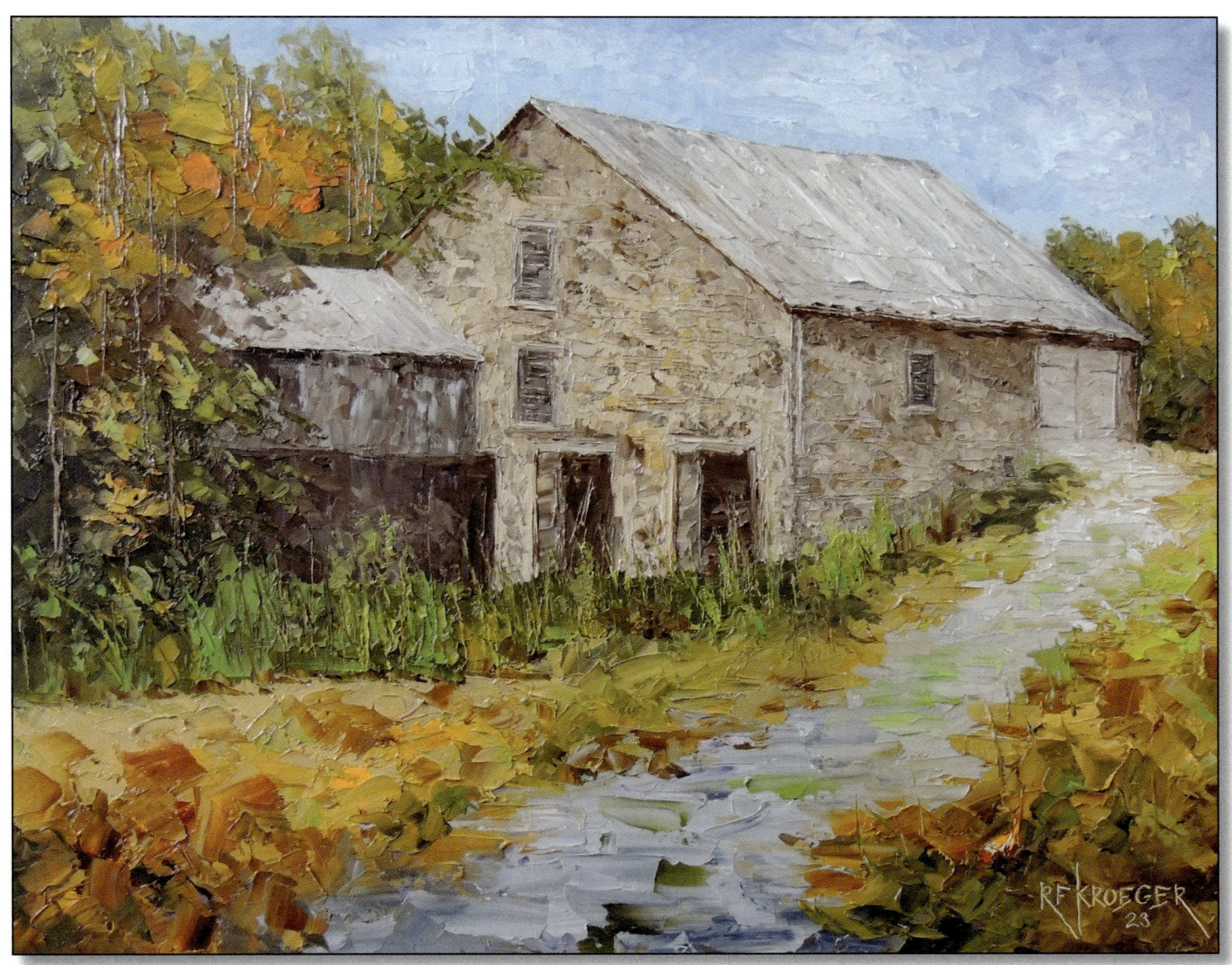

The Orphan

INDIANA

JEFFERSON COUNTY

"The Orphan"

Life can be cruel … as it was in the childhood of the farmer who built this barn in the mid-1800s, years before the Civil War started. Zephaniah Lloyd, born in Maryland in 1805, lost his mother when he was only three months old and became a full-fledged orphan when his dad died in 1810. Fortunately, his older half-brother Tubmond Wright took him under his wing and raised him.

The family name of Lloyd, a Welsh name with typical multiple consonants, traces back to Quakerism in 17th-century Britain. Quakers, especially the ones who were goldsmiths, were trusted enough for people to store their valuables with them. They also provided loans in a time before banks existed. Eventually, Welsh families

named Lloyd and Barclay evolved into financial institutions known today as Barclays Bank and Lloyds Bank … and Lloyds of London, the insurance company that will insure just about anything under the sun.

Around 1618 the first Welsh immigrants arrived in America, hoping for religious freedom since their form of Christianity did not conform to that of the Church of England. When William Penn established his large land grant in 1682 – which eventually became the colony of Pennsylvania – Quakers, both Welsh and English, once again flocked to America, especially to the region surrounding southeastern Pennsylvania, Delaware, western New Jersey, and Maryland. In fact, Welsh immigrants, taking advantage of a 1702 Penn land grant, settled in Montgomery County, Pennsylvania, and named the borough North Wales and the countryside "Gwynedd," after their homeland in Wales.

In the early 18th-century, the Lloyds were prominent

in the colony of Maryland. Edward Lloyd II was the 11th Royal Governor of Maryland from 1709 to 1714 and Edward Lloyd IV was a delegate to the Continental Congress for Maryland in 1783 and 1784.

Though Zephaniah may not have been related to these affluent Lloyds, his first name, a biblical one meaning "hidden by God" and symbolic of God's protection, hints that his parents named him for religious reasons. Indeed, his Hebrew name proved true: God did protect this five-year-old orphan. Raised by his half-brother, he certainly would have been exposed to the many stone barns of that era in that region, the nation's motherlode of stone barns.

In 1817, Zephaniah, then 12, moved from Maryland to Switzerland County, Indiana, where Tubmond began farming, with help from his younger brother. Five years later, now 17, Zephaniah moved to Jefferson County, where he remained for the rest of his life. Unfortunately, Tubmond passed away in 1828, only 39 years old.

In farm country of the early 19th century, children grew up quickly. In 1824 Zephhaniah, now 19 years old and on his own, married a local farm girl, Anna Latimore, whose father had moved here, as many did in the early 1800s – in search of cheap and fertile farmland. Together, they raised nine children. Zephhaniah lived to see all of them get married. His wife passed away in 1881.

In 1830, at 25 and married with children, he was prosperous enough to purchase 80 acres to start his own farm. Chances are good that he built a wooden barn, if the farm didn't already have one. As the years passed, Zephaniah apparently continued to do well, evidenced by his decision to build this large stone barn. Etched on a stone plaque under the peak on the barn's left-hand side, reads, *"Built By An. Rock and Jon Splez for Z. Loyd 1855."* Stonemason Charles Anthony Rock's ability to build a stone barn

exceeded his spelling skill; he misspelled Lloyd. However, according to barn scholar Greg Huber, who has inspected thousands of 18th- and 19th-century stone barns, the mason might have purposely abbreviated the name since space was limited. Interestingly, the date of 1855, representing the year of the barn's construction, likely suggests that the add-on stone shed was built later, possibly in the early 1860s. Perhaps he was doing so well that he needed the shed for more livestock.

Despite its remote location in the middle of a dense field of soybeans, the barn is architecturally remarkable as well as being one of the earliest stone barns built in this part of the Midwest, which was still Indian territory in 1830. Beginning that year and continuing for 15 years, the last of Indiana's tribes – which included the Miami, Shawnee, Illinois, Potawatomi, and Delaware – were removed to reservations further west, in accordance with the Indian Removal Act of 1830.

The datestone lists the builder as Jon Spelz, whose name derives from Middle High German spëlze and is the occupational name for a grower of spelt (a type of wheat). Perhaps Lloyd told Spelz, who was experienced in building wooden barns, about his childhood memories of the stone barns in Maryland. Unlike the traditional Pennsylvania barn, a German design and one built into a bank with a forebay on the rear side, this one does not have a forebay. Instead, the two-story barn (with an attic for hay storage), fits into a bank that slopes from right to left and has two threshing doors on the extreme right, a variation of the older three-bay English threshing barn, whose doors are normally centered. Huber explained that this position of the threshing doors is rare. In fact, he's seen only two like this, out of the many thousands of stone barns he's visited.

Inside the upper story, roof rafters rest on long plates that sit on the 18-inch-thick stone walls, an unusual variation, compared to resting directly into the stone walls, typical of most stone barns. Massive hand-hewn beams, lodged into the stone walls, extend from one side to the other, above the threshing doors, and support purlin posts, both perpendicular and canted, which, in turn, hold up the roof's sawn lumber, cut from trees of varied widths. Saw-cut beams have been placed into mortises in the hewn plates to create the haymow, hinting that there was either a sawmill close by or a portable one brought to the site. The roof, probably originally made with wooden hand-split shakes,

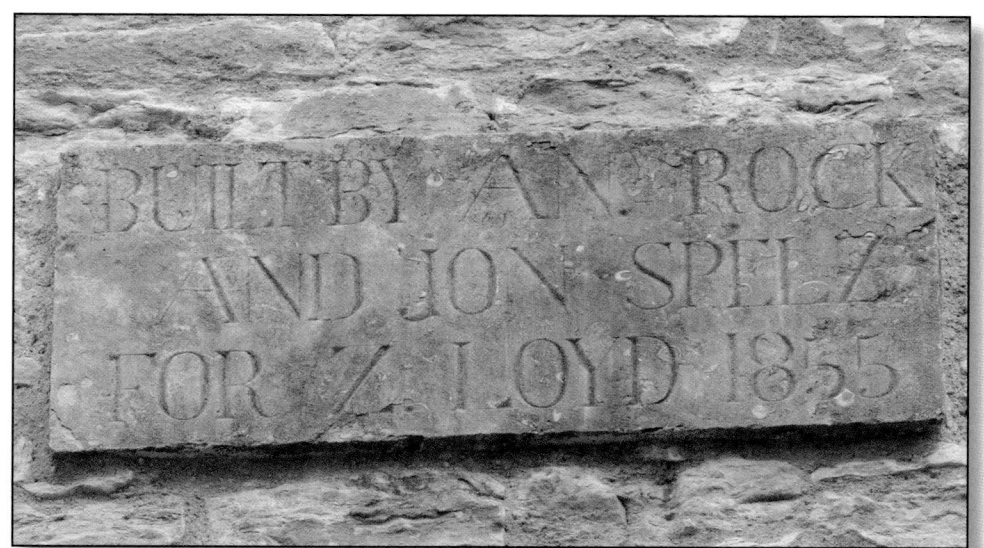

Datestone on the Lloyd stone barn, Jefferson County, Indiana.

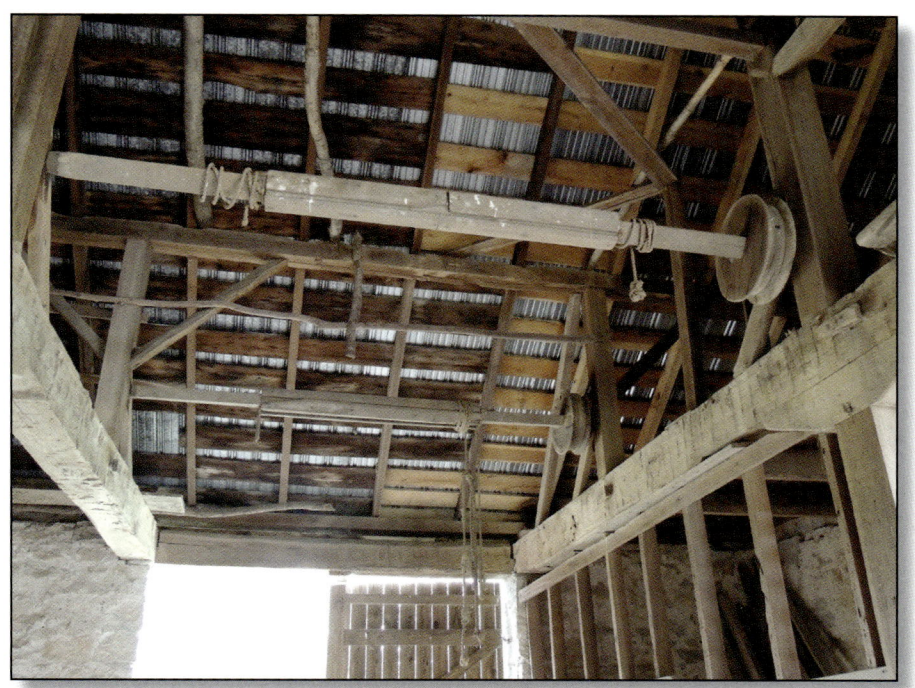

Two windlasses in Lloyd barn

is now covered with metal. When a tornado hit the barn in 2017, part of the roof suffered damage, requiring the new owners to replace part of it, which they did.

Next to the rear door stands a wooden corn crib, 9x12 feet, positioned on the floor, in a convenient spot and, being enclosed by stone on two sides, is virtually rodent-proof. Though it is often seen in 19th-century barns, this barn does not have a hay track for a hay carrier, first designed and sold by Iowa's William Louden in 1867. Instead, Lloyd or Splez built two wooden windlasses near the rear threshing door, still with rope attached.

The windlass, normally an open-spoked wheel, compared to these solid-wood wheels, is rarely seen in barns anymore. In pioneer days, catalogs didn't sell them; farmers made them. About two to three feet in diameter, the circular wheel was attached to a round shaft, which would turn as the farmer pulled on ropes fitted inside the slot in the wheel. This made hoisting easier. Wagons could be raised to dump hay into the mow, harvested crops onto the floor, or corn into the crib. If wagons or other equipment needed repair, they could be hoisted by the windlass. The windlass could also be used to raise livestock for butchering or move heavy sacks of threshed grain. It was a versatile performer.

Towards the left-hand side of the upper story, a large wooden hand-hewn lintel rests on an opening cut in the stone wall, which was presumably made to allow access to the upper floor of the shed that came later. Triangular cracking in the stone above the lintel has been repaired.

On the 60x63-foot lower level, the mason constructed three huge stone piers – one is about three feet wide – to bear the weight of the gigantic stone façade. Wooden lintels rest on these piers. Most likely, animal stalls lined the walls with wooden feeding bins, one of which lies in the haymow. Seven window openings, probably covered originally with wood, provided light and large slit ventilators with stone sills and lintels, cut into the stone walls, provided much-needed air flow. The barn was designed well.

The interesting shed, wooden on the front and made of stone on its rear wall and left side and open to the main barn on both levels, has a whimsical, Hansel-and-Gretel appearance with latticework and two entry doors. Hand-hewn timber-framed beams support the upper level and large stone quoins, next to the door on the left, are open-faced, possibly having been connected to a partial stone wall on the front side at one time. Inside a door frame, next to a large section of latticework, a giant wooden peg, about 20 inches long, protrudes from an open mortise. Perhaps the farmer hung harnesses on it. All guessing aside, why Lloyd added this shed remains a mystery.

Mr. Rock's work represents master stonemasonry. Limestone, taken from a nearby quarry, has been cut uniformly, though it remains undressed. Large, uniform quoins support the corners and there is virtually no cracking. Thanks to the current owners, the stone has been recently tuckpointed on the outside walls. They hired a barn restorer to stabilize the lower level, which showed signs of collapse under the weight of the bank.

A website, findagrave.com, featured an image of Anthony Rock's tombstone and provided the gist of his obituary, a rare look at an old barn stonemason. An article, published in the *Madison Courier* on December 23, 1911, reported that he was born in Poland in 1825, which raises the question about how he got his surname, obviously English in origin. Perhaps his mother remarried and changed her name and her son's to that of her new English husband. Fluent in three languages, Charles – or Anthony, as he was known by – immigrated to the United States with his brother, though they soon separated – with Anthony settling in Jefferson County. Nothing is known about how he learned stonemasonry, but the newspaper reported that he was "one of the very best." It's probable that he built many stone structures in the area. The article mentioned that his first work in the county came at the "big cut."

In 1836, legislators passed a bill to construct a railroad that would pass from Madison, which at the time was a major city in Indiana, through Columbus and Indianapolis, ending at Lafayette. Irish workers were recruited to build the line – as they did for canals in Ohio and Indiana – but they had to deal with rugged terrain, including a crossing over Crooked Creek. The construction lasted five years, ending in 1841, when Anthony would have been 16 years old. Working with stonemasons during this project might be how he learned how to evaluate rock types, mix mortar, and lay stone. The "big cut" refers to a 1,150-foot-long section, which required excavation of more than 250,000 tons of earth and rock.

The article explained that he also built the Landon stone mill on Big Creek and a stone house for James Jackson in Republican township, which is still standing, across the creek from the Lloyd barn. Though he probably came to Jefferson County with little money, he quickly acquired skills, which made his services in demand.

In 1856 Anthony married Rebecca Lloyd, one of Zephaniah's nine children, whom he may have met while building the barn. After her death, he married again and had three children with his new wife Susana, giving him a total of seven children. Raising two large families required substantial income, which attested to his skill in stonemasonry. The writer of his obituary commented that Anthony was a "noble man, always cheerful and in a good humor," and that he could weather the ups and downs of farming without distress. Apparently, he was also good friends with the Lloyds since, when he died at 86 in 1911, he was buried in their family cemetery alongside Zephaniah, who passed at 86 in 1892, and his son, Zephaniah, Jr., who died in 1915.

Yes, chances are good that Zephaniah was not related to the wealthy Lloyds in Maryland and that, like his stonemason friend Anthony, he had little money when he settled in the county. However, disregarding his unfortunate childhood, he enjoyed a long life, living till he was 86, at that time nearly twice the average male life expectancy of 45. In an 1885 edition of the *Madison Herald*, a reporter wrote in an article entitled, *The Old Settlers' Meeting*, that "Zephaniah Lloyd showed a pair of pants that was one hundred and twelve years old. The cotton was raised on the farm, the seed picked out, carding, dying, spinning and weaving all done by hand. The cloth was good but the fashion was very peculiar." Perhaps the pants were special enough to him to save since they may have belonged to a relative, who would have worn them in 1773.

After his son died in 1915, the farm continued in family hands, likely owned by his wife Sarah, who died in 1930. Sometime in the 1920s, the Field family took over ownership and continued to farm the 80 acres.

In 2015 the farm once again changed hands, when Amy and Brady Kress purchased the stone barn and 10 acres surrounding it. Both grew up in Dayton, Ohio, where Brady presently is the president of Dayton History, which merged with Carillon Historical Park in 2005. Part of the allure of this timber-framed stone barn traces back to Brady's childhood.

During middle school and high school, he watched many episodes of *The Woodwright's Shop*. The show, along with *This Old House*, which also began in 1979, is the longest running PBS "how-to" series and stars Roy Underhill, a master woodworker, who became Colonial Williamsburg's first master housewright. From watching this show, Brady learned the skills of timber framing, including hewing logs with a broad axe, which led to him building a log home for the Beavercreek Historical Society. He also taught early trades classes for the Centerville Historical Society.

For eight years, Brady worked as Director of Museums for the Historic Landmarks Foundation of Indiana, a nonprofit that focuses on preserving historic structures in the state. During that time, Amy and Brady began looking for investment property in farmland and, in their search, the Landmarks foundation pointed them towards the Lloyd stone barn, which they wanted a historic easement placed on. If Amy and Brady would buy it, they could work with Landmarks to place the preservation easements. During their negotiation with Don Fields, the owner, they convinced him to sell 10 surrounding acres with it.

These days, they allow the Fields family to farm the acreage in exchange for them being watchdogs and maintaining the ground around the barn. Sadly, even though lush green fields of soybeans surround the barn, arsonists managed sneak through and burn down the adjacent brick farmhouse, less than 100 yards from the barn. Fortunately, Amy and Brady plan to continue to preserve the barn, which, as most old barns do, requires annual repair. It richly deserves a listing on the National Register.

Still, questions persist. Why did Zephaniah choose stone for his barn – and such a large one (70x60 feet) at that? Did his first barn burn down? Did he remember seeing stone barns in his childhood in Maryland? And, living as a modest farmer and raising nine children, how could he afford to hire both a barn builder and a master stonemason? Was he friends with both? Did he barter for their services, offering grain, vegetables, or livestock? Many farmers in the mid-1850s traded agricultural products for services, though a large amount of cash was likely required in the case of this barn.

Regardless, his legacy stands today, a memorial to a farmer, husband, and father – one who saw all nine children get married – after rising to economic success from the humble beginnings of being an orphan.

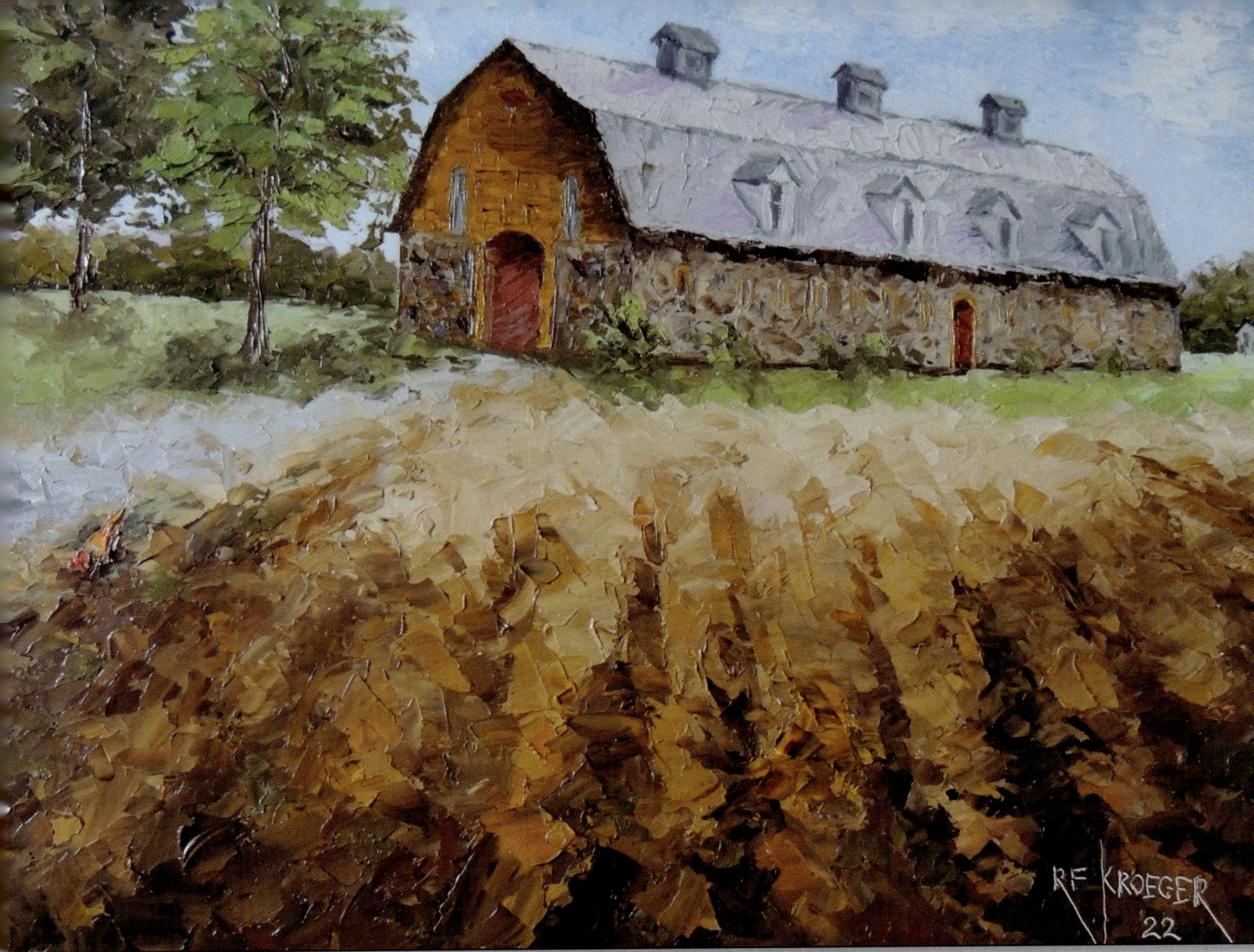

McKain's Marvel

WHITE COUNTY

McKain's Marvel

One of few existing stone barns in Indiana, this magnificent piece of architecture serves as not only a precious feather in the cap of the closest town, Monticello, but also as a national treasure. Owner Dick Hubbard is currently trying to enter it on the National Register, an honor it certainly deserves.

The barn, built in 1905, traces back to an Ohioan, Arthur Albert McKain, born in Troy, Miami County, on Ohio's western flank. Unfortunately, his father James died when Arthur was young, leaving him with the responsibility to support his mother Elvira and his older sister. Although the family lived in poverty, this difficult childhood served to teach the youngster valuable life lessons. Outside of a year in an academy in Euphemia, Ohio (a ghost town in northern Preble County), he had little formal schooling.

He began his career in the nursery business and became an owner of one in his early 20s in 1873. In those years, nurseries sold fruit trees and seeds, which may explain the abundance of fruit trees and vegetables on his farm. After he married Mary McClure, the daughter of a farmer, McKain, possibly looking for a more lucrative occupation, switched into the marble and monument business, first in 1877 in North Manchester, a town in rural Wabash County in northern Indiana. Next, he moved to Chicago. Obviously, this young entrepreneur had a knack for business.

After living in Chicago, where he established a marble yard, he moved to Indianapolis in 1881 and started a company that made large monuments, costing between $2,000 to $25,000, a fortune in the 1880s. One of his greatest achievements, the Soldiers and Sailors Monument, dedicated to the local soldiers and sailors of the Union Army in the Civil War, still stands in Winchester, Indiana. County commissioners paid McKain $100 to design the monument in 1885 and, four years later, awarded him the construction contract for $23,000. McKain finished building it in 1892. By then his reputation had spread. He then branched out into other ventures.

According to the *Arthur A. McKain Papers, 1907-1938,* stored in the archives of the Indiana Historical Society, McKain saw opportunity in producing farm equipment, since agriculture remained the predominant occupation at the turn of the century. In 1891 he founded and served as the president of the Indiana Manufacturing Company, a firm that made a straw stacker for harvesting machines. This was related to the work of inventor James Buchanan, whom he admired. McKain's patent on the stacker gave him a virtual monopoly in this field. Four years later he started – and ran – the American Buncher Manufacturing Company, which produced machines that bunched clover.

Buoyed by this financial success, he bought land near Monticello and established a dairy farm, though he never forgot his rise from poverty. As a patriot, he recruited men for the 161st Indiana Volunteer Regiment in the Spanish-American War in 1898.

But farming was not what drew him to Monticello; it was fishing on the Tippecanoe River, which flows through the town. Nor did he want farming to interfere with his many businesses and, accordingly, McKain hired two supervisors, A.W. Doyle and Van A. Douglass to manage the farm. In their archived letters to McKain, they reported taking a dairy farming course at Purdue University as well as buying a milk wagon and traveling to New York to buy cows. They also raised hogs, sheep, and chickens on this large farm, about a mile south of town.

According to Kean MacOwan's article, "History's Mysteries of White County," the McKain farm was not only the most progressive in the county but was the leader in the entire state. Its 14 buildings included not only the stone horse barn but also a cattle barn, a milking barn, a springhouse, wagon barns, a water pumping station, a family farmhouse, a guest house, and a machine shop, powered by

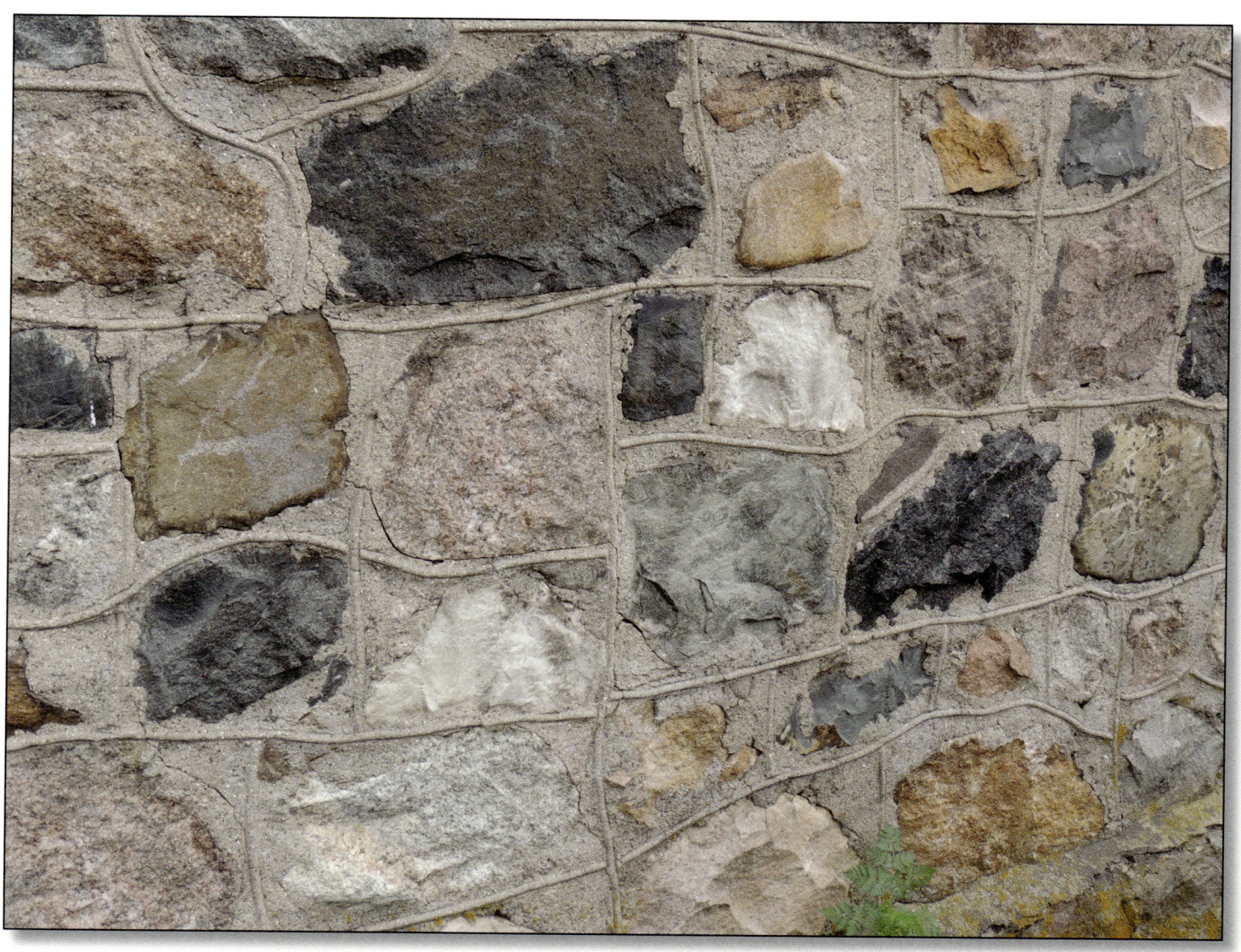

Beaded stonework, McKain barn, Indiana, 2023.

an early steam engine. Despite this sprawling farmstead, McKain's primary residence was a modest home at 1724 North Alabama Street in Indianapolis. Apparently, he and his wife didn't need a mansion to keep them happy – just as the founder of Walmart, Sam Walton, didn't need a fancy car. Despite his wealth, he drove a 1979 Ford F-150 truck for decades, which is on display in the Walmart Museum.

Along with his monument to Indiana's men of the Union Army, A. A. McKain left behind this stone barn as part of his legacy for future generations. But why stone? Well, there are two reasons: one, he could afford it and, two, he likely wanted substantial protection for his horses. Wooden framed barns were good enough for the cattle.

But what a stone barn it still is! Measuring 40x135 feet, it has plenty of room for a stable of horses – with stalls for each – and a self-supporting roof. Diagonal Y-shaped beams, all saw-cut, help support the roof, as do the rafters, which are lodged on the 24-inch-thick stone walls. Unlike any other barn, the second-floor hay mow has a cement floor, another expensive undertaking. Whoever the architect was, he or she designed it well since the roofing lumber had to be strong enough to support heavy slate, which has since been replaced with asphalt shingles. A comment on a Facebook posting claimed that the walnut timber was harvested on the farm and another person, who worked on the farm in his teenaged years, said that the farm field was rocky, a plentiful source of stone.

Indeed, mason William Hout probably used stones from these fields to craft his masterpiece, laying a distinctive beaded, raised mortar joint (assuming that the joinery is original). Such mortaring is highly decorative and rare; its excellent condition verifies the skill of this stonemason. The eave on each gable end, where doors open, typical of early Dutch barns, features a reddish-orange brick, built above the stonework. Two elongated windows, which Dick boarded up to thwart vandalism, have decorative orange brick lintels as does an elliptical All-Seeing-Eye-shaped window, also ringed with the same orange brick. Large red barn doors on each end are well protected by an arc enclosure of the same matching brick. Incredibly, the brick and stones show hardly any cracking over a century, hinting that the architect may have selected this site, based on a foundation of solid bedrock.

Two pillars, built with cobblestones and laid with matching beaded mortar, stand near the edge of the road, where a long-gone path likely led 50 yards to the barn. The pillars, likewise, are in excellent condition. The mason rotated the colors of the stones – black, red, brown, maroon, pink, tan, and beige – to add an artistic flair to his work. Smaller red doors on the wide sides have matching arched brick outlines, as do the 12 large windows. Four dormers, renovated smartly, still sit above the stone walls but the three large cupolas, another source of ventilation, were destroyed in a windstorm in 1967, according to Dick. I decided to include them in the painting.

Interestingly, another stone building, its masonry and brickwork identical to that of the barn, stands in a wooded area several hundred yards away. Judging from its construction, multiple windows, small doors, and a five-foot square chimney, it may have been a cottage that McKain stayed in when he visited the farm. Inside, we noticed an old photograph, circa 1890s, that might provide a clue to the building's past.

Over the years, the farm passed through ownership until two brothers, Melvin and Wilbur Voight, bought the farmstead and became partners in farming. In 1960 the Hubbard family acquired it. Today, Dick leases 60 tillable acres; the other 40 acres are wooded. He plans to maintain this barn, which remains in outstanding condition, a tribute to its architect, stonemason Fout, and McKain, the affluent businessman who could afford to build such a barn. Though McKain spent the main part of his life in Indiana, he reverted to his roots and was buried in Dayton, Ohio, where his wife Mary, who passed in 1928, is buried next to him.

To paraphrase one of my classmates – who returned to his rural hometown to practice – "you can take a boy out of Ohio, but you can't take Ohio out of the boy." However, though he's buried in Ohio, Arthur's work in Indiana continues to stand – his outstanding monument in Winchester and Monticello's stone barn – both genuine McKain marvels.

ILLINOIS

STEPHENSON COUNTY

Lamm's Legacy

With urbanization of America and the domination of large-scale corporate farming, it's rare to see a family maintain continuous ownership of a farm for over a century … and even rarer if the ownership nearly reaches bicentennial status. Such is the legacy of the Lamm family, whose heritage traces back to 1848, when Georg T. and his wife Gertrud Lamm founded this farm. Chances are that they started out with a timber-framed barn, which housed livestock and crops. Fourteen years later they had become prosperous enough to build this stunning stone barn in 1862, one of only a few stone barns still existing in the state.

Although German stonemasons were numerous throughout America in the 19th century – building stone houses and

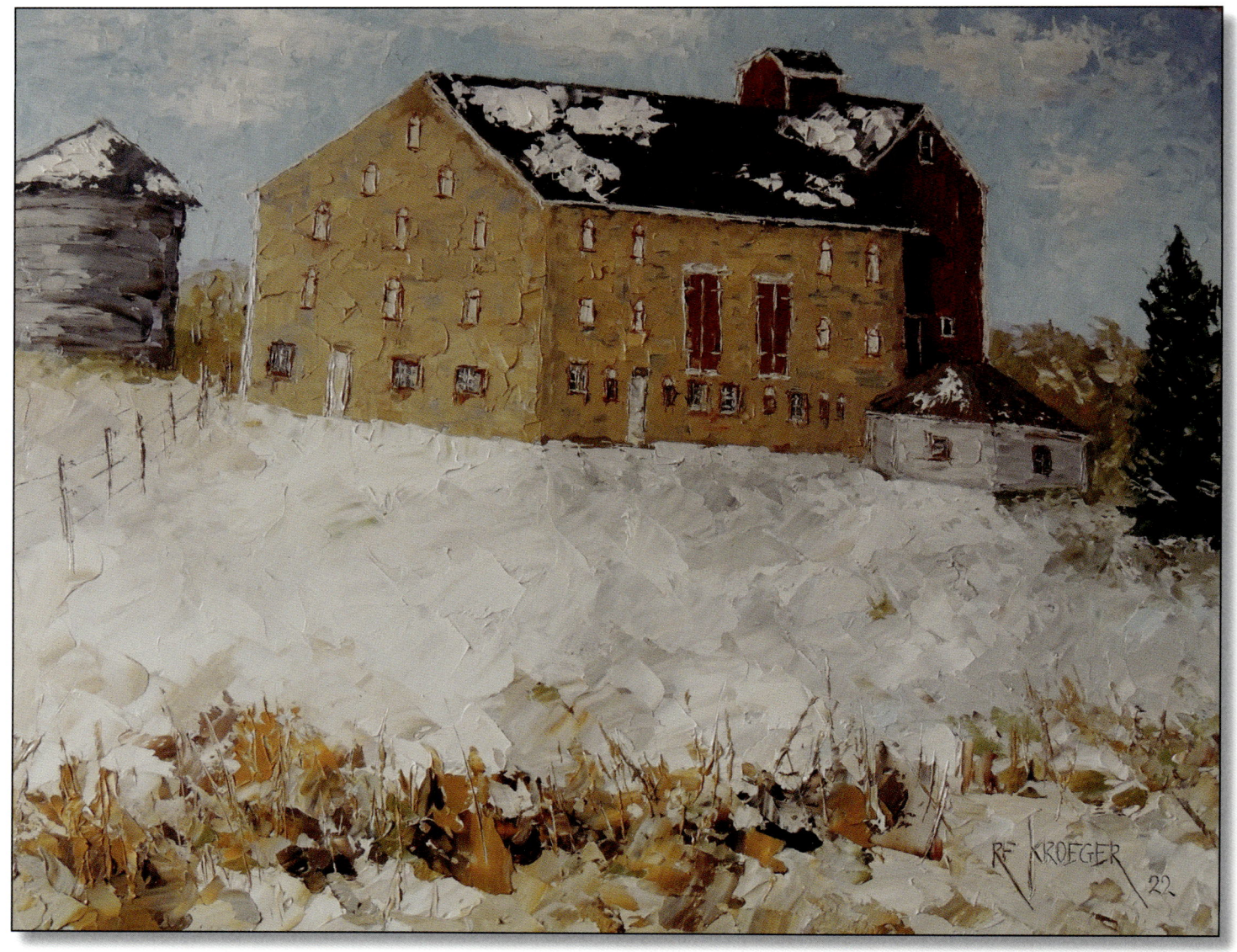

Lamm's Legacy

barns – why a mason built this one this one is puzzling. It stands out, the only stone barn in the midst of traditional timber-framed barns, and is especially unusual since, with only 80 acres, the farm wasn't a large one. Georg and Gertrud must have been inclined to build a barn for posterity and they had the resources to do it, choosing stone over wood. A photo, circa 1900, shows the farmyard full of cattle though, initially, the barn was used for both horses and dairy cattle. Hogs came later. The Lamms also raised wheat, using the two large red doors for threshing.

Eventually, the farm passed to Frank and Mary Lamm and then, in 1921, to Robert and Cecelia Lamm. Surviving the era of depressed farm prices in the 1920s and then the Great Depression of the 1930s must have been difficult, but the Lamms held on to their farm. Many unfortunate souls didn't.

In 1945 William and Florence Lamm became owners and erected a large red shed in 1950 on an end of the barn, which I decided would detract from the stone and,

accordingly, didn't include it in the painting. They had three sons, Richard, an accountant in Freeport, and William and Gerald, who farm the 1,400 acres, raising corn and soybeans.

When Georg built the barn in 1862, according to Gerald's wife Luann, he hauled stone from a quarry on the farm, which the stonemason used to build the barn the next year. Inside, hand-hewn beams are connected with mortise and tenon joints. The thickness of the stone walls – two feet tapering to 18 inches – helps to insulate during the warm summers and cold winters.

Today the Lamms, the fifth generation to own the farm, use the barn for equipment storage. Over the years, they've maintained it well, eliminating the horse stalls, strengthening weakened beams, and keeping its wood brightly painted. Two massive elevators have replaced older ones and a new roof ensures years of function, guaranteeing that the Lamm legacy will pass on to future generations.

ANTRIM COUNTY

The Lord Will Provide

Not much is known about Sam Bricker, the farm owner who built this remarkable stone barn. An undated family photo shows Sam, his wife, and their six children … and a dog on Sam's lap. According to current owners Kenn and Connie Kutzleb, the original part of their stone farmhouse dates to 1880; a newer section – with matching random fieldstone masonry – was added later.

One reference source mentioned that there was a community called Brickersville in Antrim County and that the post office was a rural one, located in the Bricker and Company general store. In fact, Samuel Bricker was appointed its first postmaster on April 20, 1902, but the post office closed three years later. This scenario could have been true since the family photo appears to have

been taken circa 1890 to 1910, based on clothing styles. Also, the farm sits on state highway M-32, a section of which was originally known as Bricker Road. The formal address of the barn is on Stanek Road, named for the large farm adjacent to the Bricker's.

Most likely, the Brickers began farming as soon as they moved into the area and built a wooden barn, though Sam may have started his general store later. He also operated a sawmill, still present on the property, though it's not operating anymore. Such entrepreneurship might have transferred to his three sons. But none wanted to continue farming.

It's also possible that the original barn burned and that Sam wanted a structure more durable, which led to his building the stone barn sometime in the 1920s. Considering the cost involved, Sam Bricker had to have been wealthy; such superb stonemasonry on a large barn was expensive.

It sits on top of a hill – with views for miles down

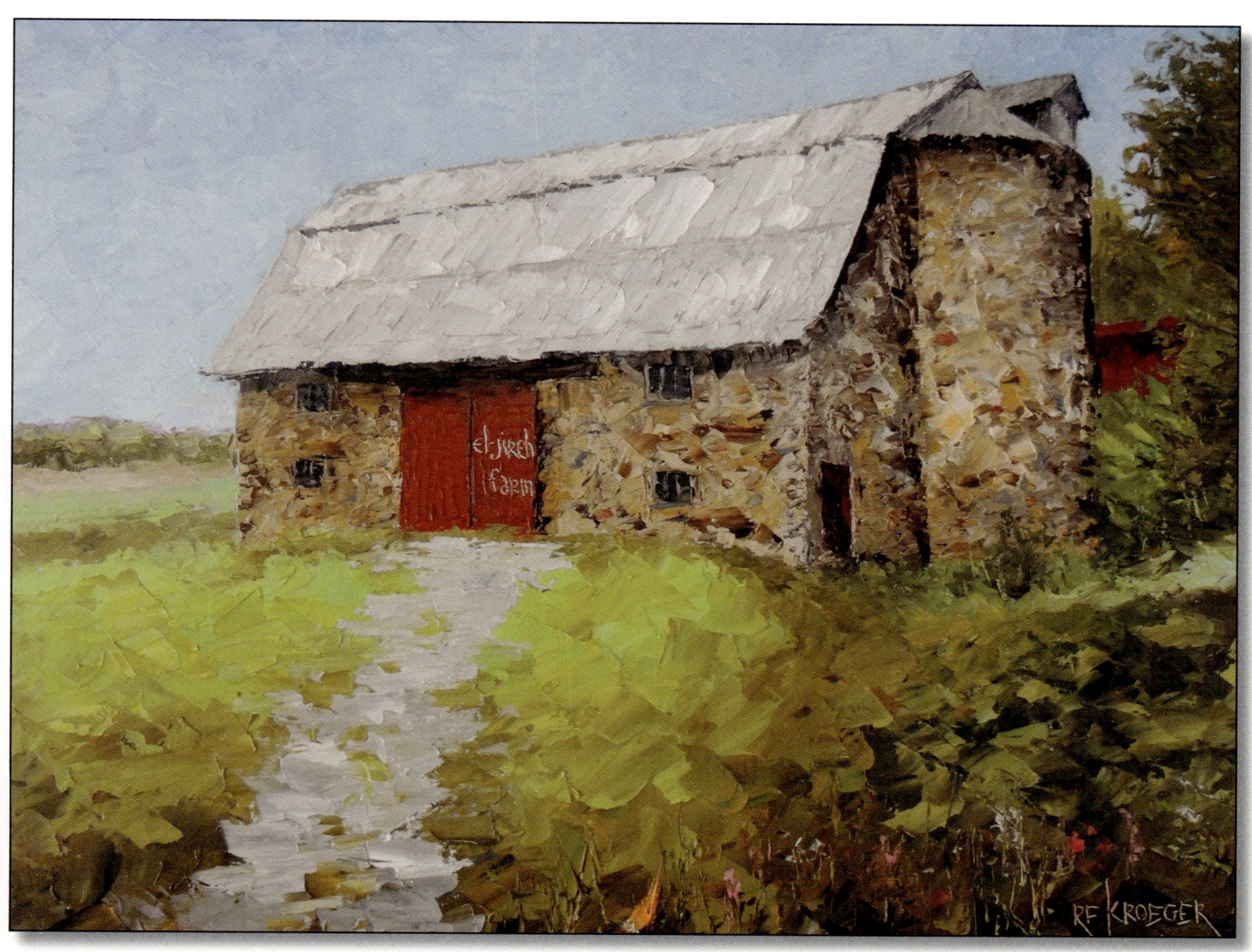

The Lord Will Provide

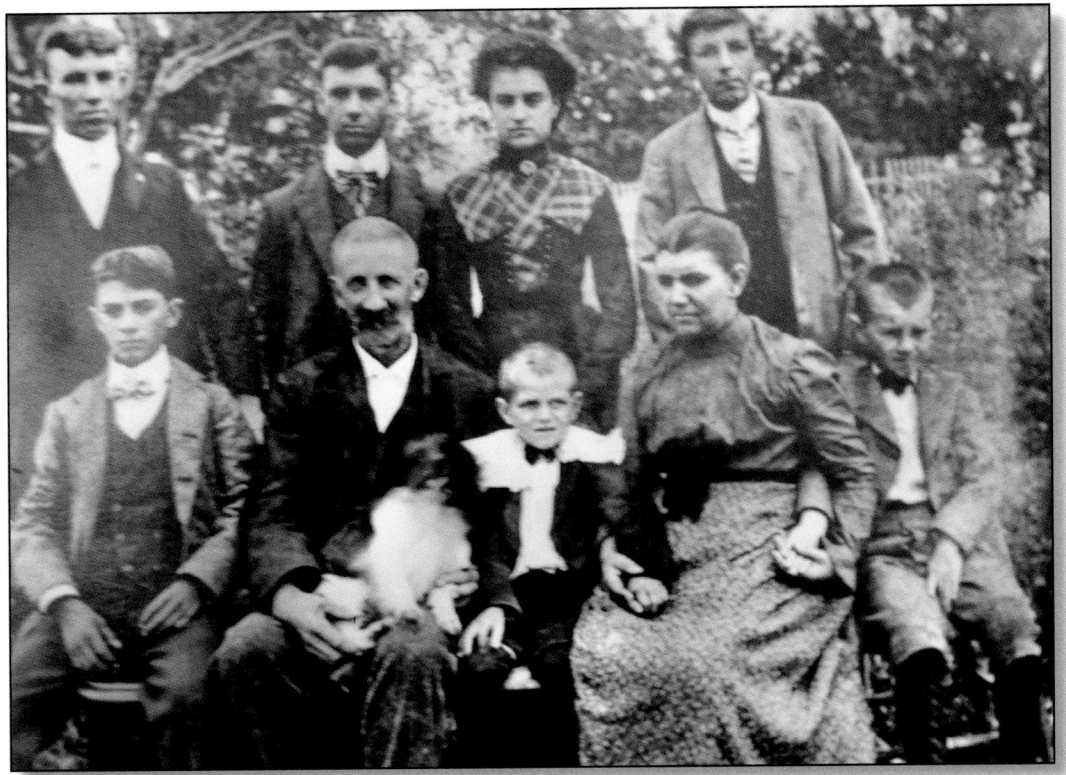

Bricker Family photo circa 1900, courtesy Kenn and Connie Kutzleb.

1920s – and possibly earlier – the farm was a productive dairy operation. Logs, half-cut, support the second floor, including the heavy stone silo, a testament to the builder's engineering skills. Multiple windows on all sides, some framed with cement sills and lintels, provided both light and ventilation, so necessary for dairy cows. On three sides, concrete sloped extensions, essentially buttresses, also adorned with fieldstones, presumably were built to prevent shifting. If so, that strategy worked; only a small corner inside shows cracking.

The stonework is outstanding. Fieldstone was probably gathered from the Bricker farm fields, as well the valley, showing fertile farm fields as well as the sawmill. Though it's unknown how many acres the Brickers farmed, judging from the size of the barn – 40x70 feet – and from the number of stanchions, the acreage must have been substantial. Today, the owners have 10 acres for agriculture and 10 acres of woodland.

Inside, the lumber appears to have come from trees on the farm, cut in the sawmill, though one major beam was partly hand-hewn and partly saw-cut. The main floor was used for hay storage but not for threshing, since there is only one main door. It's likely that the farmer drove a wagon up the earthen bank and through the door to unload the hay. The original tin roof, now a century old, has held up well; boards of random widths suggest they were cut from trees on the farm, as well. The rafters rest on the stone walls, 16 to 18 inches thick.

The stone silo, as impressive as the rest of the barn, stands half-way inside the barn, its external half showing prominently outside, capped by a wooden ventilator. Metal rungs lead to the top and are bordered with quoins of various sizes, the mark of fine masonry. Outside, next to the silo sits a red granary, which stored wheat, rye, and oats. Underneath is a cistern, which collected rainwater for the livestock.

On the lower level, accessed by wooden stairs as well as by external doors, cow stanchions line one side; some were replaced with horse stalls in the 1970s. In the

as from nearby farms – sort of a win-win solution for farmers since every spring, after winter upheaval and thawing, stones would rise to the surface, a problem for plowing. Year after year, local farmers would remove and pile the stones – to clear their fields.

Chances are that several masons – and perhaps one master stonemason – worked on the barn. Masons chose the stones carefully and artistically, alternating colors of the stones – red, burgundy, tan, serpentine, gray, and black – in random courses. Large quoins support the corners, also of various colors. Three courses of scaffolding holes remain. And some parts of the walls show different masonry techniques. One section, a cobblestone-like arrangement, resembles the barns and homes of Wayne County, New York. However, the biggest hint that a master mason was involved is the mortar, which has held up without tuckpointing; knowing the correct amount of lime to add is crucial for mortar longevity. On the other hand, very little mortar was used on the farmhouse, hinting that another mason did the work.

Though none of Sam Bricker's sons wanted to farm, they held onto it and presumably rented the land to tenant farmers. In 1972, they formed the East Jordan Development Company – with plans to develop the land into a golf course, with the stone barn becoming the clubhouse. However, such a hope never materialized and, after giving up, they sold the farm to Gale and Larraine Tinsley. They kept it until, after going through a divorce, they sold it in 1990. Thanks to Connie's parents, who saw a for sale sign and alerted them, Connie and Kenn were able to buy the farm.

But they were faced with a lot of work: the barn needed repair, as did the other buildings, and the grounds were overgrown with weeds and brush. It was a lot of work, but Connie and Kenn rose to the challenge. After transitioning through several occupations, they seem to have blossomed in caring for this historic farmstead.

Connie graduated with a master's degree in English and held teaching positions, though horticulture was her passion. She also became a massage therapist, worked as a garden manager, and was a part-time tutor. Kenn, originally from New Jersey – within sight of the famous skyline of New York City – went to college in Michigan, where he met Connie. They married in Grand Rapids and raised two sons, who were young children in 1990 when they moved from urban living to farm country.

Over the years, the Kutzlebs have taken great care of the barn, including repairing the caved-in roof, and, historically minded, they have chosen to leave the beautiful stonemasonry in its original state. They named their new home, the El Jireh Farm, a Hebrew word that means "the Lord will provide." Both Christians, they felt that God had blessed them throughout their lives and, after consulting a Jewish friend, came up with a name to reflect such good fortune.

Originally, they bred Shetland sheep and Nigerian Dwarf goats; today they have 10 sheep and four goats. Once again they've added to their work resume: Connie spins the wool and Kenn weaves it into beautiful wool blankets, mostly for family now. They also showed creativity in creating a unique barn to be home for the goats. Salvaging part of an original cement silo from an old barn that burned, they built a wooden rafter system which rests on the stone walls. The conical roof, made of repurposed metal, is capped by an antique lightning rod. In essence, since this structure houses farm livestock, it is a barn and, since it's circular, it qualifies as a round barn. Unfortunately, I didn't discover this gem until after my book on round barns was finished. Anyway, thanks to the charm of this little barn, I did its painting.

They also connected wood poles into the scaffolding holes on the rear of the barn to create an arbor for a vineyard, which yields several types of grapes. Next to the lush vines, there's a large garden, which, Kenn explained, provides plenty for him and Connie.

About 30 yards in front of a wooden chicken barn is a little building with a chimney, built circa 1900, which, as Connie explained, was probably the office for Bricker or perhaps for a hired hand. Once again, thanks to a creative moment, they raised the ceiling (apparently, Sam was a short man) and added a bed, turning this quaint apartment into an Air B&B rental. At first, they weren't sure if it would work, but, after it booked out for months in advance, they decided to limit it to only Friday and Saturday nights. Such is the power of the Internet.

Now that his farm lies in good hands, the question remains: Why did Sam Bricker choose stone for his barn? There are no stone barns close by. The massive Loeb stone barns, about 20 miles away and built in 1918, may have inspired him – their silos are made of fieldstone and have similar wooden ventilator caps. It's also possible that stone buildings closer to home had an influence.

In 1861 a group of immigrants from Bohemia, later named Czechoslovakia, arrived in Antrim City, a village that no longer exists. Word must have reached the homeland since more Czechs arrived in 1869 and formed a Bohemian settlement. Two of the settlers were Frank and Barbara Pesek, whose farm, Stonehedge, still operates today, with the original log home, stone hedge, and outbuildings.

Another stone building, which may have also motivated Sam to use stone, is a Catholic church, built originally as a frame structure in 1890, but was covered in stone in 1926, about the same time as the Bricker barn was built. Located in a community in East Jordan that's known as Praga, a name adopted from Prague, the stunning fieldstone church sits directly on M-32, only a few miles from the Bricker farm. St. John Nepomucene Church was named after the patron saint of the region (Czechoslovakia was formed in 1918). This priest was born in 1345, refused to divulge secrets of the confessional, was tortured, put in chains with a block in his mouth, and led through town before being thrown in the River Moldau. Besides the church, the region holds other stone buildings and fences, built with native fieldstone.

Today, the entrance to this farmstead, its garden beds teeming with color – as if on a cover of the magazine *Better Homes and Gardens* – is a pleasant introduction to this couple, who generously devote their time and talents to preserving the stone farmhouse and barn. They explained that their future plans are simply to take care of the farm and its buildings as they have been doing. After all, the Lord has been good to them.

CHARLEVOIX COUNTY

Loeb's Legacy

Albert Henry Loeb, born in 1868 in Rockford, Illinois, worked his way through Johns Hopkins University and became a Chicago schoolteacher while attending law school. He was admitted to the Illinois bar in 1889 and formed a partnership with a fellow law school classmate, with whom he practiced law in Chicago. His life changed in 1901 when he joined Sears, Roebuck and Company, a mail-order company started in 1893 by Richard Sears and Alvah Roebuck. Two years later, Julius Rosenwald, a wealthy clothing manufacturer, bought out Roebuck's interest, and reorganized the mail-order business. He became president of the company in 1909. When Loeb joined Sears, he blossomed in retailing and quickly rose to secretary of the company and then to treasurer and vice-president in 1908. During his career, he helped transform Sears into a mega mail-order business. By the turn of the century and after wave after wave of immigrants, companies began to realize that the American Dream – a home, a job, and a family – was becoming marketable. In 1906 William Sovereign, an advertising expert in Bay City, Michigan, noticed plans for a pre-cut boat and he figured that such a system might also work for a house. Accordingly, he had a pre-cut boathouse kit designed and, after these kits became popular, William joined forces with his brother Otto to start the Aladdin Company, which began selling pre-cut kits for cottages and small homes. Several other companies quickly followed, including Sears, which began selling home kits in 1908 … and barn kits in 1911.

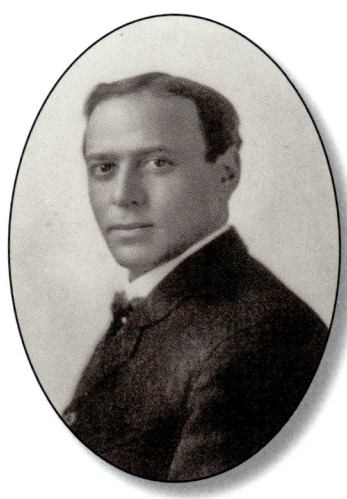

Albert Henry Loeb, circa 1900. Courtesy, Castle Farms.

During World War I, Loeb served as the acting president of Sears while president Julius Rosenwald was called to Washington to be on a War Advisory Committee in 1917. By November, Forbes magazine labeled Loeb, the "Modern Mail Order Marvel," giving him credit for taking Sears and Roebuck from a small business to a major player, one that

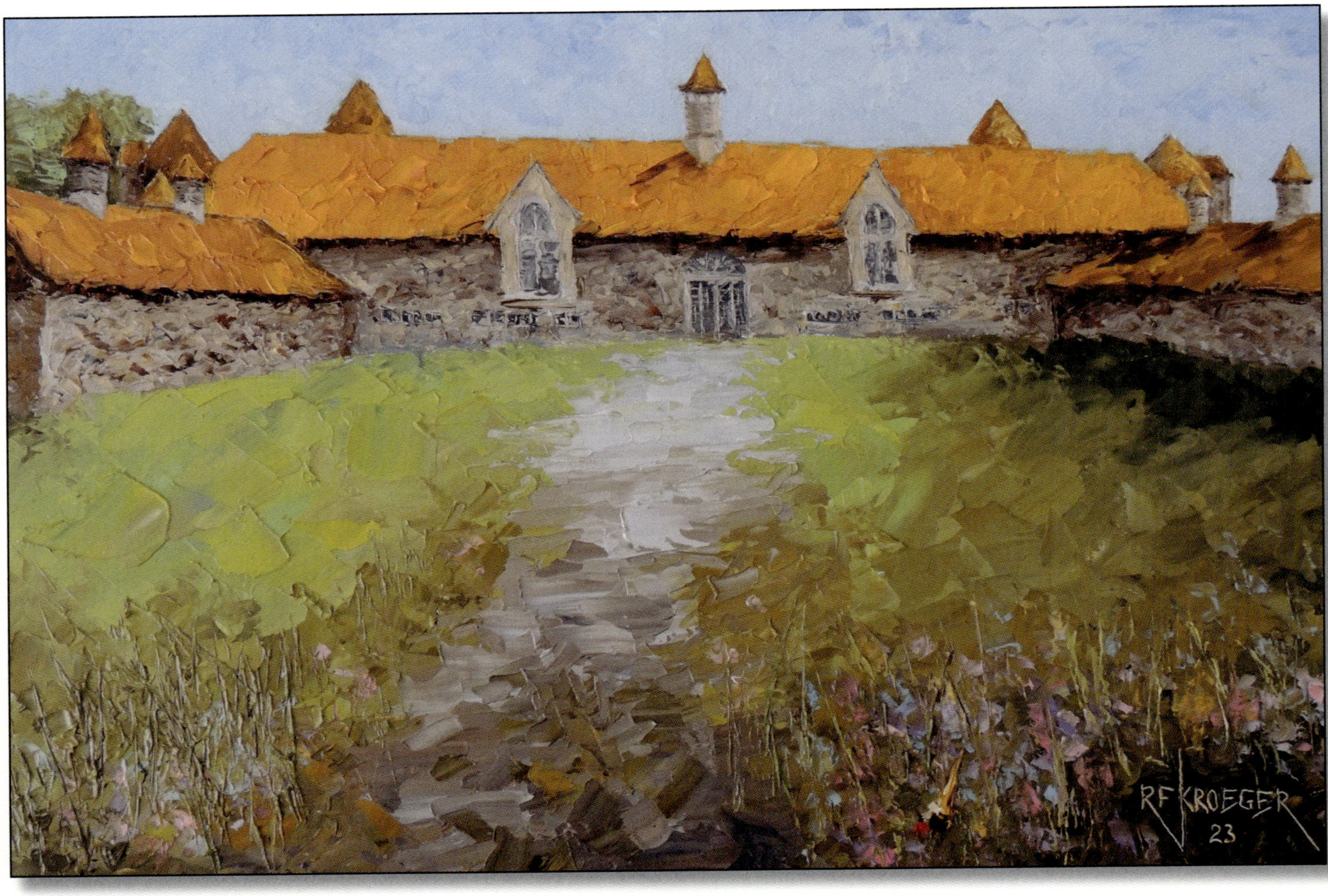

Loeb's Legacy

was doing $2.5 million per week in the mail-order business. Like Harvey Firestone, the Akron rubber tire king, Loeb wanted to sell farm equipment. Firestone grew up on a 19th-century farm in Columbiana County, Ohio, and, after becoming successful, he built a model barn complex there to teach farmers new methods, including, of course, the use of rubber on their metal tractor rims. In the early 1900s, farm tractors had metal wheels. Harvey was a born salesman.

By this time the Loeb family had become wealthy and for many years had spent summer vacations with their four sons – Allan, Ernest, Richard, and Thomas – in Charlevoix, a resort town in

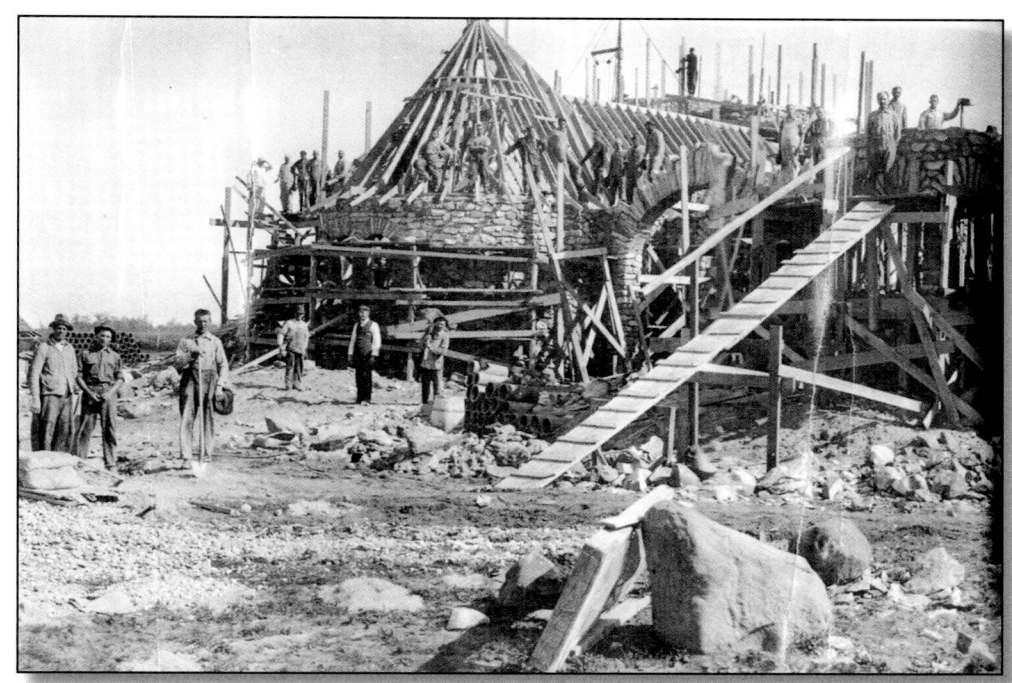

Laborers posing during 1918 stone barn construction. Courtesy, Castle Farms.

northern Michigan, where many affluent families vacationed in the early 1900s. Finally in 1917, Albert Loeb had a brain flash: combine summer holidays with work by building a farmstead that would be the envy of all and would be a chance to showcase the latest Sears farm equipment. And Charlevoix would be the perfect place.

During that summer he and his associates quietly began buying real estate around Charlevoix – beginning with 800 acres and ending with nearly 1,800 acres, including prime lakefront property. In June Albert and his wife Anna made plans and hired Arthur Huen, a prominent architect who had constructed the Loeb's mansion on Ellis Avenue in Chicago in 1910. They also wanted to hire Jens Jensen, the famous Chicago landscape architect, to design the grounds and gardens. However, since Jensen wanted to establish the farm elsewhere in Michigan, the family passed, though they used his design plans. Instead, they chose Robert Sloan, a Charlevoix city engineer, to oversee construction and to manage the farm.

Hundreds of locals were hired as well, which ingratiated the Loebs to this tiny beach community. Albert and his wife Anna had traveled to Normandy in the early 1900s – with visits to turreted French chateaus and castles – which gave them ideas to build their farm complex in stone and in a French countryside design. Heun's blueprints – fortuitously found during recent renovations – called for stones, lots of them. Fortunately, Albert came up with a win-win solution to help area farmers clear their land of rock piles, which they'd add to each spring when winter frosts forced stones up through the fields, impeding plowing. All Loeb asked was for the farmer to transport

the rocks to his property, which meant they'd have clear fields for planting and Loeb would have plenty of rocks for his farm complex and summer residence.

An old construction photo shows 22 laborers posing, almost as if they knew they were building something historically significant. One of them is carrying a hod, a V-shaped box mounted on a pole for carrying bricks, stones, or mortar, over the shoulder – often up a ladder to reach the stonemasons or bricklayers on scaffolding. Seeing that reminded me of a summer job I had, working for a construction company. To get the job, I had to join the local hod-carriers union, which cost $90, a large amount for a college kid in 1964. However, an hourly wage of $3.64 was more than enough to cover it quickly. Sadly, I didn't keep my union badge.

Started in 1917, the stone barns and mansion were finished a year later and drew praise from all corners. The horse barn with its high hipped roof was capped with a central, octagonal ventilator. Dormers featured pointed-arch windows. The dairy barn – with two wings measuring 42x198 feet – was equally impressive. It had several parts: a U-shaped section for 200 head of cattle and a dairy basement, a dormitory for single male workers, a kitchen, and four round stone silos. Initially, the family hired more than 90 people to take care of the land and livestock. They built homes on the estate to give families places to live. A couple years later, Albert built a school nearby for children of his employees.

The stonemasonry was – and still is – remarkable, even though some of it has been repaired as the result of destructive ownership during the 1970s. Most likely, at least a few of the 35 masons were master stonemasons, who were assisted by two or three apprentices. Masons received an hourly wage of $1.50 – about $33.00 in 2023 dollars – while their apprentices got 50 cents an hour. They used skill, creativity, and artistry in placing colors randomly – pink and red granite, green serpentine, tan and gray limestone, sandstone, and shale, black basalt, septarian brown stones, and even fossilized plants, called Petoskey stones, the state rock of Michigan. Differences in patterns of masonry, laid by various masons, can be seen throughout the complex. For the most part, the stones were laid intact, without any cutting.

The masons chose large rocks for quoins and, most importantly, mixed the correct amount of lime to make the mortar since there is virtually no cracking. Keystone arches, with little cement, have remained intact, much like the stone aqueducts of the Romans – built entirely without cement and still standing today. Inside the horse barn, rafters rest on the stone walls, which range from 15 to 22 inches in thickness. The pyramidal octagonal roof that originally covered the icehouse has been replaced with stone crenellations to resemble the battlements of a castle.

The Loebs also built a rectangular hip-roofed building in between the horse barns and the dairy complex, which they called the "Cheese Box," used as a refreshment stand and for sales of milk, cheese, and ice cream to visitors. Yes, these were boom years for agriculture. High prices of agricultural produce and livestock escalated throughout World War I since American farmers were supplying Europe, whose farms were essentially shut down during the fighting. However, those American farmers who borrowed money to purchase additional acreage, hoping to produce more, became sadly disappointed during the 1920s when demand fell. No one predicted that European farms would recover so quickly. Many lost their farms in foreclosure.

Though the Loebs raised crops on many of their 1,800 acres, they took pride in their purebred livestock: Duroc-Jersey hogs, Belgian horses, and Holstein-Fresian cattle, which soon began winning awards. By 1923 livestock had become a major source of income for the farm. In fact, visitors could come at specified milking times to watch Marion, their prizewinning Holstein that got milked four times a day. It ranked second in the world in milk production.

Loeb's second eldest son Ernest – after service in the army in World War I – began working on the farm in 1921. His mother Anna publicly pledged to volunteer her sons for military service, but Richard, the second youngest, did not accept her challenge. On the other hand, Ernest, now working on the farm, without pretense, lived in a dormitory with the rest of the single workers until he married in 1923. As Albert's heart condition worsened, Ernest worked

with Robert Sloan in running the farm. They started a mail order business to sell the farm's produce and dairy products and began making cheese. Two of their other sons also were doing well. But one wasn't.

In May of 1924, tragedy shocked the family as well as the Charlevoix community. Loeb's son Richard and his college friend Nathan Leopold, Jr. were accused of murdering a 14-year-old boy in Chicago. Earlier in May, before this happened, 56-year-old Albert, now retired from Sears, suffered a heart attack.

As with many affluent families, Richard was raised by a governess. Realizing that the boy had incredible intelligence, Emily Struthers pushed him relentlessly and entered him, age 12, into the innovative University High School, which he enjoyed, joining three academic clubs. However, the governess continued to drive him, which he resented; while his friends were outside playing baseball, he was inside studying and doing homework. He finished high school in two years. In college, he graduated from the University of Michigan at the age of 17 – at the time the youngest to earn a diploma from that university. After graduation, he enrolled in the University of Chicago, studying history. He had been accepted into the law school for the fall term of 1924.

However, the pressure of intense academics took its toll. An avid reader, Richard loved historical and crime-oriented detective novels, but continued to resent his governess. In college he met Nathan Leopold, also highly intelligent, academically proficient, and, likewise, came from a wealthy Jewish family in Chicago. They became friends. Nathan, on the other hand, a reserved introvert, retreated to his studies, which included reading works by the German writer and philosopher, Friedrich Nietzsche, who coined the word Übermensch in 1883, which referred to the ideal human, a superior being, often above the law. Perhaps out of rebellion against the tight control of his governess and inspired by Nietzsche, Richard and Nathan never considered the consequences of his crimes.

In late 1923 the two began to plan "the perfect crime," which they spent seven months preparing for. Their victim was a neighbor, 14-year-old Bobby Franks, son of another wealthy Jewish family. Newspapers throughout the country called it "the crime of the century," which blended seamlessly into Chicago's Roaring Twenties, teeming with gangsters such as Al Capone and Bugs Moran, the taxicab wars, and prohibition bootleggers. Chicago was anything but dull in that decade.

Newspaper headlines followed with "the trial of the century," especially after the Loebs hired Clarence Darrow, ranked as one of the most influential American lawyers of all time. Even before the trial, public consensus pointed to the death penalty, though there was no anti-Semitic backlash since all three boys were Jewish. The 67-year-old Darrow wisely changed the plea from not guilty to guilty, hoping the judge – instead of a jury – would avoid giving his clients the death penalty, which Darrow despised. Darrow's closing argument took 12 hours and stretched over three days – August 22, 23, 24 – and was published in several editions of newspapers during the 1920s and 1930s. It remains today as one of the most influential trial speeches ever delivered in a courtroom. Darrow's strategy worked; the sentence was life in prison plus 99 years. Two months later on October 28, Albert Loeb died of a heart attack.

With Albert Loeb and his incredible knack for business gone, the agricultural depression of the 1920s, and perhaps debts mounting, managing the farm became difficult for Anna, her son Ernst, and manager Robert Sloan. During this time, Ernest expanded the mail order business to include cheese, butter, honey, syrup, poultry, and eggs. But it wasn't enough to offset a national agricultural depression. At the end of the 1927 farm season, the family closed the farm and sold the livestock, after less than 10 years of operation. Though the farm became inactive during the Great Depression and the years of World War II, Anna, Ernest and his brothers continued to spend summer vacations in their Charlevoix mansion.

After the farm sale, they used the barns only for storage. Gradually, the buildings deteriorated. After Ernest died in 1961 and his brother Allan died a year later, the family decided to sell the farm complex to John Van Haver, who was happy to sign the sales contract, even though it mandated a massive clean-up. However, the Loebs kept the mansion and its acreage.

Van Haver, both an artist and a finalist in the Mr. America competition, was also a historical preservationist and understood the significance of what he purchased. Born in 1916 in Michigan, he loved history and, as he rose to the level of a top executive with the Sealed Power Corporation in Muskegon, he worked on restoring historical property in Marlborough, a Michigan ghost town. Van Haver also taught himself not only painting but metallurgy and casting as he evolved into an artist and sculptor, his second career.

When he bought the dilapidated Loeb farm buildings, he set a goal to restore them, decorate them with his metal art sculptures, offer demonstrations of his metal work at his forge, and turn the farm into a tourist destination. After spending more than three years restoring the complex, he named it "Castle Van Haver" and opened it to the public in 1966. It featured an art studio, gift shop, and art gallery. He scoured through more than 50 old barns in northern Michigan, salvaging many hand-hewn beams to decorate the ceilings of the old dairy, which he turned into a gift shop. He repurposed original tiles from the stanchions, fashioning them into a colorful herringbone pattern, still present. Today's owners have recognized his preservation efforts by dedicating the Knight's Courtyard Garden to him. Van Haver died in 2012 at 95.

In time his funds dwindled, and minimal tourist income made it difficult for Van Haver to continue to maintain the extensive grounds. One day in 1969 he consulted a local attorney for advice on declaring bankruptcy. During a "five-martini lunch" – as the lawyer's daughter later described it – the consultation turned into a sale. That attorney, Art Reibel, became the third and the least historically minded owner of the Loeb farm.

Reibel had moved his law practice from Troy to Charlevoix in 1968 and, until his lunch with Van Haver, had no intention of becoming a farm owner. Initially, he and his wife had planned to operate a riding school on the farm, as well as a tavern and a theater. However, those plans never materialized.

According to his daughter Kimberly, a random meeting changed his mind. A couple of Californians paid a visit and had ideas of turning the grounds into a venue for rock concerts, which were in their infancy; in 1969 the iconic Woodstock festival lasted three days on a farm in Vermont and attracted over 400,000 rock fans. After the meeting, the Reibels were interested and held their first concert in 1976, and, though the grounds weren't big enough to attract a Woodstock-sized crowd, they did hold 17,000 at one point, enough to be a nuisance in this quiet beach town resort. Traffic congestion, noise, crime, drunkenness and drug use, and countless scantily-clad hippies created headaches for locals and vacationers. The Reibels gave the complex a new name, "Castle Farms," though it was anything but a farm in his ownership. Ignoring the historical value of the cow barn, Reibel dismantled its stone walls to provide more space for concert goers and he erected a massive 50-foot-wide steel and concrete stage for the performers in the cow pasture.

During these years – lasting from 1976 to 1993 – over 120 acts played here, including Ozzy Osbourne, Aerosmith, Def Leppard, Sting, Bob Dylan, and almost every other big-name group of that era. These concerts, held weekly from June through August, turned the normally blissful vacation spot into a nightmare; pristine Charlevoix became littered with beer cans, cigarette butts, empty booze bottles. Roads, normally filled with families eager to head to the beach, were stuck in gridlock.

Marion Township tried to shut the concerts down, enacting a law for a mass gathering permit. When that didn't work, locals tried other methods – without success.

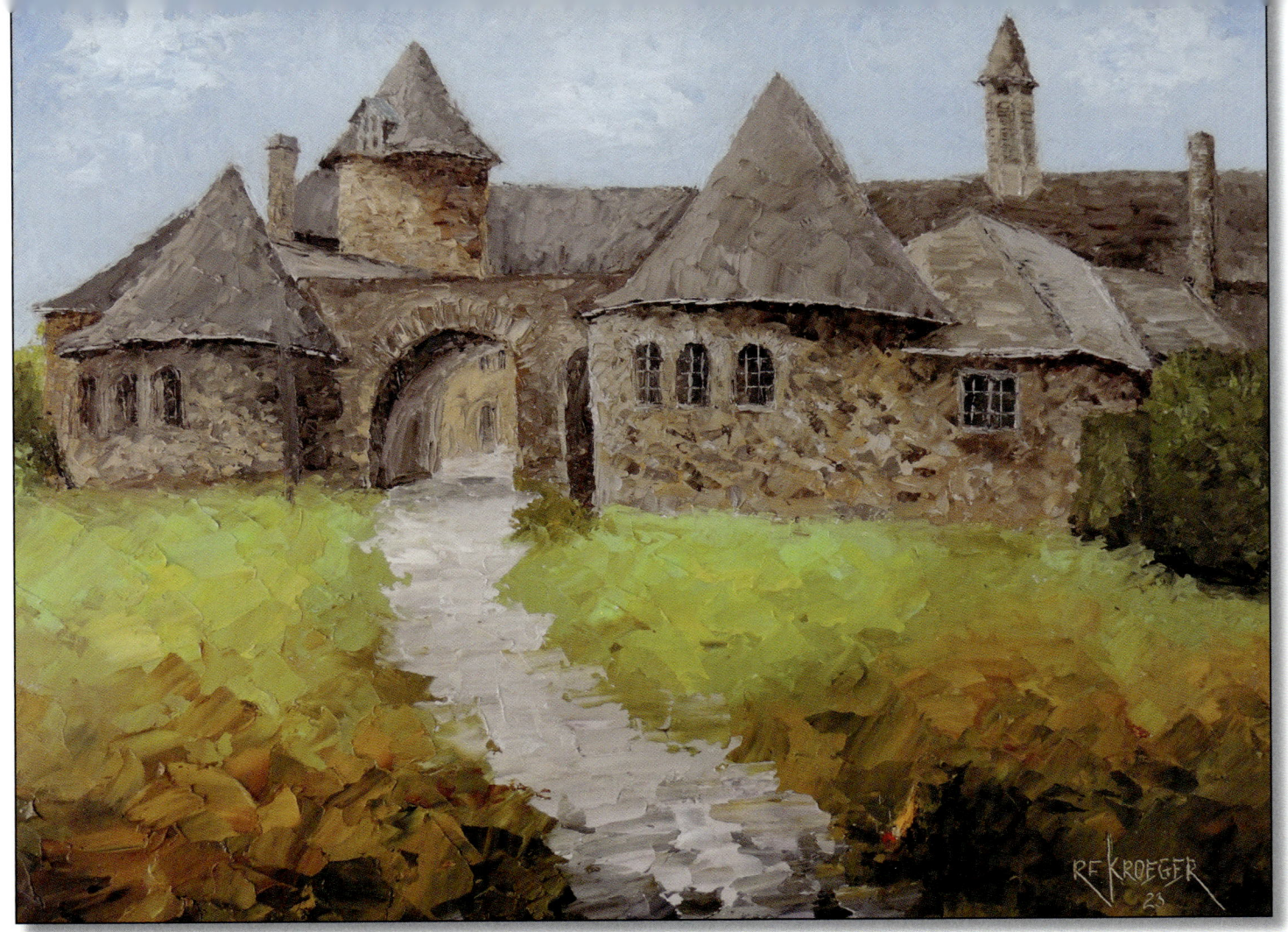

Loeb's Legacy, II

Art Reibel, an attorney, was familiar with the law, especially after having served as a Charlevoix County district court judge. Eventually Michigan's state bar investigated whether he used his office as judge to further his own interest, especially considering that he often ruled in favor of the concert venue in cases brought on by the township.

According to David Miles, director of the Charlevoix Historical Society, the traffic, noise, health complaints, fights, public urination, drunkenness, and rude behavior were beyond obnoxious. "Charlevoix was just a mob scene," he said. Fortunately, as the rock scene evolved, groups wanted bigger spaces than Castle Farms could accommodate. Oddly enough, even though Reibel had not maintained the buildings, a local group, Friends of the 4-H, got the Loeb farm listed on the National Register in 1995, perhaps realizing such a recognition was long overdue. Art Reibel, 66, died in 1999 and no one wanted to take over his rock concert business. The property was for sale.

Unfortunately, the farm buildings had deteriorated badly and roofs of the towers and barns had collapsed. Other roofs were sagging and countless windows were broken. However, most of the stone walls, built by master stonemasons a century earlier, remained intact. These farm buildings, once shining masterpieces of Charlevoix, had become public eyesores. In fact, if the property had been left to worsen, the ground would have turned into just another roadside pasture. Enter owner number four – Linda and Richard Mueller – who purchased the 37-acre farm for $300,000 at an auction in 2001.

Linda, who grew up in Lakewood, a suburb of Cleveland, visited the Loeb farmstead in the early 1960s with her boyfriend Richard, whose family had a summer home in Charlevoix. She and Richard, high school sweethearts, married in 1969, the same year that Reibel bought the farm. Over the years, on her visits to Castle Farms, she dreamed of owning it one day. But that would be an expensive proposition.

Her husband Richard began working in 1967 at a Domino's Pizza, a company started in 1960 by Tom Monaghan with a single store in Ypsilanti, Michigan. Eventually, their ownership of over hundreds of Domino's afforded them the assets to restore the Loeb farm. "In the first 30 years, I helped him in his business.

Then, 10 years ago, Richard said it was my turn to pursue my dream," Linda wrote in her book, *For the Love of a Castle.*

With an interest in history, castles, and travel, Linda and Richard traveled throughout Europe – in Germany, France, the British Isles, and Ireland. In all, Linda visited over 160 castles, which had become her passion. But, unlike the showpieces she visited, the Loeb farm needed help … lots of it. It would be a noble and gigantic undertaking.

Fortunately, she hired the right folks – AZD Associates-Architects, a full-service architecture and design firm, located near Detroit. In the beginning, the property needed extensive repair and rebuilding and the monstrous concert stage had to be dismantled. There were no heating or cooling systems, no electricity or plumbing. For public visits, restrooms were required.

Linda wanted the complex to return to its original design and hoped to use correct materials to achieve this. She set a rehab plan for 10 years, but it took only four. After years of working with these architects – and spending millions of dollars (about 18 to be exact) – her dream came true. Livestock areas in the barns were repurposed into banquet halls, dancing rooms, and offices. When possible, original construction details were followed since Heun's original blueprints were found. Linda's two books detail the restoration, as well as her extensive collections.

One wing of the cow barn, formerly filled with stanchions for 200 dairy cows, now houses a museum-quality exhibition of antique bridal gowns, some dating to 1830. Another wing is devoted to huge quilts, including a few made by Linda. One, displaying the history of the farm buildings, took Linda five years to knit.

Other halls feature historic photos of the farm, Linda's collection of Royal Commemorative China, models of European castles, artifacts from the 1918 Sears catalog, and antique wedding cake toppers. The original blacksmith shop – with its circular stone forge – has been converted into a World War I museum – since that is when this farm was established. In another hall, thanks to generous donations from John Van Haver, his metal sculptures are displayed, including heraldic crests and arms, catapults, emblems, and other pieces cast in aluminum and bronze.

While these collections and the stone barns are reasons enough to visit – about 100,000 visit annually – the major draws are weddings and reunions, which bring guests from as far away as Alaska, Hawaii, and Africa. Several rooms can hold weddings – from 200 to 350 people. At the time of our visit in July 2023, the complex was booked

through 2024 and into 2025. It's a perfect place for a fair maiden to be wed to her knight in shining armor.

The landscaping is breathtaking. KP Landscaping Company, the firm that designed the grounds – in accordance with what Linda observed during her visits to European castles – currently maintains the gardens, ponds, and fountains. They employ two full-time landscapers to care for the grounds and four "flower ladies" to tend to the flowers, which have been chosen from Proven Winners varieties since 2022. The colors are spectacular. Tours of the buildings and grounds can be booked online.

In the thousands of old barns I've visited, this restoration is by far the best of them all. Many barns, including round and stone ones, unfortunately, have been lost – to old age or Mother Nature, or have been purposely dismantled for parts. Accordingly, it's refreshing to witness such a spectacular historical restoration.

Awards quickly followed. In 2006, when Castle Farms opened, it won the Governor's Award for Design Excellence from the Michigan Historical Society. Three other awards came that year: the Ambassador Award from the local chamber of commerce, the M award from the Masonry Institute of Michigan, and the Margaret Duerr Book Award. For nearly every year since 2008, Castle Farms has been recognized for its weddings by The Knot, a national site that rates wedding venues. When I asked our knowledgeable tour guide Jessica Anderson about succession plans, she explained that the Mueller children will continue to operate the facility, ensuring its historical preservation.

Today Castle Farms has been restored to its glory of a century ago. The stone barns, once vacant for decades, have been given a new purpose in hosting weddings, family reunions, or corporate events. It's a tourist attraction, too – with the state's largest outdoor model railroad, featuring over 2,500 feet of track, all thanks to Richard's love of model railroading. A red Welsh dragon stands proudly in the background of the complex and a fountain shoots up a column of water, like the scene at the palace of Versailles. Tour guides take visitors around the complex, explaining its fascinating stories. In fact, Castle Farms has its own wine label – 1918 Cellars – named in honor of the founding date. Wine lovers can taste eight wines in a tasting room.

Thanks to Linda and Richard Mueller, this national treasure has been preserved – its history, its stone barns, and its masterful stonemasonry – a fitting tribute to its founder Albert Loeb and his incredible vision. Though Albert Loeb died over a century ago, ending a life so well lived, his legacy lives on.

WISCONSIN

IRON COUNTY
Little Finland

Like Finland, northern Wisconsin and Michigan's Upper Peninsula have cold weather and lots of snow. In fact, this area, known as Iron Country, gets more snow than anywhere else east of the Mississippi River – not ideal for farming crops. The region was, however, full of iron and copper deposits, earning this county the name "Iron." After more than a century of mining iron ore in this region, ending in the 1960s, the famous 2,000-foot ore dock in Ashland was dismantled in late 2013. In 2024, thanks to a charitable trust, plans are underway to redevelop the historic dock as a public space.

Copper mining in this region dates to 3,000 B.C. when Native Americans dug it out of small pits. Mining also flourished from 1845 to the 1960s, attracting European immigrants. Along with the Irish, fleeing from the potato famine, Germans, and Scandinavians began to colonize this area. Immigration of the Finns peaked from 1890 to 1920. One of them built this barn.

In 1902 the Annalas were among the first five families to settle the rural countryside near Hurley, land that had been cleared by logging. Rocks and boulders, left behind by the glaciers, were plentiful. Besides long winters and a short growing season, the soil was clay-based, not conducive to crop raising. That meant dairy farming.

Matthew Annala, a Finnish carpenter and stonemason, quickly decided on that option, in hopes of supporting his wife and 12 children. By 1917 – when he began working on the barn – he had built several buildings, including the Oma (a Finnish word for "our home") School, which has since become the town hall. According to his daughter Mildred, he chose a circular design after visiting round barns in east

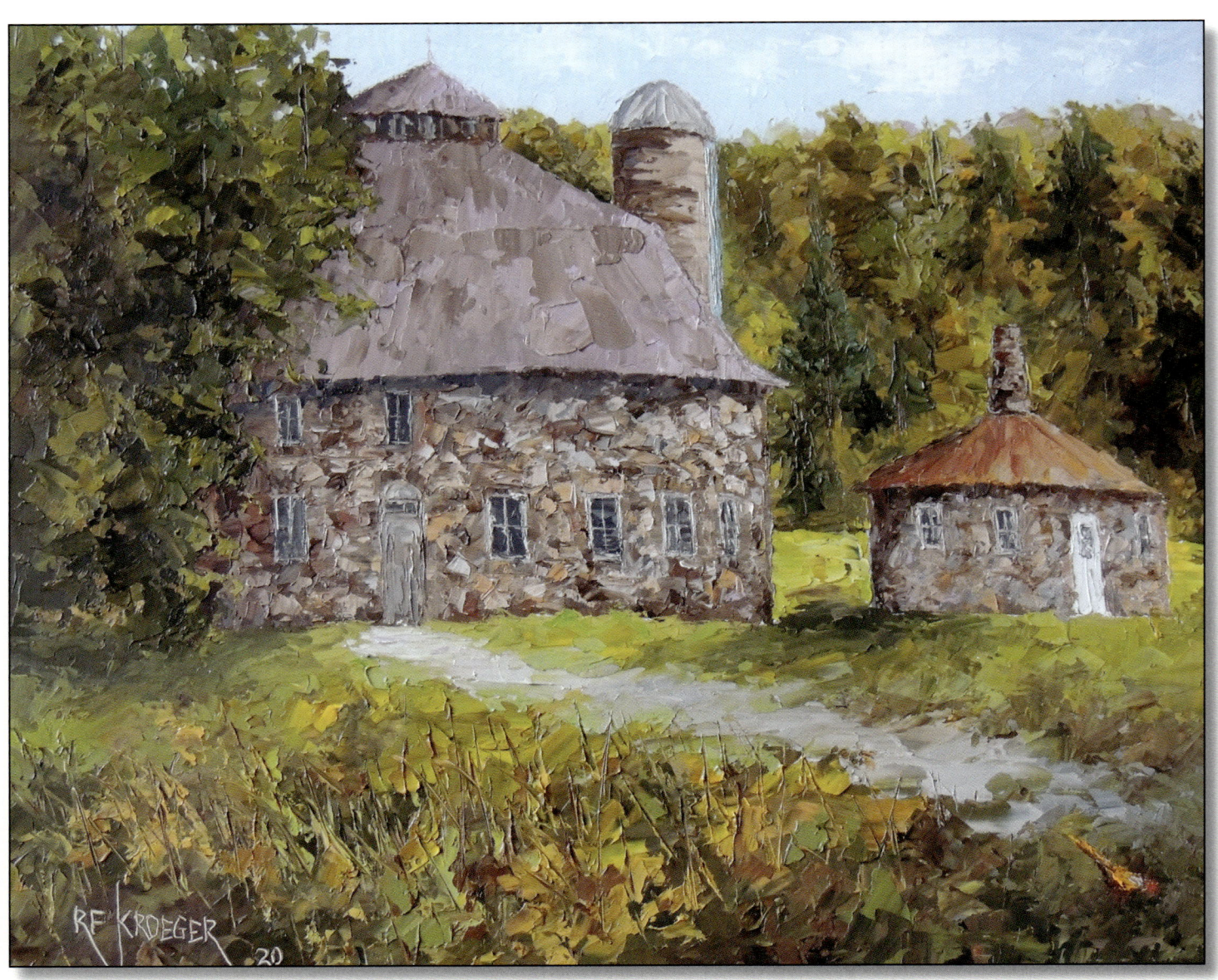

Little Finland

central Wisconsin, a state that exploded with the circular design and central silo, thanks to Professor Franklin King's articles. Also, concerned about the destruction caused by tornadoes, Annala decided to make his barn tornado-proof and, with a never-ending supply of rocks, he built his barn with fieldstone. Though many of Wisconsin's barns have fieldstone foundations, this is the only round one with complete walls of stone.

One of his daughters explained his method: heating the boulders in a fire and then dropping them in cold water – to make them crack. Matthew then used his stonemasonry skills to fit the pieces tightly next to one another, creating a two-foot-thick wall of stone, one requiring little mortar. She explained that engineering professors would bring their students to view the free-standing roof, which converged on the central silo – with only a drum and hoop support of hemlock rafters. Annala and his sons worked on the barn during summer seasons, beginning in 1917 and ending in 1921. Oddly, though his barn was an esthetic masterpiece, it didn't prompt other farmers to follow his lead. Most chose a conventional wooden design. By the 1920s, farm journals were publishing reports that proclaimed the round barn design to be more costly and perhaps less efficient than the traditional rectangular shape.

The barn's size, 60 feet wide and 60 feet high, was large enough for a small dairy herd; its 24 metal cow stalls circle around the white-painted fieldstone silo. After years of success in the dairy business, in 1928 he built a 15-foot high circular milkhouse – with matching fieldstone – so that fresh milk could be piped from the barn directly for bottling and shipping. His plan was to fashion the fieldstone chimney into a milk bottle but he never finished, possibly due to the emergence of the Great Depression.

Still, during these hard times, Mr. Annala continued to improve his barn, adding a clay tile silo around 1938. In 1943 he built a 40-foot-long ramp of fieldstone that led to the double-door entrance of the second level. The haymow could hold 100 tons of hay. Stalls for the bull and calves were located beneath this ramp.

During WWII the family delivered their own milk but stopped the bottling process by the mid-1940s. As the typical Wisconsin dairy herd increased in size, the farmer would often add an extension to his barn to accommodate increased production. However, the Annala barn's stone walls made that difficult and its dimensions limited the number of cows it could hold, eventually leading to the family's exiting the business and selling the farm in 1973.

The next owner, Paul Janoska, must have felt a sense of history when he secured a listing for the barn and milkhouse on the National Register in 1979, though the nomination form noted that the gambrel roof was in poor condition.

In fact, when photographer Frank Hutton visited the barn in the 1980s, he began to observe a gradual deterioration and, worried about vandalism and fire, he placed the barn high on his bucket list. In 2011 he visited again and was lucky to find the new owner, Paul Bauschke, not only at home but gracious enough to permit him to take photos in various seasons.

The Bauschkes purchased the farm in 2003 and have taken good care of it, using it mostly for storage. They hired professional restoration workers to bring it back to life, which was costly, though Paul refitted the windows by himself. Its fieldstone walls, bursting with multi-colored stones fitting together like clockwork, revive the memory not only of this master stonemason and his sons but also of the early Finnish immigrants who settled here, in little Finland.

OCONTO COUNTY
Mesenkamp's Marvel

This stunning stone barn still stands, located in the town of Chase, a small town of 3,300, about 20 miles north of Green Bay, where the average high in January is 26 degrees. Thanks to the Wisconsin glaciers, which ended about 11,000 years ago, rocks and boulders (some gargantuan) rise to the surface each spring, a nightmare for farmers, who must remove them before plowing their fields, but a great source of building stones for stonemasons. Such stones adorn all four walls of this barn.

In 1857 Nathan B. Chase, a lumber baron from Canada, moved to Wrightstown, about 20 miles south of Green Bay, and established a sawmill. Six years later he moved to what has become the town of Chase and transported his sawmill to the Little Suamico River. The Chase and Dixie Sawmill employed many; lumbering was a major force in the local economy. In 1870 Nathan's son Jasper and a partner took over the sawmill.

In October 1871, the famous Peshtigo Fire destroyed thousands of acres of prime timber, effectively ending the lumber industry here, but, on a positive note, it cleared the land for raising crops. Two years later, locals established the town, originally called St. Nathans but changed to Chase in 1890, perhaps to honor Nathan and his sons. Two years later he died.

Earlier, in 1876, Chase and his two sons founded the extensive Chase Valley Brickyards and in 1880 he organized the Chase Valley Glass Works. Diversifying came in handy since the fire and the 1877 Pensaukee tornado effectively ended the lumber industry in this region by the 1880s.

In the 1890s and early 1900s, the J.J. Hof Land Company purchased much of the deforested land and sold lots, encouraging European immigrants, particularly Polish, to

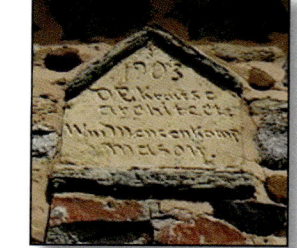

start farms in the Chase area – especially in Pulaski, about five miles south of Chase.

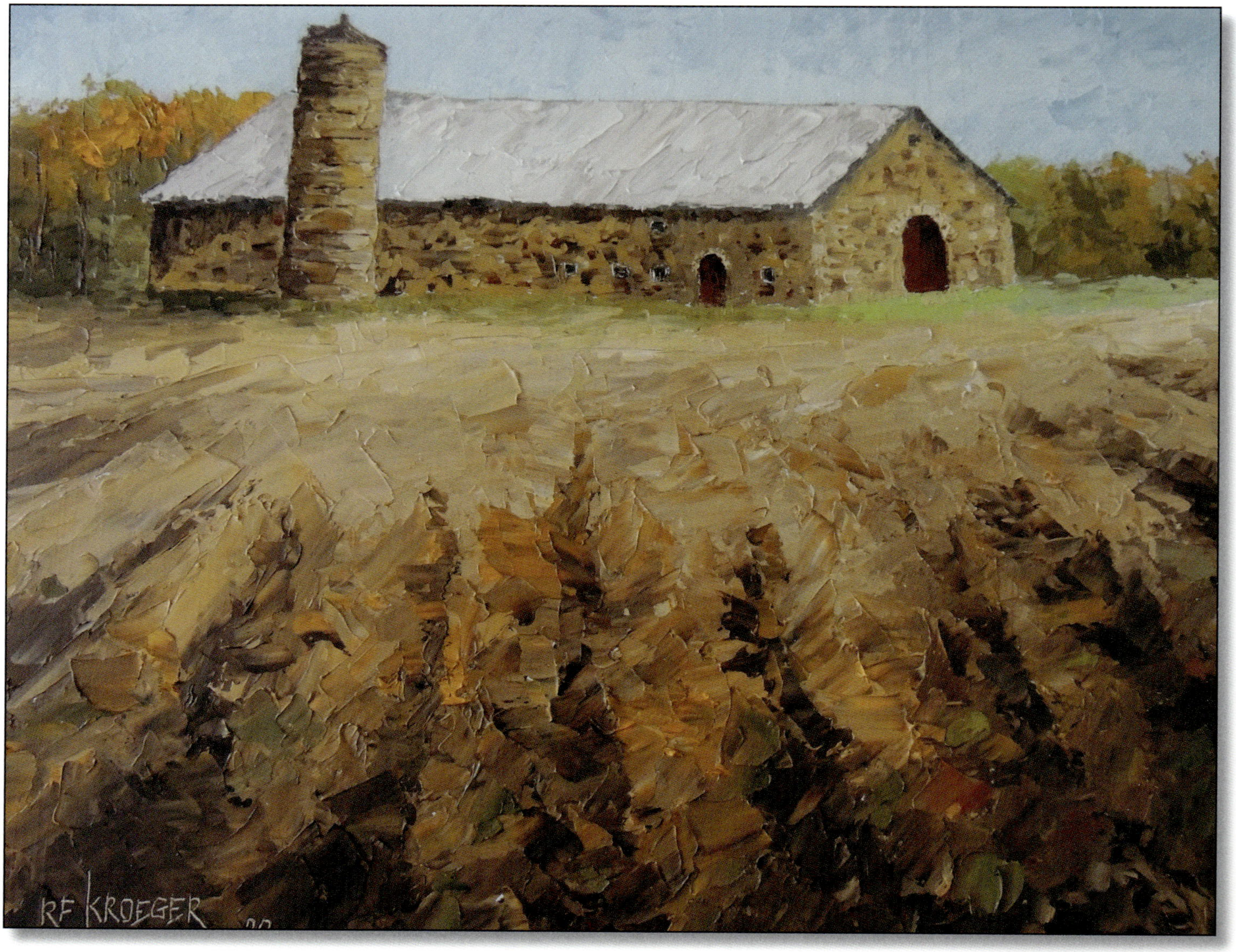

One of the early settlers, though not enticed by the Hof Company, was Daniel Krause, Sr., who immigrated here from Germany in 1867. Lincoln's Homestead Act of 1862 was working. Krause bought a farm in 1870 and sold it six years later to his son Daniel Krause, Jr., who took it over, married, and raised nine children. Besides farming and producing maple syrup, the family owned a sawmill and a farm implement business. Apparently, their hard work paid off; by 1903 they were affluent enough to afford to build this impressive stone barn, most likely replacing an earlier-built wooden one. Two years later Daniel, Sr., died.

Replace parentheses with italics. The date stone on the barn reads, *1903 D.E. Krause architect Wm Mensenkamp mason.* Listing the mason on the stone was generous of Krause, since master stonemasons seldom received credit for their work. And what a job William Mensenkamp did!

It's probable that the Krauses did not hire an architect since the barn was a basic rectangular shape with a gable

Above: Mesenkamp's Marvel **Right:** *Date stone, Krause barn, 1903. Courtesy Town of Chase, Wisconsin.*

roof. It's more likely that father, son, and the stonemason Mensenkamp collaborated on the design of the 100x60-foot barn. They built walls two-feet thick from rocks and stones from the fields, a much less expensive alternative to buying quarried rock and a far more attractive one – the variegated colors are striking. Stones such as granite, quartz, gneiss, gabbro, schist, hornblende, mica, and feldspar, ranging from a few inches to a foot in diameter, make the walls a joy for anyone to look at. Corner quoins were cut from large fieldstones, requiring expert stonemasonry.

Keystone-laid arched limestone lintels frame the main end doors (a Dutch barn design) and the side man-doors. Brick arches frame the many windows. Inside, an unusual half-stone wall separates the threshing area from the stable.

Feed could be dropped over the edge and pushed through wooden-hinged doors into the stable. Hay was lifted up with a rope and pulley from wagons, which could enter one door and exit through the other. It was then moved via a track system along the peak of the roof.

Hand-hewn roof rafters rest on the two-foot-thick stone walls, but they're also supported by central canted queen posts. A large cement ring remains in the threshing section and may have been the foundation of a cistern. Another clever idea was a water pump connected by an underground pipe to a hand-dug stone-lined well, which was located about 50 feet from the barn. Later, a 50-foot cement silo was added, most likely around 1910, as many were built in Wisconsin at that time.

Why did the Krause family choose stone for their barn? First, they could afford it and, secondly, they began breeding shorthorn cattle. Knowing Wisconsin's winters can be brutal, they might have wanted the best possible barn for their stock. They also had dairy cows, following the example of most Wisconsin farmers who were switching from wheat to dairy in the late 1800s. And, with nine children, Daniel Krause may have looked at this stone barn as an investment for the future of his family.

But for some reason, possibly due to the beginning of depressed farm prices after World War I, Daniel sold the farm in 1920, only 17 years after he built the barn. From 1920 to 1954 the farm went through 11 owners – including a sheriff's sale during the Great Depression, an all-too-often occurrence. Such a sequence of multiple ownership usually results in deterioration of the farmhouse and barns. This situation was no different.

Fortunately for this classic stone barn, two bachelors, brothers Casey and Stanley Frysh, bought the farm in 1954. Thankfully, they continued its upkeep – never an inexpensive task – and worked the farm for the next 50 years. In the early 1990s the north wall, 100 feet long, began to tilt outward, causing cracks in the foundation. Not long after that, a tornado ripped off part of the roof. But the brothers Frysh rose to the challenge and hired Orvil Krueger, "The Building Doctor," whose company uprighted the wall and added concrete and steel beams for support. In 2000, thanks to the Pulaski Area Historical Society, the barn was listed on the National Register.

After the brothers passed away, a niece became the stone barn's new owner and, apparently not interested in farming, sold the farm to a developer. Oops. But the developer, upon learning of the community's attachment to this barn, sold it to the town in 2007.

The little town of Chase had a tough task: restore the barn and turn it into an event center, an educational museum, and a city park – a costly proposition. They quickly discovered that the Portland cement used in the 1995 repair was not the right choice – it was too rigid and allowed moisture to penetrate, resulting in more deterioration. Good stonemasons know that just the right mixture of lime putty mortar has a lower compressive strength than cement and will allow the old mortar to expand and contract without causing damage. But fixing this problem was not simple.

Realizing the importance of the barn, the National Trust for Historic Preservation featured it on the cover of its 2009 Midwest Office Annual Report, a nice honor for the barn as well as for its new owner. But there was still the major hurdle of money.

A matching grant challenge in 2009 from the Jeffris Family Foundation of $143,000 requested Chase to raise $287,000 by June 2012. Bruce Jeffris, retired CEO of the Parker Pen Corporation, passed on his philanthropic ways to his family. Bruce and Eleanor Jeffris, and their son Tom founded the Jeffris Family Foundation in 1979.

Finally, after three years, the Chase Stone Barn Preservation Project met its fundraising goal of $530,000 – through grants, donations and multiple fundraisers. In 2014 the general contractor, IEI, completed the restoration.

The town still plans to convert the barn's stable area into a rustic agricultural museum, showcasing antique farm equipment and the pioneering lifestyle of early settlers, along with a geologic history of the fieldstones. They hope to turn the acreage into a public park with walking paths, a stone bridge over a creek, and a play area for children. Field trips from area schools will be encouraged.

Chase will make the barn available for events, such as weddings, family reunions, company picnics, and farmers' markets. One such event – showing how a community can spend a cold evening together on a snowless January day – featured fireworks behind the stone barn, a fitting tribute to not only the town's preservation success but a way to honor their prized gem, Mesenkamp's marvel.

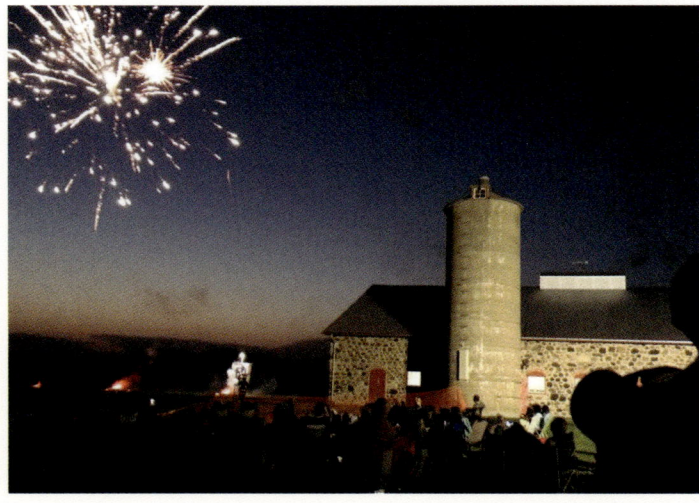

Fireworks celebration, Krause barn. Courtesy of Town of Chase.

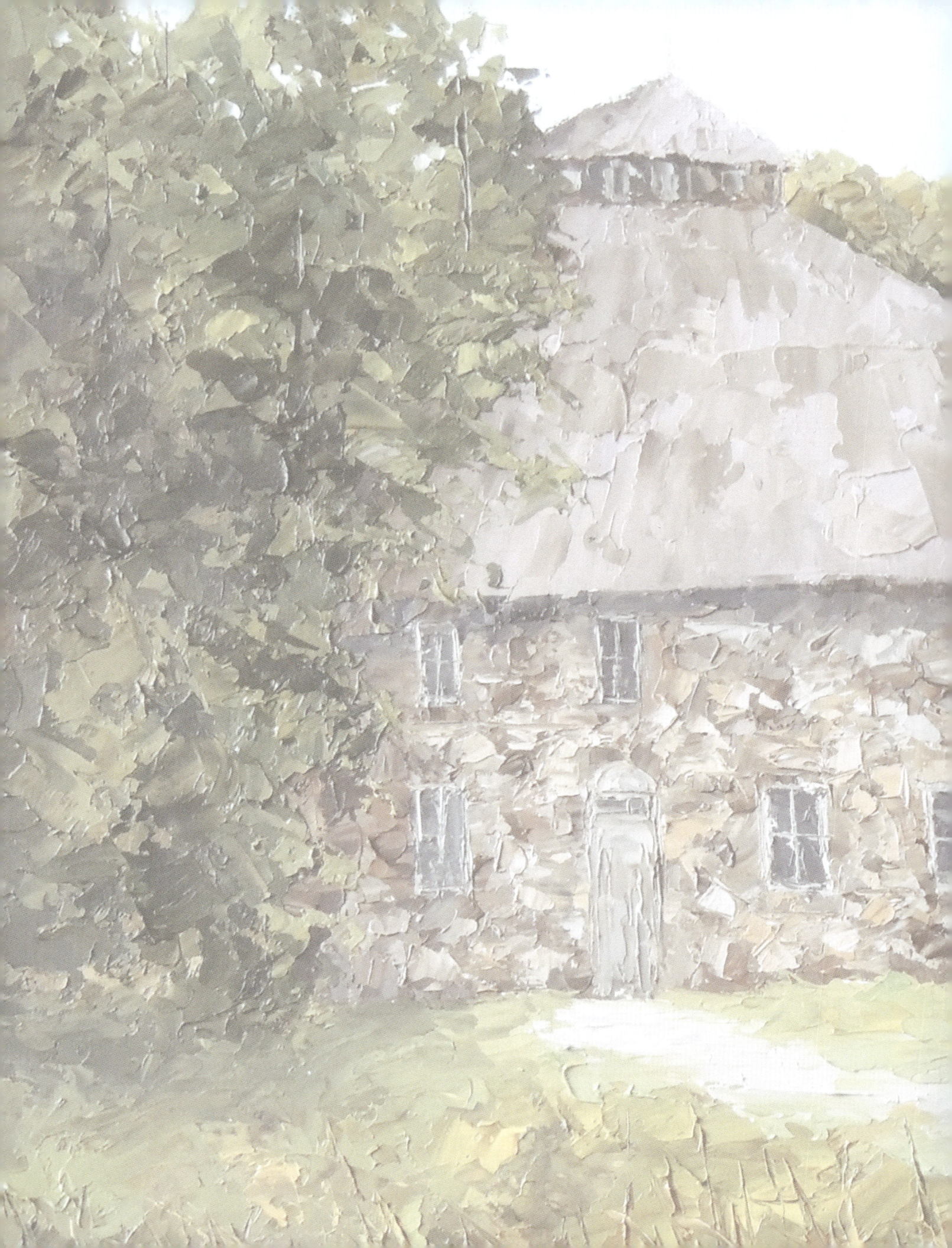

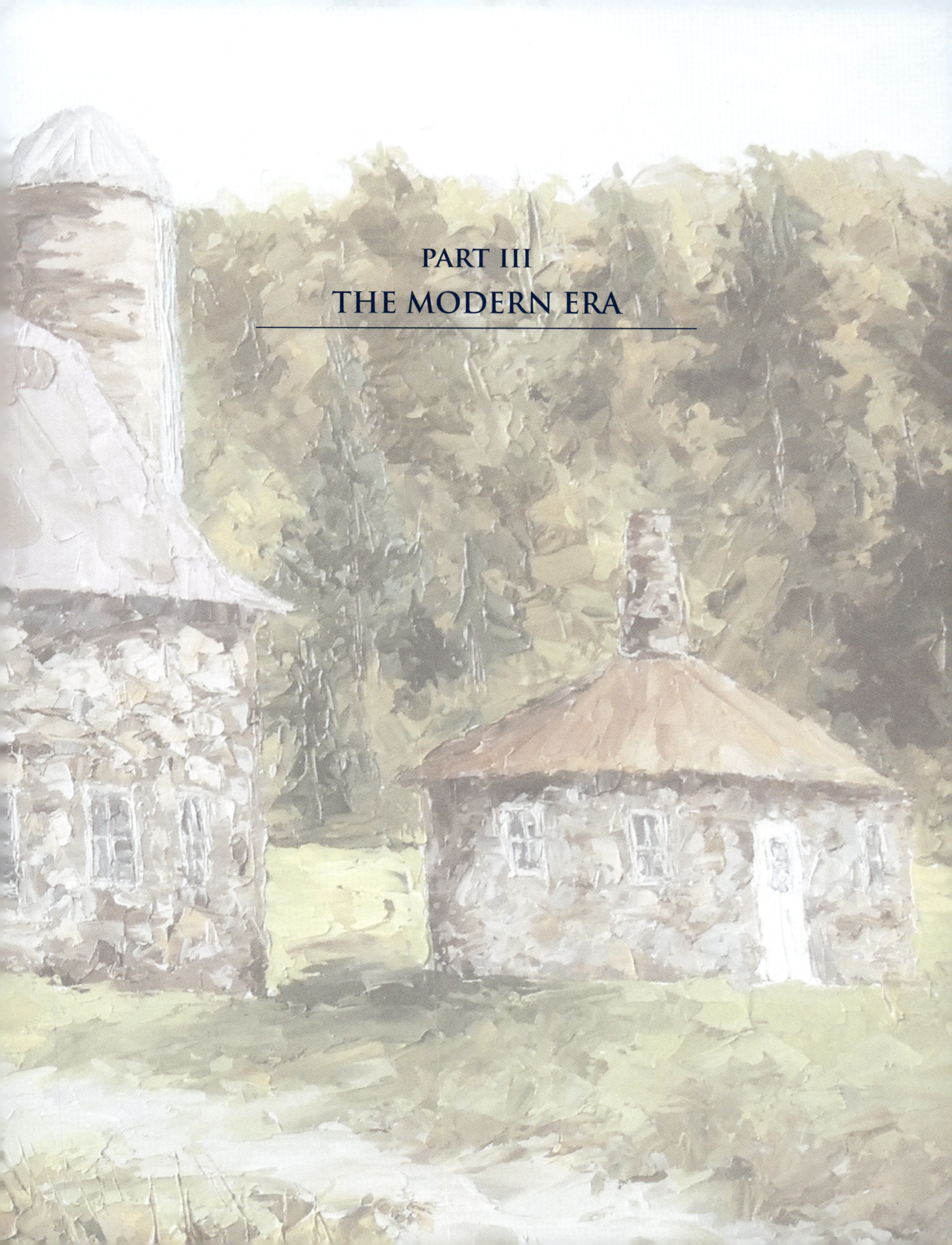

PART III
THE MODERN ERA

8. CONTEMPORARY

Though many old wooden barns have deteriorated, have been dismantled for their ancient lumber, or currently are in various states of collapse, stone barns seem to buck this trend. Still, it's much less expensive to erect a modern pole barn, one large enough to house huge farm equipment, than it is to build a wooden barn of a comparable size, much less a stone barn. But there are exceptions.

Wisconsin's Dick Schwab built six stone round barns in Iowa, beginning in 1991. Owner of a construction company, Dick got the idea to build a barn when a storm toppled some large trees on his rural property, about three miles northwest of Iowa City. Intrigued by the logs, he took them to a sawmill and eventually used them to build three rectangular wooden barns from 1985 to 1987. Those led to more ideas.

"This rectangular, square stuff is kind of boring. Anybody can build rectangular barns," he said in a newspaper interview. So, he began building round barns … six of them … out of stone from the famous Anamosa quarry in Iowa. He finished his first one, with a 40-foot diameter, in 1991 and ended in 2011 with his sixth one, his masterpiece, with a diameter of 100 feet. The Johnson County Conservation Board acquired five of the stone barns, thanks to a generous offer from Dick, with plans to make a pioneer village surrounding them. To honor his work, a photo of two of his barns grace the cover of my book, *Round Barns of America*.

Dick, not a stonemason by trade, explains that he learned by doing and has laid over 800,000 pounds of split-faced veneer limestone from the Anamosa Quarry. Humbly, he considers himself to be a five on a stonemasonry scale of 0 to 10. According to him, "The art of stonemasonry is dwindling. There are some 8s and 9s, but not many masters left." How true. Today's stonework, often done with artificially produced stone, doesn't require expert placement.

A few miles south of Mason City, Iowa, Dale Mills and his wife Judy run a B&B called the Cupola Inn. When the owner of a nearby damaged barn was about to bury the stones from the barn, Dale offered to take them, which he used to build a small round stone barn in 2002. As

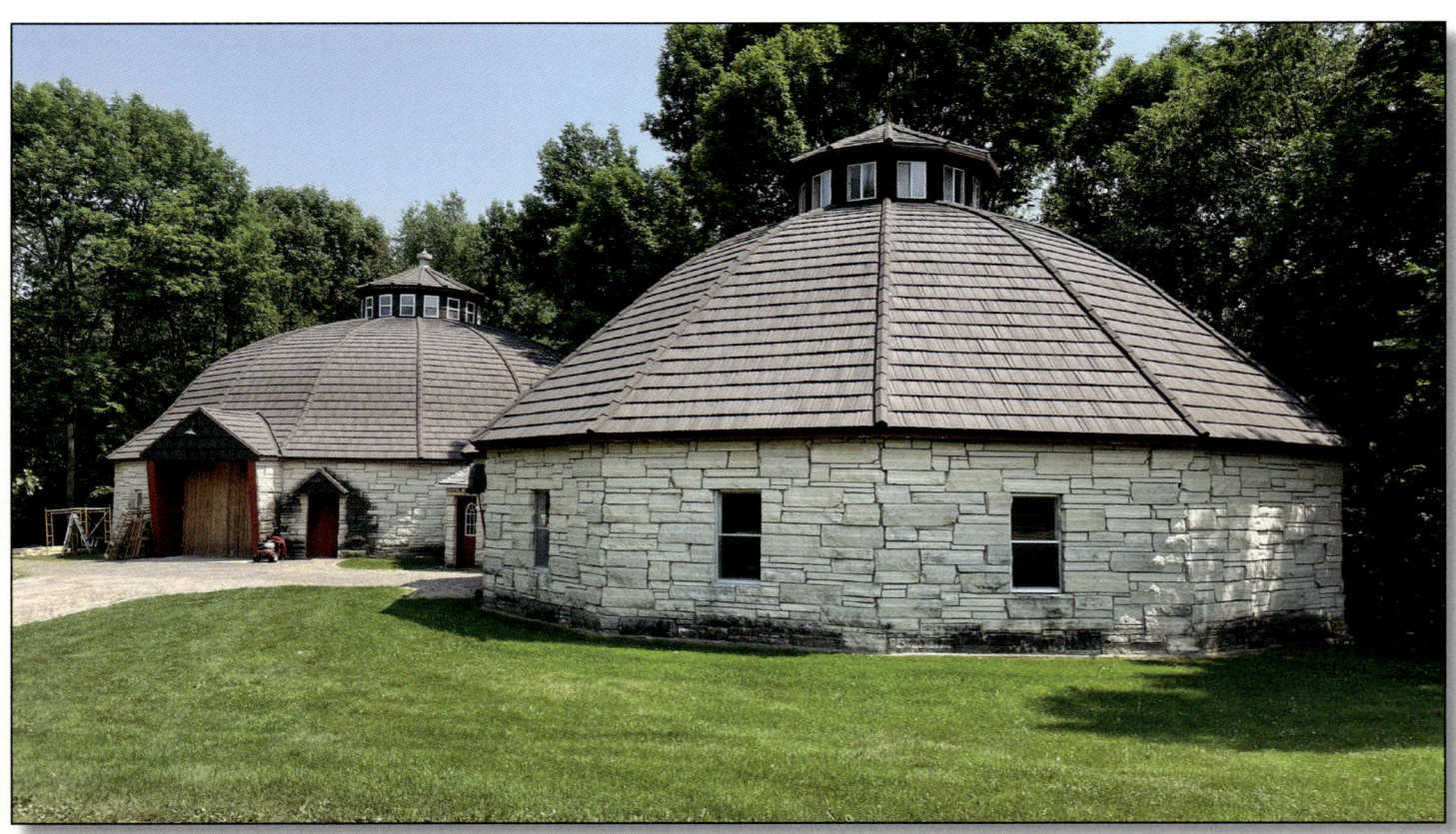

Dick Schwab round barns, Iowa. Courtesy of Johnson County Conservation Board.

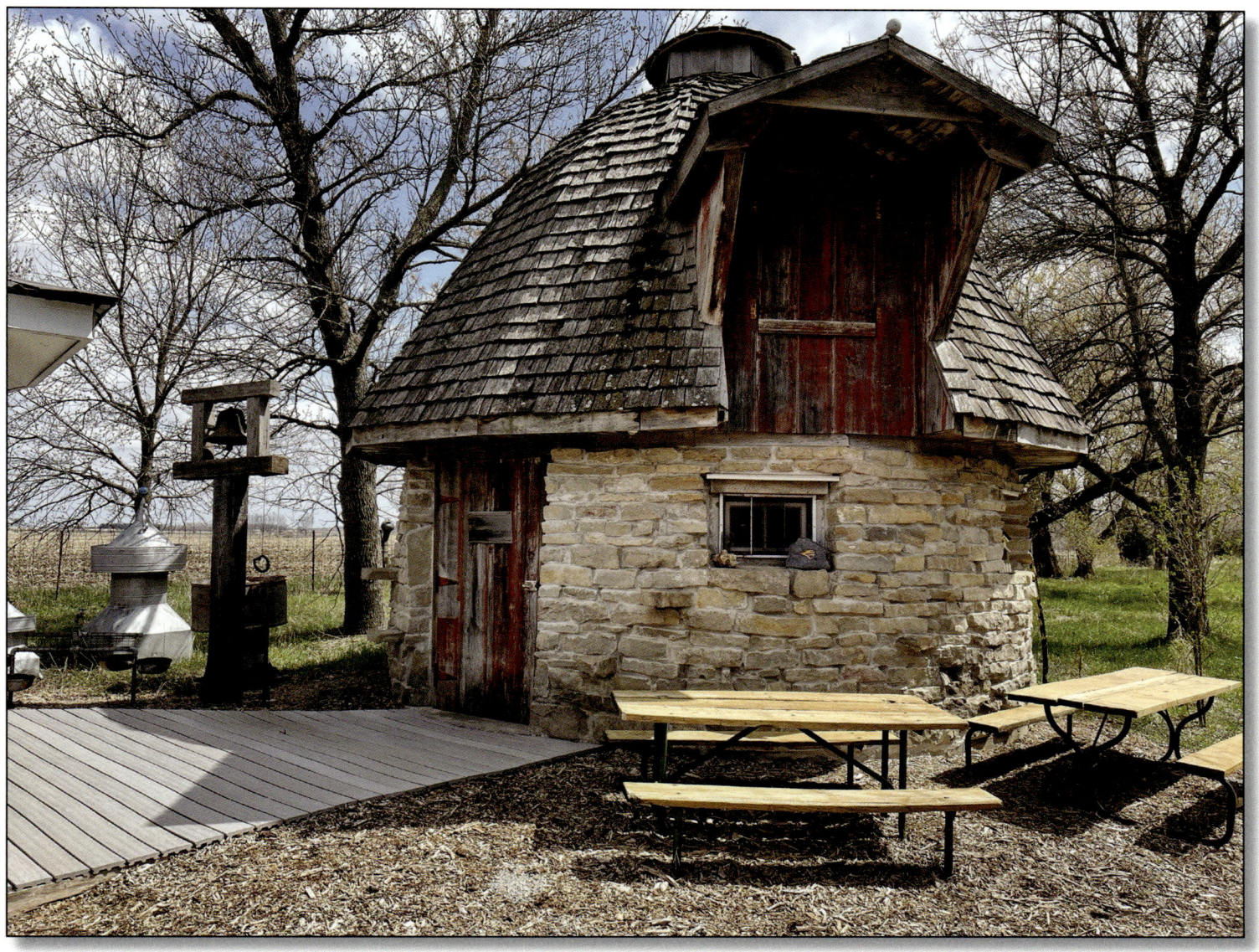

Cupola Inn, Mason City, Iowa. Courtesy of Dale and Judy Mills.

he explained, "I had never laid a brick before, let alone irregular native limestone, but after talking to a friend, I knew what to avoid." He fashioned the cupola out of cedar shingles and decided to use the 24-foot-diameter barn as a seasonal breakfast room, right next to his B&B rental. Dale calls this "an Iowa ingenuity special barn."

Over the past several decades there's been renewed interest in the ancient skills of wooden timber-framing as well as in the art and science of stone craftsmanship. A nonprofit, the Dry Stone Conservancy (www.drystone.org), is the only organization in the country devoted solely to dry stone masonry. With a goal of preserving the art and craft of masonry without mortar, the group certifies three levels of masons: basic, journeyman, and master craftsman.

Vermont's Stone Trust also offers education, workshops, and certification in dry stone walling. Groups such as the International Masonry Society and The European Association of Stonemasons and Sculptors – as well as many

others – offer certification and education, hoping to preserve this ancient art.

And on another bright note, many stone barns have been converted into museums, offices of historical societies, and event centers. But repurposing an old barn isn't a new trend. In the late 16th century in Holland, Dutch Catholics were suppressed and lost their churches. So, they celebrated Mass in their barns. Sects of the Amish religion held their services in barns well into the 1800s.

A stone barn in New Hampshire has been marvelously adapted into a vacation rental with 22 guest rooms. In Iowa an old stone barn now holds a brewery. The New York State Historical Association has moved their offices into the stone barn complex in Cooperstown. And, in rural and suburban areas young couples are choosing to get married in old barns, a growing trend that gives a new purpose to an old barn and helps to preserve its story – as does this book.

AFTERWORD

While traveling around Ohio in search of old barns in each of the state's 88 counties, I decided that the Kindelberger barn in Monroe County, the first stone barn I'd seen, would represent that county in my book, *Historic Barns of Ohio*. That happened in 2015. Despite having printed directions and a gps system in my car, I got lost in the hills of this scenic countryside, which is rightfully called the "Switzerland of Ohio." A few years later when I paid another visit to Gary and Marge, the fifth generation of ownership, I got lost again. But, this stone barn, deservedly listed on the National Register, was worth the trouble. At the time I didn't realize that it would be the first of over 90 that I'd record in my stone barn project.

Over the next 10 years I continued documenting old barns that I found in Ohio and Indiana, while doing barn tours and using the paintings for fundraisers for historical societies. When a representative of the History Press contacted me, I agreed to write a book on Ohio barns. After the book copy was finished, stories of old barns kept emerging and one, in particular, could have been easily adapted into a movie. That prompted me to ask the History Press about writing a second book. However, the rep explained to me that the press didn't want any competition since the first book was doing so well. It sold out of its first printing within a year.

So, I asked if the press would be willing to publish a book on round barns, which I had been working on for several years. No, again, was the reply; the History Press does not publish books with a national scope. When I asked for referrals, John directed me to several publishers. I chose Acclaim Press, a tiny publisher in Missouri, for two reasons. First, the sample book they sent had excellent color reproduction and, two, they print full-color in the USA. (Most full-color coffee-table-sized books are printed overseas.) The first printing sold out within nine months.

After I discovered other stone barns, I began thinking about devoting a book to them. Part of this motivation began in the summer of 2021 when a Cincinnati-area lady contacted me after reading a review of my Ohio book in our newspaper. She said she had a stone barn. Sure, I thought. But, after seeing her photos, I visited the barn and marveled at the creek rubble stone construction and its story, which traced perhaps as far back as Sir Francis Drake and his medieval tithe stone barn at Buckland Abbey in Cornwall.

Though I didn't have access to a listing of stone barns – as I did in the round barn project – I looked for them state by state, mostly through state historical societies, state historical preservation offices, and National Register listings. As I muddled through these sources, I wondered if I'd find the same level of stories as in the round barn project. I was pleasantly surprised by what I found.

And, even though I couldn't visit each barn, I often talked with the owners. In some cases I traveled. I marveled at two in Michigan, a good eight-hour drive from Cincinnati, but more than justified. In fact, one of them graces the book's cover. I took a long road trip to northern Missouri and the German immigrant niche in the city of Hermann, where I met two of the most interesting historic barn lovers I'd come across. On the same trip I drove north into Iowa for a terrific tour with Jack Smith, president of the Iowa Barn Foundation. That area in eastern Iowa is full of limestone quarries, the source of stone for its many stone barns, including the remarkable prison complex in Anamosa.

I also had a chance to visit barns in nearby Indiana and Kentucky, though I regretted not being able to see the one whose walls were still embedded with irons rings used to hold slaves. My college roommate, Dr. Pat Lang, took me to the Shaker barns near his home in western Massachusetts and eastern New York. He also scouted the Hay barn in New Hampshire.

However, by far the most interesting trip I made was to six counties in southeastern Pennsylvania, essentially bedroom communities of Philadelphia but also unquestionably the motherlode of stone barns in America. In my research and from other sources, I knew that these six counties had hundreds of stone barns and that their masonry was almost always exquisite. But seeing is believing and, when I visited, I became a believer. I also was surprised that typical suburban sprawl hadn't moved north from the big city environs of Philadelphia. This region still maintains a bucolic flavor and countless historical societies have worked hard to preserve the rich history, going back to the 1680s and William Penn. It is one of the most remarkable havens of antiquity in our country.

I was also fortunate to have traveled – with my oldest son Rob – to southwestern England and its three counties – Somerset, Devon, and Cornwall. Besides playing golf, we witnessed several majestic stone buildings and barns, the precedents of their counterparts in early America. The most impressive was the great barn at Glastonbury Abbey, completed in the 1340s.

In the early years while I was working on this barn project of painting old barns and writing about them, I understood *how* this started, but I didn't fully understand the main reason behind my passion. Why was I, a suburbanite, going from rural town to town, touring the countryside with barn scouts, and recording these forgotten symbols of early agriculture? Finally, it clicked. After purchasing *Edward S. Curtis Portraits*, my second book on the work of Edward Curtis, photographer of Native American tribes at the end of the 19th century, whose thousands of images are stored in the Library of Congress, I read one of his quotes: "The passing of every old man or woman means the passing of some tradition, some knowledge of sacred rites possessed by no other." Curtis felt compelled to document the lives and customs of "one of the greatest races of mankind" and, thanks to the patronage of J.P. Morgan and the support of President Theodore Roosevelt, he recorded a way of life that has disappeared.

I then realized *why* I was capturing images of old barns, which are vanishing rapidly from rural landscapes, a trend that most folks in the suburbs and cities know little about. My hope is that my work will help to preserve a small piece of America's rich agricultural heritage. In 50-100 years from now, when most of the old barns are gone, if someone sees one of my paintings and reads its essay, he or she will understand the role that the old barn, "the money maker," played in the early years of our country.

BIBLIOGRAPHY

Andrzejewski, Anna, ed. 2017 *Folk Farmsteads on the Frontier: North Dakota Field School 2017*. Madison, Wisconsin. University of Wisconsin, e-book.

Apps, Jerold W. 2010 *Barns of Wisconsin*. Madison, Wisconsin: Wisconsin Historical Society Press.

Arthur, Eric and Witney, Dudley 1981 *The Barn: A Vanishing Landmark in North America*. Toronto, Canada: Galahad Books.

Bek, William Godfrey 1907 *The German Settlement Society of Philadelphia*. Philadelphia: Americana Germanica Press.

Bonham, Ken 2015 *A Big Book of Barns*. Online flip book.

Burnett, Robyn and Luebbering, Ken. 1996 *German Settlement in Missouri*. Columbia, Missouri: University of Missouri Press.

Cramb, Ian 2021 *The Art of the Stonemason*. Lanham, Maryland: Stackpole Books.

Dregni, Michael, ed. 2002 *This Old Barn: A Treasury of Family Farm Memories*. Stillwater, Minnesota: Voyageur Press.

Endersby, Elric, Greenwood, Alexander, and Larkin, David 1992 *Barn: The Art of a Working Building*. New York, New York: Houghton Mifflin Company.

Endersby, Elric, Greenwood, Alexander, and Larkin, David 2014 *Barn: Preservation & Adaptation*. New York, New York: Rizzoli International Publications, Inc.

Eckes, Alfred E. 2020 *Stone And Architecture In The Flint Hills*. Manhattan, Kansas. New Prairie Press, Kansas State University Libraries.

Falk, Cynthia G. 2012 *Barns of New York: Rural Architecture of the Empire State*. Ithaca, New York: Cornell University Press.

Fink, Daniel 1987 *Barns of the Genesee Country: 1790-1915*. Geneseo, New York: James Brunner, Publisher.

Flynn, Brenda 2015 *The Complete Guide to Building With Rocks and Stone*. Ocala, Florida: Atlantic Publishing Group, Inc.

French, Giles 1964 *Cattle Country of Peter French*. Portland, Oregon: Binfords and Mort, Publishers.

Haney, Chuck 2007 *Big Sky Barns*. Helena, Montana: Riverbend Publishing.

Hanou, John T. 1993 *A Round Indiana: Round Barns in the Hoosier State*. West Lafayette, Indiana: Purdue University Press.

Hanou, John T. 2020 *A Round Indiana: Round Barns in the Hoosier State, Second Edition*. West Lafayette, Indiana: Purdue University Press.

Hoots, Greg 2020 *Two Barns in Wabaunsee County*. Flint Hills Special Digital Magazine: Flint Hills Special, January 24, 2020.

Hoots, Greg 2020 *The Peter Thoes Barn*. Flint Hills Special Digital Magazine: Flint Hills Special, March 19, 2020.

Huber, Gregory D. 2017 *The Historic Barns of Southeastern Pennsylvania*. Atglen, Pennsylvania: Schiffer Publishing, Ltd.

Huger, Lucie F. 2001 St. *Albans: History and Folklore of a Missouri River Town*. Kirkwood, Missouri: Fairfield Publishing Company.

Hughes, Graham 1985 *Barns of Rural Britain*. London: The Herbert Press.

Jackson, Jacqueline D. 2011 *The Round Barn: A Biography of an American Farm*. Beloit, Wisconsin: Beloit College Press.

Kauffman, Henry J. 1992 *Architecture of the Pennsylvania Dutch Country - 1700-1900*. Lancaster, Pennsylvania: Olde Springfield Shoppe.

Kautz, Donald 2023 *Mills of Lancaster County*. Morgantown, Pennsylvania: Masthof Press.

Kekel, Nikolas 2019 *The Crescent Farm Rock Barn*. Paper written for a course, Introduction to Public History, at Kennesaw State University: Georgiahistoricalsociety.com.

Kennedy, Stephen M. 1988 *Practical Stonemasonry Made Easy*. Blue Ridge Summit, Pennsylvania: Tab Books, Inc.

Kirk, Malcolm 1994 *Silent Spaces: The Last of the Great Aisled Barns*. Boston, Massachusetts: Bullfinch Press, Little, Brown and Company.

Kroeger, Robert 2022 *Round Barns of America – 75 Icons of History*. Morley, Missouri: Acclaim Press.

Kroeger, Robert 2021 *Historic Barns of Ohio*. Charleston, South Carolina: The History Press.

Launey, John Pitts 2007 *First Families of Chester County Pennsylvania*. Westminster, Maryland: Heritage Books, Inc.

Leffingwell, Randy 1997 *The American Barn*. Osceola, Wisconsin: MBI Publishing Company.

Marshall, Howard Wight 1995 *Paradise Valley, Nevada*. Tucson, Arizona: The University of Arizona Press.

McGready, Blake 2016 *Abigail Hartman Rice, Revolutionary War Nurse*, article in *Journal of the American Revolution*, an online publication of www.allthingsliberty.com.

McKee, Harley J. 1973 *Introduction to Early American Masonry*. Washington, D.C.: National Trust for Historic Preservation.

McPhee, John 2002 *The Founding Fish*. New York, New York: Farrar, Straus and Giroux.

McRaven, Charles 1989 *Building With Stone*. New York, New York: Lippincott & Crowell.

Mohr, Marsha W. 2010 *Indiana Barns*. Bloomington, Indiana: Indiana University Press.

Mueller, Linda and Paterka, Kathleen Irene 2012 *For the Love of a Castle*. Boyne City, Michigan: Harbor House Publishers.

Mueller, Linda and Paterka, Kathleen Irene 2022 *For the Love of a Castle II*. Boyne City, Michigan: Harbor House Publishers.

Nagy, John Charles and Goulding, Penny Teaf 2006 *Acres of Quakers*. Chester County, Pennsylvania: Willistown Township Historical Commission.

Noble, Allen G. and Cleek, Richard K. 1995 *The Old Barn Book*. New Brunswick, New Jersey: Rutgers University Press.

Noble, Allen G. and Wilhelm, Hubert G.H., eds. 1995 *Barns of the Midwest*. Athens, Ohio: Ohio University Press.

Peachee, Carol 2019 *Kentucky Barns*. Bloomington, Indiana: Indiana University Press.

Pendleton, Philip E. 1994 *Oley Valley Heritage, The Colonial Years: 1700-1775*. Kutztown, Pennsylvania: The Pennsylvania German Society.

Pennypacker, Samuel W. 1872 *Annals of Phoenixville and Its Vicinity*. Philadelphia: Bavis and Pennypacker.

Philbrick, Nathaniel 2016 *Valiant Ambition: George Washington, Benedict Arnold, and the Fate of the American Revolution*. New York, New York: Viking.

Ravenswaay, Charles 1977 *The Arts and Architecture of German Settlements in Missouri: A Survey of a Vanishing Culture*. Columbia, Missouri: University of Missouri Press.

Reed, David 2002 *The Art and Craft of Stonework*: New York, New York: Lark Books.

Schmidt, Carl F. 1966 *Cobblestone Masonry*. Rush, New York: Fishell-Van Wagenen.

Schuler, Stanley 1984 *American Barns*. West Chester, Pennsylvania: Schiffer Publishing.

Scott, Donald H. 1997 *Barns of Indiana*. Virginia Beach, Virginia: The Donning Company.

Shewmaker, Melba and Harris, Monte K. 2016 *Barns of Benton County, Arkansas*. Bentonville, Arkansas.

Sloane, Eric 1954 *Eric Sloane's America*. New York, New York: Promontory Press.

Sloane, Eric 1965 *A Reverence for Wood*. Mineola, New York: Dover Publications.

Sloane, Eric 2001 *Eric Sloane's An Age of Barns*. Minneapolis, Minnesota: Voyageur Press.

Smith, Regina C. et al. 1983 *Prehistory and History of the Winnemucca District. Cultural Resource Series, Monograph No. 6*. Reno, Nevada: Nevada State Office of the Bureau of Land Management.

Sobon, Jack A. 2019 *Hand Hewn*. North Adams, Massachusetts: Storey Publishing.

Soike, Lowell J. 1983 *Without Right Angles: The Round Barns of Iowa*. Des Moines, Iowa: Iowa State Historical Department.

Steccato, Jeffrey 2019 *Barns Across America*. Buffalo, New York: Amherst Media.

Sommer, Robin L. 1997 *The Old Barn Book*. Barnes and Noble.

Spencer, Brenda R. 2007 *Kansas Historic Barns Survey, 2007*. Topeka, Kansas: Kansas State Historical Society.

Skinner, John S., ed. *The American Farmer*, 1827. Volume 9, Number 3. Rural Economy, "Shakers' Barn." Baltimore, Maryland.

Stonemasons of Muskingum County, Ohio, in the 1800s. 1997. Zanesville, Ohio: Muskingum County Genealogical Chapter of the Ohio Genealogical Society.

Triumpho, Richard 2004 *Round Barns of New York*. Syracuse, New York: Syracuse University Press.

Weber, Susan, Ames, Kenneth L. and Wittmann, Matthew, eds. 2012 *The American Circus*. New Haven, Connecticut: Yale University Press.

Wheeler, Kenneth H. and Cowart, Jennifer Lee 2013 *Who Was the Real Gus Coggins?: Social Struggle and Criminal Mystery in Cherokee County, 1912–1927*. The Georgia Historical Quarterly, Vol. 97, No. 4 (Winter, 2013), pp. 411-446. Savannah, Georgia: Georgia Historical Society.

Whitney, Charles W. and Gray, Pamela W. *Ohio Barns: Inside and Out*. Mt. Vernon, Ohio: Gray's Venture.

Youngblood, Wayne L. 2017 *Edward S. Curtis Portraits*. New York, New York: Chartwell Books.

Ziminski, Andrew 2020 *The Stone Mason: A History of Building Britain*. London: John Murray Publishers.

ABOUT THE AUTHOR

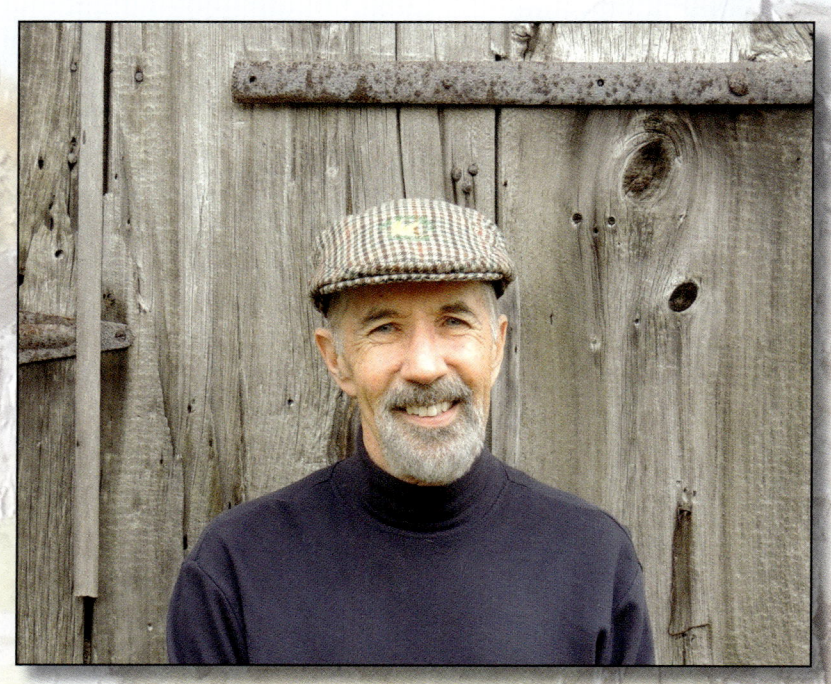

Robert Kroeger. Photograph, David Bimschleger

Dr. Robert Kroeger, a native of Youngstown, graduated from Ohio State University's College of Dentistry, served seven years in the US Navy and ended with the rank of lieutenant commander. He and his late wife Brenda moved to Cincinnati where they raised five children and Dr. Kroeger practiced general dentistry from 1977 to 2010, when he retired. He and his wife Laura also live in Cincinnati, where they enjoy spending time with grandchildren.

Kroeger is a second-generation artist, though, unlike his father Francis, who held an art degree from Notre Dame, his professional art career blossomed later in life. Though he did not immediately follow in his father's footsteps, Robert's career as a dentist allowed him to study color values and facial esthetic principles in smile design. He is the author of *Historic Barns of Ohio*, a book that features a barn, its painting, and its essay in each of Ohio's 88 counties. His second effort to preserve barn history, *Round Barns of America*, a full-color book, features the paintings and essays of 75 circular and polygonal barns, built from the east to the west coast, including 11 in Ohio.

Dr. Kroeger has also written two books on dentistry and seven books on golf in Scotland, England, Wales, and Ireland, including *To The 14th Tee*, *The Links of Wales*, *The Golf Courses of Old Tom Morris*, *Golf on the Links of Ireland*, *Golf on the Links of England*, *Complete Guide to the Golf Courses of Scotland*, and *The Secrets of Islay*. This is his third book on old barns but hopefully not his last. His storytelling, books, and nearly all of his paintings support historical societies, museums, and libraries in fundraising events throughout Ohio and Indiana. He continues to search for forgotten old barns and their stories and can be contacted via the website, www.barnart.weebly.com.

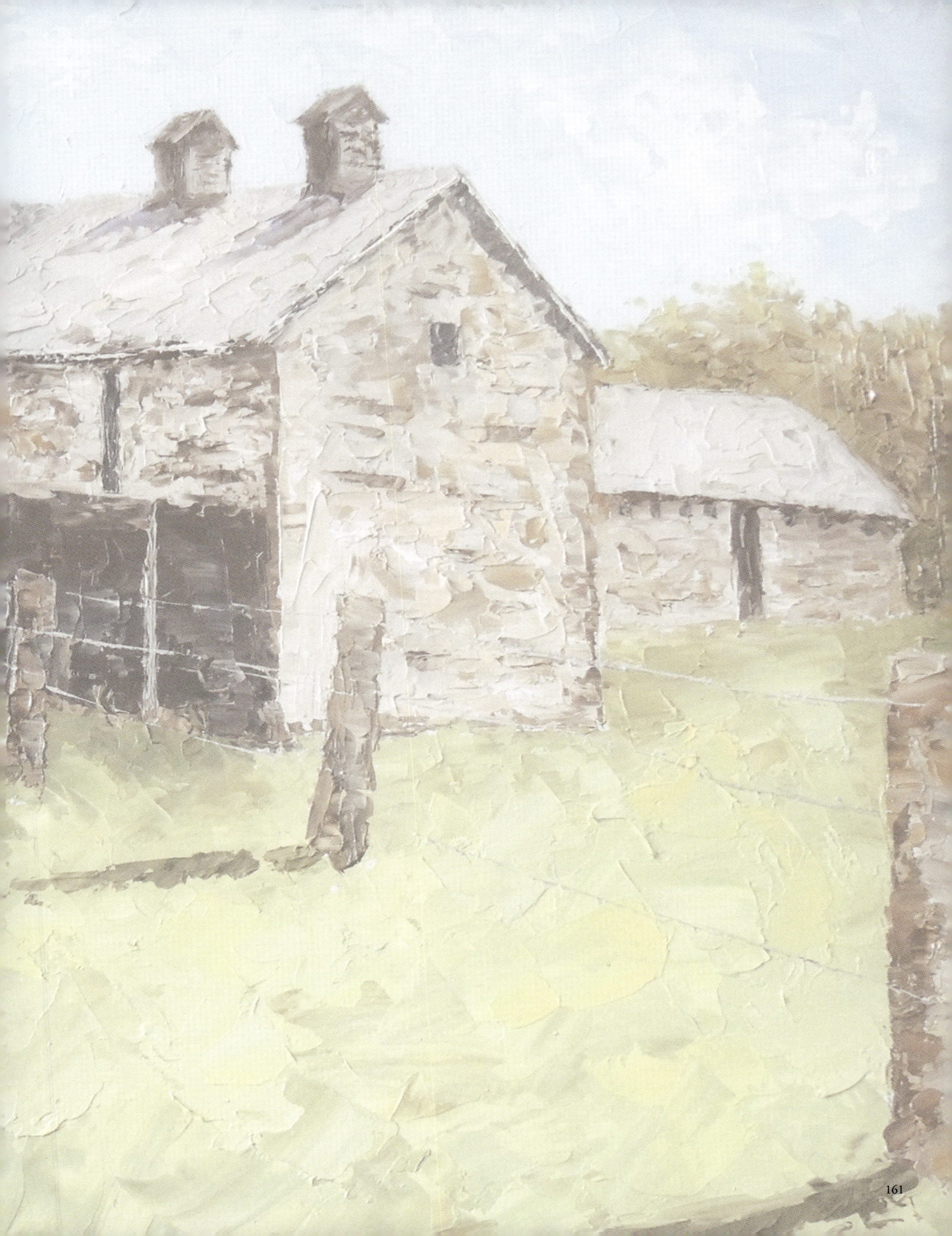

INDEX

A

Abenaki Native Americans 35
Abraham Lincoln: A History 36
Acadia National Park 31
Acres of Quakers 68
Adams, Reuben 50
Adamson, Hannah 74
Aerosmith 143
Agricultural Society of Albemarle 110
Aladdin Company 140
Alcock, Nat 17
Allen, Andrew 79
Allen, Hezekiah 55
Allentown, Pennsylvania 7, 8
Allerton Farm 70
Alloway, New York 50
American Anti-Slavery Society 74
American Barns and Covered Bridges 7
American Buncher Manufacturing Company 134
American Express 34
American Farmer 110
American Stove Company 114
An Age of Barns 7, 11
Anamosa Quarry 152
Anderson, James 72
Anderson, Jessica 145
Anderson, Wayne 15
Angell, Israel 78
Annala, Matthew 146, 147
Annala, Mildred 146
Annals of Phoenixville and its Vicinity, The 73
Antrim County, Michigan 137
Arthur A. McKain Papers, 1907-1938 134
Art of the Stonemason, The 14, 18
Arts and Architecture of German Settlements

in Missouri: A Survey of a Vanishing Culture, The 20
Ashlar 20
Aspdin, Joseph 16
Asplundh, Meredith 94
Astor, J.J. 40
Astor, John Jacob 50
Atlanta Constitution 116
AZD Associates-Architects 145

B

Baker Farm 101
Baker, Bruce 3
Baldwin Farm 70
Ball, Berenice 66, 67
Bank of Ball Ground 119
Bank of Bristol 53
Bank of Cherokee 117, 119
Bannister, Turpin 56
Bar Harbor, Maine 31, 32
Barclays Bank 129
Barn for All Reasons, A (painting) 62
Barn, Proseus 50
Barns of Chester County 66
Barraud, Anne 109
Barto, Pennsylvania 59
Baseball Hall of Fame 46, 47
Battle of Brandywine Creek 72
Battle of Culloden 91
Battle of Fallen Timbers 27
Battle of Germantown 73, 78
Battle of Hastings 22
Battle of Long Island 95
Battle of Monmouth 74
Battle of Monocacy 100
Battle of Paoli Tavern 72

Battle of Princeton 91
Battle That Saved Washington, The (painting) 99
Baumberger, Beverly 125
Baumberger, Frederick, Jr. 125
Baumberger, Gary 17, 125, 126, 127
Baumberger, Marge 17
Baumberger, Marjorie 125, 126, 127
Bauschke, Paul 147
Bay City, Michigan 140
Beautiful Bremo (painting) 108
Beavercreek Historical Society 132
Bell, H.J. 128
Benedictine Abbey 22
Benedictines 22
Bennett, Abraham 68
Bennett, Rebecca 68
Berks County, Pennsylvania 58
Berkshire County, Massachusetts 41, 42
Best Farm 101
Best, David 100
Best, John 100, 101
Bethlehem, Pennsylvania 63
Big Book of Barns, A 67
Billboard Barn, The (painting) 30
Birmingham Friends Meeting 66
Bishops of Exeter 24
Black Hills of South Dakota 21
Blenke, Joseph 128
Blue Rock Farmhouse 70
Blumer, Abraham 82, 83, 85
Blumer, Henry 83
Blumer, Susanna 83
Bonham, Ken 8, 66, 67, 68, 123
Borglum, Gutzon 21

Bradford Township, Pennsylvania 70
Bradley, Morris 56
Brady, Mathew 46
Brandywine Conservancy 72
Brandywine Creek 65
Brandywine River 69, 70
Brandywine, The (painting) 69
Bremo Plantation 109, 110
Bremo Trees 110
Bremo Trust 110
Bricker, Sam 137, 138, 139
Bricker and Company general store 137
Brien, John 100
Brinton Quarry 58
Bristol, Rhode Island 53, 54
Bristol County, Rhode Island 53
Bronescombe, Bishop Walter 24
Bronstein, Jesse B. 84
Bronstein, Jesse B. Jr. 85
Brown, John 105
Buchanan, James 134
Buckland Abbey, Devon 123
Bucks County, Pennsylvania 60, 62
Buffalo Livestock Journal 121
Buffington, Thomas 70
Burgess Lea Press 61
Burgess, Richard 60
Burkholder, Christian 81
Burlington, New Jersey 45
Burra Burra Copper Company 113
Burr, Milton 107
Butler, New York 49
Butter Valley Golf Course 59
Buttress 20

C

Caesar, Julius 22
Caldwell, J.D. 126
Camp Springs House 128
Camp Springs, Kentucky 127, 128
Camp Springs (painting) 127
Camp Springs Winery 128
Campbell, Wallace Jr. 116
Campbell County, Kentucky 127
Cann, Harry 71
Canton, Georgia 115, 118
Canton Cotton Mills 118
Cargoll barn 17, 24, 25
Carillon Historical Park 132
Carnegie, Andrew 10, 50
Carnegie Corporation 108
Carter, George Sr. 70
Carter, Mike 96
Carter, Thomas 96
Carter-Worth Farm 70
Cascade Barn 44
Cassidy, Joe 69
Castle Farms 4, 143, 144, 145
Castle Van Haver 143
Catalogue of Cruck Buildings, A 18
Cedar View Farm 90
Center Bridge Historic District 60
Centerville Historical Society 132
Centre Bridge (painting) 60
Centre Bridge, Pennsylvania 60, 61
Century, The 36
Champlain, Samuel de 30
Chapman, John 63
Charlemagne 22

Charles River 34
Charlestown Village, Pennsylvania 72
Charlevoix, Michigan 4, 141
Charlevoix County, Michigan 140
Charlevoix Historical Society 144
Charter of Privileges 87
Chase, Jasper 147
Chase, Nathan B. 147
Chase and Dixie Sawmill 147
Chase Stone Barn Preservation Project 149
Chase Valley Brickyards 147
Chase Valley Glass Works 147
Chase, Wisconsin 147, 148, 149
Cheney, Benjamin Pierce 33, 34
Cheney, Elizabeth 34
Cherokee County Board of Education 119
Cherokee County, Georgia 115
Cherokee County Historical Society 119
Cherokee Federal Savings Banks 119
Chesapeake and Ohio Canal 103
Chester County Barn, A (painting) 67
Chester County Hospital Foundation 79
Chester County, Pennsylvania 26, 27, 57, 58, 65, 66, 76
Chickies Creek 81
Chiefly Cobblestone (painting) 48
Children of the Mist (painting) 111
Children's farmyard 40
Chittenden County, Vermont 38
Christ and Holy Trinity Church 56
Cistercians 22
Civil War 31, 75, 101, 110, 113
Civilian Conservation Corps 96
Clark, Ambrose Jordan 46
Clark, Chester 49

Clark County, Ohio 121
Clark, Edward 46
Clark, Edward Severin 46
Clark, Jack 8
Clark, Jenny 8
Clark, Stephen 46
Clark, Stephen C. 47
Claytor, Archer 69
Claytor, Warren I. 3, 8, 11, 57, 66, 68, 69
Cleveland Builders Supply Company 114
Cleveland Chair Company 113
Cleveland Coal and Feed Company 114
Cleveland Hosiery Mills 113, 114
Cleveland Woolen Mills 113
Clinton, DeWitt 48
Coates, Sarah 74
Cobblestone Buildings in Wayne County, New York 50
Cobblestone Masonry 49
Cobblestone Quest: Road Tours of New York's Historic Buildings 27, 48
Cocke, Clara 110
Cocke, John Hartwell 108, 109, 111
Cocke, Philip 110
Cocke, Richard 109
Coggins, Augustus (Gus) Lee 116, 117, 118, 119
Coggins, Daisy 118, 119
Coggins, Frank 117
Coggins Marble Factory 117
Coggins, Rol 116, 117
Coley, Ebenezer 55
Coley, Michael 55
College of New Jersey 91
College of the Atlantic 32
Colt, Russell 54
Colt, Samuel 53
Colt, Samuel Pomeroy 53, 54
Colt State Park 54, 55
Colt, Theodora DeWolf 53
Columbia County, New York 43

Commercial Solvents Corporation 85
Concord, New Hampshire 35
Conestoga Creek 81
Cooks Creek 62, 63
Coon, Halsey 51
Cooper, Elizabeth 46
Cooper, James Fenimore 10, 46, 47
Cooper, William 45, 46
Cooperstown, New York 45, 46, 47, 153
Coplay Cement Company 16
Cornwall, England 24
Cornwallis, General 70
Courses 20
Cramb, Ian 14, 16, 18, 68
Craters of the Moon National Monument 15
Crescent Farm 116, 117, 118, 119
Crossing the Delaware (painting) 94
Crossroads of the American Revolution 94
Cruck 20
Cryptic Coggins (painting) 115
Culpeper family estates 105
Cultivator 110
Cupola Inn 152, 153
Curtis, Edward 155
Curtis, Paul 55
Custer, John 72

D
da Costa, Mathieu 30
Darby, Charlotte 56
Darke, Samuel 106
Darrow, Clarence 142
Darrow School 44
Daughters of the American Revolution, Abigail Hartman Rice Chapter 78
Dayton History 132
Deal, Nancy Ceperley 96
Deerslayer, The 46
Def Leppard 143
DeLancey, Susan Augusta 46
Delaware Canal 61
Delaware River 62, 94, 95
Deming, William 42

dendrochronology 22, 24, 66
Devlin, Caryn 50
DeWolf, George 53
DeWolf, James 53, 54
DeWolf, Mark Anthony 53
Dierberg, Jim 8
DiMaria, Joan 3
Distillers, The (painting) 89
Dixie Foundry 114
Dixie Products 115
Domino's Pizza 144
Donaldson family 102
Dorr, George B. 31
Dorset, England 68
Dorset Field Club 40
Douglass, Van A. 134
Dowdell, Ralph 96
Doyle, A.W. 134
Drake, Anna 123
Drake, Daniel 123
Drake, Francis 122
Drake, Isaac 122
Drake, Lawrence 74
Drake, Thomas 122
Drake, William 123, 125
Drake, William II 122
Drake barn 122, 123
Drake's Dazzling Delight (painting) 122
Dressed Stone 20
Dry Stone Conservancy 20
dry stone masonry 20
Duncan, Renee 32
DuPont's Eastern Laboratory 84
Durell family 61
Dylan, Bob 143

E
Eakin, Elizabeth 63
Eakin, John 63
Early, Jubal A. 100
East Jordan Development Company 138
Eastburn, David 97
Eastburn, Joseph 97, 98, 99
Eastburn Lime Kiln 98
Eastburn-Jeanes Lime Kilns Historic District, Delaware 97
Eastman, Samuel 37
Edgewater Hall 118, 119
Edward S. Curtis Portraits 155
Eight Oaks Distillery 90

Elijah's Exquisite Example (painting) 75
El Jireh Farm 139
El Paraíso, Peru 21
Elm Bank Horticulture Center 34
Emery, John 123
Emery, John Josiah Sr. 32
Emery, Sophia 31
Emperor Trajan 22
Ensminger, Robert 11, 66, 67
Ensminger, Robert F. 57
Eric Sloane's An Age of Barns 44
Erie Canal 49
Erie Canal Commission 48
Etowah River 116
Europe 22
European Association of Stonemasons and Sculptors 153
Evans, Frederick W. 43
Evans, Oliver 90
Everglades Club 40

F
Fackenthal, O.B. 63
Fairfax, Thomas 105, 106
Fairfield County, Connecticut 55
Fairman, Thomas 72
Fargo, William 34
Farmers' Museum, The 45, 47
Farmin's Finest (painting) 55
Favre, Dr. 34
Fells, The 36, 38
Fenimore, Elizabeth 45
Fenimore Art Museum 47
Fenimore farm 46, 47
Fields, Don 132
Firestone, Harvey 141
Fisher, Joseph R. 102
Fisher, Martin 102
Fluvanna County Historical Society 110
Fluvanna County, Virginia 108
For the Love of a Castle 145
Ford, Henry 116
Founding Fish, The 61
Fowler, Orson 121
Fox, George 65
Fox Meadow Farm 80

Franklin, Benjamin 83
Franks, Bobby 142
Frederick County Agricultural Society 101
Frederick County, Maryland 99, 100
Frederick, Maryland 100
Freed, Christina 87
Freed, Peter 86
Freeman, Rich 27, 48
Freeman, Sue 27, 48
Fremont, John 93
Friends of the 4-H 144
Frysh, Casey 149
Frysh, Stanley 149
Fry, Stan 34
Funk, Abraham 62, 63

G

Gagliardi, Eugene 66
Gagliardi, Jean 66
Gamble, Robert 117
Gambrill Mill 101
Gardner, Tim 94
Gardner Seveney Sports Complex 53
Garfield, James 37
Garrett, Isaac 68
Garrett, Samuel 68
Garrett family 68
Gasconade County, Missouri 19, 27
Gehman, Christopher 59
Gehman farm 59
Gehman, Joel M. 59
Gehman, Johannes 59
Gehman, John 58, 59
Gehman, Lydia 59
Gehman's Glory (painting) 58
Gehman's Mennonite Church 59
Genesee Farmer, The 49
Gentleman Farmer 20
Georgia Farm 70, 71, 72
Georgia Historical Quarterly, The 118
German Settlement Society 27
Gilmore barn 121
Glastonbury Abbey barn 18, 23, 24
Glastonbury Abbey, Somerset County 20, 22
Glen Farm 3, 51, 52, 53
Glen-Worth Farm 70
Goforth, William 123

Goodman, Jacob 81
Goodnight, Charles 10
Goodrich, Daniel 42
Gott, Julia 31
Granite Monthly, The 37
Granite State, The (painting) 33
Granville Gray 9
Great Barn, The 123
Great Depression 27, 71, 74, 75, 90, 96, 102, 107, 108, 114, 118, 143, 147, 149
Greeley, Horace 36
Green Acres Program 55
Greenberg, Herman 102, 103
Greenwood, John 95
Gregg, Hannah 111
Gregg, John 111
Gregg, Thomas Jr. 111, 112
Gregg, Thomas Sr. 112
Gregg, William 111
Gulf Stream, Florida 41
Gus Coggins brass band 116, 117
Guth, Lorenz 83
Guth, Lorenze 82

H

Hadley, Olive 31
Hall family 113
Hall, Alice 68
Hall, Herbert 9
Hall, Samuel 68
Hall, Sarah 68
Hall, Terri 113
Hall, Thomas 68
Hamilton County, Ohio 18, 19, 123
Hamilton, Ohio 122
Hammond, George Francis 36
Hampshire County, England 33
Hancock County, Maine 30
Hancock County Trustees of Public Reservations 31
Hancock, Massachusetts 42
Hancock Shaker Village 42
Hands to Work … Hearts to God (painting) 41
Harding, Micajah 50

Hardin, John Henry 119
Hardwick Stove Company 113
Harleysville, Pennsylvania 86
Harper Mule Company 119
Hartford, Connecticut 15
Hartman, Abigail 76
Hartman, Johannes 76, 78, 79
Harvey, Abraham 95
Harvey, Moses 95
Havermeyer, Theodore 40
Hay, Charles 35
Hay, Clarence 35, 36
Hay, Helen 35
Hay, John 36, 37, 38
Hay, John Milton 35
Hays, Clara 36
Hays, Clarence 37
Hays Heavenly Haven (painting) 35
Heckler, Abraham 87
Heckler, Angeline 87
Heckler, David 87
Heckler, George 87
Heckler, George P. 87
Heckler, James Y. 86
Heckler Plains Folklife Society 88
Heckler stone barn 88
Heckler's Heritage (painting) 86
Hemsher, Barbara 89
Hemsher, Daniel 89
Hendricks, John 106
Henricks, James 106
Henry VIII 22
Heppner, Leianne Neff 3
Hereford Township, Pennsylvania 59
Hermann, Missouri 11
Herr, Christian 81
Herr, Hans 81
Herr, Rudolph 81
Herr, Samuel 80, 81
Hicks, Orrin 50
Higgins, Israel 31
Highland Farm 34
Hillsborough County, New Hampshire 33
Hine, Lewis 114
Historic Barns of Ohio 9, 154
Historic Barns of Southeastern Pennsylvania, The 8, 57

Historic Landmarks Foundation of Indiana 132
History Cherokee 119
History of Chester County 70
Hoare, Samuel 79
Hockensmith, Mary Frances 107
Hockensmith, Robert A. 107
Hockensmith, Samuel J. 107
Hockman, Gordon 107
Hockman, Jerry 107
Hodkensmith, Pauline 107
Hoffman, Adam 88
Hoffman, Carol 59
Hoffman, Erwin 59
Hoffman, Robert 59
Holmes, F.B. 84
Holmes, Louisa 110
Holmes, Thomas 70
Holme, Thomas 57, 72
Home for All, A 121
Hope Valley Community Church 60
Hout, William 135
Howard, Ezekial 79
Howe, Wallis E. 54
Howe, William 70, 77
Hubbard, Dick 133, 135
Huber, Greg 8, 11, 26, 57, 64, 66, 83, 87, 88, 93, 130
Hubicky, Ilko 87
Hubicky, Paracia 87
Hubicky, Paul 87
Huen, Arthur 141
Hunters Mill Historic District 59
Hutton, Frank 147

I

Indiana Historical Society 134
Indiana Manufacturing Company 134
Industrial National Bank 54
Industrial Trust Company 54
International Masonry Society 153
Iowa Barn Foundation 155
Iron County, Wisconsin 146
Isadore Baumann House 128

J

Jackson, Andrew 125
Jackson, James 132
James River 110
Jamestown, Virginia 109
Janoska, Paul 147
Jeanes, Abel 97, 98, 99
Jeanes, Elizabeth 97
Jefferis, Emmor 70
Jefferis, Robert 70
Jefferson County, Indiana 129, 130
Jefferson County, West Virginia 105
Jefferson, Thomas 21, 25, 56, 68, 109, 113
Jeffris, Bruce 149
Jeffris, Eleanor 149
Jeffris, Tom 149
Jeffris Family Foundation 149
Jenkins, Allston 72
Jensen, Jens 141
Jeras-Blumer Barn (painting) 84
Jeras Corporation 83, 85
Jeras-Troxell Barn (painting) 85
Jewell, Edward 93
J.J. Hof Land Company 147
John Hay National Wildlife Refuge 37
John Heinz National Wildlife Refuge 72
Johnson County Conservation Board 152
Johnson family 61
Johnson Ferry 94
Johnson Ferry House 96
Johnson, Garrett 94, 95
Johnson's Ferry 95
Johnston, Forney 110
Johnston, Frances Benjamin 108
Johnston, Joseph F. 110
Johnston, Joseph F. Jr. 110
Johnston, Joseph Fortney 110
Jones, Griffith 72
Jones Mercantile Company 118, 119
Jones, Paul 118
Jordan Reformed Church 82

K

Kanawha Canal 110
Kauffman, Christian 81

Kauffman, Jacob 81
Kaufmann, Elizabeth Cheney 34
Kautz, Donald 80
Kearny, Stephen 93
Keating, Dan 53
Keller, John 81
Kennedy, Samuel 78
Kent, Ann 55
Kent, Mary 55
Kilns of New Castle County, The (painting) 97
Kimberton Hunt Club 79
Kindelberger barn 126, 154
Kindelberger farm 17
Kindelberger New (painting) 124
Kindelberger stone barn 10, 17
Kindelberger, Frederick Jr. 127
Kindelberger, Frederick, Sr. 125
Kindelberger, Margartha 125
Kindelberger, Mary 125
Kindelberger, William 126
King, Clarence 36
King, Franklin 42, 147
Kneip, Johannes 88
Knight's Courtyard Garden 143
Knipe, Anna 89
Knipe, Christian 89
Knipe, David 89
Knipe, Joseph 88, 90
Knipe, Joseph Jr. 90
Knox, Henry 95
Kooker, Jacob 63
Kooker, Jacob Jr. 63
Kooker, Jane 63, 64
Kooker's Tavern 63
Koontz, Elizabeth 85
Kort Grocery 128
Kort, Peter 128
KP Landscaping Company 145
Krause barn 148, 149
Krause, Daniel Jr. 148, 149
Krause, Daniel Sr. 148
Kress, Amy 132
Kress, Brady 132
Kroeger, Bob 3
Kroeger, Brenda 160
Kroeger, Francis 160
Kroeger, Laura 9, 160

Kroeger, Robert 7, 8, 160
Kroeger, Rob 155
Kröger, Gerhardt 11
Kröger, Joseph 11
Krueger, Orvil 149
Kutzleb, Connie 137, 138, 139
Kutzleb, Kenn 137, 138, 139

L

Lafayette County, Wisconsin 66
Lafayette, Marquis de 33, 70
Laird, William 71
Lake Champlain 38, 40
Lamm, Cecelia 136
Lamm, Florence 136
Lamm, Frank 136
Lamm, Georg T. 135, 136
Lamm, Gerald 136
Lamm, Gertrud 135, 136
Lamm, Luann 136
Lamm, Mary 136
Lamm, Richard 136
Lamm, Robert 136
Lamm, William 136
Lamm's Legacy (painting) 136
Lancaster County, Pennsylvania 80
Landis, John 81
Landis, Nelson 82
Landis, Sylvia 82
Lang, Pat 8, 155
Lapp, John 125
Last of the Mohicans 46
Latimore, Anna 130
Lauterborn, Mike 56
Leaser, Frederick 83
Leavitt, David 44
Lederach, Pennsylvania 86
Lee, Anna 110
Lee, Mother Ann 42, 43
Lee, Robert E. 100, 109, 110
Lehigh County, Pennsylvania 16, 57, 82
Lehigh River 62
Lenox, Massachusetts 44
Lentz, Ann Mary 100
Leopold, Nathan Jr. 142
Levis, Samuel 68

Lewis Farm 101
L'Hermitage 100
Lincoln, Abraham 21, 36
Lincoln, Robert 36
Lincoln, Willie 36
Linden Place 53, 54
Little Conestoga River 80
Little Finland (painting) 146
Lloyd barn 131
Lloyd, Edward II 130
Lloyd, Edward IV 130
Lloyd, Rebecca 132
Lloyd, Sarah 132
Lloyds Bank 129
Lloyds of London 129
Lloyd, Zephaniah 129, 130, 132
Lloyd, Zephaniah Jr. 132
Loeb, Albert Henry 11, 140, 141, 142, 143, 145
Loeb, Allan 141, 143
Loeb, Anna 141, 142, 143
Loeb, Ernest 141, 142, 143
Loeb, Richard 141, 142
Loeb, Thomas 141
Loeb's Legacy (painting) 140
Loeb's Legacy, II (painting) 144
Lonas, W.H 115
Lord Will Provide, The (painting) 137
Louden, William 131
Loudon County, Virginia 7, 27, 111
Lower Salford Historical Society 88
Lower Salford Township, Pennsylvania 86, 87
Lucky Hill Farm 71
Lucky Hill Farm (painting) 71
Luther, Martin 81

M

MacGregor, Rob Roy 112
MacOwan, Kean 134
Madison Courier 131
Madison Herald 132
Madison, James 92, 109
Magic Chef 114, 115
Mahoning County, Ohio 15

Maine Coast Heritage Trust 32
Maine Farmland Trust 31
Mainland, Pennsylvania 86
Manchester, Isaac 53
Mandell, Alice 79
Mandell, Harvey 79
Man for All Seasons, A 65
Manly-Anthony bank 119
Manor Township, Pennsylvania 80
Marek, Catherine 64
Marietta, Ohio 125
Marion, New York 50
Marion Township, Michigan 143
Maris, Christian 15
Maris, Jonathan 68
Maris, Robert 68
Maryland-National Capital Park and Planning Commission 102
Mary M. Rupp, Inc. 90
Mason City, Iowa 152, 153
Mason, John 33
Mason Phelps 53
Masonry Institute of Michigan 145
Maurer, Andrew 59
Maytag 115
McClatchy, Vince 69
McClellan, George B. 100
McClure, Bob 121
McClure, Marjorie 121
McClure, Mary 133
McClure Center for School Programs 40
McConkey, Samuel 96
McKain barn 134
McKain, Arthur Albert (A.A.) 133, 134, 135
McKain, Elvira 133
McKain, James 133
McKain, Mary 135
McKain's Marvel (painting) 133
McKinley, William 36, 37
McPhee, John 61
Medical College of Ohio 123
Meigs County, Tennessee 7, 113
Meigs, Return Jonathan Sr. 113

Mensenkamp, William 148
Mercer County, New Jersey 91, 95
Mercer, Forrest 34
Mercer, Hugh 91, 95
Merrimack County, New Hampshire 35
Mesenkamp's Marvel (painting) 148
Michigan Historical Society 145
Mickley, John Jacob 83
Mickley, Sarah 83
Miles, David 144
Mill Gut bridge 54
Mills, Dale 152, 153
Mills, Judy 152, 153
Mills of Lancaster County 80
Milner, John 66
Milner, Wynne 66
Minnich family 84
Miradero 41
Mischka, Joe 3
Mitchell, Joseph 61
Mittelberger, Gottlieb 76
Monadnock Conservancy 34
Monaghan, Tom 144
Monocacy National Battlefield Cultural Resource Division 101
Monroe County, Ohio 10, 125, 154
Monroe, James 95
Montgomery County, Maryland 102
Montgomery County, Pennsylvania 72, 86
Monticello 109
Monticello, Indiana 133, 134
Moore, Adam 90
Moore, Ann 90
Moore, Avril 93
Moore, Daniel 90
Moore, Joseph K. 90
Moore, Thomas 93
Morgan, J.P. 10, 50, 155
Morrison barn 50
Morrison, Jacob 50
Morris, Robert 79, 119
Mosul, Iraq 21
Mount Desert Island, Maine 31
Mount Lebanon, New York 11, 27, 43, 44
Mt. Monadnock 35
Mt. Rushmore 21

Mucarella, Grace 90
Mueller, Linda 3, 144, 145
Mueller, Richard 144, 145
Muhlenberg, Henry 76
Murphy, Glenn 121
Musser, Yost 81
Myers, Martin 106

N

Nassau Hall 93
National India Rubber Company 54
National Park Service 100, 101
National Register 19, 32, 37, 38, 42, 43, 47, 50, 54, 55, 56, 58, 59, 60, 61, 64, 66, 69, 74, 75, 79, 82, 90, 93, 96, 97, 100, 103, 107, 108, 110, 115, 119, 121, 127, 128, 132, 133, 144, 147, 149
National Rubber Company 54
National Trust for Historic Preservation 149
Natural and Statistical View, or Picture of Cincinnati and the Miami County 123
Natural Lands 72
Natural Lands Trust 72, 79
Neilson, John 109
Nelson, Samuel 46
New Castle County, Delaware 97
New Jersey Division of Parks and Forestry 96
New Lebanon, New York 11, 42
New York State Historical Association 47, 153
New York Times 51
New York Tribune 36, 50
Newman, Paul 56
Newport County, Rhode Island 50
Newport International Polo Series 53
Newport Polo Club 53
Newport, Rhode Island 53
Newton, Massachusetts 37

Nicholson, Alexander 110
Nicolay, John 35, 36
Niemcewicz, Julian 100
Nietzsche, Friedrich 142
Noble, Allen 11
Noll, Fannie 82
Noll, Grant 82
Non-Freezing Powder Company 84
Northeast Creek 32
Nyland, Henry 34

O

Oak Grove Restoration Company 104
Oakhurst Links 40
Oconto County, Wisconsin 147
Odgers, Julian 24
O'Grady, Tom 3
Ohio Company Land Office 125
Ohio-Erie Canal 61
Old Kennett Meetinghouse 70
Old Settlers' Meeting, The 132
Oley Valley Historical Society 71
Olmsted, Frederick Law 38
O'Neill, Emily 79
O'Neill, Gail 79
On the Shores of Shelburne (painting) 38
Orcutt, Don 87
Orphan, The (painting) 129
Ort brothers 128
Osbourne, Ozzy 143
Otsego County Historical Society 47
Otsego County, New York 45
Otsego Hall 45
Otter Creek 32
Otto, Bodo 78
Owen, Cindy 32
Owen, Harry 32

P

Paine, Richard 31, 32
Paine, Sophia 31
Paine, Thomas Jr. 31
Paine, Willis 31, 32
Palladio, Andrea 25, 68, 109
Pannebecker, Hendrick 72, 74
Paoli Massacre 78

Pardee, Ario 93
Pardoe, Dr. 93
Park, Willie, Jr. 40
Parker Pen Corporation 149
Patchin, Farmin 56
Paterson, New Jersey 54
Patowmack Canal 103
Patriotism Personified (painting) 91
Paxson, Henry 60
Paxson, Isaiah 61
Paxson, Thomas 61
Peale, Rembrandt 48
Penn, John 62
Penn, Thomas 62
Penn, William 57, 62, 65, 72, 79, 87, 88, 129, 155
Pennebecker, James 79
Pennebecker, John 79
Pennebecker, Joseph 79
Pennsylvania Barn, The 57, 66
Pennsylvania Mutual Fire Insurance Company 75
Pennypacker, Elijah 76
Pennypacker, Elijah Funk 74
Pennypacker, George 79
Pennypacker, Joseph 74
Pennypacker, Matthias 72, 73, 74
Pennypacker, Mrs. S.W., II 73
Pennypacker, Peter 73
Pennypacker, Samuel 73, 74
Pennypacker, Samuel W. 15
Pennypacker Mills 73
Pequea Creek 81
Perkins, Jacob 88
Pesek, Barbara 139
Pesek, Frank 139
Peterborough, New Hampshire 34
Peterloon Estate 123
Petty, William 38
Philadelphia Conservationists 72
Philadelphia, Pennsylvania 63, 72
Phoenixville, Pennsylvania 72
Pickering, Charles 72
Pickering Creek 72

Pike Creek Valley, Delaware 15
Pikeland Company 76
Pittsfield, Massachusetts 27, 41, 42
Polk County, Tennessee 113
Polk, Thomas 83
Pope family 119
Pope, John Russell 52
Poppasquash Farms district 54
Portland cement 16
Portsmouth, Rhode Island 3, 51, 53
Portsmouth's Gentleman Farmer (painting) 51
Potato Creek 113
Potomac Company 103
Potomack Navigation Company 106
Potomac River 103, 106
Powell, David 86
Price, Bruce 32
Princeton Township, New Jersey 93
Princeton University 91
Prohibition Party 75
Proseus, J.F. 50
Pueblo, Colorado 10
Pulaski Area Historical Society 149
Pulaski, Wisconsin 148

Q

Quaker Country (painting) 64
Quoins 20

R

Raht, Julius 113
Rarest of the Rare (painting) 120
Ravenswaay, Charles 20
Reading, John 60
Reading's Ferry 60
Red Hill, Pennsylvania 60
Reese, Matt 3
Reibel, Art 143, 144
Reibel, Kimberly 143
Reiff, Hans 86
Renwick, James Jr. 103
Revere, Paul 87
Revolutionary War 27, 63, 70, 78, 83, 87, 113
Rhymer, Clara 114

Rhymer, Stephen Bradford 113
Rhymer, Zola 114
Rice, Abigail 78
Rice, Benjamin 78
Rice, John 76, 78
Rice, Zachariah 76, 78, 79, 80
Richard, Peter 59
Ringen, John 114
Ritter, Andrew 128
River, Elk 70
Robertson, Robert 38, 40
Robinson, Doane 21
Rob Roy 112
Rock, Charles Anthony 130, 131, 132
Rock, Susana 132
Rockefeller, John D. 38
Rockefeller stone barn 27
Roebuck, Alvah 140
Roebuck and Company 140
Roe Cobblestone Schoolhouse 14
Rohrer, Cheryl 81, 82
Rohrer, Doug 81, 82
Rohrer, Ken 81, 82
Rohrer, Paul 82
Roosevelt, Franklin 121
Roosevelt, Theodore 21, 37, 155
Rosenwald, Julius 140
Ross, Alexander 72
Round Barns of America 9, 152
Rowe Farm 36
Rubber King of Bristol, The (painting) 52
Rubble 20
Ruins of lime kilns 16
Rupp, Ernest 90
Rupp, Eva Babette Metzger 90
Rupp, George 90
Rupp, Mary 90
Ryman, Daisy 116
Rymer, S. Bradford Jr. 115

S

Sagatuck Bank 56
Salisbury, Eben 31
Samuel Hall farm 68
Sanger, Prentice 37
Saunders, Margaret Anne 107
Scattene, Frank 83
Schmidt, Carl 49

Schmidt, Gloria 3
Schuykill Fishing Company 69
Schuylkill Friends Meeting Cemetery 75
Schuylkill River 61, 74
Schuylkill Township, Pennsylvania 74
Schwab, Dick 27, 152
Scott, Sir Water 112
Seagraves, Kathleen 59
Sealed Power Corporation 143
Sears 140
Sears, Richard 140
Seisholtzville, Pennsylvania 59
Seneca Creek 103
Seneca Historic District 103
Seneca Quarry 103
Seneca Sandstone (painting) 102
Seneca Stonecutting Mill 103
Seventeen Children (painting) 77
Sfrock family 64
Shaker barns 26
Shaker Community, Inc. 42
Shaker Museum 45
Shaker round stone barn 27
Shaker stone barn 11, 27
Shaking Quakers (Shakers) 41
Shank, Joe 121
Shaw, John 90
Shea, Charles W. 31, 32
Shea, James M. 31, 32
Shelburne Farms 38, 40, 41
Shelburne, Vermont 38
Shenandoah Junction, West Virginia 105
Shenandoah Valley, West Virginia 107
Sheridan, Wyoming, County Fair 121
Shipley, Elizabeth 68
Shipley, William 68
Shuler, Gabriel 79
Shuller, William 79
Siddington Tithe Barn 66, 67
Silver Creek 63
Silver Linden Farm 7, 27, 111
Simon, Menno 81

Singer, Isaac Merritt 46
Singer Sewing Machine Company 46, 47
Skippack, Pennsylvania 72
Slack, James 95
Sloane, Eric 7, 11, 44
Sloan, Robert 141, 142, 143
Smith, Jack 8, 155
Smith, Samuel 50
Smithsonian 103, 104
Smithsonian Castle 14
Snyder, Ferdinand 107
Snyder, Henry M. 107
Snyder, Jacob 106, 107
Snyder, John Jr. 106
Snyder, John Sr. 106
Snyder, Lizzie 107
Snyder, Maria 107
Snyder, Susan 107
Snyder Farm 107
Society for the Protection of New Hampshire Forests 37
Society of Friends 65, 74
Sodus, New York 50
Solebury Township, Pennsylvania 60
Somerset County, England 20, 22
Somerset Rural Life Museum 22
Somes, Abraham 31
Sons of the American Revolution 38
South Bend, Indiana 11
Southern Planter 110
South Whitehall Township, Pennsylvania 82
Sovereign, Otto 140
Sovereign, William 140
Spirit of Democracy, The 126
Splez, Jon 130
Springfield Township, Pennsylvania 62, 63
Springtown, Pennsylvania 62, 63
Springtown Water Company 63
Spy, The 46
St. Andrews Golf Club 40, 50
St. Augustine 22
St. Benedict of Nursia 22
St. Columba 22
St. Columban 22

St. Croix Island 30
St. Dunstan 22
Stephenson County, Illinois 135
Stevens, Thaddeus 74
Stewart, Elliot 121
Sting 143
St. John Nepomucene Church 139
Stockton, John 91
Stockton, John Potter 93
Stockton, Mary 92
Stockton, Richard 91, 92, 94
Stockton, Robert 92, 94
Stockton, Robert F. 92, 93
Stockton, Samuel Witham 92
Stone Barn Farm 31
Stonebrook Winery 128
Stone, Clara 36
Stonehedge 139
Stoner, John 87
St. Peter's Cemetery 78
Stroud, Dick 72
Stroud, Morris W. III 71, 72
Stroud Preserve 72
Stroud Water Research Center 72
Struthers, Emily 142
Stuart, Gilbert 46
Surry County, Virginia 109
Survival (painting) 105
Susquehanna County, Pennsylvania 58
Susquehanna River 66, 81
Swenson family 33
Switzerland County, Indiana 130
Sylvanside Farm 113

T

Taft, William Howard 38
Tanner, Oliver P. 44
Taylor, Abiah 65, 66
Taylor, Abiah III 65
Taylor, Abiah Jr. 65
Taylor, Anne 65
Taylor, Arthur 40
Taylor barn 26
Taylor-Cope Historic District 66
Taylor, Edith 52
Taylor, Henry Augustus Coit 50, 53

Taylor, Jacob 50
Taylor, John 65
Taylor, Mary 65
Taylor, Moses 50, 52
Taylor, Reginald 52
Taylor, Samuel 65
Taylor's Run 65
Taylor stone barn 27
Tellurium Gold Mine 93
Tennessee Magic (painting) 112
This Old House 132
Thomas, John 31
Thomas, Linda 66
Thomas Farm 101
Thomlinson, Samuel 95
Thomson, Mr. & Mrs. Joe 75
Tile Makers, The (painting) 73
Tinker Dam Farm 74
Tinsley, Gale 139
Tinsley, Larraine 139
Tippecanoe River 134
Titusville, New Jersey 94
Trail, Charles E. 100
Travis, Dale 10
Treasure in Cooperstown, A (painting) 45
Trenton, New Jersey 95
Trewithen Estate 24
Trojan Powder Company 85
Troxell family 84
Turrets 32
Turril, Anna 122
Tusculum 92, 93, 94
Tustin, Joseph 79
Twain, Mark 10
Twining, Stephen 62, 63
Twin Ridge Orchard Company 107
Tyler, President 93

U

Underground Railroad 74
Underhill, Roy 132
Uniroyal 54
United States and Canada Express Company 34
United States Fish and Wildlife Service 37
United States Golf Association 40

United States Rubber Company 54
University of Cincinnati College of Medicine 123
University of Cincinnati's Daniel Drake Center for Post-Acute Care 123
University of Virginia 109
Upper Gwynedd Township, Pennsylvania 88
Uthe, William 128

V

Valley Campaign 107
Valley Forge, Pennsylvania 73, 78
Van Haver, John 143
Van Haver, Jon 145
Vanderbilt, Cornelius 38
Vanderbilt, Eliza "Lila" 38
Vanderbilt, William 38
Vanderbilt University 38
Varnum, James Mitchell 53
Vermont's Stone Trust 153
Vernacular 20
Vernfield, Pennsylvania 86
Vincendière, Victoire 100
Vincendière's family 99
Virginia Department of Historic Resources 108
Vitruvius, Marcus 15
Voight, Melvin 135
Voight, Wilbur 135

W

Wagner, Marc 108
Wagner Palace Car Company 38
Walking Purchase 62, 63
Wallace, Lew 100
Waln, Nicholas 57
Walton, Sam 135
Warren, Russell 53
Washington, George 21, 51, 62, 70, 72, 73, 77, 78, 89, 91, 95, 96, 103, 105, 109
Washington Crossing Park Association 96

Washington Crossing State Park 96
Washington Hall 78
Wasserman, Max 37
Watervliet, New York 42
Wayne, Anthony 78, 87, 123
Wayne County, New York 14, 47, 49
Webb, Alec 40
Webb, Derick 41
Webb, James Watson 38
Webb, Lila 40
Webb, William 40
Webb, William Seward 38
Webster, Daniel 33
Wellesley, Massachusetts 34
Wells Fargo Company 34
Wells, Henry 34

Wellstar Health System 119
Well Sweep Farm 36
Westbrook Farm 68
Westport, Connecticut 55
Westport Historical Society 56
Westport Museum 56
Wheeler, Julia 56
Wheeler, Lewis 56
Wheeler, William B. 56
Whirlpool 115
White County, Indiana 133
White Horse Farm 74, 75
White Sulphur Springs, West Virginia 40
Whitacre, James 70
Whiting, Frank 46, 47
Whittaker, James 43
Whittaker's Wisdom (painting) 43

Whittier, John Greenleaf 76
Who Was the Real Gus Coggins?: Social Struggle and Criminal Mystery in Cherokee County, 1912–1927 118
Wickersham, George 43, 44
Wilhelm, Hubert 11
William the Conqueror 22
Williams, John S. 45
Williamson, Colonel 50
Williamson, New York 50
Willistown Conservation Trust 57
Wilson, George 62
Wilson, Nan 107
Wilson, Woodrow 31
Winchester, Indiana 133

Windom Mill 82
Windom Mill (painting) 80
Wistar, Caspar 62
Witherspoon, Anne 92
Witherspoon, Elizabeth 91
Witherspoon, James 94
Witherspoon, John 91, 92, 94
Woodstock Equestrian Park 102, 104
Woodward, Joanne 56
Woodwright's Shop, The 132
Worth, Ebenezer 70
Worth, John 70
Worth, Paschall 70
Worth, Thomas 70
Worth family 71
Worth-Jefferis Rural Historic District 69
Worthington Farm 101
Wray, Colorado 119

Wright, Tubmond 129, 130
Wrightstown, Wisconsin 147
W. S. Webb & Company 38

Y
Yankee Magazine 37
York Hill Farm 105, 107, 108
York Hill Orchard & Farm 107
Young, William 102
Ypsilanti, Michigan 144

Z
Zion's Reformed Church 83
Zirkman family 68